TRAJECTORIES OF DECLINING AND DESTRUCTIVE CAPITALISM

RESEARCH IN POLITICAL ECONOMY

Series Editor: Paul Zarembka

State University of New York at Buffalo, USA

Recent Volumes:

Volume 35: The Capitalist Commodification of Animals – Edited by B. Clark and T. D. Wilson

Volume 36: Imperialism and Transitions to Socialism – Edited by R. Herrera

Volume 37: Polish Marxism after Luxemburg – Edited by J. Toporowski

Volume 38: Imperialism and the Political Economy of Global South's Debt – Edited by Ndongo Samba Sylla

Volume 39: Value, Money, Profit, and Capital Today – Edited by Rémy Herrera

EDITORIAL ADVISORY BOARD

RESEARCH IN POLITICAL ECONOMY VOLUME 40

TRAJECTORIES OF DECLINING AND DESTRUCTIVE CAPITALISM

EDITED BY

RÉMY HERRERA
CNRS (National Center of Scientific Research), France

emerald PUBLISHING

United Kingdom – North America – Japan
India – Malaysia – China

Emerald Publishing Limited
Emerald Publishing, Floor 5, Northspring, 21-23 Wellington Street, Leeds LS1 4DL

First edition 2025

British Library Cataloguing in Publication Data
A catalogue record for this book is available from the British Library

ISBN: 978-1-83549-203-1 (Print)
ISBN: 978-1-83549-202-4 (Online)
ISBN: 978-1-83549-204-8 (Epub)

ISSN: 0161-7230 (Series)

Printed and bound by CPI Group (UK) Ltd, Croydon, CR0 4YY

INVESTOR IN PEOPLE

CONTENTS

ABOUT THE EDITOR

Rémy Herrera (France) is an Economist and a researcher at the National Centre of Scientific Research (CNRS). Graduated from a Business School (*École supérieure de Commerce*, 1988), the Institute of Political Studies (*Institut d'Études politiques*, 1990) and the University of Paris 1 Panthéon-Sorbonne (Master of Philosophy, 1994; PhD in Economics, 1996), he supervises students in PhD at the *Centre d'Économie de la Sorbonne*. He started working in financial audit (1988), at the Organization for Economic Cooperation and Development (OECD) (1992–1997) and for the World Bank (1999–2000). He was a member of the CNRS National Committee (2000–2005) and of the Scientific Council of Paris 1 (2001–2006). He taught at various universities in France (especially Paris 1 [1993–2013]) and abroad, including the Universities of Aleppo (1998), Cairo (1999–2000), Vitoria in Brasil (2006), Complutense in Madrid (2009–2013), and Lingnan in Hong Kong (2018). He was an adviser to research programmes at the Chubu University (Nagoya). He is or has been associated with: Third World Forum (Dakar), Union of Radical Political Economics (New York), International Initiative for Promoting Political Economics (London), *Sociedad de Economía Política Latinoamericana* (São Paulo), *Consejo Latinoamericano de Ciencias Sociales* (Buenos Aires), and *Asociación Nacional de Economistas de Cuba* (Havana). He was the World Forum of Alternative's (WFA's) executive secretary. He is also a member of the Global University for Sustainability and of the International Observatory of the Crisis. He organized the 'Marx in the Twenty-First Century' seminar at La Sorbonne. He regularly works with the Centre Europe-Tiers Monde (Geneva), supporting it in its advisory role to the Human Rights Council of the United Nations.

ABOUT THE CONTRIBUTORS

Demba Moussa Dembele (Senegal), an Economist-researcher, is a member of the Council for the Development of Social Science Research in Africa (CODESRIA) and the Third World Forum (FTM). He has a PhD in Financial Economics from the Pierre et Marie Curie University, Paris and an MBA in International Trade and Finance from the American University (Washington DC). He is a former research associate at the Institute of International Finance (Washington DC). He is currently the Chair of the African Association for Research and Cooperation in Support of Endogenous Development (ARCADE).

Marcelo Dias Carcanholo (Brazil) is a full Professor at the School of Economics of the Fluminense Federal University (UFF) – Rio de Janeiro, Brazil – and a member of the Interdisciplinary Centre for Studies and Research on Marx and Marxism (NIEP-UFF). He is a member of the International Observatory of the Crisis.

Frédéric Farah (France) is a member of the team EA 7418 *Philosophie, Histoire et Analyse des Représentations Économiques* (PHARE) at the University of Paris 1 Panthéon–Sorbonne. His latest book is *Fake State: L'impuissance organisée de l'État en France* (2020), written with Olivier Delorme (H&O, Saint-Martin-de-Londres, France).

Hugo Figueira de Souza Corrêa (Brazil) is a Professor at the School of Economics of the Fluminense Federal University (UFF) – Rio de Janeiro, Brazil – and a member of the Interdisciplinary Centre for Studies and Research on Marx and Marxism (NIEP-UFF).

Ben Fine (United Kingdom) is an Emeritus Professor of Economics, School of Oriental and African Studies (SOAS), University of London, and a Visiting Professor, Wits School of Governance, University of Witwatersrand in Johannesburg (South Africa). He has been the Chair of the International Initiative for Promoting Political Economy (iippe.org) and the fourth in his series of volumes of edited articles on the *Critical Reconstructions of Political Economy* is in press with Brill. He was a contributing editor to the Macroeconomic Research Group (MERG) Report of 1993, commissioned by the *African National Congress* (ANC) to offer progressive post-apartheid options, but it was discarded.

Thierry Madjid Labica (France) teaches British Studies at Université Paris Nanterre. He is a member of the editorial board of the online journal *Contretemps, revue de critique communiste,* to which he has been a regular contributor. He has co-edited several books, with M Bertrand and C. Crowley, *Ici notre* *défaite a commencé: la grève des mineurs britanniques, 1984–1985*, Syllepse, 2016. He is the author of *L'hypothèse Jeremy Corbyn. Une histoire politique et sociale de la Grande-Bretagne depuis Tony Blair*, preface by Ken Loach, Demopolis, 2019.

André Gilles Latournald (France) is a Doctor in Economic Sciences. He works at the National Institute for Young Blind People in Paris. Since 1995, he has taught at the University of Paris 1 (Panthéon-Sorbonne). He is a specialist in Adam Smith; his work focuses on liberalism, economic policies, econometrics and epistemology.

Dic Lo (China) is a Political Economist specializing in China and world development. His works have been published in scholarly journals both in Chinese and English. He has been with School of Oriental and African Studies (SOAS), University of London, for almost 30 years. He is currently with the Economics School (Lingnan College) of Sun Yat-Sen University in Guangzhou.

Zhiming Long (China), is a Tenured Associate Professor in Economics and a doctoral supervisor at the School of Marxism at the Tsinghua University in Beijing. He is an Associate Editor of the book series *A Comprehensive Study on the World Dissemination of Marxist Classic Literature* (100 volumes). He has a PhD in Economics from the University of Paris 1. His research focuses on China's Economy, World Economics and Quantitative Marxian Economics.

Juan Pablo Mateo (Spain) is currently an Associate Professor at the Complutense University of Madrid. His research is focused on the theory of crisis, the tendency of the profit rate and the core/periphery relation within the unequal development of capitalism. His last book is *The Theory of Crisis and the Great Recession in Spain* (Palgrave, 2019), with articles in the *Review of Radical Political Economics, Capital & Class, Science & Society, International Review of Applied Economics*, among others.

Jérôme Maucourant (France) teaches at the Université Jean Monnet in Saint-Étienne, France, and is a member of the team UMR 5206 *Triangle* (École normale supérieure of Lyon). He is the host of the *Prolégomènes* website (jerome-maucourant.com/). One of his last publications is the chapter 'Karl Polanyi on Money', In Michele Cangiani and Claus Thomasberge (Eds.), *The Routledge Handbook on Karl Polanyi*, pp. 206–216, Routledge, London and New York, 2024.

Surajit Mazumdar (India) is a Professor at the Centre for Economic Studies and Planning (CESP), Jawaharlal Nehru University, New Delhi, India, since 2014. He had previously served on the faculty of several other institutions in Delhi too. His academic research has focused on the Political Economy of Indian Development, with special focus on the Corporate Sector, Industrialization and on Globalization and its impact on the Indian Economy.

Seeraj Mohamed (South Africa) is Deputy Director for Economics in the South African Parliamentary Budget Office. He is an Adjunct Professor at the School of

Government at the University of the Western Cape. Before that, he was an Associate Professor of Economics at the University of the Western Cape and the Director of the Corporate Strategy and Industrial Development Research Programme at the University of the Witwatersrand in Johannesburg. In 1993, he was a Research Trainee in the Macroeconomic Research Group (MERG) project commissioned by the *African National Congress* (ANC) to offer progressive post-apartheid options, which they rejected. (*His article expresses his own views and not those of his employer*).

Farhang Morady is an Associate Professor in International Development at the University of Westminster in London. His research focuses on the intersection of global politics and the economy, particularly emphasizing the Middle East and its developmental issues. He has collaborated with academics from Southeast Asia, the Middle East and Latin America to produce scholarly works in English, Turkish and Spanish. His most recent publication, *Contemporary Iran: Politics, Economy, Religion*, was published by the Bristol University Press in 2020.

Maxence Poulin (Canada) is a PhD student at the University of Quebec in Montreal. He graduated in Political Science from the University of Montreal. His research focuses on socialist transitions in the Global South, imperialism and socialist China. His current research analyzes the dynamics and contradictions arising from the articulations among socialism, capitalism and imperialism in modern socialist China.

Poeura Tetoe (France) has a multidisciplinary background, notably in anthropology and economics. She graduated from the University of Paris 1 where she obtained a Master's degree in development economics and the *École des Hautes Études en Sciences Sociales* (EHESS). She is originally from Tahiti where she currently lives, after having lived for a long time in New Caledonia, but also stayed in Papua New Guinea during her studies.

Ying Yue (China) is a doctoral candidate specializing in modern and contemporary Chinese history at Tsinghua University. She has co-authored *The Origin of the Family, Private Property and the State: A Study on Ravé's French Translation* (Liaoning People's Publishing House, 2023). Her article *Gender, Family, and Political Power Construction* is to be published in the *Journal of China Women's University*.

Paul Zarembka (United States) is a Research Professor of Economics at the State University of New York at Buffalo and, since 1977, has been Series Editor of *Research in Political Economy*. He published in mainstream economics and edited *Frontiers in Econometrics*, before moving into Marxist political economy. Along with numerous articles and presentations, he was an editor and a contributor for *The Hidden History of 9–11* (Seven Stories Press, 2nd edition, 2008). In 2021, he published *Key Elements of Social Theory Revolutionized by Marx* (Brill hardcover, Haymarket softcover). Among other indices, he has appeared Marquis *Who's Who in the World*.

Chen Zhang (China) is a PhD student at Peking University. She specializes in French imperialism and State-led and social anti-imperialist movements in West Africa. She published papers on Canadian neo-fascist social movements and the CFA (zone franc de la Communauté financière en Afrique, or *franc zone of the Financial Community in Africa*) franc in Francophone Africa. Her current research analyzes anti-French imperialism social movements in contemporary Senegal.

Shaozhi Zhong (China) is a graduate student at the School of Economics at Renmin University of China and Kyushu University in Japan. His primary research interests lie in historical and comparative political economy.

PRESENTATION

This new volume of *Research in Political Economy* is devoted to themes related to various 'trajectories of declining and destructive capitalism', within the framework of contemporary Marxism. To discuss these themes, we brought together 15 texts, written by 20 social scientists from 10 countries. These authors are, for some, internationally renowned and experienced personalities and, for others, young researchers starting their careers, but all working in their own way to strengthen Marxism in order to apply its powerful methods to the interpretation and, above all, the transformation of the world. Their contributions deal with 12 economies, covering five continents: Germany, Great Britain, France, Spain, Senegal, South Africa, Lebanon, Iran, India, Papua New Guinea, Australia and Chile in the current period or very near past – plus two other countries, China and Cuba, in their more distant past preceding their respective socialist revolutions. In addition, the cases of Palestine and Israel, but also of Ukraine, are addressed in a final postscript written by Paul Zarembka.

Capitalism has always been destructive, since its origins. Let us take as examples the process of enclosures which, at the very centre of the world system, closed access to land to peasants, expelled many of them from their countryside, pushed them into an exodus towards the miserable slums of the working-class neighborhoods of industrial cities and threw their children into the throes of 'dirty work' during the First Industrial Revolution, or, more massive still, the processes of primitive accumulation at the time of the great 'discoveries' and the colonizations, accompanied by the variations of modern slavery, from *encomienda* imposed on Amerindians to 'black birding' suffered by the Oceanians, through the deportations of forced laborers from Africa to plantations of the Americas for centuries or, later, through the recruitment of Indian ryots or Chinese coolies. And what about the immensely devastating effects of imperialism on the peoples who were its victims or the human cataclysms of the World Wars, which were inter-imperialist clashes?

Nevertheless, these calamities were associated, in the northern countries, with high economic growth rates, productivity gains, technological innovations or even infrastructure construction and job creation. But present capitalism is now declining at the core of the global system, where economic growth of low intensity or close to zero prevails. Japan or, in Europe, Germany (and recently France), have been experiencing recession for years, Canada is almost there – the United States owing its relative 'dynamism' only to wealth transfers from abroad and its (still for a while) hegemonic position over the world system. Most of the indicators went haywire: drops in economic growth rates, consumption, trade; operating deficits of industrial companies; losses of jobs, housing, savings – the worst consequences of the structural crisis of capitalism still being borne by the poorest among the working classes. However, today, on a global scale, capitalism is above all destructive for individuals, societies and the environment.

The damages include a generalized malaise, pains in life, bad feelings in the workplace and phenomena of individual psychological collapse. This is about the combined effects of tension and stress caused by the threat of unemployment and pressures exerted by evaluation methods, leading to heightened competition between workers within a same production unit. From there comes a rupture in the bonds of respect, loyalty, conviviality and solidarity between colleagues. Hence the appearance of distrust among them, fear at work, self–control, reciprocal surveillance or pathologies of loneliness, accompanied by feelings of moral betrayal of oneself, awareness of a lie in the face of the requirements of 'total quality' and 'certification by the market.' Hence also – in a universe where the mobilization of energies is permanent, instability and flexibility become normalized, and collective spaces for thinking and acting together are shrinking –, a loss of moral reference points, of the sense of responsibility and of motivation to regain the tools to transform human relationships at work. Not to mention the hardening of labour conflicts and forms of repression against workers who resist and those who defend them. In this context, cases of suicide at work (wage earners, peasants) or elsewhere (unemployed) have multiplied.

On the scale of society, the damage caused by capitalism, under the effect of the concentration of private ownership of means of production and the logic of maximizing immediate individual profit, is innumerable at the levels of families, ethical values, political life, institutions – the State seeing its perimeter less reduced than its repressive functions reinforced to the detriment of its social ones – and, of course, the economies. The downward pressure on the rate of profit is incessant, despite its counter-trends. But the rise of credit allows capital to accumulate in various forms of money capital. The current crisis is reflected in explosions of fictitious capital, however, associated with real devaluations. In capitalism that throws workers into competition, pits people against each other, fuels racism and far rights, its neoliberal form leads all countries into a destructive spiral which pushes to make labour markets more flexible, to lower the 'cost of work', to privatize and outsource. Social rights and public services are dismantled. Trapped in a systemic crisis, capital no longer finds solutions and is much more dangerous. Between business bankruptcies and mass unemployment, bank destabilization and stock market crashes, the probability of a worsening of the systemic crisis of capital is high. The conditions are ripe for the contradictions of the capitalist system to become even more accentuated.

Let us take a concrete example, among others, of such contradictions. For decades, the peasantries of the capitalist world have been suffering an intensification of attacks by capital on their land, natural resources and means of production. These attacks have also been eroding national sovereignty, destroying communities, devastating ecosystems and threatening the survival of huge numbers of human beings. While agricultural production far exceeds needs, billions of people on earth today continue to suffer from undernourishment, most of them being peasants. Besides, the expansion of cultivated areas worldwide has been accompanied by a decline in peasant populations relative to those in cities, which absorb massive flows of rural exodus, mainly into overcrowded and unsanitary slums. Furthermore, a growing proportion of land is cultivated by transnational firms which no longer intend their agricultural production for household food consumption, but for agro-fuels or industrial outlets. In most southern countries which find themselves excluded from the benefits of capitalist globalization, growing agricultural exports derived from rental crops coexists with increasing imports of basic food goods.

Today, we are dealing, within the power of finance itself, with a systemic crisis: capital does not find internal solutions to the contradictory dynamics it deploys. Among the options for exiting the crisis which are considered by the dominant fractions of neoliberal globalist capital, there is unfortunately that of the war economy, i.e. a sector which programmes the destruction of human lives, as well as material and natural wealth. Militarization is the mode of existence of financial oligopolies' capital. Overaccumulation is the chronic disease of capitalism, from which it cannot escape and which in the long term marks its structural tendency to enter into crisis – and even decadence. To avoid this overaccumulation, a drastic, dramatic solution exists: the devaluation of capital through its massive destruction, and this is the terrain of war – even if, ultimately, imperialist wars further aggravate the imbalances of capitalism. An illustration of this extreme violence is given by the current drama experienced in Gaza by the Palestinian people, already the victim of a colonization and apartheid project, unconditionally supported by US imperialist hegemony and its northern allies, maintaining a permanent war and leading to what the International Court of Justice itself considers a 'plausible risk of genocide.'

And how can we not talk about environmental disasters directly caused by the capitalist system? Nowadays, the general public is widely aware of the deterioration of the state of the planet and the global risks that result from it. This is the case of the 'greenhouse effect' and the expected manifestations of global warming linked to anthropogenic gas emissions. The effects of climate change are already perceptible, and in most ecological scandals, those responsible are clearly identifiable. Capitalism has become a threat to humanity as a whole – its neoliberal form only aggravating its impact. Climate crisis multiplies the risks of ecological disasters, but also of wars for access to natural resources – with their consequent migrations. The present situation resembles the beginning of a process of slow, gradual, huge collapse of the oligopolistic-financialized stage of capitalism. The latter, however, will not fall of its own accord; only popular struggles, massive, convergent and organized, will succeed. Thus, we have to get out of capitalism in order to finally open post-capitalist transitions made of authentically social or, better still, socialist alternatives.

Rémy Herrera, July 9, 2024

PART I

PAST, (PRE-REVOLUTIONARY) SOUTH

REPUBLICAN CHINA AS A UNITY OF OPPOSITES: AN ANALYSIS OF THE ESSENCE OF SEMI-COLONIALISM AND SEMI-FEUDALISM FROM 1911 TO 1949

Maxence Poulin[a] and Chen Zhang[b]

[a]*University of Quebec in Montreal, Canada*
[b]*Peking University, China*

ABSTRACT

This chapter argues that the destruction of the Chinese economy and the immiseration of the productive classes of the country during the Republican era were caused by contradictions arising from the forceful articulation of the Chinese social formation to imperialism. We further argue that imperialism, as an external factor, could only cause the stagnation of the Chinese economy because of the particular essence of the modes of production found within Chinese imperial society at the end of the Qing dynasty (1644–1911). The critical internal factors were strong bureaucratic and feudal modes of production, which left merchant capitalism unfree to develop. When imperialism opened China to the international capitalist market, Chinese merchant capitalists served as a bridge between imperialism and Chinese feudalism. Their growing influence tended to reinforce their capitalism's feudal and bureaucratic appearances. The articulation of this comprador capitalism with the State-based mode of production and feudalism created, during the Republican era, bureaucratic–capitalism, which increased the exploitation of working people by the State, landlords, and capitalists. This articulation of feudalism, bureaucratic–capitalism, and imperialism was the root cause of the underdevelopment of the Chinese economy.

Trajectories of Declining and Destructive Capitalism
Research in Political Economy, Volume 40, 3–18

Published under exclusive licence by Emerald Publishing Limited
ISSN: 0161-7230/doi:10.1108/S0161-723020250000040001

Keywords: Chinese social formation; imperialism; Chinese feudalism; comprador capitalism; bureaucratic capitalism

INTRODUCTION: CHINA AS A UNITY OF OPPOSITES

Wide debates about the nature of the Chinese mode of production are ever-present in both academic and political circles. For some, China is a land where capitalism reigns as the market and a capitalist class are found within it. For others, socialism is still in power as the land and heaviest industry still function based on socialist relations of production, maintained by political power in the hands of the Communist Party of China. This debate on the essence of the Chinese social formation can be extended over time. It surged during the Republican era when feudal lords and the comprador bourgeoisie were in power. For some Marxists like Chen Duxiu, China had already attained capitalism and needed a socialist Revolution to put the working class in power (Chen, 1932; especially: 'Capitalism or the City Dominated Feudalism'). For Mao Zedong, this was only partially true. While capitalism did exist in China, the country remained a semi-feudal and semi-colonial social formation (Mao, 1928; especially 'Feudalism Was Not Yet a Dying Force'). This apparent logical contradiction only reflects the dialectical contradiction that rests on the Chinese social formations: multiple modes of production seem to coexist in China. Mao grasped the dialectical aspect of the question, as he regarded the essence of a thing as being dependent on the kind of relations found between its inner aspects. China could be conceptualized as being both feudal and capitalist.

This chapter argues that the destruction of Chinese society, of its productive forces and its productive classes, was caused by capitalism. Our analysis rests on a dialectical understanding of China as a unity of opposite modes of production in interrelation. The immiseration of the Chinese people can only be understood when conceptualized as a dynamic created by the contradictory relations of the multiple modes of production found in the Chinese social formation during the Republican era. When Chinese society is viewed as a unity of contradictory modes of production, the dynamics that led to the decrease in the quality of life of the Chinese people can be explicitly located in the governing laws of the dominant mode of production in China, in the laws of the subordinate ones, and in their relations with each other. During the Republican era, three major modes of production were found in the Chinese social formation: feudalism, bureaucratic–capitalism, and imperialism.

Using untranslated Chinese Marxist documents, we will, in the following few sections, describe each mode of production found in China in that period, explain their main class relationships, their main contradictions, their productive forces, their superstructures, and the transformations that occurred from the end of the Qing Empire (1644–1911) to the eve of the Revolution. We further argue that the root cause of the destruction and stagnation of the Chinese social formation of the Republican era with a dominant bureaucratic mode of production is found in imperialism, understood as the global system of trade and exchange of commodities extending from rich imperialist countries and imposed by force on other nations.

THE CHINESE FEUDAL AND BUREAUCRATIC MODES OF PRODUCTION

The Feudal Mode of Production

For the official interpretation of feudalism by the Communist Party of China in Chinese history, feudalism lasted from the beginning of the Zhou dynasty (1046 BC–256 BC) right until around the first Opium War (1839–1842) (Dirlik, 1997, p. 49). During the Republican era, Mao described the evolution of his society towards socialism as facing two great mountains that needed to be overcome: imperialism and feudalism (Mao, 1971, p. 321). Feudalism stayed entrenched in many parts of the country even after the Revolution of 1911. However, the idea that feudalism is a eurocentric concept that cannot apply to the history of China is still widespread. This is explained by the fact that feudalism is mainly described in political terms as a method of government (Strayer, 1965, p. 13), a fragmentation of authority (Bloch, 1961, p. 446), or a fragmentation of political sovereignty based on a regime of politically constituted property (Wood, 2011, p. 167).

The issue with these conceptualizations is that they stem from a Weberian view, situating the determining factor of history in the political sphere, in the constant struggle for the control of the State (Weber, 1995, p. 347). For most Marxists, the essence of a unity is found within its economic base, not its superstructure. The fact that China does not share the particular political State machinery of feudal Europe does not mean that it does not share its essence. Feudalism has a universal essence with specific laws of motion. However, it also possesses multiple appearances that are formed depending on the concrete conditions in which this mode of production is found. For Chinese Marxists, European feudalism is but one of a kind, and Chinese feudalism is as much indicative of the essence of feudalism as the European one (Dirlik, 1997, p. 55).

The essence of feudalism for most of Chinese history takes the appearance of the landlord economy created by the disintegration of a European kind of feudalism of the Zhou dynasty when hereditary property was transformed into a system of private ownership where land could be freely bought and sold. The characteristic of this type of feudal mode of production is the absence of obligations towards the landlords. The landlords' economic exploitation of the peasant tenants took the form of rent in kind and money rent. The creation of this appearance of feudalism is explained by the increasing power of commercial capital, which articulated itself to the feudal natural economy in a social formation that had no developed industry. This meant that capital in a social formation dominated by feudalism took the appearance of a commercial capitalist mode of production that produced very little, as no industrial base was available to subsume, and as a result, only transformed available feudal products into commodities. Land thus became the commodity of choice for the dominant classes to invest in, as pure money profit could be achieved. The governing law of this feudal mode became the accumulation of land by lords and merchants for achieving high rates of profit, which caused an important polarization of the land and of money wealth, a decreasing rate of free peasants, and an increasing rate of tenants and slaves.

The State was a key factor in the exploitation of the peasantry even after the Xinhai Revolution of 1911. It was, however, more than just the political arm of the landlord class. The Chinese dynastic State and the Republican State, after it, contained in themselves a State-based mode of production, which we termed in the Chinese case the *bureaucratic–landlord* mode of production. Its main economic function was the exploitation of the peasantry by the imposition of a tax for the reproduction of a bureaucratic landlord class. In contrast, its secondary functions were the organization of infrastructure projects and industries. The producing class of this mode of production was the free peasantry, which suffered a rate of exploitation as high as the tenants (Zhufu, 1981, pp. 10–20).

In 1902, during the Qing dynasty, free peasants with the best fields had to pay a tax of 0.4 yuan per *mu* (亩, a Chinese unit of measurement of 666.67 square metres) of land to the central State. From 1929 to 1931, this tax increased 3 to 12 folds depending on the locality (Zhang, 1957b, p. 16). Local governments were also charging additional taxes and fees imposed on most daily activities. During the Qing dynasty, the local governments' fees imposed on peasants were lower than those imposed by the central government by law. However, they grew in proportion during the Republican era. In 1915, the additional taxes and fees were only 27% of the central tax per *mu* that peasants generally paid. In 1933, they increased to 500% more than the central tax per *mu* (Zhang, 1957b, p. 21). The reason for the increases in these fees is because of the military competition between warlords. As the country was divided between competing local feudal landlord forces consolidated in the power of powerful warlords, the war for control of the territory and taxes took place between different warlords and the Guomindang Party. As a result, the war effort increased the feudal extortion of peasants by many folds (Zhang, 1957a, pp. 557–580).

When the Guomindang took over and reunited the country, this prime characteristic of the bureaucratic–landlord State did not go away. Rather, this type of economic exploitation grew larger than during the Qing dynasty and the warlord era (Zhang, 2002, p. 138). The Xinhai Revolution inaugurated the transformation of the bureaucratic–landlord mode of production towards a bureaucratic–capitalist mode of production wherein the bureaucratic class progressively created surplus value through State-protected capitalist enterprises.

The Bureaucratic–Landlord Mode of Production

The period of the warlord State was a transitory one between bureaucratic–landlordism and bureaucratic–capitalism, where feudalism became increasingly important. Warlords were the main military force backing the Republic of China and the bureaucratic–capitalist mode of production. As the Xinhai Revolution succeeded because a large group of feudal aristocrats leading the Beiyang army rebelled against the Qing Empire not to establish a bourgeois Republic but to consolidate their power over their Manchu bureaucratic overlord, some of the most powerful landlords of the country were in places of high power. The most powerful landlords became warlords, acting as governors of the provinces of the former empire. They also individually held a considerable amount of land. Big landlords held, on average, 10,000 *mu* of farmland (Zhang, 1957a, pp. 14–16).

In addition, the exploitation rate of the peasantry increased as the warlord State demanded that peasants prepay the taxes for multiple years. As an extreme example, the warlord State in Sichuan demanded peasants pay more than 30 years' worth of their annual central tax from 1926, up to 1957. As most peasants could not pay, they had to relinquish their land, which was transferred directly to the warlord or influential local landlords (Zhang, 2002, p. 138), weakening the bureaucratic mode and strengthening feudalism. Even though their personal power rested on their property, their power as warlords was brought about by the need for the landlord class to suppress peasant resistance when the Xinhai Revolution made the bureaucratic State too weak (Xie, 2019, p. 72). They acted first and foremost to protect the interests of their class against peasants by keeping intact the feudal relations of production found in the villages (Li, 1930).

The increased exploitation of the peasantry created by the alliance of capitalists, imperialists, and landlords generated a large supply of landless peasants and unemployed workers for recruitment in the warlords' armies (Chen, 1980, p. 72). The number of soldiers under the command of various warlords grew from 500,000 in 1916 to 2 million in 1928 (Qi, 1991, p. 71). As Mao pointed out, at the time of the Beiyang government (1912–1928), the landlords and the bureaucrats were the dominant class of China, and warlords were their political arm. When the Guomindang took over (in 1928), most warlords were integrated into the party's governing structure, and an alliance was formed between the big Chinese bourgeoisie and the landlords (Mao, 1991, p. 601). The effect of the Xinhai Revolution was to weaken the bureaucratic State to consolidate the power of the landed aristocracy and its feudal mode of production, causing the increased power of the comprador bourgeoisie, which took hold of the bureaucratic State.

Chinese feudalism during the Republican era still found its essence in the relation of production between peasants and landlords, embodied in sharecropping and money rent. In 1934, 10% of the big landlords and rich peasants controlled 68% of the land, while 70% of peasants only had 17% of the land (Zhang, 1957a, p. 747). During this period, landlords dramatically increased their wealth and power as the amount of land in their hands grew. The landless peasants and the agricultural proletariat reprensented 28% of the total number of peasants. In comparison, the free peasantry was 49%, the sharecroppers were 28%, and 23% of peasants were at the same time free and sharecroppers in 1912. In 1947, the share of landless tenants increased to 33%, that of free peasants decreased to 42%, and the share of mixed peasants increased to 25% (Yan, 2012, p. 276). Sharecropping was an important, though not predominant, relation of production in the feudal mode of production still at the end of the Qing dynasty, where landlords took around 40%–70% of the products cultivated by peasants (Zhang, 1957a, pp. 96–97).

Even though money rent was already an important aspect of the Chinese feudal mode of production, it took an unprecedented proportion near the coast where commercial capital was more developed and imperialism strongly influenced the economy. In 1934, the average proportion of money rent became 21% of total rent, while 79% was paid in kind. In an area of Jiangsu with an undeveloped commercial economy, money rent was only 23.5% of the total, while in a commercially developed area, the percentage increased to 48% (Yan, 2012, p. 290). When a landlord became very large, his desired choice of rent was the money rent as opposed to rent in agricultural products (Zhang, 1957a, p. 266), as most were already well established in the cities (Zhang, 1957a, p. 305) where the commercial economy was more developed and where the money form of value held considerable power.

Money rent and rent-in-kind both increased during this period. On average, money rent grew by about 103% from 1910 to 1930 (Yan, 2012, p. 318). This price increase in rent is partly explained by the deflation of foodstuff prices during the 1920s and the 1930s, which created a tendency for the landlords to increase the rents to maintain the profit rate of their land (Zhang, 1957b, p. 267). As the data show, rents were becoming increasingly expensive for peasants. For comparison, yearly land rents in China during the Republican period were about 15%–20% of the value of the land, while those of Western Europe during the 18th and 19th centuries were about 3%–5% (Zhang, 1957a, p. 112). This shows that the Chinese peasantry was more exploited than in the past by their feudal lords and was more exploited than their Western European counterparts.

The result of this feudal exploitation of the Chinese peasantry by private landlords and the bureaucratic State was an increase in the debt level of peasants. In the 1930s, 50%–70% of all peasants were indebted. Two types of debt existed: money debt, the secondary one, and the debt in foodstuffs, the main one. Even though the money debt's interest rate was high, at a yearly average of 30%, the foodstuff debt was considerably higher, ranging from 30% to 500% yearly. The debt in foodstuff shows that many peasants at the time could not produce enough to pay for the fees and the rent and had to resort to borrowing food from their landlords to survive. In contrast, the free peasantry had to resort to borrowing money debt to pay for the taxes and later mostly borrowed money to repay old debts. The rate of exploitation of the peasantry increased as the main lenders, landlords, rich peasants, and local capitalists tended to shorten the debt repayment time from 10–12 months to 1–3 months. The interest rate in the villages of China increased between 1909 and 1934 from a minimum of 10% to a maximum of 400% yearly (Yan, 2012, pp. 340–349). The extremely high interest rate was accompanied by a clause that made peasants unable to repay the entirety of their debt in a certain amount of time, around three years in Fujian, forfeit their land to the lender (Zhang, 1957a, pp. 551–555). This led to an increase in the rate of landless peasants and sharecroppers.

Usury Capital in Bureaucratic China

At the core of this relation is found usury capital. It belongs, with commercial capital, to the 'antediluvian forms of capital which long precede the capitalist mode of production and are to be found in the most diverse socio-economic formations' (Marx, 1991, p. 728). They are here subordinated forms, or modes of production, articulated to social formations where small peasant production predominates. Usurer capital's organic class relation is not found within the confines of the real capitalist mode of production, but rather in the modes of production preceding it, in this instance, the Chinese feudal social formation. It is a social relation where capital does not yet subordinate the producer as in modern capitalism but only takes control of the surplus labour without altering, in the short term, the relations of production (Marx, 1991, pp. 729–730). Consequently, this type of usury capital in China should be understood in the confines of the relations of production existing in a social formation dominated by feudalism and the bureaucratic modes of production.

As the data shows, the rate of interest of usury capital in the heart of Chinese feudalism, the villages, became so high during the warlord and Guomindang eras that most of the surplus labour of the free peasantry was taken by this kind of capital. In the 1930s, 56% of these free peasants had money debts, and 48% were food borrowers (Zhang, 1935). The income of four-fifths of peasant families was less than the minimum necessary to feed a family (Tawnky, 1937, p. 90). The income of the Chinese peasantry was low and, in many cases, even negative (Zhang, 1957a, pp. 473–475). As Marx (1991, pp. 730–731) explained, the consequence of usury capital is to impoverish the mode of production without necessarily causing an evolution towards a new mode of production, as it does not revolutionize the productive forces but only separates the producers from their means of production. In China, most landless peasants were not absorbed in the new capitalist mode of production as the cities did not have enough industrial capital to employ them. However, they could only be absorbed incompletely as sharecroppers in the feudal mode or soldiers for the warlords (Zhang, 2002, p. 132).

As China was a semi-feudal and semi-colonial social formation, the root cause of the increased importance of usury capital is found in the articulation of feudalism with imperialism, the international capitalist mode of production. Chinese feudalism at the time was highly dependent on money as the bureaucratic State and landlords required taxes, fees, and rents to be paid in this form, as the money economy was increasingly developed on the coasts. As Marx explained, usurer generally articulates itself in relations of production where money plays an important role, like the tax farmers of ancient Rome (Marx, 1991, p. 734). The money form of value and, as we will see, the commodity form of production play an important role in the growth of usury and in the separation of producers from means of production.

One of the appearances that the entry of the modern capitalist mode of production took in the feudal villages is banking capital. As peasants in the 1930s became too poor to pay the State tax, the Guomindang government wanted to restore their ability to produce and pay taxes to save itself from a financial crisis. The main goal was to improve peasants' agricultural productivity and root out usury capital from the countryside to restore its subjects' ability to pay the central tax (Luo, 1983, pp. 600–603). This was done by introducing banking capital, which was organically tied to the free peasantry, producers working with their own means of production, as opposed to the sharecroppers of the feudal mode tied to usury capital and the landlord class. As we said, the interest rate of money debt was considerably lower than that for borrowing products, mainly by sharecroppers. As Marx (1991, p. 730) pointed out, the lower level of interest in money lending compared to usury, found mainly in food lending in China, reflects the fact that banking capital only has a secondary function in the modern capitalist mode of production, taking only one part of the whole surplus value from the producers, while usury takes typically all the surplus value from them. Usury capital inhibited the appearance of agrarian capitalism, while banking capital could articulate itself to the peasantry and help create a class of capitalist peasants. Banking capital increased differentiation in the countryside.

This could only be done because commodity production became widespread in the Chinese countryside following the imperialist aggression of the 19th century, taking hold not among feudalism's main class, the landlords, but rather among the free peasantry, articulated to the bureaucratic mode of production (Xue, 1983, pp. 514–516). It expanded rapidly in the 1920s and 1930s when the rate of commercialization of the peasantry attained an average of 40% and as high as 70% in areas specialized in cash crops. In 1922 and 1923, the rate of commercialization of the rich peasants was the highest, selling 62% of their products on the market while also being the most insulated from the market for their consumption, only buying 6.5% of their total food consumption. On the other hand, poor free peasants had to rely on the market to buy 58.7% of their food intake, while selling 57% of their production (Yan, 2012, pp. 327–329). This shows that, in theory, banking capital could be set loose in the countryside and increase the productivity of the free peasantry, who were mainly integrated into the market while creating capitalist relations of production in agriculture.

This did not happen. The agricultural banks of China only lent in 12 cotton-producing provinces, an important cash crop for imperialist countries, and only to middle and rich peasants. In contrast, poor and landless peasants and sharecroppers were entirely excluded from the arrangement (Zhang, 1957b, pp. 183–193). Because banking capital excluded much of the peasantry, bureaucratism and feudalism remained the predominant modes of production in the Chinese countryside. Usury capital was, therefore, still the predominant form of capital in the countryside. In the 1930s, the sharecroppers and their associated mode of debt, in food, were still the predominant relation of production, being about 70% of the peasantry, while money debtors represented about 30% of the total (Yan, 2012, pp. 342–343). As a result, bank capital mainly went into the hands of feudal landlords who could increase their holdings by buying the land of poor peasants (Wang, 1983, pp. 578–580). In this case, banking capital did not result in the advancement of capitalist relations of production in the countryside but only in the strengthening of the number of sharecroppers and landless peasants and the concentration of land under landlord domination.

Quality of Life of Peasants and Productive Forces in Republican China

Another indicator of the transition from feudalism and the bureaucratic–landlord mode to capitalism was the growth of the agricultural productive forces, which was also absent. The productivity of agriculture dropped during China's Republican era. The farm tools and farm fertilizers used by peasants of this era were the same as the ones used by their peers of the Qing dynasty. They were productively highly inefficient, as no industrial fertilizers or modern farming tools or machines were utilized (Zhang, 2002, p. 129). During the Republican era, new agriculture tools like pumping machines and threshing machines existed in port regions connected to the world market. Still, only a very few of them were used. Tractors only appeared in imperialist farms operating in China and in the very few Chinese capitalist farms. Chinese agriculture was devoid of any mechanization, as data shows that from all the machines imported to China, the share of agricultural machinery was only 0.74% in 1912 and 1.81% in 1931. Most of the tools used by peasants were the ox-drawn plough and the wooden waterwheel, which were mostly the same ones used 1,000 years ago. When merchant capitalists went to the countryside to sell modern machines and tools, peasants could not afford any of them as they were too poor and their land too small to use them.

As a result, the most common tool of peasants during the 1920s and 1930s were their hands and feet (Zhang, 1991, pp. 45–46). This is explained by the fact that as peasants at that time grew poorer, about 50% lost their oxen and had to sell their basic agricultural tools to survive (Zhang, 1957b, p. 858). This caused a decline in agricultural productivity, as the yield per *mu* of land in 1936 fell by 20% compared to 200 years before, and by 1946, the productivity was even lower than that of the Han dynasty (206 BC–220 AD) (Wu, 1985, pp. 205–206). Productivity could also hardly increase as there was a trend towards reducing farm size, from 202.5 *mu* on average in 1890 to 138 *mu* in 1933 (Yan, 2012, p. 286). With this reduction in farm size also came a 300% increase in the amount of uncultivated arable land from 1914 to 1930 (*Wang Yanan Collection*, 1988, p. 277). In a contradictory way, as the productivity of agriculture lowered, the share of agriculture in China's total value of exports grew from 39% in 1910 to 45% in 1930 (Yan, 2012, p. 72), while the number of self-sufficient peasants declined, causing the need for China to rely on food imports as imperialism made cash crops very important in agricultural production.

BUREAUCRATIC CAPITAL: ON THE BORDER OF FEUDALISM AND IMPERIALISM

Bureaucratic Capitalism

An important growth of the capitalist mode of production occurred in the Chinese social formation since the imperialist aggressions of the 19th century. The main appearance of the capitalist mode of production during the Republican era took the form of bureaucratic capital, which is, in essence, comprador capital merged into the bureaucratic superstructure. The nature of this capital cannot be separated from imperialism. It was birthed in its modern form because of the articulation of the international capitalist market and the Chinese bureaucratic-landlord mode of production, uniting four classes into an alliance: the comprador bourgeoisie, the feudal landlords, the bureaucrats, and the capitalists from imperialist countries.

There are four main aspects of bureaucratic capital. The first is the bureaucracy. Bureaucrats in feudal China were more than simple feudal intellectuals of the superstructure. Their position as bureaucrats was in itself a class that guaranteed a portion of the surplus of the free peasantry taken through the central tax and other forms of State-organized labour. As bureaucracy is a class created through its political privilege to access the surplus of the productive population, bureaucratic capital is based on capital enjoying the political privilege of extracting profits. Here lies the second aspect: the monopoly rights of bureaucratic capital. It acquires this right through political privilege in the bureaucratic superstructure of the owner of the capital. As a consequence, it suppresses non-bureaucratic capital owners while extracting profits for itself (Yan, 2012, p. 153). The third aspect is the linkage between the Chinese social formation and imperialist countries, where Western capital needed native capitalists to acquire materials and sell commodities in its interest. The fourth aspect is the primitive accumulation of capital through the exploitation of peasants.

The essence of the bureaucratic–capital mode of production can, therefore, be summarized as a frozen transitory phase between the bureaucratic–landlord mode of production and State capitalism, controlled by a bureaucratic superstructure with the main aim of serving imperialism, extracting monopoly profits for bureaucrats and keeping intact feudalism in China by suppressing the rise of industrial capitalism in the country.

Bureaucratic capitalism originated in the reform movement of the Qing dynasty in the 1860s when a group of officials saw that Western military and economic superiority came from its industries and wanted to pursue the industrialization of arms production to protect the Chinese social order. Before the articulation of the international market with the Chinese social formation, bureaucratic capital mainly took the form of usury, a capital wholly dependent on the feudal mode of production for its production of surplus value, but only after the Opium War and the large-scale appearance of a comprador capitalist class did bureaucratic capital begin to take industrial and commercial forms (Xu, 1949, p. 9). These forms resulted from merging bureaucrats' feudal capital, the comprador's commercial capital, and State loans. They developed industries near the coast of China (Chan, 1977, pp. 428–430), importing machinery from the West to accumulate capital. They were China's first large-scale modern industrial capital, taking a State-bureaucratic form. They were not focussing on developing consumer and productive goods but on producing military goods.

At the time of the Beiyang government, the nature of bureaucratic capital only changed insofar as landlord bureaucrats transformed into a comprador bourgeoisie, not only accumulating capital through the bureaucratic exploitation of peasants but also through bridging the feudal Chinese economy to the imperialist markets. Their main aim was to help imperialist countries acquire cheap raw material from the feudal mode of production, buy imperialist commodities, and serve other functions facilitating the activities of foreign businesses in China. The competition among foreign capitalists was fierce in China, and the country was never under the rule of only one power; compradors were needed to link Chinese feudalism and foreign capitalism. China's currency was not standardized, measurements were different, and the market was not unified. This is why banking became a critical facet of bureaucratic capital, as Chinese institutions were needed to transfer foreign capital in and out of China (Xu, 1949, pp. 11–13). As a result, bureaucratic capital tended to develop its banking functions.

As bureaucratic banking capital became critical, the transformation of merchant and usury capital into bureaucratic–capitalism was done in China without transforming the feudal mode of production into capitalism as feudalism and the bureaucratic landlord or bureaucratic–capitalist modes of production are not in antagonism with feudalism but are instead in a relation of mutual interdependency. As Andréani (2022, p. 260) put it, the bureaucratic State is rarely the only mode of production in a social formation as it enters into relation not only with the free peasantry but also with a landlord mode of production. This transformation occurred in the 1930s and 1940s when most of the native capital was concentrated in the property of four prominent families in control of the Guomindang government. This bureaucratic–capitalism originated in the surplus produced by peasants that landlords, warlords, and bureaucrats took and invested in the bureaucratic banks. It, however, kept its landlord and feudal character as this capital flowed back into agriculture under the form of usury and land grabbing by wealthy landlords rather than in industry. Consequently, feudalism was strengthened while the landlord and comprador nature of this type of bureaucratic–capital severely hampered the growth of agrarian and industrial capitalism.

Bureaucratic–Capitalism in Antagonism With the Chinese Productive Forces

Bureaucratic capitalism is in an antagonistic relation with the development of national capital and of the productive forces. This is explained by the different class nature of these two kinds of capital: the foundation of bureaucratic capitalism rests on landlord and comprador property. In contrast, the foundation of national capitalism rests strictly on capitalist property. As these different kinds of property belong to opposite classes, their interests and the motions set in place by their property are also opposite. Bureaucratic landlordism takes its power in the exploitation of peasants through its monopolization of land and by taxes. At the same time, comprador capitalism derives its wealth from its role of facilitating the imperialist exploitation of China. Bureaucratic capitalism as a blending of those two kinds of property was in antagonism with the development of a purely national capitalist mode of production which could, politically, endanger the power of bureaucratic landlords and compradors, and economically, destroy the monopoly of foreign capitalists, compradors and bureaucrats. As a result, the rise of industrial capitalism and the productive forces was blocked in China by the alliance of feudalism, bureaucratic capitalism, and imperialism.

Although always dominant in its relationship with other kinds of capital, the predominance of bureaucratic capital was only realized during the war. Whereas bureaucratic capital was predominant in 1894, accounting for 62% of total capital (Wu, 1991), in 1935, private capital's value grew to 88% of the total capital. This was no small feat, as between 1890 and 1913, the capital gained from the commissions of Chinese comprador capitalists working for imperialists, at 5% of the value of imported and exported goods, without accounting for their commercial profits and their salaries, was six times higher than all the capital invested in industrial and mining enterprises by Chinese bureaucratic and private capitalists. This immense comprador capital was only very partially invested in modern industry. Rather, it was invested in land and usury of the feudal economy for higher returns (Writing Group for Capitalist Production Relations in Old China, 1977, pp. 38–41).

Capitalism proper was a growing force. However, bureaucratic capital overtook it, and its value grew to 80% of total capital after the war. During the war, the average value of each bureaucratic factory was two million yuan, and the number of workers employed in each factory on average was more than 100. In comparison, the average value of factories of private capital was only 200,000 yuan, and on average employed half of the number of workers of bureaucratic factories (Chen, 1961a, pp. 1419–1421). This was achieved through political power, as taxes on private national capital were eight times higher than on bureaucratic capital, and bureaucratic monopolies were imposed on major industrial sectors (Yan, 2012, p. 153). There was also widespread acquisition of medium and small enterprises by bureaucratic capital (Xu, 1949, p. 98).

Banking became even more entrenched in bureaucratic hands when the four wealthiest families of China took control of the new central bank and announced a new currency at a time when high inflation made the silver price of commodities very high and when the United States and United Kingdom began to amass all the silver they could find. The new yuan was soon the only available currency in China (Writing Group for Capitalist Production Relations in Old China, 1977, p. 55). The already weak Chinese industrial sector became monopolized by bureaucratic capital. Controlling banking, usury, commerce, and industry, it combined into a financial capital that blocked the establishment of capitalism proper in China.

As a result, the productive forces and the quality of life of workers could not increase and, in many cases, they even regressed. The total value output of capital goods was only 17% of the total industrial production, while that of machinery only accounted for 0.9% in 1933. Most of the machinery imported by Chinese capitalists was outdated, which resulted in very low productivity in the industrial sector, where the productivity of an average Chinese worker was only 1/19th of an American one (Chen, 1961b, pp. 8–10) as compradors were not importing much means of production. Although its shares in total imports grew from 8.1% in 1873 to 52.8% in 1947, most imports served to produce luxury for the higher classes, not for the mass production of commodities for the producing classes. The proportion of machines and tools in total imports stayed very low throughout the period, from 1.5% in 1910 to 8.2% in 1947. China would remain an unindustrialized importer of consumer goods (Yan, 2012, pp. 70–73).

Compared both to a full colony, India, and to poor eastern European countries, China lagged in industrialization (Chen, 1961b, pp. 1–3). This accumulation of capital by the bureaucratic and imperialist classes and of land by feudal lords created a large decline in workers' real wages in China. As feudal lords took peasants' land, and the State and usury capital bankrupted the free peasantry, a growing reserve army of labour appeared in China, which lowered the salary of the Chinese working class. In 1928, the approximate figures for the rate of unemployment were in the range of 25%–33% in China. In Shanghai, where most capitalist employment was found, the number of unemployed jumped from half a million in 1933 to two million in 1947. Even though workers' nominal wages increased until the war with Japan in 1928, real wages decreased due to inflation and increased taxes. Workers could hardly afford their necessities as the price of cloth, coal, and rice rose more rapidly than their wages. The number of families by houses doubled from 1935 to 1938.

After the war, real wages in Shanghai were about half what they were in 1941 (Writing Group for Capitalist Production Relations in Old China, 1977, pp. 341–359). Real wages of workers in the main coastal cities of China were on the same par with those of European countries not yet industrialized in the 18th century and slipped only during the 19th century at the time of the imperialist invasion, only to increase very slightly until the 1910s (Allen et al., 2007, pp. 27–31). This drop in workers' quality of life during the beginning of the 20th century tells us that international capital and bureaucratic capitalism in China were the root causes of the increased immiseration of the productive classes of China. Additionally, the stagnant rate of industrialization of bureaucratic capitalism articulated with a slowly disintegrating feudal mode of production kept alive by the alliance of the feudal landlords, bureaucratic landlords and capitalists, and imperialists caused the stagnation of both the productive forces and the relations of production in the Chinese social formation.

The Role of Imperialism in China

We analyzed the internal modes of production in China to understand the origin of the motion in the Chinese social formation at the beginning of the 20th century. Contradictions found in a unity are primarily determined by its internal aspects. We, however, must not neglect the role of imperialism, for it is the variable that explains the continued dominance of feudalism and the weakness of Chinese capitalism. Economically, imperialist forces controlled much of the industrial capital found in China. By 1920, foreign capital controlled 99% of China's iron ore and pig iron, 93% of the railway, 76% of the coal, and much of the commerce done in the waterways (Walker, 1999, p. 14). Most of the imperialist investments were made on the coast. Shanghai, in 1929, received 76.6% of all British investment, the dominant imperialist power in China. The power of their capital extended far beyond the coast and dug deep into the feudal hinterland (Osterhammel, 1984, p. 266).

Bureaucratic capital was the link between imperialist forces and Chinese production, a force in the process of the formal subsumption of labour under capitalist circuits (Karl, 2017, p. 127). Far from having only an economic role, the political aspect of this alliance was paramount to protect the economic exploitation of the Chinese social formation. Popular resistance to imperialist exploitation was overcome using both foreign and bureaucratic troops. British capital repeatedly used feudal authorities and their own marines to massacre strikers (Osterhammel, 1984, pp. 277–278).

The economic exploitation of China by imperialist countries took two forms. The first one is the superexploitation of the Chinese labour force, whereby foreign capital gains higher profits by paying the workers in the periphery below the cost of the reproduction of labour (Smith, 2016, pp. 241–243). This is a form of direct exploitation of the workers by the bourgeoisie of another country and can only happen when direct investment is made in the country. As the data shows, imperialists already had investments in China used to manufacture goods. However, this form is still secondary to the structural one, the second form, whereby the wealthy imperialist social formations structure the world market in two camps, one which manufactures and gains surplus value, and the other which only gives raw materials and buys manufactured goods (Yan, 2012, p. 79). This serves, firstly, to create a market for finished products manufactured in rich capitalist countries while creating a source of cheap raw materials. Secondly, as Grossman and Kuhn (2021, p. 371) pointed out, the formation of a world market creating a relation between industrialized and non-industrialized countries permits the transfer of value to the rich countries through the equalization of the profit rate between social formations with different organic compositions of capital.

As this relation does not require both aspects to be completely capitalist but rather only requires them to be articulated through the international capitalist market, it is in the interests of imperialist countries for feudalism with strong comprador elements to survive and dominate colonial social formations. It is the structural relation, the relations of production between the Chinese and imperialist social formations, that explains not only the other forms of imperialist exploitation but also why feudalism was still important, why the bureaucratic mode of production was still the dominant mode of production in China, why the capitalist mode of production did not develop as it did in Europe and Japan, and why the Chinese productive classes were exponentially poorer as capitalist' influences entered their social formation.

CONCLUSION

In this chapter, we analyzed the Chinese social formation as a unity of opposite modes of production. Three modes of production were articulated in the social formation during the Republican era: feudalism, bureaucratic–capitalism, and imperialism. During the Republican era time, feudalism became the predominant mode of production. This type of feudalism, however, had different characteristics than classical Chinese feudalism as it mutated due to the transformation of bureaucratic–landlordism into bureaucratic–capitalism due to its articulation with imperialism during the 19th and 20th centuries.

Whereas classical feudalism tends to keep its social order stable by limiting the exploitation of its productive classes, the kind of feudalism and the bureaucratic mode of production found in China under the Beiyang and Guomindang governments were antagonistic with the reproduction of Chinese society itself. The productive forces of agriculture regressed while peasants could not reproduce themselves as a class, forcing many into the ranks of the proletariat. The root cause of this destruction of bureaucratic society is to be found in critical aspects internal and external to the chinese social formation. The internal aspect is comprador capitalism, at its base merchant capitalism generally found within most feudal societies that morphed with the bureaucratic State into bureaucratic–capitalism when Chinese merchant capitalism articulated itself to the international capitalist economy and gained the dominant class position in China.

This specific articulation between feudalism and imperialism, done through comprador capitalism, created the stagnation of feudalism by blocking the birth of industrial capitalism in China. This permitted imperialist countries to extract value from China at a time when monopoly capitalism was causing a lowering of their national profit rates. As the Japanese experience showed, peripheral countries could develop industrial capitalism. China and most countries of the Global South were robbed of this possibility by imperialism.

Therefore, imperialism, as understood as the extension of the political and economic systems of developed capitalism worldwide, forcefully articulated itself to the Chinese bureaucratic–feudal social formation, causing the breakdown of the old feudal economy. It shaped and maintained an alliance of feudal and bureaucratic landlords and capitalists and created an economic system that caged China into a non-industrialized economy with labour freed from feudalism but unabsorbed by industry and with raw resources widely available for exploitation by the imperialist bourgeoisie.

REFERENCES

Allen, R., Bassino, J., Ma, D., Moll-Murata, C., & Zanden, J. (2007). *Wages, prices, and living standards in China, Japan, and Europe, 1738-1925*. Discussion paper series. Department of Economics (University of Oxford). https://ora.ox.ac.uk/objects/uuid:2649015b-12b5-4e65-a83e-538b3a3aaed0

Andréani, T. (2022). *Matérialisme Historique: Les Concepts Fondamentaux Revisités*. Ouverture Philosophique. L'Harmattan.

Bloch, M. (1961). *Feudal society*. Routledge.

Chan, W. K. K. (1977). Bureaucratic capital and Chou Hsüeh-Hsi in late Ch'ing China. *Modern Asian Studies*, *11*(3), 427–439. https://doi.org/10.1017/S0026749X00014219

Chen, D. (1932, November 17). Who can save China? How can China be saved? [In Chinese]. *Marxists.org*. https://www.marxists.org/chinese/chenduxiu/marxist.org-chinese-chen-19321117.htm

Chen, Z. (1961a). *Documents on modern Chinese industrial history* [in Chinese] (Vol. 3). SDX Joint Publishing Company.

Chen, Z. (1961b). *Documents on modern Chinese industrial history* [in Chinese] (Vol. 4). SDX Joint Publishing Company.

Chen, Z. (1980). *Military and gentry power* [in Chinese]. SDX Joint Publishing Company.

Dirlik, A. (1997). 'Feudalism' in twentieth century Chinese historiography. *China Report*, *33*(1), 35–66. https://doi.org/10.1177/000944559703300103

Grossman, H., & Kuhn, R. (2021). Henryk grossman works. In *The law of accumulation and breakdown of the capitalist system, being also a theory of crises* (Vol. 3, J. Banaji & R. Kuhn, Trans.). Brill. https://doi.org/10.1163/9789004449978

Karl, R. E. (2017). Compradors: The mediating middle of capitalism in twentieth-century China and the world. In *East-Asian marxisms and their trajectories*. Routledge.

Li, S. (1930). The fundamental problems of the Chinese revolution [in Chinese]. *Bolshevik*, *3*, 2–3.

Luo, G. (1983). Credit co-operation and rural finance in China [in Chinese]. In M. Xue & H. Feng (Eds.), *Selected papers from rural China*. People's Publishing House.
Mao, Z. (1928, October 5). Why does the red regime in China exist? [In Chinese] *Marxists.Org*. https://www.marxists.org/chinese/maozedong/marxist.org-chinese-mao-19281005.htm
Mao, Z. (1971). *Selected readings from the works of Mao Tsetung* (1st ed.). Foreign Languages Press.
Mao, Z. (1991). *Selected works of Mao Zedong* [in Chinese] (Vol. 2). People's Publishing House.
Marx, K. (1991). *Capital: A critique of political economy* (Vol. 3) Reprint edition. Penguin Classics.
Osterhammel, J. (1984). Imperialism in transition: British business and the Chinese authorities, 1931-1937. *The China Quarterly*, *98*, 260–286.
Qi, X. (1991). *Warlord politics in China* [in Chinese] (Y. Yang & Y. Xiao, Trans.). China Renmin University Press.
Smith, J. (2016). *Imperialism in the twenty-first century*. Monthly Review Press.
Strayer, J. R. (1965). *Feudalism*. D. Van Nostrand Company.
Tawnky, R. H. (1937). *A memorandum on agriculture and industry in China* [in Chinese] (Z. Tao, Trans.). Cheng Chung Book Co.
Walker, K. L. M. (1999). *Chinese modernity and the peasant path: Semicolonialism in the Northern Yangzi delta*. Stanford University Press.
Wang, Y. (1983). Usury capitalism [in Chinese]. In M. Xue & H. Feng (Eds.), *Selected papers from rural China*. People's Publishing House.
Wang, Y. (1988). *Wang Yanan collection* [in Chinese] (Vol. 3). Fujian Education Press.
Weber, M. (1995). *Économie et Société* (Vol. 1, Les Catégories de La Société). Librairie Plon.
Wood, E. M. (2011). *Citizens to lords: A social history of western political thought from antiquity to the late middle ages*. Verso Books.
Writing Group for Capitalist Production Relations in Old China. (1977). *Capitalist relations of production in old China* [in Chinese]. People's Publishing House.
Wu, H. (1985). *A study of grain production in China throughout the ages* [in Chinese]. China Agriculture Press.
Wu, C. (1991). Estimates of capital integration and the value of industrial, agricultural and transport output in modern China [in Chinese]. *Research on Chinese Economic History*, *3*, 23–26.
Xie, G. (2019). *The study of the CPC's anti-feudal struggle thought from 1912 to 1949: A study based on the nature of society* [in Chinese]. Working Paper. Gannan Normal University.
Xu, D. (1949). *Theory of bureaucratic capital* [in Chinese]. Haiyan Bookstore.
Xue, M. (1983). Agricultural commercialisation and rural markets [in Chinese]. In M. Xue & H. Feng (Eds.), *Selected papers from rural China*. People's Publishing House.
Yan, Z. (2012). *Selected statistics on modern Chinese economic history* [in Chinese]. China Social Sciences Press.
Zhang, P. (1935). China's agricultural economy in the 23rd year of the Republic of China [in Chinese]. *Orient Magazine*, *33*, 13.
Zhang, Y. (1957a). *Documents on modern Chinese agricultural history* [in Chinese] (Vol. 2). SDX Joint Publishing Company.
Zhang, Y. (1957b). *Documents on modern Chinese agricultural history* [in Chinese] (Vol. 3). SDX Joint Publishing Company.
Zhang, Y. (1991). The state of agricultural productivity in modern China in customs reports [in Chinese]. *Agricultural History of China*, *2*, 42–48.
Zhang, F. (2002). *Social evolution and revolution in modern China* [in Chinese]. People's Publishing House.
Zhufu, F. (1981). The economic history of China: Some special problems. *Modern China*, *7*(1), 3–30. https://doi.org/10.1177/009770048100700101

CHINA AND MARXIST POLITICAL ECONOMY CONFRONTING WORLD CAPITALISM: REVISITING THE 'SOCIAL NATURE' DEBATE OF THE 1930S–1940S

Dic Lo[a] and Shaozhi Zhong[b]

[a]*Sun Yat-sen University, China*
[b]*Renmin University of China, China*

ABSTRACT

Marxist political economy in the 20th century had to confront the historic task of theorizing capitalism on the world scale. What was at stake was not just the theoretical construct about the capitalist mode of production, or the historical developments in the core capitalist regions of Western Europe and North America, but rather the entire world transformed and reigned by the system of capitalism. An essential constituent of this task concerns the nature of the peripheral societies of the system, and China was at the heart of it. In relation to the twists and turns of anti-capitalist revolutions that overwhelmed the country in the first-half of the century, a range of important theories were developed in Chinese Marxism in the 1930s and 1940s. These theories turned out to be necessary for guiding the revolutions that successfully led to the founding of the People's Republic. They also appeared to be of general importance for Marxist political economy. The exposition on issues of imperialism, compradorization of capital, super-exploitation of labour, the state and modernization, etc., has had far-reaching implications for subsequent theoretical developments. Discernibly, these contributions from China were a precursor of relevant post-war developments in Marxist political economy including those on the world system, dependency, the articulations of modes of production, and uneven development.

Trajectories of Declining and Destructive Capitalism
Research in Political Economy, Volume 40, 19–36

Published under exclusive licence by Emerald Publishing Limited
ISSN: 0161-7230/doi:10.1108/S0161-723020250000040002

Keywords: China; Marxism; world capitalism; anti-capitalist revolutions; political economy; history of thought; economic history; peripheral societies

INTRODUCTION: THE INTELLECTUAL CONTEXT

Despite the worldwide presence, indeed prevalence, of the communist movement in the 20th century, Marxist political economy at least in terms of its mainstream seemed to have experienced a 'nationalistic turn'. The analyses of capitalism tended to take a comparative perspective, as if capitalism is just a set of national models rather than a world-dominating system. This, in a sense, could be deemed a submission to the ideological hegemony of world capitalism.

Post World War II, amid the prevailing Cold War between the capitalist camp and the USSR-led socialist camp, Soviet-type theory seemed to assume the position of orthodoxy in Marxist political economy. Its mission was to serve as the guidance for the modernization drives of the countries within the camp. Representative of the theory was Stalin's (1986) canonical work, *Economic Problems of Socialism in the USSR*, and the subsequent 1957 Soviet official publication, *Political Economy: A Textbook*. The focus of these texts was on socialist construction within the framework of 'one-country socialism' – that is, socialist construction without full consideration of the ubiquitous existence of world capitalism.

Not by coincidence, in the capitalist camp, amid the formation of what later came to be known as the Golden Age of Capitalism which started in the early 1950s, modernization was portrayed as the normalcy under the 'right' policies. And the 'right' policies referred to those of imitating the model of the advanced capitalist countries. The promise from all these was economic 'take-off' (Rostow, 1990) and 'convergence' to the income levels of the advanced countries (Solow, 1956). Thus, in a spirit that is similar to its Soviet counterpart, the message from the capitalist orthodoxy was that every country could achieve modernization by means of imitating the political-economic models of the 'exemplar' countries in the camp. Put another way, both the socialist and capitalist camps indulged in promoting the transplantation of the respective political-economic models of the advanced to the latecomer countries.

The 'nationalistic turn' was a far cry from the classical protagonists of Marxist political economy in the early decades of the 20th century. Revolutionaries such as Lenin, Luxemburg, Trotsky, and Bukharin, and even reformists like Kautsky and Hilferding, put great emphasis on the 'global' nature of modernization – and, by extension, of socialist construction. Much depends on the position of the country in the world economy, especially its connection with imperialism. A country that aspired to socialist construction would inevitably confront the threat from imperialism, including the threat of war.

In the context of this general post-war setting, Baran (1957) was one of the very few political economists to preserve the classical tradition and go against the current of the time. He creatively shifted his focus to underdeveloped countries, pointing out that due to fundamental differences in their own political-economic structures from those of developed capitalist countries, they cannot simply escape the poverty trap through institutional transplantation. Baran also revived the concept of 'imperialism' in the Western context, pointing out that exports and investments thereof are nothing but imperialist drives. And these are inevitable choices for monopolistic capitalist countries under the pressure to digest economic surplus (Baran & Sweezy, 1966).

Following Baran, subsequent radical scholars cited historical data and real-world cases to deepen the study of 'backwardness' as an outcome of imperialism. The emergence of the Dependency School and World-System Analysis in the 1960s and 1970s in the English-speaking world represented this development. Intellectually, the development drew on and systematized a range of theoretical positions from various sources far afield, particularly from Latin America. In terms of its geographical focus, the development progressively expanded the scope from Latin America (Dos Santos, 1970; Frank, 1967) to the rest of the underdeveloped world (Arrighi & Saul, 1973). Eventually, the relevant studies were systematized to give rise to theoretical constructions at the global level (Amin, 1977; Emmanuel, 1972; Wallerstein, 1974). The endeavours of this development deserved the title of *Radical Global Political Economy*. The associated scholars shared a range of theoretical positions, notably the following: first, capitalism is a world system and must be examined from a global perspective; second, this world system embodies a centre–periphery structure; and, third, the world economy is essentially characterized by the exploitation of the periphery by the centre and the dependence of the periphery on the centre. Integrating into the world economy will tend to exacerbate the centre-periphery, rather than bringing about convergence.

Brewer (1990, p. 137) pointed out that after experiencing the 'rupture' of the 1930s and 1940s, the theory of imperialism transited from 'classical' to 'modern' or that of 'Neo Marxism' (see also Noonan, 2017, p. 8). The transition, starting with Baran's *The Political Economy of Growth*, marked the shift in intellectual visions: first, in the post-war world dominated by the United States, systemic wars and revolutions were no longer the most pressing issues; second, monopoly capitalism was no longer imperative for plundering via wars but rather for coping with growth stagnation; and finally, underdeveloped countries, rather than the semi-developed countries focused on by Lenin (1960) in *The Development of Capitalism in Russia*, became the formal subjects of study because of their different growth logics from those of developed countries.

This stock-taking by Brewer and the like seems being limited by their vision both geographically and intellectually. The judgement over the so-called 'rupture' of the 1930s and 1940s might be true in the theoretical developments in the core capitalist countries. But that need not be true in the broader world. After all, it was the peripheral societies of the world that had the far more pressing needs of theorizing imperialism and underdevelopment. The intellectual developments thereof might end up in 'theories in concrete' that are an inextricable part of particular revolutions in specific contexts. For understanding the real world, these theories are no less important than the 'theories in abstract' developed in the core societies. This latter kind of theories have often tended to focus on issues of inter-imperialist rivalry whilst ignoring the broader and more fundamental issues of imperialism and underdevelopment (see, e.g., Callinicos, 2009). Such an inclination embodies the character of the 'nationalistic turn'.

Once the vision is broadened geographically and intellectually, it is possible to posit that Marxist theory of imperialism has actually exhibited a lineage of development from the classics to the modern. This is not just the lineage from Lenin and Luxemburg to Baran and Frank, in the form of 'theories in abstract'. It is also in the form of 'theories in concrete' developed in the diverse settings of peripheral societies. Latin American theories of dependency has been influential in this regard (Marini, 2022). Less well-known, but not less influential in practices although not necessary in scholarly knowledge, is the theories derived from and guiding China's revolutions in the first-half of the 20th century.

In this article, we seek to demonstrate that precisely in the 1930s and 1940s, a host of Chinese radical thinkers devoted great intellectual efforts to apply classical theories of Marxist political economy to the revolutionary praxis of the time. In so doing they had to confront enormous complexities and challenges, and therefore the compelling need for re-conceptualizing and re-formulating the classics. In the event, it turned out that a range of theoretical views were generated from their innovations. These views were quite systematic, encompassing the core concepts, arguments, and logical reasonings of subsequent intellectual developments in the 1960s and 1970s including the theories of dependency and the world system. After all, in the world over the first-half of the 20th century, China was the country that experienced possibly the largest scale of the crucible of world capitalism and the revolution against it. The intellectual endeavours were entirely motivated and driven by the needs of the time.

THE PRELUDE: THE FRIENDS AND ENEMIES OF THE REVOLUTION, 1919–1927

Almost immediately following the October Revolution in Russia in 1917, Marxism was systematically introduced into China and became increasingly influential. Intellectuals of different political orientations sought to analyze Chinese realities through the lens of Marxism. It can be said that their understanding of the political-economic crises in the realities deepened along with the spread of Marxism. They needed the new inspirations for coping with the crises they were confronted with.

The concerned intellectuals mostly tended to treat China as an integral part of the world. This character was part and parcel of the political atmosphere of the time amid the eruption of anti-imperialist sentiment associated with the May Fourth Movement in 1919. China as nominally a member of the victorious countries in the First World War was dealt a heavy blow and humiliation in the post-war peace settlement. It was denied getting back its territories that had been occupied by Germany in the name of concessions, which were decided by the Paris Peace Conference to be transferred to Japan. In the view of the Chinese people, the Treaty of Versailles not only laid bare the ugly face of Western powers but more fundamentally the unjust nature of the existing world system. Qu Qiubai (1899–1935), who was later to adventure to 'seek truth' by visiting Russia and to become a member of the leadership of the Communist Party of China (CPC), aptly made the point: 'the Chinese nation has been exploited for decades and only now has it begun to realize the essence of colonisation. The deep pains of imperialist oppression have awakened the people from the nightmare of empty democracy' (Qu, 1982, p. 34).

Also in 1919, Dai Jitao (1891–1949), who was later to become representative of the far rights of the ruling nationalist party Kuomintang (KMT), published an article entitled *Tracing the Root Causes of China's Disorders From an Economic Perspective* in the journal *Jianshe* (*Construction*). In this article, he explicitly tried to dissect Chinese realities within the framework of historical materialism. His judgement was that China's chaos and crises at the time were not simply a matter of 'political bankruptcy' or 'intellectual bankruptcy', but rather of 'issues of material living' (Dai, 1919, p. 350). Specifically, he attributed the economic chaos and crises to the transformation of the laborers with the formerly cottage industries and agricultural producers into unemployed individuals owing to the oppression from foreign machine-made goods.

Alongside the efforts of Chinese intellectuals, guidance from the Communist International to the CPC newly founded in 1921 became an important source for understanding imperialism and China. In his *Report of the Commission on the National and Colonial Questions* at the Second Congress of the Communist International in July 1920, Lenin pointed out that 'in this age of imperialism, it is particularly important for the proletariat and the Communist International to establish the concrete economic facts and to proceed from concrete realities, not from abstract postulates, in all colonial and national problems'. He also noted that the bourgeoisie of the exploiting countries and the colonial countries have close relations. Hence, the bourgeois of the oppressed countries often, and in most cases, on the one hand, support national movements, but on the other hand, act according to the will of the imperialist bourgeoisie – that is, they join in opposing all revolutionary movements and revolutionary classes (Lenin, 1966, pp. 240–242). It can be said that in the initial revolutionary practices, Lenin's theory of the 'imperialism–colonialism relationship' provided a basic framework for understanding the nature of the Chinese society. On this basis, the CPC established its view and position regarding the historical stage of the Chinese society and the imminent revolutionary tasks for itself. Thus, in the first anti-imperialist and anti-feudal democratic revolution platform passed by the CPC Second National Congress in 1922, the chief targets of the revolution were 'capitalist imperialism and the feudal forces of warlords and state bureaucrats' (Party History Research Center of the CPC Central Committee, 2011, p. 79).

Under the guidance of this platform, the CPC started the process in 1923–1924 to cooperatively join forces with the KMT in launching the national liberation revolution. Imperialism as a target of the revolution was clearly stated in the platform. The target 'feudal forces', in contrast, only referred to warlords and bureaucrats without further extending to include the landlord class.

Various CPC leaders during this period elaborated on Lenin's position for applying the theory to the concrete situations of imperialism and China. In May 1923, the party mouthpiece *Xiangdao* (*The Guide*) published an article by Cai

Hesen (1895–1931), entitled *The Relationship Between the Chinese Revolutionary Movement and the World.* Cai pointed out that

> ...when the capitalist countries have a revolution, the international bourgeoisie often aids each other (as in France and the United States) to counter the international feudal forces. When the colonies and semi-colonies have a revolution, the international bourgeoisie not only does not help the local immature bourgeoisie to overthrow the feudal forces but instead aids the feudal forces in oppressing the democratic revolution. (Cai, 1979, p. 187)

Qu Qiubai (1985, p. 25), in another article entitled *Various Ways of Imperialist Aggression in China* and published in July 1923, highlighted the concept 'surplus capital'. Developed capitalist countries, when reaching the stage of the dominance by finance capital, tend to exhibit the following character: 'Domestic production exceeds their domestic consumption capacity. All capital could not be fully accommodated in the production agencies, so they invade the colonies'. Qu (1985, p. 30) moved on to propose that developed capitalist countries inevitably seek to open up new markets and get hold of cheap raw materials and labour. In this connection, imperialism not only cultivated 'puppet rulers' in politics, aligning with warlords and bureaucrats, but also controlled the lifelines of China's industries. He reached the concluding judgement: 'The more the Chinese private economy develops, the more it depends on British and American finance capital, and the weaker the national economy reaching the point of bankruptcy'.

The May 30th Massacre in Shanghai in 1925, and the series of similar events that followed including the Shakee Massacre in Guangzhou on the 23rd June, laid bare the antagonism between imperialism and the Chinese people. They also made it apparent the nature of the warlord regimes as accomplices of imperialism. Nevertheless, despite this general atmosphere of the radicalization of politics and the rise of the revolutionary movement, the question remained unresolved as to who would be leading the revolution. Indeed, what was the nature of the on-going revolutionary movement? It appeared to be an unclear and uneasy mix of three different revolutions: a democratic revolution against feudal warlords, a national liberation revolution against foreign aggressions, and a communist revolution against the bourgeoisie. The complex realities posed an urgent task for clarification.

Earlier in the same year 1925, the CPC Fourth National Congress had already categorized the Chinese bourgeoisie into two distinctive blocs: the 'big comprador class' and the 'newly emerged industrial national bourgeoisie'. The former bloc was deemed reactionary, while the latter could be united for the revolution (Party History Research Center of the CPC Central Committee, 2011, p. 155). Yet, amid the increasing division between the KMT and the CPC at the top level, there was a trend of radicalization among the communists from the grassroot upwards targeting at the landlord class. Reflecting this trend was the launching of the journal *Zhongguo Nongmin* (*Chinese Peasants*) in 1926. Its first issue carried Tan Pingshan's article *the Peasant Question in the Chinese Revolution* and Mao Zedong's *An Analysis of the Classes in the Chinese Society*. They both included the landlord class in the bloc of counter-revolutionaries. Mao (1965a, pp. 13–14) categorically stated: 'in economically backward and semi-colonial China the landlord class and the comprador class are wholly appendages of the international bourgeoisie, depending upon imperialism for their survival and expansion', and 'their political representatives are the *Étatistes* and the right-wing of the KMT'. According to Mao, the national bourgeoisie (i.e., the 'middle bourgeoisie') was full of wobbles in the revolution and could easily disintegrate at any moment.

Meanwhile, the political spectrum of the various classes in the Chinese society had already been delineated by the CPC. The focus of the debate thus shifted to how to 'cut' this spectrum. After the cut, the revolutionary task was to unite the left in opposition to the right. The crucial issue was where the 'cutting point' should lie. With the rapid progress of the on-going national liberation revolution (known as the 'Northward Expedition') and the tremendous development of labour movements following the Great Guangzhou–Hong Kong Strike in 1925–1926, this issue increasingly sparked debates among radical thinkers.

The situation also reflected the internal debate within the Communist International between Stalin and Trotsky on the Chinese revolutionary. Stalin had always had a positive attitude towards the cooperation between the KMT and the CPC. The cutting point he set was basically consistent with the Second Congress of the CPC, namely, to unite the left wing of the KMT in opposition to imperialism and warlords. He emphasized that due to the weakness of the national bourgeoisie in the era of imperialism, the proletariat could strive for leadership in the revolution but should not withdraw from the KMT. In a speech at the end of 1926, he praised the KMT-led revolution army for being 'inspired by an ideal, by enthusiasm, in the struggle for liberation from imperialism; in the fact that they are bringing China liberation'. In his view, as the exploitation of the proletariat by the bourgeoisie in the era of imperialism had been transformed into the oppression of the colonies by the capitalist powers, the national liberation movements of all colonies and semi-colonies themselves constituted 'a blow at imperialism'. Anti-imperialism represented a transitional stage towards socialism (Stalin, 1954, pp. 377–379).

Trotsky, in contrast, placed the cutting point between the national bourgeoisie and the proletariat, calling the cooperation between the KMT and the CPC '(communists) flirting with the Three Principles of the People' (Trotsky, 2011, p. 12). He denied that the on-going national liberation revolution could at any rate transcend class struggles. From the perspective of world revolution, he pointed out that the bourgeois nature of the KMT determined that it would inevitably turn to side with imperialism and confront the proletariat. Therefore, he advocated that the CPC should withdraw from its alliance with the KMT.

Notwithstanding this division in the communist leadership, the alliance persisted until its abrupt termination in 1927 marked by the bloody suppression of the communists and the KMT left-wing by the KMT mainstream that turned out to be indeed siding with imperialism as well as the landlord class. The real intense and meaningful theoretical debate then started to take shape.

DEBATING IMPERIALISM AND LATE DEVELOPMENT, 1927–1933

On April 12, 1927 in Shanghai, the KMT mainstream led by Chiang Kai-shek started its party-purging drive in the form of a large-scale massacre of Communists and left-wing KMT members. The KMT–CPC alliance came to an end. It became an immediate issue for the CPC to redefine the revolution and to re-focus its mission.

Shortly after the April 12th Incident, Trotsky published an article entitled *The Chinese Revolution and the Theses of Comrade Stalin*, in which he harshly criticized the China policy of the Communist International, stating that it was based on 'a policy that proceeded from an abstract conception of national oppression without its class refraction and reflection' (Trotsky, 1967, pp. 19–20). In Trotsky's view, under the influence of imperialism, China's productive forces had already developed to become capitalist in character. Both the comprador bourgeoisie and the national bourgeoisie were dependent on the fate of imperialism, and there was no clear division between them. As part of the world proletarian revolution, the working class and peasantry in China should oppose all the bourgeoisie and landlords. With the revolutionary path in the cities blocked, the best way out was to conduct a thorough agrarian revolution in the countryside.

Stalin rejected Trotsky's position, resorting to the concept of 'the feudal remnants'. Trotsky allegedly had the view that 'the feudal remnants' did not exhaustively encompass all the targeted enemies of the revolution. Stalin interpreted that this means Trotsky 'either refuses altogether to recognize the existence of the feudal remnants in China or does not attach decisive importance to them'. Hence, it is asserted that Trotsky 'underestimates the agrarian revolution in China, does not understand the bourgeois–democratic character of that revolution, denies the existence of the preconditions for an agrarian movement in China, and underestimates the role of the peasantry in the Chinese revolution' (Stalin, 1953, pp. 293–297).

Irrespective of the conclusions of the debate in Moscow, and the validity of the respective arguments by Stalin and Trotsky, the realities of Chinese revolution had to undergo fundamental changes. Following the disastrous failures of the series of urban uprisings in 1927–1928, the revolution had to re-constitute itself in the countryside focussing on the agrarian question. This posed a serious challenge to the perceived wisdom of Marxism–Leninism, which had hitherto centred on promoting the proletarian revolution in the urban areas. The division among radical intellectuals thus inevitably deepened, resulting in the first ever systematic debate over the nature of the Chinese society.

As reckoned by Wang Yichang (1932; see also Dirlik, 1989; Wen & Huang, 2004), the protagonists in the debate fell into three different camps. The first was KMT radicals known as the *New Life School* and represented by thinkers such as Tao Xisheng (1899–1988), Chen Gongbo (1892–1946) and Gu Mengyu (1888–1972). Their theories centred on the argument that the class structure in China was vague and indeterminate. The second was official CPC thinkers and fellow travelers, known as the *New Current School* and represented by Guo

Moruo (1892–1978), Li Lisan (1899–1967), Pan Dongzhou (1906–1935), and Wang Xuewen (1895–1985). They advocated the theory of the 'semi-feudal society'. The third was formal or self-labelled Chinese Trotskyists, known as the *Dynamism School* and represented by writers such as Ren Shu and Yan Lingfeng (1904–1999). Following Trotsky, they maintained that the Chinese society had already become largely capitalist.

The position of the KMT radicals was basically to highlight the vagueness of the relationship between the economic and the political, in order to deny the Marxist call for class struggles. This position was based on quite sophisticated theories as well as empirical analyses. Tao Xisheng argued that neither Bukharin's theory of 'the feudal remnants' nor Trotsky's thesis of 'capitalist transformation completed' were applicable to the Chinese realities. The realities, in this view, were such that China had ended the feudal system defined as the supreme powers of lordship long ago after the Zhou Dynasty (i.e., from 256 BCE onward) though had remained a pre-capitalist society all the way until the modern times. A system of free trade of land and agricultural products had prevailed, and the landlord class had been able to prosper. The accumulation of wealth in the hand of landlords had relied on the sale of agricultural surplus in the market, which required the transformation of landlords into 'merchant capitalists' or their alliance with merchant capital. This system was qualitatively different from the feudal lordship in mediaeval Europe.

The separation of political power and economic domination in the Chinese society presented a further complexity that was immediately relevant to rejecting the call for class struggles. The main component of the bureaucracy–gentry stratum that dominated politics was actually from the landlord class. Yet, the stability of its political dominance had to be based on the agricultural sector, and that's why it had to often act with hostility towards commerce. The complex relationship between the landlord class and merchant capital – economic alliance cum political conflict – necessitated the actual outcome that capital accumulation via commerce had to be spent on purchasing lands and exploiting farmers. This was the only possibly safe 'investment strategy' with respect to the reproduction and persistence of the traditional Chinese social formation (Tao, 2010).

The intrusion of imperialism only reinforced the complexity. The merchant capital class with its flexibility quickly allied with international finance capital to became comprador. The landlord class was squeezed as its agricultural foundation was undermined by the competitive pressure of imported goods. It had to largely increase its exploitation of the peasants, and to move towards warlordization under the direction of imperialism. Meanwhile, the capital accumulated by these two social strata had to be spent on imported goods or transformed into banking capital that was subordinated to international finance capital. This was due to the underdevelopment of domestic modern industries, which could not withstand the internationalized competition. The bureaucracy–gentry political elite, in the face of the collapse of the traditional power structure, also had to become dependent on the warlords and ultimately the imperialist powers. On the whole, both before and after imperialist intrusion, the accumulated capital in China could not be invested in productive uses but only in speculative activities.

The Chinese social formation was characterized by 'a society dominated by the landlord class under commercial and financial capitalism' (Tao, 1930a; see also Tao, 1930b).

The preceding theory advocated by the KMT radicals clearly had its political and policy conclusions. It implies that the paramount task of modernization confronting the Chinese society was to achieve national unity and enhance state capacity. This entailed eliminating the barriers erected by imperialist forces, cancelling the privileges of international finance capital, and transforming the land and money capital accumulated by landlords and merchants into productive industrial capital. In this connection, a revolution led by the KMT had the advantage of providing the necessary foundation for the development of productive industrial capital. The KMT state would not hinder the expansion of merchant capital. It would rather guide the expansion in the direction of investing in industrialization. With hindsight, it can be said that the theory of the KMT radicals is broadly in the same spirit of what has come to be known as the model of the Developmental State in the second-half of the 20th century.

Meanwhile, the position of CPC thinkers and fellow-travelers remained basically in line with Stalin. Pan Dongzhou (1930) provided a nuanced interpretation of the nature and role of commercial capital in traditional China. Commercial capital had been indeed in an alliance with landlords. But it did not actually occupy a dominant position in the economy. Nor could its expansion in the modern times represent China's entry into the capitalist stage. After all, unlike industrial capital, 'commercial capital is a medium of exchange that can exist under various production methods... Commercial capital itself cannot represent a certain production method, and its role vacillates along with the production methods. It cannot independently determine a social system' (Pan, 1930, pp. 3–4).

It is clear that, in the view of Pan and the like, the nature of a particular social formation is determined by its mainstream mode of production. In the case of traditional China, this took the form of agricultural production under the dominance of landlords which appropriated the surplus products through land rents. This, essentially, was feudalism. Pan pointed out that the expansion of commodity relations meant that the exploitation of peasants by feudal landlords in China would not normally stop at the level of use values but would pursue money. This way, the commodification of surplus products remained in the exchange field. It did not fundamentally change the mode of production and exploitation. It thus would not change the feudal nature of traditional China. This nature basically remained after the intrusion of imperialism, as capital accumulation basically remained in the fields of commerce and money instead of penetrating into production. What was new was just the emergence of comprador and usurious capital, which served as the main agent for linking up the articulation of different modes of production in China in the modern times. Politically, therefore, the conclusion is clear. Redirecting capital into productive uses is of secondary importance. What is needed for modernization is a bourgeois–democratic revolution overthrowing the feudal orders of the landlord class.

Chinese Trotskyists similarly insisted on the imperative of class struggles, but at the same time denied that the Chinese social formation was mainly feudal in nature. Yan Lingfeng (1931) contended that the capitalist mode of production had already become the mainstay. Specifically, in the era of imperialism, international finance did not seek to preserve the feudal relations of production in China. It has rather fostered the accelerated development of the capitalist mode of production. This contention was substantiated by three related arguments. First, in the era of imperialism, capitalism had become a world system incorporating all the countries. Second, imperialist dominance in the world entailed capital export instead of commodity export, and hence its drive to establish the capitalist mode of production in the colonial and semi-colonial societies. Third, within the Chinese society, the capitalist mode of production would continue to spread until it transformed all the other modes that were relatively backward. It might be true that non-capitalistic economic activities had remained ample quantitatively, but the capitalist mode was the most dynamic and would eventually conquer the society. Sharing this essentialist contention, Ren Shu (1930) pinpointed its political implication: in view of the realities, all the capitalist elements (domestic or foreign) could only bring about disasters to the proletariat class, so they must be opposed.

It can be said that the position of Chinese Trotskyists is essentially a restatement of the classical theory of imperialism. It centres on the postulate that the capitalist mode of production would eventually and inevitably dominate all the societies in the world. Hence, its political message was that the Chinese revolution must be an inextricable part of the proletarian revolution worldwide against capitalism. The conclusion that logically followed was that the agrarian revolution in the Chinese countryside might be able to gain supports from the poor peasants, but it would remain backward if it were to be disconnected from the leadership of the urban proletarian.

WHAT IS CAPITALISM, AFTER ALL? DEEPENING THE DEBATE, 1933–1937

The review in the preceding section highlights the contrasting stances on the Chinese realities, which are mainly political messages in nature. Further theoretically deepening the debate took place in the subsequent years of 1933–1937, mainly between the CPC writers and the Trotskyists. The former group was mainly based on the journal *Rural China*, while the latter group on another journal *Chinese Economy*. The debate centred on the notion of the 'semi-colonial and semi-feudal society' versus that of the 'semi-colonial and semi-capitalist society'. Behind this division is the political question that evolved from 'whether the agrarian revolution is progressive' to 'whether the agrarian revolution is needed'.

There was no division over the descriptive characteristics of the realities. Both sides shared the perception that the Chinese agricultural economy was in bankruptcy and the rural society was disintegrating. Meanwhile, modern production facilities had gradually penetrated to the countryside. Amid the Great Depression in the world economy from 1929, capital in China had no viable profit opportunities in the cities and thus had to turn to the countryside as its outlets. The phenomenon of 'capital going to the countryside' was mainly in the form of banking capital. Thus, the pressing question that confronted radical intellectuals of the time was: what was the nature of China's rural society that was now dominated by finance capital with the emergence of mechanized production? What to be done to save the rural society from its peril?

The debate now concerned different characterizations and interpretations of the realities, not just different political stances. The Trotskyists insisted on upholding the core postulate that 'the nature of the society is determined by the kind of productive forces that are the most advanced'. Given that the Chinese society has already become capitalist, the rural economy too has been dominated by the working of capitalism. Put another way, Zhang Zhicheng (1934) asserted that 'China's peasant economy nowadays is essentially a peasant economy of the capitalist epoch, just like the peasant economy that continues to exist in imperialist countries'. As a backward sector, the peasant economy was bound to be undermined and eliminated along with the expansion of capitalism. Ultimately, it would be replaced by large-scale capitalist farms, i.e., 'agricultural capitalism' as understood at that time. Wang Yuquan (1934) further contended that whilst it was true that the mainstay of the peasant economy was with small-scale intensive farming, that did not imply that it was at any rate feudal. What makes agriculture capitalist is the mechanization of production technology and the commercialization of agricultural products, both of which, in this view, were developing fast in China.

It appears that the thesis of 'capitalist transformation completed' advocated by the Trotskyist *Chinese Economy* School was based on its characterization of both the productive forces and the relations of exchange in the Chinese realities at that time. Theoretically, these two categories are quite far apart, but they are just replicas of the two stages of 'capital export' and 'commodity export' in Lenin's theory of imperialism. In their interpretation of Marxist classics, the spread of capitalism across the world normally occurs through the mediation of commodity exchanges and the replication of production technology. During this process, the gap between advanced and backward societies continues to exist, but this might be just evidence of Trotsky's 'uneven and combined development' on the world scale. This is a process of various modes of production not only intermingling with each other but also dragging each other, and ultimately undergoing continuous transformation driven by the most developed forces of production (see Howard & King, 2014, chapter 12).

The CPC-related *Rural China* School provided a distinctively different theory about the Chinese realities. The associated writers insisted on the characterization of the rural society as semi-feudal. Qian Junrui (1908–1985, alias Tao Zhifu) proposed that, in the debate, the division between the two schools had been due to two fundamentally different interpretations of Marxist political economy: whether the nature of a social formation is determined by the forces of production or by the relations of production. The *Rural China* School clearly took the position that the relations of production are primary. Yet, behind the division there was an even more complex question concerning the relationship between the forces and relations of production. It seemed that somehow there was a presumption of one-to-one correspondence between the two categories held by the Trotskyists, so that the more advanced productive forces were treated as tantamount to the more advanced productive relations – i.e., the capitalist versus the pre-capitalist. The *Rural China* School disagreed. It contended that the productive forces only demarcate the scope for the relations of production that could actually be of diverse forms and contents. With hindsight, this contention seems to be in a spirit that is similar to a well-known thesis in post-war Marxist theory – namely, Louis Althusser's (2014) thesis that 'the productive forces establish limits, and the relations of production play a decisive role'. The implication is that, to approach the question of determining the nature of a social formation, it necessarily requires first analyzing its relations of production in concrete, as is proposed by Qian and associated writers (Tao, 1935).

What were the dominant relations of production in rural China, then? Based on extensive field surveys and research work, Xue Muqiao (1904–2005, alias Yu Lin) reached the conclusion that rural China was still in a transition stage where capitalist elements were in embryonic forms and feudal remnants were still predominant. In a later text published in 1937, Xue further raised four criteria for the judgement that rural China was still mainly feudal in nature: the predominance of a self-sufficient economy, the combination of agricultural and handicraft production, the possession of most lands with landlords and the super-exploitation of peasants thereof, and the landlords' possession of extra-economic coercive powers.

The labelling of the realities described above as '(semi-)feudal' was based on defining feudalism as a system where the appropriation of the surplus product takes the form of land rents. Xue (1937) proposed that in a feudal society, there are normally two main methods of surplus extraction: forced-labour rents or the '*corvée* system', and money rents or the 'levy system'. If left to develop spontaneously, the *corvée* system would be more easily transformed into capitalism because the landlords had already concentrated a high portion of the means of production. When political changes end the feudal system, the *corvée* system is likely to be transformed into the labour repayment system, where farmers become wage laborers working on the landlords' farms and receiving monetary wages. In contrast, the levy system is likely to be transformed into sharecropping, where landlords lease most of the lands to the peasants and use usurious loans to put them under control. Xue pointed out that both forms of surplus extraction existed extensively in the Chinese realities at that time. The hereditary feudal system had gone, but exploitation via extra-economic coercions and land-based controls continued to be pervasive. Hence, the mainstay of rural China should be deemed semi-feudal rather than capitalist. It was true, though, that embryonic forms of capitalism were developing fast in the meantime. The emergence of capitalist farms and the transition from sharecropping to capitalist lease operations were symptoms of this development.

How about the impact from imperialist intrusion? Is it true that, despite the semi-feudal nature of its rural society, China as a whole had become capitalist following its incorporation by imperialism into the world market? Once again, there is the most fundamental question regarding what is meant by capitalism. The almost consensus view among protagonists of the 1933–1937 debate was that China's integration into the world market had been mediated mainly by commercial capital. Now, in the perspective of the *Rural China* School, this entailed the 'commodification of the economy' at the level of exchange. That was not yet capitalist, because capitalism necessarily requires commodification at the level of production – particularly the commodification of labour power.

Qian Junrui made the point that 'whether China is already under the control of world finance capital is one issue, but whether China's mode of production has already become capitalist is another' (Zhou, 1935). Xue (1937) likewise posited that 'whether capital dominates the exchange process is one thing, but whether it dominates the production process is another'. Similarly, monetization of the surplus product in the market is qualitatively different from appropriation of surplus value from laborers. It might well be true that the world system as a whole is capitalist, and colonies and semi-colonies play an important role in the system by providing cheap raw materials and labour. But that does not necessarily trivialize the investigation into the social nature of a particular nation. Qian provided a justification for his inquiry, of which the reasoning goes in the following way (Tao, 1935, p. 141). Well before the formation of the world market, China had maintained an independent economy over a long historical epoch. It had continued to basically maintain a domestically integrated national economy in the modern times. Hence, integrating into the world market need not erase the specificity of domestic contradictions in the country. To study the dynamics and consequences of social changes, it is necessary to take as its starting point of sufficiently analyzing the 'internal causes'.

The preceding exposition by Qian Junrui could be seen as a 'theory in concrete' in nature, in the sense that it treated the analysis of the specific domestic contradictions as the first step towards fuller investigations of capitalism and modernization. Sun Yefang (1908–1983) moved well beyond this to attempt constructing a 'theory in abstract'. Would China's semi-feudal rural society be transformed into capitalist over time, through the working of the capitalist world system? Put another way, would capitalist transformation gradually move from exchange relations to production relations due to the process of imperialist 'capital export' as characterized by Lenin? In his pioneering work published in 1935, Sun (1998) dissected the logic of the rule of finance capital over pre-capitalist relations. Following Marxist classics, Sun divided the evolution of the economic relationship between the capitalist core and the colonies into three stages: commodity capital, industrial capital, and finance capital. There is no reason, and no evidence in actual history, that along with the progress from the commodity stage to the finance stage the social nature of colonies must become progressively capitalist. So long as China's (semi-)feudal exploitative relations could maintain ultra-low labour and raw material costs, imperialist finance capital had no incentive to change them. To the contrary, it would tend to preserve the exploitative relations by supporting China's (semi-)feudal ruling elite. So, in the end, there had been the amalgamation of the rule of finance capital and the perpetuation or even re-creation of pre-capitalist relations in China.

From this exposition Sun Yefang raised a couple of theses that are discernibly precursors of post-war Marxist political-economic theories of imperialism and under-development. The first concerns unequal exchange, which is claimed to be a general existence in the commodity export stage of world capitalism. In relation to unequal exchange is parasitic comprador capitalists appropriating the main part of the surplus left after imperialist appropriation. Underpinning unequal exchange is what later labelled 'uneven development' by Samir Amin (1977), meaning the prevalence of qualitatively different types of exploitative relations in the imperialist countries versus the colonies. Xue Muqiao (1937) actually pointed out that the relationship between colonies (or semi-colonies) and imperialist countries cannot be viewed simply from the perspective of the division of labour and beneficial reciprocity. The exploitation of the former by the latter is different from 'the urban exploiting the rural'. This, again, is due to the perpetuation of different types of exploitative relations. Higher rates of the surplus value typically can be maintained in colonies owing to feudal or semi-feudal exploitation.

Uneven development persists even in the capital export stage of world capitalism. Above all, there is no competition on equal footing between domestic and international capitals. International capitals typically have far more monopolistic power owing to their scale and technological advantages. Historically, and in an extra-economic sense, international capitals enjoyed all kinds of privilege and special rights. They were in control of the strategic sectors of the Chinese economy, especially in finance, transport, and modern industries. The railway system that existed, for example, was built in a way that served mainly international trade – so that its transportation cost was far lower than that of domestic trade. To further worsen the unevenness was the tendency of the domestic political-economic elite, which appropriated the main part of the economic surplus left after imperialist appropriation, typically spending the surplus on luxurious consumption or turning it into speculative capital. Industrialization was thus squeezed due to the insufficiency in both productive investment and market outlets.

Sun Yefang and Xue Muqiao both found that once finance capital penetrated the countryside of China and other (semi-)colonies, it inevitably exploited the peasants in a way that is even more brutal than the feudal remnants. In the areas dominated by concentrated land ownership, international capital tended to ally with local landlords and comprador capital in large-scale farming. The production of such business entities tended to be devoted, as far as possible, to providing cheap and abundant primary commodities to the imperialist economies. They therefore also tended to use forced labour, in different forms of semi-slavery, instead of free-wage labour. In comparison, in the areas with decentralized land ownership, where sharecropping prevailed, landlords tended to rely on usurious capital for raising exploitation. They tried as far as possible to appropriate the surplus products of small-scale peasants. The land rents thereof were mostly pre-capitalist in nature (Sun, 1998; Xue, 1937).

CONCLUSION: REVOLUTION RENEWED AND THEORY BUILDING TO CONTINUE

Japanese imperialist aggression of China entered the stage of full-scale wars in 1937. From that point onward, radical writers concerned with the political economy of imperialism and modernization had to devote their maximum efforts to the immediate needs of revolution. And it was mainly political leaders that took up the task of distilling the theories generated in the intellectual debates into even more concrete guidelines for the praxis of revolution.

In December 1939, Mao Zedong published his major work *The Chinese Revolution and the Chinese Communist Party* (Mao, 1965b). This together with another subsequent text, *On the New Democracy*, contain the main insights of the debates. First, it is stated that pre-modern China had been a feudal society ruled by the landlord class. There were also progressive developments of commodity relations, which imply that pre-modern China had already 'carried within itself the seeds of capitalism, and China would of itself have developed slowly into a capitalist society even without the impact of foreign capitalism'. Second, imperialism had caused the disintegration of the self-sufficient economy, promoted the development of industry, and, at the same time, colluded with feudal forces to suppress the development of national capitalism, thus pushing China to become a semi-colonial cum semi-feudal society. Third, the 'cutting point' of China's class spectrum was within the bourgeoisie class. The Chinese society in the modern times was divided between the agents of revolution – i.e., the proletariat, peasants, petite bourgeoisie, and national bourgeoisie – and the targets of revolution including imperialism, the landlord class and comprador capitalism. Fourth, in relation to the specificities of China's social formation and class structure, the revolution needed for promoting modernization could only be a New Democratic Revolution. Such a revolution would need to have the double characteristics of having the workers-peasants alliance as its leadership, on the one hand, and the promotion of capitalist development, on the other hand.

The combination of these views represents a guideline for the Chinese revolution that is fundamentally different from that of Stalin, Trotsky, or indeed the whole tradition of classical Marxist political economy. The challenge to all the strands of Marxism is that this guideline seems to have led to the success of the Chinese revolution, which was of the largest scale among all the revolutions against world capitalism in the 20th century. A separate challenge to China itself, however, is that the guideline does appear to embody an intrinsic contradiction which would inevitably play out after the revolution. This is the contradiction between the political and the economic. The former entails the leadership of the CPC representing the workers-peasants alliance, while the latter requires the revolution and the newly established state power to promote capitalist development. The turns and twists of

Chinese political economy since the early 1950s until the present time can be seen in this light.

Intellectually, it can be posited that the contradiction with the revolution guideline is to some extent ascribable to its underpinnings as mainly essentially 'theories in concrete'. The question as to 'what is capitalism', and with it all the issues concerning the driving forces of and hurdles to late development, has remained unresolved in the debates reviewed above. That is why the same question and its related issues have emerged time and again in the post-war epoch across different parts of the world, for want of the 'theories in abstract'. The debate on whether capitalism constitutes a world system connected by the process of exchange, or as a set of models defined by the relations of production, was revived in the 1970s – in the form of the debate between dependency writers and mainstream Marxist scholars including Brenner (1977), Laclau (2018), and Warren (2020). The emphasis on distinguishing capitalism from the market-commodity economy has passed on from the historiography of Braudel (1992) to the world system school. The phenomena of imperialist finance capital dominating late-comer economies, suppressing their national industry, pushing for super-exploitation, and blocking productive investment have been highlighted by dependency theorists such as Marini (2022) and Frank (1967). The perpetuation or even re-creation of pre-capitalist social relations in backward countries and the 'compradorization' of the ruling elite thereof have been of granted with systemic importance in the theory building by scholars like Baran (1957). Unsurprising, all these issues and theoretical views were already visible in China in the 1930s and 1940s, which is a reflection of the harsh realities after all.

REFERENCES

Althusser, L. (2014). *On the reproduction of capitalism*. Verso.

Amin, S. (1977). *Unequal development: An essay on the social formations of peripheral capitalism*. Monthly Review Press.

Arrighi, G., & Saul, J. S. (1973). *Essays on the political economy of Africa*. Monthly Review Press.

Baran, P. A. (1957). *The political economy of growth*. Monthly Review Press.

Baran, P. A., & Sweezy, P. M. (1966). *Monopoly capital: An essay on the American economic and social order*. Monthly Review Press.

Braudel, F. (1992). *Civilization and capitalism 15th-18th century (vol. 3: The perspective of the world)*. University of California Press.

Brenner, R. (1977). The origins of capitalist development: A critique of neo-Smithian Marxism. *New Left Review*, *104*, 25–93.

Brewer, A. (1990). *Marxist theories of imperialism: A critical survey*. Routledge.

Cai, H. (1979). *Collected works of Cai Hesen*. Hunan People's Publishing House.

Callinicos, A. (2009). *Imperialism and global political economy*. Polity Press.

Dai, J. (1919). Tracing the root causes of China's disorders from an economic perspective. *Jianshe*, *1*(2), 345–365.

Dirlik, A. (1989). *Revolution and history: Origins of Marxist historiography in China, 1919-1937*. University of California Press.

Dos Santos, T. (1970). The structure of dependence. *American Economic Review*, *60*(2), 231–236.

Emmanuel, A. (1972). *Unequal exchange: A study of the imperialism of trade*. Monthly Review Press.

Frank, A. G. (1967). *Capitalism and underdevelopment in Latin America*. Monthly Review Press.

Howard, M. C., & King, J. E. (2014). *A history of Marxian economics* (Vol. 1, pp. 1883–1929). Princeton University Press.

Laclau, E. (2018). Feudalism and capitalism in Latin America. In P. F. Klarén & T. J. Bossert (Eds.), *Promise of development* (pp. 166–190). Routledge.
Lenin, V. I. (1960). *Collected works* (Vol. 3). Progress Publishers.
Lenin, V. I. (1966). *Collected works* (Vol. 31). Progress Publishers.
Mao, Z. (1965a). *Selected works of Mao Tze-tung* (Vol. 1). Foreign Languages Press.
Mao, Z. (1965b). *Selected works of Mao Tze-tung* (Vol. 2). Foreign Languages Press.
Marini, R. M. (2022). *The dialectics of dependency*. Monthly Review Press.
Noonan, M. (2017). *Marxist theories of imperialism: A history*. I.B. Touris.
Pan, D. (1930). The nature of the Chinese economy. *Xin Sichao, 5*, 4–23.
Party History Research Center of the CPC Central Committee. (2011). *History of the communist party of China* (Vol. 1). History of Chinese Communist Party Publishing House.
Qu, Q. (1982). *Selected poems and writings of Qu Qiubai*. People's Literature Publishing House.
Qu, Q. (1985). *Selected works of Qu Qiubai*. People's Publishing House.
Ren, S. (1930). *Introduction to the study of the Chinese economy*. Shenzhou Guoguang Society.
Rostow, W. W. (1990). *The stages of economic growth: A non-communist manifesto*. Cambridge University Press.
Solow, R. M. (1956). A contribution to the theory of economic growth. *Quarterly Journal of Economics, 70*(1), 65–94.
Stalin, J. V. (1953). *Works* (Vol. 8). Foreign Language Publishing House.
Stalin, J. V. (1954). *Works* (Vol. 9). Foreign Language Publishing House.
Stalin, J. V. (1986). *Works* (Vol. 16). Red Star Press.
Sun, Y. (1998). *Complete works of Sun Yefang*. Shaanxi Economic Publishing House.
Tao, X. (1930a). Chinese merchant capital and landlords and farmers. *Xinsheng, 3*(2), 2–16.
Tao, X. (1930b). *Retrospect and prospect of Chinese issues*. Xin Shengming Bookstore.
Tao, Z. (1935). The nature of Chinese rural society and the problem of agricultural transformation. *Zhongguo Nongcun, 1*(11), 1–33.
Tao, X. (2010). *Historical analysis of Chinese society*. Yuelu Press.
Trotsky, L. (1967). *Problems of the Chinese revolution*. The University of Michigan Press. https://www.marxists.org/archive/trotsky/1932/pcr/index.htm
Trotsky, L. (2011). *Trotsky on the Chinese revolution (1925-1927)* [Translated from Russian to Chinese by Shi Yongqin]. Shaanxi People's Publishing House.
Wallerstein, I. (1974). *The modern world system*. Academic Press.
Wang, Y. (1932). History of Chinese social history. *Dushu Zazhi, 2*, 2–3.
Wang, Y. (1934). Several important issues in the study of China's rural economy. *Zhongguo Nongcun, 2*(9), 1–9.
Warren, B. (2020). *Imperialism: Pioneer of capitalism*. Verso.
Wen, L., & Huang, D. (2004). *The debate on the nature of Chinese society and social history in the 1920s and 1930s*. Baihuazhou Literature and Art Publishing House.
Xue, M. (1937). *Feudal, semi-feudal, and capitalist*. Heibai Press.
Yan, L. (1931). *Research on China's economic problems*. Xin Shengming Press.
Zhang, Z. (1934). The current stage of Chinese rural economy. *Zhongguo Jingji, 2*(7), 1–8.
Zhou, B. (1935). Discussion on the nature of Chinese rural economy. *Zhongguo Nongcun, 1*(9), 1–10.

GENDER AND CLASS LIBERATION: THE WOMEN'S LIBERATION MOVEMENT IN YAN'AN PERIOD (1937–1948)

Ying Yue

Tsinghua University, China

ABSTRACT

This chapter explores the women's liberation movement during the Yan'an period (1937–1948) under the Communist Party of China (CPC). It examines how Marxist theories on gender and class were practically applied to revolutionary activities in rural China. By encouraging women's participation in production and integrating them into social and economic activities, the CPC sought to reform family structures and achieve gender equality. The Large-scale Production Campaign of 1943 and subsequent policy adjustments significantly transformed ethical and familial norms, promoting the establishment of new democratic family models. This effort aimed to balance public and private interests, advancing both women's liberation and broader social transformation. The study demonstrates that revolutionary China could promote women's liberation within the framework of class revolution, particularly benefiting rural women at the grassroots level.

Keywords: Communist Party of China; gender; equality; women's liberation; family; labour; marxism; Chinese revolution; social classes; Yan'an period (1937–1948)

INTRODUCTION

In early 1937, the Communist Party of China (referred to as CPC hereafter) established a revolutionary regime in Yan'an (located in the Shaanxi province, in the heart of the country) as its command centre, beginning the 'Yan'an period'

Trajectories of Declining and Destructive Capitalism
Research in Political Economy, Volume 40, 37–54

Published under exclusive licence by Emerald Publishing Limited
ISSN: 0161-7230/doi:10.1108/S0161-72302025000040003

that lasted for more than 10 years. Marxist theory on women's liberation holds that private ownership and class exploitation are the fundamental reasons for women's oppression, and unequal possession of means of production leads to female oppression in feudal and capitalist societies. Through revolutionary practice in rural areas, the CPC increasingly realized the relationship between gender and class issues. This article explores how the CPC used 'women's participation in production' as a medium to balance multiple interests in gender negotiations between two forces inside and outside households, exploring ways to rebuild a more equal family structure. It also proves that it is feasible for 'Revolutionary China' to promote women's liberation under the framework of class Revolution, especially for rural women at the grassroots level.

The Large-scale Production Campaign launched since 1943 and adjustments made to women's work have brought significant changes to ethical concepts within families in the Shaanxi-Gansu–Ningxia Border Region, creating an atmosphere conducive to establishing new-style democratic families. Compared with the old feudal, poor, and backward families, elements such as democratic elections, family meetings, meticulous division of labour, and distribution of benefits according to work constitute the 'new' type of family. The CPC attaches importance to family building in revolutionary base areas. On the one hand, it is to help people live a better family life. On the other hand, it is also to explore the relationship between the collective and the individual by re-examining the public and private spheres; conveying the spirit of public–private balance, public interests taking precedence over private interests. The CPC hopes to promote women's liberation and social transformation through family reform, as well as to promote social change through the renewal of family forms.

EARLY WOMEN'S LIBERATION THEORY OF THE CPC

The introduction of Marxist feminist theory in China is closely linked to the Russian October Revolution. As the Russian women's liberation movement gained more attention in China, some socialists and communists began distinguishing between two types of feminist movements abroad: bourgeois feminism and socialist or proletarian feminism. This differentiation is also known as third-class versus fourth-class women's movements (He, 2009, p. 145). The views on women held by Marx, Engels, and important leaders in the Soviet Union allowed early Chinese Marxists to form a preliminary understanding of gender issues within proletarian women's movements. In other words, only through the proletarian women's movement can complete female liberation be achieved; its revolutionary goal is not men but rather overthrowing class oppression, developing productive forces to eliminate poverty ultimately leading towards class emancipation for all humanity and gender equality.

From the beginning of its establishment, the CPC has supported the principle of gender equality. Several key founders of the CPC were supporters and advocates of feminism during the May Fourth Movement. After accepting Marxism, they began to guide feminist debates towards socialist demands and shifted their focus to advocating for the elimination of private ownership and class differences (Wang & Gao, 2016, p. 7). They recognized that gender liberation is closely linked to class liberation and that women couldn't be excluded from the proletarian Revolution.

Xiang Jingyu and Yang Zhihua were female communists who made important theoretical contributions to early women's liberation thinking in the CPC (Archives Bureau, 2011). Xiang Jingyu was the first Central Women's Minister during the Great Revolution, and Yang Zhihua served as the Secretary of the Women's Committee of the Central Bureau of Shanxi–Hebei–Shandong–Henan Region. Based on their practical experience in women's movements during this period, they explored theories combining Marxism with Chinese revolutionary practice for women's liberation, providing several feasible strategies and specific approaches for liberating Chinese women in urban areas under their guidance.

It was not until the focus of the CPC's Revolution shifted from cities to rural areas that the women's policy guidelines were adjusted to better suit Chinese local conditions. With the progress of land reform in Soviet Areas, women there gradually gained liberation and showed impressive performance in the Revolution, which strengthened the CPC's determination to accelerate bringing rural women into the revolutionary ranks. Issued in December 1931, 'Resolution of the CPC on Expanding the Struggle of Labouring Women' pointed out that labouring women should be attracted to actively participate in land reform and all mass organizations' work within Soviet Areas, and firmly opposed mistakes that only confined women's work to marriage issues (Archives Bureau, 2011, p. 772). In Soviet Areas' land reform, the CPC deepened Marxist theory on women's liberation, especially realizing that it was necessary to break free through struggles for gender equality and closely combine women's liberation with social development.

The CPC's emphasis, reflection, and theoretical construction on women's work in rural revolutionary base areas were not only related to the economic blockade of the revolutionary base areas and the Anti-Japanese War but also had a driving factor that could not be ignored, namely the theoretical war between the Kuomintang and the CPC. When there were differences between both parties during the Anti-Japanese United Front, they would compete for discourse power over Chinese women's role positioning.

Since the late 19th century, there have been several debates in Chinese politics and academia regarding 'Virtuous Wife and Good Mother'. The early camps involved reformists, progressives, revolutionaries, etc., which remained at an ideological level. After the outbreak of the General Anti-Japanese War, this debate on 'Virtuous Wife and Good Mother' reflected surface-level differences between the Kuomintang and the CPC regarding united front policies and women's movements. At a deeper level, differences in women's policies pointed towards each party's different governance structures.

In the early 1940s, the CPC conducted a deeper exploration and implementation of Marxist women's theory localization in the Shaanxi–Gansu–Ningxia Border Region. They sought a balance between labour and new-style families, believing that women should step out of their homes and contribute to the war effort. In addition, as liberating all humanity was the ultimate goal of their struggle, women's liberation was also part of the proletarian Revolution. Liberating women from their homes was also necessary for achieving class and national liberation.

OUTDATED LABOUR ETHIC

Before the full development of the women's liberation movement, obstacles preventing women in the Shaanxi–Gansu–Ningxia Border Region from leaving their homes to participate in labour were not only due to objective factors such as feet-binding that limited their mobility but also due to backward attitudes towards labour.

Firstly, regardless of gender, the lack of labour enthusiasm among farmers was a common phenomenon in rural areas of Northwest China. This could not be simply summarized as backwardness or laziness of the people. The first problem was the lack of production materials. As Han Ding wrote when investigating the land reform movement in Zhangzhuang, Lucheng County, Shanxi Province, before the land reform, at least half of the population had five months each year with nothing to do because they lacked funds for handicraft production or other sideline businesses after autumn harvest (Han, 1980, p. 38). Similar situations could also be applied to the Shaanxi–Gansu–Ningxia Border Region where farmers had nothing to do except for spring ploughing and autumn harvesting.

Secondly, changing old labour concepts among the masses was not an overnight task; ideas that belittled labour persisted until the mid-1940s. In 1943, Ai Siqi criticized many people and intellectuals who still held 'remnants of old labour concepts'. For example, some people believed that poor peasants worked hard to pay rent but still could not feed themselves; they were contributing their 'labour fruits' to exploitative classes who enjoyed them without working hard themselves. It showed that labour had nothing to do with personal 'happiness' and 'well-being'. The continuation of this old thinking affected mass enthusiasm for work during the wartime period, especially their production enthusiasm for public labour. People easily accepted new ideas about enjoying their own fruits from their own labour but did not understand how helping the border region government fight against war by paying taxes was related to future victories in war and national liberation as well as long-term interests for the masses. Ai Siqi specifically pointed out the issue of cadres neglecting labour and not actively participating in production and economic work in women's work, emphasizing that this was a mistake of not taking labour as a source of honour and being detached from the working people (Ai, 1943).

Thirdly, the influence of feudal backward thinking was particularly strong in Northwest China, where there was discrimination against women going out to engage in productive labour. Women going out to work were considered unlucky. Superstitious beliefs such as 'women working in the fields will result in less or no harvest', 'women digging wells won't get water and will bring bad luck', 'if a woman goes to the field, there will be three years of drought' and 'women planting grains won't grow' were widely spread among farmers. In families where men were scarce, women had no choice but to go down to the fields for farming. They often sneaked around and hid when they saw someone coming, afraid of being seen and ridiculed by others. The Shaanxi dialect saying 'no matter how cowardly a man goes to a county, no matter how good a woman goes to a pot' also reflected that most rural women did not participate in labour production outside their homes (Zhou & Liu, 2016, p. 141).

Mao Zedong believed that if the CPC wanted to mobilize rural women to participate in production, it was inevitable that they must gain sympathy from men and gradually persuade them to agree with women's participation in production (All-China Women's Federation, 1991, p. 261). Deep-rooted gender discrimination powerfully hindered women's willingness to go out for work. They found it difficult to obtain social recognition especially when facing opposition from their husbands. Even if they had no choice but to go out to work due to livelihood pressures, it was still hard for them to be regarded as an honourable thing by those around them.

In the investigation of the Suide Area (Shaanxi) in early 1943, the Women's Federation of the Border Region pointed out that women's capacity in production was not limited to 'cooking, sewing, mending clothes, and raising children', and that the government expected women to participate in social production to achieve both family prosperity and help with the Anti-Japanese War and aid for the CPC. Women's work must be guided towards participation in production, improving their morale for production, and overcoming obstacles encountered during production; only then could they gain support from women and approval from men (Zhao, 1943). The cadres who participated in this investigation realized that it was urgent to break down rural discrimination against women participating in social labour and overcome ideological constraints, which were more pressing than enhancing women's ability to engage in social labour.

'1943-DECISION'

On February 26, 1943, 'The Decision of the Central Committee of the CPC on the Current Guidelines for Women's Work in the Anti-Japanese Base Areas' (referred to as the '1943-Decision') was officially issued, becoming an important milestone in guiding women's work by the CPC. The '1943-Decision' summarized the achievements and problems of previous women's work, and proposed a new direction for the women's work in the future to prioritize production.

After the implementation of the '1943-Decision', making economic production the primary task for rural women's work became a consensus among female cadres. Cadres went deep into each household, using simple and easy-to-understand language to help women establish a sense of pride in labour, explaining the relationship between participating in production and liberating themselves. In response to the characteristics of rural women who loved singing and watching dramas, the CPC compiled a large number of popular songs, folk songs, and rhymes that were easy for the masses to learn and sing, promoting the elimination of feudal superstitions that prohibited women from going out. They also paid attention to establishing labour models to eliminate old-fashioned ideas that discriminate against women's labour (Zhou & Liu, 2016, p. 144).

Agnes Smedley believed that the CPC liberated women from their families by organizing them into textile cooperatives, which greatly changed rural women's spiritual outlook. Before the war they were 'shy girls' who were reluctant to speak up; now they were 'new-type females' working hard in production – 'a new kind of person' (Smedley, 2017, p. 397). The transformation of the CPC's concept on female labour had brought more connections between Chinese rural women and society. By comparison, at that time in the United States, the Los Angeles authorities excluded women from participating in work. Gathering places for upper-middle-class women in some US regions were usually clubs which was completely different from cooperative societies in the Chinese countryside (Smedley, 2017, p. 510).

The '1943-Decision' effectively linked the relationship between women's liberation, labour, and family. Participating in social production labour was a prerequisite and important way for women's liberation. The document indicated that in the future, the new direction of women's work was to prioritize 'production' and eliminate all erroneous views that underestimate economic and production work. Having economic discourse power was directly related to improving the status of women's families, cultivating women's confidence and sense of ownership, enhancing their enthusiasm for participating in public affairs such as politics and meetings, and was conducive to consolidating the new democratic regime in border areas.

Under the mobilization of women's cadres, many districts and townships had established women's cooperative production organizations to provide women with production materials, impart textile and other technologies, and repurchase primary processed products. With a comprehensive production, supply, and sales one-stop service, women's fear of difficulties and the misunderstanding of 'being public' (meaning leaving their private homes, working in the government or factories) or serving the public were dispelled. In labour competitions, female labour heroes also emerged. The CPC emphasized setting up models of female laborers. News propaganda about them and literary works adaptations improved the enthusiasm for work among many women. Unlike the late 1930s, in the 1940s, the CPC gradually ceased to use marital freedom as a major criterion for evaluating the degree of women's liberation, pointing out that only production was the fundamental way for women to break free from feudal oppression.

WOMEN'S TEXTILE MOVEMENT

Compared to the late 1930s when women were mobilized to participate in agricultural labour, the '1943-Decision' and related research reports regarded women's home textile production as important content. The income from women's spinning could even exceed that of men's farming, thus greatly improving the status of women in their families. The change in mobilizing women was related to the strategic position of the textile industry in the border areas.

Northern Shaanxi Area was vast but sparsely populated, with poor land and impoverished people, and its traditional small-scale peasant economy characterized by 'men ploughing and women weaving' did not apply here. Before the war, local women lacked cotton-spinning habits, and rural household textile production disappeared due to a large influx of foreign cloth. More than half of all counties did not master spinning. Except for grain and wool, everything else needed for daily use from cotton cloth to needles was dependent on imports (Shaanxi Provincial Archives, 2016, p. 2). Originally, the government had laid a certain foundation for textile industry development in border areas, but it was almost destroyed due to the dumping of foreign cloth sales, warlord devastation, and drought attacks. From the land reform until the early stages of the General Anti-Japanese War, emphasis was placed on promoting food production in border areas while military personnel relied entirely on imported fabrics (Shaanxi Women's Federation, 1985, p. 385).

In summary, the economic blockade imposed by the reactionary forces of the Kuomintang, the encirclement and suppression by the Japanese puppet regime, and the frequent occurrence of natural disasters in the border areas resulted in a shortage of cotton raw materials. As a result, there was a great shortage of cotton, cotton yarn, and fabric in the border areas, with prices skyrocketing and resulting in a chain reaction of the widening scissors gap between fabric and grain prices. Lack of clothing and wearing less was a common phenomenon. People who couldn't buy cotton would wear woolen blankets all year round. The so-called 'fur all over the day, fur all over the mouth at night' (Shaanxi Provincial Archives, 1981, p. 42). Since the early 1940s, the increase in cloth prices had far exceeded that of grain prices. Consequently, the amount of cloth that could be exchanged for one year's worth of millet had decreased year by year. In 1937, one bucket of millet could be exchanged for one piece of '38-Old-Cloth', but by 1940 it could only be exchanged for 0.45 pieces. The vast majority of farmers felt the difficulty of dressing, and the proportion of clothing expenses in their annual expenses was increasing, with some areas even accounting for over 30%. And the poorer the farmers, the heavier the burden of clothing (Shaanxi Women's Federation, 1985, p. 386).

Although the Women's Federation of the Shaanxi–Gansu–Ningxia Border Region advocated the formation of textile groups in 1940, mobilizing women to engage in textile and learning textile, the true widespread launch of the women's textile movement was after the 1942 Border Region Senior Cadres Conference. Two months later, the '1943-Decision' which promoted the textile industry was not only to point out a new direction for the advancement of the women's movement but also to respond to the textile production issues in the border areas mentioned in Mao Zedong's report on *Economic and Financial Issues*. With the help of State-owned textile factories, textile women, and civil cooperatives, 250,000 pieces of 'Large-Cloth' were supplied to the people, the military and public officials, striving to achieve full self-sufficiency in the border areas (Shaanxi Women's Federation, 1985). The main body of the folk textile industry was women, so women's participation in the Large-scale Production Campaign after 1943 was mainly reflected in their involvement in the folk textile industry.

Mobilizing women's textile enthusiasm was not easy, and it could be said that the effectiveness of the CPC's mobilization of women's labour in the late 1930s was not satisfactory. In February 1943, the newspaper *Liberation Daily* published a history of the development of women's textiles in Yan'an South District Cooperative. In the beginning, it was mentioned that a year ago, there was no page on the economic statistics table of Yan'an South District Cooperative for women's textiles. Local women refused the call from officials to encourage them to spin, citing their inability to do so, lack of cotton, and fear of becoming public officials. In 1939, the labour union and the women's federation jointly formulated a plan to develop women's textiles, but it failed in rural rumours – 'spinning threads for public households will turn them into public servants', 'it will be our job in the future', 'whether we have time or not, we cannot stop spinning in the future'. Therefore, even if women at home had a lot of leisure time, they mainly spent it on hanging out and chatting (Mo, 1943).

There used to be no textile women in Erxiang, Liulin District, Yan'an County. Although the Women's Federation of Erxiang had already organized a spinning group, women were also unwilling to learn. Even the promise of 'spinning one kilogramme to earn one kilogramme' was of no use. Women's reasons were 'too stupid to learn', 'lack of time', and 'spinning threads just earns little money', but in reality, they were afraid of 'living in the factory', 'spinning must be done even during busy farming months after learning how to spin', and 'earning money but wife runs away' (Zhao, 1943).

How could the CPC help women eliminate old and backward labour concepts, develop an interest in textiles, and even develop the idea that textile production could be linked to self-liberation? The survey report provided some answers. In the report named *A History of Women's Textile Development*, there was a refugee woman who took the lead in trying it out. She received spinning wheels and bouncy cotton from a cooperative, and in just six months, she not only made enough money for the whole family to eat but also put on new clothes. What's more, they did not become 'public family members'. In the face of vivid examples, the women's doubts were dispelled, and they took the initiative to learn spinning from this woman. The cooperative provided them with production materials, and in just one year, not only did the whole township spin yarn but also promoted it to the entire district. The experience of the women's textile industry in Yan'an South District Cooperative pointed out the direction for the Women's Federation, as it linked women's liberation and economic interests to some extent. Therefore, it was very popular among rural women, and the work was not as difficult as most people imagined. It attracted the cadres to investigate and study local work, summarize the experience, and promote it.

The most significant measure was to establish models of women's labour. The stories of Ma Xinger and other labour heroes were passed on among the women in the Erxiang of Liulin District, Yan'an County, which improved the enthusiasm of women to participate in textile. Cadres also focused on the stories of local model workers when conducting research.

Since the convening of the Border Region Senior Cadres Conference and the release of '1943-Decision', the folk textile industry had made significant progress.

Encouraged by the CPC, cotton planting was promoted on a larger scale to provide two sets of summer clothes and one set of cotton clothes for each resident and soldier every year. A considerable amount of cotton yarn was mainly spun by women's cooperatives and supplied to many new textile factories for weaving (Israel, 2015a, p. 125).

The specific steps taken by the CPC to mobilize women's spinning were as follows: through consumer cooperatives that existed in every village, women in border areas were encouraged to spin cotton. With support from government banks and large stocks of cotton, cooperatives lent raw materials and spinning wheels to women. Cadres required that women borrow two pounds of cotton and return one pound of cotton yarn. The rest was used by women themselves at home. In this way, housewives could rely on themselves to provide clothing for their families without spending any money then, which was a major item in farmers' households in the past (Israel, 2015b, p. 244).

In 1942, there were 75,000 women involved in spinning and 13,500 involved in weaving. In 1943, these numbers increased dramatically with 133,457 women participating in spinning while those who wove cloth rose to 39,038 people. In 1944, these figures respectively reached up to 152,645 people engaged in spinning while those who weaved cloth increased up to 60,548 people. The amount of yarn spun in 1944 exceeded that of 1943 by two times and the fabric production was three times that of 1943 and eight times that of 1942 (Shaanxi Women's Federation, 1985, p. 390).

These achievements were inseparable from the special progress of the folk textile industry. The vast majority of textile women were from middle and low-income peasant families. These households couldn't fully solve their food problems through agricultural production alone, so they must rely on supplementary income. The '1943-Decision' pointed out the way out for the household textile industry. In many households, textile income could even exceed agricultural income, accounting for more than 50% of the total annual household income (Shaanxi Women's Federation, 1985, p. 392). In order to solve the problem of textile raw materials in poor peasant households, people not only relied on women's production cooperatives organized by cadres but also spontaneously formed small-scale textile cooperatives with several people as units to jointly solve raw material tools and commercialization problems. They were dispersed in their own private households to spin (in order to take care of the elderly and children at the same time), earning money according to labour remunerations so that those without capital could also produce independently (Shaanxi Women's Federation, 1985, p. 394).

ESTABLISHING NEW-STYLE FAMILIES

Due to the impact of the overall crisis related to the Anti-Japanese War, since the 1940s, the economic production in border areas has been closely linked with women's work and family transformation. In this context, 'family' was not only a concern for female workers but also a basic unit of the CPC's economic development plan. Therefore, the border area called on women to actively participate in household handicrafts, sideline businesses and other production activities. The release of '1943-Decision' further systematically explained the interrelationship between women, families and production, pointing out that there was a close relationship between women's liberation and family production. On this basis, the CPC began to promote a new style of democratic family reform, partly implementing the democratization of family life, allowing women to not only play an important role in textiles, handicrafts and household chores but also to have equal democratic rights within the family, thus taking a constructive step towards the goal of women's liberation. Incorporating the spirit of democracy into family units was also a concept of social life for the masses guided by the theory of new democracy.

Starting from March 1944, the *Liberation Daily* successively published typical reports reflecting the new atmosphere of families in the Shaanxi–Gansu–Ningxia Border Region. The renovated new-style families had four characteristics: first, it was about the democratization of family organizational life, the implementation of an electoral system in the home, and the right of women to speak. The second was a precise division of labour in production, with men engaged in heavy physical labour such as agriculture, transportation, and hiring, and women engaged in textile, handicraft, and household care. This allowed both men and women to do their best, fully utilized labour and greatly increased the income of the whole family. The third was to practice thrift. The fourth was to implement a division of labour reward system. The new-style family could break through the obstacles of the parental system, achieve the effects of family harmony, mutual assistance, and economic prosperity. Party cadres needed to promote the spirit of the new democratic family and helped farmers carry out family reform, mainly reflected in helping farmers formulate production plans and participating in democratic family meetings. In addition, the new style of family not only created a democratic atmosphere within the home but also radiated to the outside, driving assistance to the entire village and helping to transform the lazy people in other households.

During his inspection in Yan'an, Gunther Stein paid special attention to the transformation of peasant family life by the CPC. In his view, the transformation method was neither revolutionary nor interfering with people's private lives, but gradually overcame the 'old and backward traditions' of Chinese families in the implementation of the new democratic reform policy, forming the 'new family life of the new democratic vanguard'. Specific measures included the new agricultural production method of village-wide cooperation, universal suffrage for men and women, and the new habit of openly discussing issues, which allowed a democratic spirit to penetrate families. In summary, he believed that the attitude of the CPC towards families was positive. Even among lower-level party members, there was no tendency to dissolve or weaken the importance of families in the new society (Stein, 2015, p. 103).

Shaping a democratic family style was the central task of the CPC in constructing a new style of family. The specific approach was to replace the patriarchal system with democratic leadership through family meetings, open selection, discussion and review (Zhang & Zhang, 2021). The concept of democracy within families didn't grow naturally but was instead implanted by the CPC (Zhou, 2017). Therefore, we cannot ignore what 'democracy' means in the political context envisioned by the CPC, which may explain why they persisted in implanting democracy into family units despite internal and external challenges during the war.

'The New Democratic Theory' proposed that the Chinese Revolution should be carried out in two steps. The first step was to establish a new democratic society governed by a united 'governance' of various classes in China and led by the Chinese proletariat. The second step was to establish a socialist society (Mao, 1991, p. 672). At the Constitutional Promotion Conference in 1940, Mao Zedong emphasized the relationship between the Anti-Japanese War and democracy. The Anti-Japanese War was aimed at national independence, in other words, China's current main task was to undermine imperialism and feudalism, and strive for independence and democracy. He said, 'Without democracy, resistance against Japan will fail. Without democracy, resistance against Japan cannot continue. With democracy, we will resist for eight or ten years, and we will win' (Mao, 1991, pp. 731–732).

Mao Zedong pointed out that the essence of a democratic regime was to improve the economic life of people and enhance their political consciousness, both of which were part of the Anti-Japanese War. To improve living conditions, the first was to reduce the burden that landlords placed on farmers, that is to say, to implement rent and interest relief. The second was to reduce the burden that the government placed on farmers, that is, to implement streamlining of military and administrative measures and develop a part of the public sector of the economy. The third was to conscientiously assist farmers in developing agricultural and sideline production (Mao, 1996, pp. 1–2). These democratic measures clarified the relationship between economic production and democratic construction, which could provide a deeper understanding of the relationship between economic development measures in transforming households and household democratization.

The degree of women's liberation is a natural measure of the overall liberation of society. Influenced by Marxist theory on women's liberation and the actual Revolution in China, the CPC had a clear understanding of the women's movement and revolutionary process. The core meaning of the new-style family was democratization. From newspaper reports, it could be seen that the level of domestic democracy was particularly reflected in how much freedom oppressed groups such as women had obtained. During the process of family reform, women should be able to participate in productive labour, have the right to speak and have economic rights (such as being allowed to save their own private money and participate in production rewards). Therefore, studying new-style families cannot avoid studying the relationship between women's liberation, democracy and family reform.

For women in revolutionary base areas, the implementation of democracy had significant distinctions in different places. In the public sphere, women's democratic rights were guaranteed by legal systems. 'The Shaanxi–Gansu–Ningxia

Border Election Regulations', promulgated in 1937, officially granted women equal political participation rights. In the first democratic election activities at the end of the 1930s, many women participated in elections and began to exercise their democratic rights. In 1941, the government launched a second round of elections, namely 'three-thirds system' democratic elections. This time it attached particular importance to mobilizing women to participate in elections. Both the number of female candidates and those elected as female representatives at all levels greatly exceeded that of the first election.

In the private sphere, the process of women's struggle for democratic rights within the family was complex and tortuous. There were contradictions between relevant laws and traditional families that were difficult to reconcile, and female cadres in particular faced conflicts between ideals and reality. In exploration, the CPC gradually realized that the benign connection between women's liberation, production and democracy could not be separated from 'family' as a place or hub. Based on resuming the path of liberation through labour in the '1943-Decision', the CPC further localized the Marxist theory of women's liberation and officially proposed building a new type of family in 1944, which more clearly presented relationships among women's liberation, democratic construction, labour production and family transformation.

In summary, the transformation of the family essence is to eliminate feudal family relationships that involve personal dependence. In terms of women's liberation, this means breaking the shackles of male dominance over their wives rather than eliminating the form of the family itself. The form of the family still exists, but its essence has changed. Women are no longer dependent on men and have independent production capabilities and opportunities. Family members work together and accumulate wealth collectively. Some Western sociologists (see, e.g., Baker, 1979; Cohen, 1970, 1976; Freedman, 1979; Gallin & Gallin, 1982; Harrell, 1982; Wolf, 1985) have proposed an economic household model for Chinese families, which considers them as economic cooperatives with common income and expenditure plans, shared property, and a joint household economy where individual incomes must be included (Yan, 2017, pp. 15–16).

The labour system promoted by the CPC in rural areas gave women working rights while preserving their traditional way of life. This was a quite gentle form of women's liberation movement that also helped maintain social stability. Its result was not massive destruction or disintegration of family forms (Cai, 2018, p. 269). In Zhao Shuli's novel named *Sanliwan*, during the agricultural cooperative movement stage in 1950s China, old forms of families still existed. Transforming traditional families also meant changing traditional inheritance practices.

LABOUR AND FAMILY

This article believes that two of the distinct conflicts between Marxist women's theory and Western feminist theory lie in the differences in views on 'labour' and 'family'. Marx found through investigating cotton mills that due to changes in labour organization, women were included in the employment scope, so they had a relatively independent economic status, and ultimately men and women tended to be closer to each other in social relations (Marx, 2014, p. 15). Engels believed that the primary prerequisite for women's liberation was their involvement in public affairs (Engels, 1972, p. 72). The promotion of investigation and research is the practical path for the CPC to develop proletarian women's liberation theory and determine Marxist women's theory. In the investigation, the CPC found that the answer to women's liberation was economic production. Women should gradually resist feudal bondage in production practice, a process known as women's socialization. Women should enter into public labour fields. The Shaanxi–Gansu–Ningxia Border Region investigation reports show that the spinning movement gradually developed into a comprehensive movement for fighting for women's interests. Taking cultural education as an example, at first, there was not much enthusiasm among women for learning literacy because they felt it was useless and would delay household chores time. However, since joining the spinning ranks, they had become interested in arithmetic literacy to count money.

Under the background of capitalist production mode, 'labour' has been divided into different levels. Adam Smith distinguished 'productive labour' and 'unproductive labour', with women's household chores belonging to the latter as they do not produce exchange value (Song, 2016, pp. 54–55). Compared with productive labour, it is considered inferior or low-value work. This conception has denied the value of women's domestic labour in general for thousands of years. Such a view was popular during the May Fourth Movement, which led to a necessity for women to leave their homes if they were deemed worthless there.

The liberation movement for women in the 1920s merged with youth ideological liberation movements, and the issue of women was not an independent problem but accompanied by calls from intellectuals for breaking down dual structural oppression from both patriarchal and marital authority on women. They called on women to step out of their homes. At that time, literary themes about female liberation mainly focused on love and marriage while describing 'home' as a place where females are oppressed. However, historical facts have proven that leaving home did not necessarily lead to a bright future for these women. As Lu Xun pointed out, there were only two possible outcomes: either degradation or return home. Some male intellectuals advocated for female 'runaways', which was essentially not due to concern over Chinese female oppression but rather stemmed from learning Western civilization considerations instead. However, western capitalist societies at that time had also failed to prepare housewives for entering workplaces properly (Smedley, 2017, p. 510).

The May Fourth Movement inspired women to step out of their families; but where should they go? How can women avoid the consequences of 'degradation' (i.e., having to engage in lowly or even unethical work, and becoming the bottom of society) or 'returning home'? This question needs to be answered in the process of exploring the sinicization of Marxist women's theory. The adjustment of the direction of women's liberation work in Yan'an period shows that the CPC has opened up sufficient space for women's liberation within the original Marxist framework, and has linked women, families and the country together by mobilizing women's production. In the 1940s, while mobilizing women to participate in the production labour and movement, the government put forward the slogan of 'new-style families', allowing women's domestic labour value to be 'seen' through official channels, and advocating for 'family harmony' and 'building new-style families' through propaganda and other means. The degree of women's liberation should be within the range that families can tolerate, and female cadres should not create tense relationships between women and their husbands and mothers-in-law.

During the early period of reflection on women's work, the CPC believed that what families needed was transformation rather than abandonment. Some cadres only saw the constraints imposed on women by the semi-feudal family system and regarded the family as a prison for women. They did not consider how to transform families in the new democratic society but simply tried to free women from their shackles (Zhang, 2013, p. 224). Several seemingly progressive women's work actually had a negative impact on the household economy and rural women's status in households, especially causing new psychological distress for young women and reducing their acceptance within families. In rural areas, simple application of theories such as economic independence and gender equality could easily lead to marital discord and conflicts between mothers-in-law and daughters-in-law, often triggering contradictions among the masses and between the masses and cadres. Due to the unfavourable work route for women in the early stage, which was not conducive to uniting male farmers or stabilizing rural areas, starting from the actual needs of the Anti-Japanese War, the CPC finally resumed the dialectical path of women's liberation of 'going out of the family' and 'consolidating the family' in 1944. Many clues about the transformation of rural families and the collective life of rural women in China during the collectivization period of the 1950s had already emerged in the Yan'an period.

CONCLUSION

Since modern times, with the introduction of Marxism to China, 'women' have become a conceptual group associated with several important social liberation issues. Women and labour, women and socialism, women and class, and so on, are all topics of concern to early Marxists in China. The CPC has inherited the women's liberation thoughts of Marx, Engels, Lenin, etc., since its establishment. However, it is worth noting that the exploration of women's liberation theory by the CPC also underwent a gradual localization process. It was not until the 1940s, under the background of the construction of the Shaanxi–Gansu–Ningxia Border Region, that the shift in women's work marked its maturity and influenced the participation of working women in the socialist construction cause after the founding of New China.

Before the Great National Revolution (1924–1927), the women's liberation theory of Chinese intellectuals was relatively limited to gender equality and exposure of accusations against the feudal system. After the Great Revolution, with the successive blows to the women's movement in reality, many intellectuals who were baptized by the Revolution turned to Marxist women's liberation theory, using class struggle theory to view women's issues, and began to agree with the women's movement resolution of the Second National Congress of the CPC. Especially, women's liberation must be accompanied by labour liberation. Only when the proletariat obtains power can women truly be liberated (Archives Bureau, 1991, p. 88).

Sun Yat–sen's early idea of gender equality, which was based on the Western bourgeois concepts of natural human rights, freedom, equality and universal love, gradually lost its persuasiveness. It emphasized calling on women to strive for equal rights to education, economy, and political participation with men, and hoped that women would also assume equal responsibilities and obligations with men in national construction. However, in reality, the Nationalist government led by the Kuomintang deviated from this original intention and did not consider the liberation of women as part of the revolutionary task. Some intellectuals also chose to be inclusive and absorbed various theories as their theoretical foundation for women, discussing both 'human rights' and 'social assistance', integrating applied social system theory with human evolution theory (Han, 2003).

When the revolutionary base of the CPC shifted from cities to rural areas, and the main target of the women's movement shifted from female workers to rural women, the CPC felt the importance of changing economic dependency relationships for the vast number of working women from the land reform. The Marxist theory of women's liberation holds that private ownership and class exploitation are the fundamental reasons for women's oppression. Due to the unequal ownership of means of production, women are in an oppressed position in both feudal and capitalist societies. Through the revolutionary practice in rural areas, the CPC has become increasingly aware of the relationship between gender issues and class issues: class liberation restricts gender liberation (meaning that the priority and importance of class liberation often limit the process and intensity of gender liberation), while gender liberation is subordinate to class liberation (He, 2012). The protection of women's rights is not the decoration of progressiveness political power and civilization, but the revolutionary process integrated into social liberation. Rural women are one of the bravest parts of the struggling farmers. Ignoring and absorbing them into the movement will inevitably reduce the strength of the rural revolution. Men are not the objects of women's struggle, but comrades in the proletarian revolution. Male farmers who oppress rural women are essentially also oppressed by landlords and gentry. Therefore, in the 1930s, the CPC led the women's movement in Soviet Areas towards the agrarian Revolution.

From a theoretical perspective, the liberation of women required that the CPC could not simply emphasize the commonality of class while ignoring the gender specificity of women's oppression. In light of the realities of the Chinese Revolution, especially during the General Anti-Japanese War, the CPC sought to establish and consolidate an anti-Japanese national united front by striving for class unity and gender cooperation. It searched for a balance between cooperation and independence in history and reality. The embodiment of this balance was centred on production-oriented ideas about women's liberation in the 1940s, which not only improved women's economic status but also served to support war efforts through labour productivity. This idea and practical path towards women's liberation partially eliminated several tense situations between male–female gender camps in border areas since the late 1930s (mainly manifested in divorce), promoted unity and cooperation among revolutionary forces, strengthened female power within revolutionary classes, and provided more solid social foundations as well as broader development space for women's liberation (Peng & Wan, 2021).

Undeniably, the above theory has been questioned by feminists (see, e.g., Johnson, 1985; Stacey, 1984) who believe that Chinese rural women bear dual responsibilities (to participate in social labour production and bear the burden of household chores). Moreover, based on the Marxist theory of women's liberation, the premise for women to leave their homes should be that socialized large-scale production allows them to break free from heavy household labour. Obviously, at that time, the Shaanxi–Gansu–Ningxia Border Region did not reach this level of productivity. In addition to the questioning by feminists represented by Ding Ling, the CPC also had to engage in a debate against the trend of 'women returning home' in the Nationalist-controlled areas, in order to consolidate the enthusiasm of women to participate in social production during the Anti-Japanese War and not give up any forces that could be united.

Despite persistent questioning by feminists about the CPC's theory of women's liberation, the CPC has not stopped exploring and practicing the path of women's liberation. After the victory of the Anti-Japanese War, the CPC continued to promote the process of women's liberation and raised the status of women to a new height. In December 1948, the Central Committee of the CPC issued 'The Decision on the Current Work of Rural Women in Liberated Areas', which inherited and developed the important spirit of the '1943-Decision' mentioned previously. Especially after the establishment of the People's Republic of China in 1949, the CPC incorporated women's liberation into the overall plan of national development, improving women's status an important part of the country's modernization process, and strengthening theoretical research and practical exploration of women's issues. In this process, the CPC deeply recognized the mutually reinforcing relationship between women's liberation and socialist construction, actively promoted the improvement of women's status and the development of social productivity, accelerated the process of socialist construction, and also provided broader development space for women's liberation. During this process, the CPC focused on improving the status of women through their participation in social production, and actively explored ways for women to participate in the country's political, economic and cultural life.

REFERENCES

Ai, S. (1943, April 8). Establish a new concept of labor [in Chinese]. *Liberation Daily*, *688*, 1.

All–China Women's Federation. (1991). *History materials of Chinese women's movement (1937–1945)* [in Chinese]. China Women Publishing House.

Archives Bureau. (1991). *Selected works of the central committee of the CPC* [in Chinese] (Vol. 1). Central Party School Press.

Archives Bureau. (2011). *Selected works of important documents since the founding of the CPC* [in Chinese] (Vol. 8). Central Party Literature Press.

Baker, H. (1979). *Chinese family and kinship*. Columbia University Press.

Cai, X. (2018). *Chinese socialist literature and cultural imagination (1949–1966)* [in Chinese]. Peking University Press.

Cohen, M. L. (1970). Developmental process in the Chinese domestic group. In M. Freedman (Ed.), *Family and kinship in Chinese society* (pp. 21–36). Stanford University Press.

Cohen, M. L. (1976). *House united, house divided: The Chinese family in Taiwan*. Columbia University Press.

Engels, F. (1972). *The origin of the family, private property and the state* [in Chinese]. People's Publishing House.

Freedman, M. (1979). The family in China, past and present. In G. Skinner (Ed.), *The study of Chinese society: Essays by Maurice Freedman* (pp. 273–295). Stanford University Press.

Gallin, B., & Gallin, R. (1982). The Chinese joint family in changing rural Taiwan. In S. Greenblatt, R. Wilson, & A. Wilson (Eds.), *Social interaction in Chinese society*. Praeger.

Han, D. (1980). *Fanshen: A documentary of revolution in a Chinese village* [in Chinese]. Beijing Publishing House.

Han, H. (2003). The practice of the China women's movement in respect of the buildup of the basic women-oriented theory [in Chinese]. *Journal of Chinese Women's Studies*, *2*, 10–16.

Harrell, S. (1982). *Ploughshare village: Culture and context in Taiwan*. University of Washington Press.

He, L. (2009). *The rights of women in the Republic of China under the influence of western waves* [in Chinese]. Jiuzhou Press.

He, L. (2012). The dissemination and influence of Soviet Russia's women liberation concept in China at the beginning of the twentieth century [in Chinese]. *CPC History Studies*, *12*, 78–87.

Israel, E. (2015a). *I visit Yenan* [in Chinese]. New Star Press.

Israel, E. (2015b). *The unfinished revolution in China* [in Chinese]. New Star Press.

Johnson, K. A. (1985). *Women, the family, and peasant revolution in China*. University of Chicago Press.

Mao, Z. (1991). *Selected works of Mao Tse–tung* [in Chinese] (Vol. 2). People's Publishing House.

Mao, Z. (1996). *Collected works of Mao Tse–tung* [in Chinese] (Vol. 3). People's Publishing House.

Marx, K. (2014). *1844 manuscripts of economics and philosophy* [in Chinese]. People's Publishing House.

Mo, A. (1943, February 28). A history of women's textile development in one page [in Chinese]. *Liberation Daily*, *649*, 4.

Peng, D., & Wan, J. (2021). The intersection of gender and class: A brief discussion on the early ideology of women's work in the CPC [in Chinese]. *Hubei Social Sciences*, *10*, 123–130.

Shaanxi Provincial Archives. (1981). *Compilation of historical materials on finance and economy in the Shaanxi–Gansu–Ningxia border region during the anti–Japanese war period* [in Chinese] (Vol. 9). Shaanxi People's Publishing House.

Shaanxi Provincial Archives. (2016). *Compilation of historical materials on finance and economy in the Shaanxi–Gansu–Ningxia border region during the anti–Japanese war period* [in Chinese] (Vol. 3). Changjiang Literature and Art Publishing House.

Shaanxi Women's Federation. (1985). *Documentation of women's movement in the Shaanxi-Gansu-Ningxia border region* [in Chinese]. Shaanxi Women's Federation.

Smedley, A. (2017). *Battle hymn of China* [in Chinese]. Beijing Publishing House.

Song, S. (2016). *China and women in "Western Mirror"* [in Chinese]. Social Sciences Academic Press.

Stacey, J. (1984). *Patriarchy and socialist revolution in China*. University of California Press.

Stein, G. (2015). *The challenge of red China* [in Chinese]. Shanghai Scientific and Technological Lite Rature Press.

Wang, Z., & Gao, Y. (2016). *Translating feminisim in China* [in Chinese]. Fudan University Press.

Wolf, A. (1985). Chinese family size: A myth revitalized. In J.-C. Hsieh & Y.-C. Chuang (Eds.), *The Chinese family and its ritual behavior* (pp. 30–49). Academia Sinica.

Yan, Y. (2017). *Private life under socialism* [in Chinese]. Shanghai People's Publishing House.

Zhang, W. (2013). *The limits of liberation* [in Chinese]. China University of Political Science and Law Press.

Zhang, Y., & Zhang, J. (2021). Between family and country: Traditional family reformation and mass mobilization by the Communist Party of China during the war of resistance against Japanese invasion [in Chinese]. *Journal of Southwest University (Social Sciences Edition)*, *47*(3), 208–218.

Zhao, F. (1943, March 8). Women's production in Erxiang, Liulin district, Yan'an county [in Chinese]. *Liberation Daily*, *657*, 4.

Zhou, L. (2017). Conflict and amalgamation: Reforms of Chinese communist party's family policy during the war against Japanese invasion [in Chinese]. *Journal of Chinese Women's Studies*, *3*, 40–48.

Zhou, L., & Liu, N. (2016). *Research on the women's movement in China during the anti–Japanese war period (1931–1945)* [in Chinese]. Capital University of Economy and Business Publishing House.

A BRIEF ACCOUNT OF THE DESTRUCTION OF PRE-REVOLUTIONARY CUBA BY THE CAPITALIST SYSTEM

Rémy Herrera

CNRS (National Center of Scientific Research), France

ABSTRACT

We would like to show here not only how capitalism was fundamental in the structuring of the Cuban economy and society but also how violent this influence was during the pre-revolutionary history of this country. Destruction of Amerindian societies and annihilation of the native populations, massive deportations and over-exploitation of African slaves in sugar cultivation, misery of small farmers of Spanish origin and rural exodus, harsh living and working conditions of sugar proletarians, waves of emigration, bloody wars of independence, US military occupations, ferocious repressions of popular revolts and succession of dictatorships, confinement in economic underdevelopment, political submission, social inequalities and cultural alienation, such was the fate that capitalism reserved for the people of Cuba before the victory of their Socialist Revolution.

Keywords: Cuba; capitalism; slavery; sugar production; mono-export specialization; US imperialism; high finance; neocolonialism; pre-revolutionary period

INTRODUCTION: MAIN HISTORICAL FEATURES

Cuba was, in 1492, the first large 'discovered' land on the other side of the Atlantic; and also the place where the original Amerindian–Cuban population was almost totally decimated, from 1511 onwards, the date of the effective conquest of the island, between extreme colonial violence and demographic chaos. At the very end

Trajectories of Declining and Destructive Capitalism
Research in Political Economy, Volume 40, 55–64

Published under exclusive licence by Emerald Publishing Limited
ISSN: 0161-7230/doi:10.1108/S0161-723020250000040004

of the 18th century, the island was to be specialized in sugar production, and, by the early 19th century, elevated to the rank of the world's leading exporter of sugar. Under the combined effects of external shocks and internal factors that liquidated the old relations of production and unleashed new productive forces, this specialization was revealed through a strategy of integration into the capitalist world system that placed the colony in a dominated but dynamic position.

In contrast to the genuine development of society, this strong growth of the economy was only possible through the over-exploitation of the local populations, and then of imported workers. Cuba is, in the world, the territory where capitalist modern slavery has lasted the longest: almost four centuries. The second colony to introduce slavery, in 1511, or even 1503, after Hispaniola, Cuba was the penultimate to abolish it, in 1886, just before Brazil. It was the place where the deportation of African workers was the most massive in all of Hispanic America, with, according to our own calculations (Herrera, 2025), the cumulative flow of slaves having probably exceeded one million people. The peak of the slave population was recorded in the 1841 census, with more than 436,000 individuals, for a total Cuban population of one million inhabitants at that date, 60% of whom being black.

Cuba is also the territory where Spanish colonization lasted the longest in history, from 1492 to 1898. Its end was a late, slow and particularly painful decolonization, involving several wars of independence. The last of these, which took place between 1895 and 1898, saw the arrival of a Spanish occupying army of almost 300,000 men, or one soldier for every five inhabitants, a record then unequalled in the annals of world repression. It was at this moment of vulnerability that the United States chose to wage there the first imperialist war in its history, with the aim of securing total control of the island, trying to break the Cuban popular nationalist movement and confiscating hard-won independence.

The period was indeed a turning point in history: that of the emergence and rise to power of the major US financial groups. However, Cuba's dependence on the United States predates its military submission in 1898. From the end of the 18th century, the island, detached from the Spanish imperial monopoly by the English, was connected to the interests of the Anglo-American hegemonic classes and gradually anchored to the US economy. As a result, it was very early on placed, under the form of the very political domination of Spanish colonization, in close economic dependence on the United States – which was also a slave-owning society until the second half of the 19th century (Herrera, 2025). Shortly after US independence in 1776, Cuba became the leading foreign market for US commodities, and found the United States to be the main outlet for its exports. For a long time, this dependence was based on the exchange of raw sugar for the means to produce it, including slaves.

The military occupation of Cuba by the United States in 1898, at the end of the war of independence, was in fact the continuation of a long series of aggressions on its part throughout the 19th century, and continued with several recurrent armed interventions until 1922 – and even 1933. At the time, it guaranteed the penetration of the island's property structures and, through public debt, of its State itself, which US capital came to dominate completely. The part of the territory that the United States took from the island, i.e., Guantánamo Bay, has still not been returned to the Cuban people.

As a matter of fact, Cuba is the first – and to date, the only – victorious Communist Revolution in the Americas since 1959. The product of a long process of national identity construction, solidly constituted, the Cuban Revolution is to be interpreted as the culmination of the struggles of a proletariat – in the Marxist sense of the term – which finally succeeded in building a workers–peasants front through the convergence of demands for (i) the equality of all human beings, (ii) national liberation, and (iii) social progress. It is the merger of these struggles that precisely defines the Cuban communist project. And it is from a centuries-old perspective and in the continuity of the slave revolts and wars of independence that we can understand the profound motivations of the multiracial and rebellious Cuban people's adherence to this project. In addition to its early and resolute combativeness, what characterizes it is the deployment and realization of radically anti-capitalist requests that are interwoven and always inserted, not without complexities, into anti-racist and anti-imperialist struggles.

Finally, Cuba is the country that has suffered, and continues to suffer, the longest embargo imposed by the US administration in history: from 1962 to the present day. Condemned by an overwhelming majority of the member countries of the United Nations (Herrera, 2004), it remains in force by the sole will of Washington, causing cruel suffering to the Cuban people (Campbell, 2021). In return, Cuba knew how to respond to this imperialist hatred by taking the ethic of solidarity to the highest level of generosity and courage through its internationalist missions.

THE COLONIAL PERIOD (1492–1898)

On the eve of the *conquista* of 1511, Cuba had an Amerindian population of several tens of thousands. These peoples suffered the most violent demographic shock in modern history. Following the conquest, the decline in this population, all causes combined, was probably of the order of 10 to 1 in two generations. By 1530, the number of Amerindo–Cubans had fallen to around 15,000, and by the very beginning of the 17th century to between 1,000 and 2,000 (out of a total island population of 12,000). So Cuba's modern history began with an immense and dramatic demographic chaos. And it was in the midst of this tragedy that the colonial lands were forcibly taken over, along with what was amalgamated with them, both above and below. This original appropriation of land was accompanied by that of the mines and, as a result, the subjection of the Amerindian populations.

It was not just Diego Velázquez and his 300–man crew who landed in Cuba in 1511 – the date of the start of its colonization – but, with them, an expanding Europe, with its social structures undergoing deep changes. At the same time as original accumulation was taking place and the world capitalist system was taking shape, it was this Europe that created, in the Americas, a new colonial organization, still largely feudal though already proto–capitalist, geared towards supplying the metropolis and the international markets of the time; a social formation of the seigniorial type of subjugation, distribution and putting to forced labour of the indigenous populations, for the benefit of the great landowners and merchants. Most local production was based on the *encomienda* regime, applied in Cuba from 1513. By the end of the 16th century, the latifundium extended over almost the entire western part of the island.

Cuba's production cycles were successively driven by exports of gold (from 1511 to 1540) and copper (from 1530 to 1610), followed by timber and leather (Le Riverend, 1965). None of these cycles, nor the later ones linked to coffee and tobacco, were to lead to the start of an accumulation of local capital likely to trigger a process of industrialization. For they all began with looting and ended with non-industrialization. The deportation of black African slaves began to make up for the lack of indigenous labour. Slaves were probably brought to Cuba before the year 1511 and sent to the goldfields. Spain, like much of Western Europe, was only able to lay the foundations of capitalist industry in the 16th century by subjugating the New World colonies, in all sectors. Consequently, the process of industrialization stalled on the island, where the economy was placed, in the long term, on a trajectory of underdevelopment. In Cuba, and especially around the port of Havana, an economy of maritime and commercial services (repairs, supplies, etc.), both civil and military, was set up to organize the conquest and colonization of the American continent. From the outset, Cuba's regional integration was centrifugal and disarticulating.

What is essential, however, is to understand that the Cuban colony had to constitute itself as an export economy, based entirely on slavery. Although slavery had been instituted since the *conquista*, its large-scale extension was closely linked to the boom in sugar cane plantations and the production and export of sugar. In other words, the expansion of slavery can be explained – here is the key historical turning point – by the rise in power of the large sugar landowners and their strategy of connecting to the world market. Such strategy involved integrating the Cuban colony into the capitalist world system, through an alliance established between the dominant Creole classes and the over-dominant classes of the centre (first Spanish, then English–US).

And what is important to note is the decisive importance for the island of this specialization in sugar, which took place between 1750 and 1850. By the middle of the 19th century, it had become the world's largest exporter of sugar. The basis of this vertiginous expansion was the slavery system, extended on such a large scale that it distorted the entire colonial structure, making the conditions for class struggle much more complex.

If Cuba was able to be specialized in the mono-export of sugar, thanks to an international alliance between dominant classes that led to the extension of slavery, it is because external shocks forced it to do so, setting the island, from the second-half of the 18th century onwards, on a dynamic productive and commercial trajectory, but one that was extremely violent for its people – and above all its black population – and lastingly handicapping its long-term development. The first of these shocks was the military occupation of Havana by the English in 1762, whose impact was to increase slave imports and liberate trade; the second was its connection to the market of the United States from 1776 to 1783, with the island falling into a new dependency, of an economic nature, more pervasive than Spanish political domination; and the third was the Haitian war of independence, which broke out in the summer of 1791 and eliminated the island's main competitor in the international sugar market.

These shocks came and amplified specific internal conditions of the colony, both physical (topographical, climatic, agrological, etc.) and, above all, socio-economic (i.e., the conversion of large landowners to sugar growers, the ousting of competitors producing tobacco or coffee, the resurgence of the latifundio, etc.), making Cuba an ideal sugar island. These changes, which freed up land and manpower for sugar production, boosted Cuba's growth of productive forces, integrated the relations of slave domination into *capitalist* relations of exploitation, and eliminated archaic relations of production. All this could be achieved by liberalizing trade, turning land into a commodity and pushing all human beings – and not just slaves – into the market sphere.

In Cuba, between the 1750s and 1850s, sugar production and export volumes rapidly took on the form of exponential curves. This dazzling expansion of the sugar sector, despite recurring crises, transformed the old colony, which had been stagnant at the beginning of the 18th century, into the world's largest exporter of sugar during the first-half of the 19th century. To guarantee these profits, the pace of slave deportations had to be stepped up. The total number of slaves deported from Africa and landed alive in Cuban ports can be estimated at at least 1.1 million between 1511 and 1886 (Herrera, 2025) – that is, a demographic drain on the African continent that was probably twice as great. Slavery weighed heavily on all other employment statuses, including of course wage labour.

Nevertheless, slavery was not abolished in Cuba until 1886. In the end, it was wage labour that was to support the revitalization of modernized sugar production, soon to be directly controlled by US interests. The great transformation of the sugar industry took place in the last-third of the 19th century: the substitution of the masses of slaves by those of agricultural wage-earning workers, multicoloured and miserable proletarians on whom capitalist monetary constraint was now permanently exercised.

Spain kept its army of occupation on the island in an attempt to crush the troops of the Cuban Liberation Army when the (second) war of independence broke out in 1895. In the second-half of the 19th century, the metropolis tried to promote a vigorous colonial policy of settlement from Spain.

The fundamental phenomenon lies in the fact that, under the surface of colonial political domination, Cuba had become economically dependent on the United States since the end of the 18th century. For a long time, the closeness of these ties was largely due to the combined efforts of their respective dominant classes to consolidate slavery. The island's dependence was initially commercial, before becoming industrial and, finally, financial. Cuban exports, mainly unrefined sugar, were sent for 65% to the United States in 1850. By 1875, nearly 85% of them were going to this country. In 1895, the imbalance had become extreme: 90%. By this time, the island was the second largest foreign market for US commodities. The centre on which the Cuban periphery depended was no longer the old colonial metropolis, but the hegemonic power in the making of the capitalist world system. In reality, it was a case of 'annexation to the US market'.

By the end of the 19th century, the logic of colonial capitalism had been pushed to its ultimate limits. Cuban sugar production collapsed with the second war of independence, which began in 1895. It was a bloody war. Between 300,000 and 400,000 Cubans died during the conflict, most of them civilians. The United States intervened and confiscated the Cuban victory and the country's independence (Herrera, 2025). The new aspect of the Spanish–US war was that it was the very effect of the push of US financial capital, and the condition for its 'imperialist' expansion abroad.

THE IMPERIALIST PERIOD (1898–1958)

It was only when the transition to wage-labour and the ruin of the local capitalist nuclei that had managed to emerge were considered definitive that the agents driving the movements of finance capital in the United States took the decision to penetrate the property and State structures in Cuba. Although US investment had been arriving in Cuba since the 1880s, this control over Cuba did not really take place until 1914. Cuba's external profile, rigidly mono-export and multi-import, had already become fixed in the polarizing relations maintained throughout the 19th century with the great owners of US industry and banking, who became the owners of high finance before the turn of the 20th century, and explaining the growth in outlets and financing obtained by the sugar sector, the engine of the island's economy.

Subjugation went through hidden mechanisms in economic relations, especially trade and monetary relations. A Treaty of Reciprocity had been signed between the two countries in 1902, which obliged Cuba to grant US exporters, by lowering customs tariffs, privileges guaranteeing exclusivity of the Cuban market for thousands of commodities, but which prevented the island's economic diversification. US capital poured in. The imperialist push operated like a modern *conquista*. Its protagonists were J.P. Morgan & Co. and the Rockefeller groups – the latter structured around the National City Bank, on the one hand, or, on the other, around Standard Oil and the Chase Manhattan Bank. These financial giants, backed by the Washington administration, took total control of the island (Herrera, 2005).

The conquest was carried out under military occupation (from 1898 to 1902, from 1906 to 1912, in 1917…) and in a dollarized Cuban economy – placed under a de facto protectorate. Its methods, those of the original accumulation, combined violence, theft and corruption. Between 1898 and 1913, the advance of finance operated in all sectors: mining, telecommunications, transport, sugar plantations and plants, tobacco, tropical fruits, etc. From 1914 to 1929, the main protagonist of this assault was named John Pierpont Morgan. Between world war, stock market speculation and the 'dance of millions', US high finance took hold of the sugar sector and controlled its destiny from 1921 onwards. The capital ownership structure was held by various US companies, themselves in the hands of high finance.

By 1925, Cuba ranked third recipient country of US capital exports in the world, just behind Canada and Germany. The effect was an unprecedented surge in sugar production volumes. The growth rates in sugar exports, expressed in value, were simply prodigious. For, in 1920, Cuba's exports per capita were greater than those of England. Nevertheless, this boom had little to do with an entrepreneurial spirit; rather, it translated the plundering behaviour of US financial tycoons. The intrinsic logic of the latter was to secure control of already existing production units to extract maximum profits from them, which were repatriated to the United States, rather than to participate in the extension of the productive apparatus or its more intensive exploitation. The project to develop the national economy was not part of this vision.

The banking liquidation law of 1920 had revealed the bankruptcy of local banks, which were quickly absorbed by the financial oligopolies of the North. And the Cuban State had itself fallen into financial dependence on the United States through the public debt. So corporate finance was on the scene. It took over the entire Cuban economy – starting with sugar. But this process did not allow the Cuban sugar sector to industrialize, by refining its sugar; hence the incredible situation to which the world's leading exporter of raw sugar was reduced by having to import a luxury product from the United States: refined sugar!

The backbone of the economy, sugar was under the control of US high finance, i.e., the most powerful owners of the world's dominant capital. And it was this capital which, as a result, controlled the employment, status and – if necessary – import flows of the workforce used on the island, where this sector, at harvest time, concentrated a large mass of workers. However, one of the original features of Cuba was that, after the abolition of slavery, the workforce employed in the sugar sector was made up of salaried workers, both farm labourers and workers in the sugar centrales, which had become true factories. All together, they therefore formed, in rural areas, a proletariat – in the Marxist sense of the term.

At the beginning of the 20th century, the wages paid to cane cutters were extremely low, often below the subsistence level, which left them with no reserves for the periods of the year when they remained unemployed. In addition to the fact that it reduced the risks of uprisings or escapes, wage employment transferred part of the cost of reproducing the labour force to the workers themselves. During the harvests, which lasted a maximum of 5 months per year, generally from February to June, it relieved the owners of the sugar plantations and/or plants from the need to maintain the workforce by providing the latter with food, clothing and housing; and during the off-season, lasting about 8 months, it saved employers from having to find a way to keep workers on the plantations – the capitalist monetary constraint, which forces them to work hard to earn their living, operating. The use of seasonal immigrant workers to lend a hand to local agricultural workers divided the Cuban proletariat, and primarily black workers.

All that remained for Cuba as a perspective for its future was the development of underdevelopment. The economy was hyper-specialized in terms of its domestic production and foreign trade: sugar then represented up to a third of the gross domestic product (GDP) and more than three-quarters of the country's exports. It was vulnerabilized to price volatility. Cuba was thus totally dependent on the goodwill of its main client... and owner. The United States did not just buy sugar; it had appropriated almost everything on the island that generated profits. Adjusting to fluctuations in the foreign market required the setting aside of numerous lands, unavailable for growing food crops. The paltry amounts of land taxes that sugar producers had to pay also encouraged them to keep land unoccupied, always available for growing cane. Labour was underemployed. Inactive for most of the year and without the possibility of alternative employment, workers were suddenly mobilized in mass during harvest time (or *zafra*); hence a structurally high unemployment rate and strong seasonal variability in their income.

In Cuba, once the option of industrialization was ruled out, investment opportunities quickly reached saturation. Inflows of foreign capital would slow down in the sugar sector. From 1925, no sugar plant was built – until the Revolution of 1958. Pre-revolutionary Cuba was sinking into structural stagnation, socially harsh and politically troubled. The exhaustion of its capitalist 'model of development', extensive, extroverted, disjointed, was obvious. The trend in the growth rate of sugar production over the period 1898–1958 was clearly oriented downwards.

Under these conditions, the capitalist crisis of 1929 came to hit an already fragile and dramatically subjugated Cuban economy. In Latin America, it is Cuba that was hardest hit. The island had the economy most closely integrated with the United States, itself the country most affected of all Western powers. Cuba found itself in a situation of extreme vulnerability to variations in export revenues, 80% of which were sugar and 75% of which were directed to the United States. And the local authorities were dispossessed by Washington of the commercial, monetary, budgetary, fiscal or industrial and agricultural policy tools which could have protected their society in the face of the shock of the crisis. The strategy of the Cuban government – imposed from the outside – was that of ever greater economic integration with the United States, and an anchor in the 'dollar zone'. Order therefore had to reign there.

The Cuban economy being firmly anchored to US high finance, there was no longer any need to keep too tight the political ties attaching it to their army. The Platt Amendment was repealed in 1934 – although without the return of the Guatánamo military base. Simultaneously, quotas were assigned to Cuban sugar producers by the Jones–Costigan Act of 1934. This device locked the island into the export of raw sugar. Furthermore, it also forced it to sell part of its production on the 'free' market, exposed to high price variability. The large unsold surpluses had to be sold on this market, which caused prices already falling even further to fall, and allowed the United States to impose readjustments leading to lower guaranteed prices. At a time when the Cuban State seemed to be gaining political autonomy and having more national sovereignty, due to the repeal of the Platt Amendment by Washington and the renunciation of military interference, in fact its economic dependence, precisely financial and commercial dependence, increased, becoming more opaque, because paradoxical, combining both liberalism and interventionism.

The 'sugar factory' of the Caribbean, the island was like the overseas projection of the continental territory of the United States, shaped in the very organization of productions in the North, operating in the service of the accumulation of US capital, translating the regionally integrated character of the genesis of imperialist surplus value. The Cuban dominant classes, led from outside, were corrupt; capital flight was massive; and social inequalities were enormous.

The long history of a country stuck in underdevelopment by the international division of labour characteristic of the capitalist world system was thus sealed; a country condemned in this way to non-industrialization, or to successive deindustrializations which prolonged those of the colonial period, from copper foundries to shipyards, from leather to tobacco, and now even to the sugar sector itself. The Cuban economy was thus seeing segments of industrial activities confiscated; segments which would have allowed the adaptation of its productive apparatus to domestic consumption, as well as any possibility of articulating these productions with those of local agriculture in order to satisfy the fundamental and urgent needs of the people. In short, the island did not consume what it produced, nor did it produce what it consumed. The irrationality of peripheral capitalism was glaring.

In Cuba, the failure of the capitalist strategy commanded from the United States was clear. On the island, adjustments to external shocks were carried out in the most violent way for its population: by increasing unemployment and underemployment and by falling wages, therefore by a deterioration in the living conditions of Cuban workers.

In turn, the governments of the Cuban dominant classes which succeeded at the head of the State, pro–US and united by their submission to imperialism, despite their differences, hardened the dictatorship, through a policy of State terror, as popular protests mounted. Linked to President Fulgencio Batista himself (in business and friendship), the godfathers of organized crime operated in Cuba on conquered territory.

After 1945, the United States resumed its direct investment flows (Pino Santos, 1973). The few spaces of enrichment that it tolerated for the local bourgeoisie were enough to docilize the latter. In the mid–1950s, the empire of the Rockefellers expanded immeasurably, in all directions: sugar, mining, energy, railways, automobiles, tropical fruits, finance, especially with Chase Manhattan and the National City Bank. It was through the latter that they owned most of their sugar properties. True masters of the Cuban economy, the Rockefellers took over from J.P. Morgan at the turn of the years 1933–1934, in the midst of the chaos of the Great Depression.

CONCLUSION: THE NECESSARY REVOLUTION

In 1957, in Havana, local decision-makers saw nothing abnormal in granting a subsidy of six million dollars, to develop the exploitation of oil deposits under their soil, to a transnational owned by John D. Rockefeller whose assets exceeded three times the GDP of the island: Esso. The Cuban State, compradorized, was no match. The allocation of resources was controlled by the adjustment of the national supply of sugar to fluctuations in world demand. Results: 600,000 Cubans (out of 6 million in total) remained unemployed outside of the harvest, the rural exodus agglutinated a crowd of landless peasants in the poor neighborhoods of large cities, departures abroad accelerated.

In the 1950s, the misery of the people was massive, and society was plagued by multiple dysfunctions: illiteracy, low schooling rates, high infant mortality rates, poor health of the population, low number of doctors, housing in poor condition, high income inequalities (Martínez, 1991). Just as much as the spirit of justice, reason itself called for a rupture.

REFERENCES

Campbell, A. (2021). Imperialism and the transition to socialism in Cuba. *Research in Political Economy*, *36*, 163–178.

Herrera, R. (2004). Why lift the embargo against Cuba? *Monthly Review*, *55*(8), 49–54.

Herrera, R. (2005). When the names of the emperors were Morgan and Rockefeller. *International Journal of Political Economy*, *34*(4), 25–49.

Herrera, R. (2025). *A people's history of Cuba: 1492 – Present – Social, economic and political perspectives*. Palgrave Macmillan. [To be published].

Le Riverend, J. (1965). *Historia económica de Cuba*. Editora del Consejo Nacional de Universidades.

Martínez, O. (1991). Desarrollo humano: la experiencia cubana. *Revista Cuba Económica*, *1*(1), 16–34.

Pino Santos, O. (1973). *El Imperialismo norteamericano en la economía de Cuba*. Editorial de Ciencias sociales.

PART II

PAST AND PRESENT, (EUROPEAN) NORTH

THE ARCHIMEDEAN LEVER OF THE FEDERAL REPUBLIC OF GERMANY: ORDO-LIBERALISM AND SOCIAL MARKET ECONOMY

André Gilles Latournald

National Institute for Young Blind People, France

ABSTRACT

This chapter explores the foundational principles of ordo-liberalism and its pivotal role in shaping the economic social market. Tracing its historical roots and philosophical underpinnings, we delve into the critical analysis of liberal thought as professed by its forefathers, Eucken, Röpke, and Rüstow. We dissect ordo-liberal philosophy and its economic theory, underscoring the deep-seated ethics of human dignity central to the economic orbit. Focussing on the operationalization and objectives of ordo-liberalism, we try to highlight the metamorphosis of juridical norms into economic rules. This chapter dissects the intricate relationship between market regulations and the State's role, interrogating modern-day applications and perceptions, particularly in mouridism economic. The concept, which played an instrumental role in Germany's post-war revival, aligns deeply with the tenets of a social market economy, presenting a counter-narrative to laissez-faire capitalism.

Keywords: Social market economy; state; liberalism; ordo-liberalism; human dignity; market regulation

INTRODUCTION

The roots of German economic liberalism are the ordo-liberal thought. More precisely, ordo-liberalism is the form in which economic liberalism was established in Germany from 1933, then imposed after the end of the war in its western part. This article lays out fundamental notions and ideas critical to understanding and

Trajectories of Declining and Destructive Capitalism
Research in Political Economy, Volume 40, 67–79

Published under exclusive licence by Emerald Publishing Limited
ISSN: 0161-7230/doi:10.1108/S0161-723020250000040005

accessing the profound philosophy encircling the ordo-liberal movement in four steps.[1] First, we examine the historical foundations of ordo-liberalism (Part I). Then we are going to explore the philosophical foundations (Part II) of the economic theory in order to highlight the metamorphosis of juridical norms into economic rules: these principles reconcile with the reality of market forces and the State's regulatory functions (a regulated and subsidiary State, a regulated social market) (Part III). Last but not least, we emphasize how ordo-liberalism coheres with present-day economic practices, propelling a dialogue on the German perspective on social market economies and their relation to newer economic paradigms like mouridism in Senegal (Part IV).

HISTORICAL FOUNDATIONS OF ORDO-LIBERALISM

An examination of the inception and expansion of ordo-liberalism within Germany sets the stage for understanding its principles. The foundational texts of Eucken and Röpke, among others, establish the ground for a discussion on the movement's ubiquity and eventual influence on Germany's post-war economic miracle.[2]

The intellectual currents that eventually crystallized into ordo-liberalism began to fiercely swirl against the backdrop of a Germany ravaged by the Great Depression and political extremism. This economic doctrine represents both a robust response to the deficiencies in contemporary economic thought and a moral indictment of the market failures of its time.

A pivotal moment in the gestation of ordo-liberalism was the convergence of ideas among its founding fathers – Walter Eucken, Wilhelm Röpke, and Alexander Rüstow – whose collective examination of the role and function of the State in economic life set the groundwork for the movement. Eucken's critical work, *Die Grundlagen der Nationalökonomie*, published in 1939 (and translated by *The Foundations of Economics*), laid the foundations of the ordo-liberal perspective by rejecting both planned economy and laissez-faire capitalism. He emphasized the importance of a strong legal framework to ensure a functional competitive market. His approach to economics was distinct in that it transcended the mere numeric lens and engaged with institutional structures and societal values, thereby merging theoretical constructs with practical policies.

Meanwhile, Wilhelm Röpke's tome *Die Gesellschaftskrisis der Gegenwart*, published in 1942 (and which can be translated by *The Social Crisis of the Present*) contributed significantly to the ordo-liberal lexicon by exploring the social dimensions of market economies. His analysis focused on the ethical and cultural preconditions for a free society, strongly arguing for the decentralization of economic power and the preservation of socio-economic diversity. Röpke's work underscored that beyond the numerical growth indices, the essence of a healthy economy lay in the maintenance of human dignity and community welfare.

These works and the efforts of others, like Franz Böhm and Hans Grossmann–Doerth, contributed to overcoming the intellectual paralysis imposed by the traditional *Methodenstreit*, or 'method dispute', that had polarized the study of national economics into historical and theoretical factions. The ordo-liberals proposed an integrated approach, refusing to see the economy as merely a battlefield for different schools of thought and instead, as a living architecture needing both foundational principles and the flexibility to adapt to real-world complexity.

Ordo-liberalism gradually gained traction, finding fertile ground amidst the ruins of World War II. The need for economic renewal provided an unprecedented opportunity to translate these ideas into practice. The reconstruction of West Germany's economy, often referred to as the *Wirtschaftswunder* or 'economic miracle', provided a vivid demonstration of ordo-liberal policies' efficacy. When Ludwig Erhard, influenced significantly by Eucken's and Röpke's acolytes, took the reins as the Minister of Economic Affairs, he laid the prerequisite of a 'socially attuned market economy', or *Soziale Marktwirtschaft*.

Erhard and his team made daring moves, such as the abolition of price controls and the creation of a strong currency (*Deutsche Mark*) to stabilize the economy and promote prosperity. The result was a spectacular period of economic growth that saw the Federal Republic of Germany emerge from the destruction of war to a position of economic prominence in Europe. Ordo-liberal ideas had not only inspired political practice but had also been proven by it.

Beyond the German landscape, the intellectual influence of ordo-liberal thinkers began to cross borders, most notably into France. It found resonance with economists like Jacques Rueff, who played a crucial role in the monetary reform of the Pinay–Rueff Plan of 1958, which helped stabilize the French economy and establish the franc as a convertible currency.

Moving into the latter half of the 20th century, ordo-liberal thought also began to pique the interest of scholars outside economics. Michel Foucault, in his 1978–1979 lecture series *The Birth of Biopolitics* at the *Collège de France*, extensively analyzed neoliberalism, including ordo-liberalism, as a critical part of his exploration of government rationality. His work not only provided a philosophical legitimacy to the study of ordo-liberalism but also reinvigorated discourse around the relationship between the state, the individual, and the market.

The unique perspective of ordo-liberals, with its harmonization of economic freedom and social responsibility, did not stay confined to academia. Its principles permeated throughout the policies of the European Union, influencing the approach to competition, State aid, and the economic framework employed for integration.

The ordo-liberal emphasis on competition policy and the regulatory role of the State in kerbing excesses stands as a sobering counter-note in an age increasingly dominated by tech giants whose monopolistic tendencies contravene the fundamental tenants of a competitive marketplace. Today, contemporary adherents and critics alike continue to debate the relevance and application of these principles in addressing the modern economic challenges, such as globalization, digitization, and escalating inequality.

In sum, the historical and bibliographical examination of ordo-liberalism uncovers a rich tapestry of intellectual rigour and moral commitment. Its genesis was not just a reactive formulation to economic and political disruptions of the early

20th century but also served as a pre-emptive doctrine that sought to prevent the recurrence of such chaos by embedding the economic postulates with a social and moral compass. The legacy of Eucken, Röpke, and Rüstow, including their foundational texts, continues to inform economic policy and thought as the intertwined discourse of markets and morality gains renewed prominence in public policy debates.

PHILOSOPHICAL FOUNDATIONS OF ORDO-LIBERALISM

We are going to explore the methodology by which ordo-liberals sought to transcend the '*Methodenstreit*', through the 'isolating abstraction' and focuses on its Kantian underpinning. This analysis leads us to sketch how these intellectual exercises aimed at constructing an economic morphology rooted in human dignity.

The ascension of ordo-liberalism can be traced back to a critical engagement with the philosophical underpinnings of economic thought. The ordo-liberals, seeking to transcend the historical-methodological impasses embodied in the '*Methodenstreit*', turned towards a nuanced approach that rested heavily on Kantian philosophy. This philosophical pivot was directed towards an abstraction that isolates, discerns, and ultimately constructs a rigorous framework that weaves ethical imperatives into the tapestry of economic policy. It is here, in this synthesis of moral philosophy and economic science, that ordo-liberalism distinguishes itself from other economic theories.

At the heart of ordo-liberal methodology is the concept of 'isolating abstraction' [*isolierende Abstraktion*], a tool that would enable economists to distill the complex phenomena of economic interactions into comprehendible and analysable components. This utilization of abstraction was heavily inspired by the epistemological inquiries of Immanuel Kant, particularly his treatise on how synthetic knowledge a priori is conceivable. The ordo-liberals adopted this idea of synthetic a priori judgement as a revelation for economic thought: the synthesis of causality does not merely emerge from empirical observation but is actively constructed through a critical process inherent to human reason.[3]

The Kantian influence is further evident in how ordo-liberals conceived of the economy as a structure shaped by 'ordo', a term resonating with natural law yet wholly embedded in the promulgation of man-made legal frameworks. The 'ordo' is not merely descriptive of what exists or what naturally evolves out of human interaction; rather, it is prescriptive, outlining an order that ought to exist based on fundamental principles derived from a metaphysically grounded understanding of human nature and dignity.

This approach demanded an integration of philosophical anthropology with economics. Human dignity, in the ordo-liberal scheme, was neither to be compromised nor subjugated to the mechanistic and utilitarian demands of market forces. The ordo-liberals posited that human beings, as rational and ethical actors, are the rightful centrepiece upon which the economy is to be modelled. This core belief shaped their understanding of competition, currency, monopoly, and State intervention, ensuring that the economic 'ordo' remained subservient to the higher ethical principles of human dignity and social justice.

The philosophical thrust of ordo-liberalism extended to its critique of both socialism and unfettered capitalism. Against the backdrop of totalitarian regimes and the ensuing economic havoc, ordo-liberals warned of the dangers of extreme economic doctrines that undermine individual freedoms and the plurality of society. In reconstructing a post-war German economy, ordo-liberal thought stressed the establishment of a 'social market economy', one that fosters competition, decentralizes power, and curbs economic excesses, ensuring that no segment of society is left at the mercy of abject poverty or socio-economic marginalization.

Walter Eucken, often hailed as the chief architect of ordo-liberal thought, contended that the economy requires a strong legal and institutional framework to predetermine the rules of the game ('*Wettbewerbsordnung*' or competitive order). This framework serves as the 'constitution' of the economic system and is vital to maintaining an environment where true competition can thrive, circumventing the formation of monopolies and cartels that distort the market and harm consumer interests.

Underpinning the ordo-liberal view is a stark cognizance of the dynamic interplay between economic conditions and societal norms. The concept of '*Wirtschaftsstil*' (economic style) was thus a pivotal construct, championed by Alexander Rüstow, to explain how every age has a distinct economic culture which shapes and is shaped by prevailing moral, political, and social circumstances. Ordo-liberals perceived themselves as cultural economists, pursuing a 'third way' that balanced the needs of individuals with those of the collective, tethered by the thread of moral philosophy.

The philosophic endeavours of ordo-liberalism did not remain an abstract discourse; they carried immense practical implications. By wielding a Kantian lens, ordo-liberals embarked on a reordering of economic science that subordinated it to ethical scrutiny. They adopted a prescriptive stance, driving forward policies that could foster socio-economic environments where human beings, rather than profit-maximization imperatives, dictated the rhythm of market life.

Furthermore, the ordo-liberal notion of 'morphology' held that economic systems must be understood in their plurality and complexity, recognizing a diverse spectrum of market structures that must be constitutionally canalized to prevent distortions. This morphological analysis acknowledges the reality of variance in market forms, from monopolies to perfect competition, and the need for judicious state intervention to prevent the ossification of any form detrimental to societal welfare.

In conclusion, the philosophical appeal of ordo-liberal thought rests in its capacity to deftly integrate the Kantian imperative of weaving abstract, a priori constructs with a pragmatic analysis of economic realities. By insisting on the synthesis of ethics and economics, ordo-liberals crafted a distinctive narrative that underscored the cardinality of human dignity, the necessity for a regulatory State, and a vision of the market as a vehicle for social welfare rather than an end in itself. It is within this confluence of philosophical rigour and economic pragmatism that the legacy of ordo-liberalism finds its resilience and enduring relevance.

ECONOMIC THEORY OF ORDO-LIBERALISM: THE METAMORPHOSIS OF JURIDICAL NORMS INTO ECONOMIC RULES

Focussing on the operationalization and objectives of ordo-liberalism, this section highlights the metamorphosis of juridical norms into economic rules. The section delineates how these principles reconcile with the reality of market forces and the State's regulatory functions (a regulated and subsidiary State, a regulated social market).[4]

The economic theory of ordo-liberalism, developed amid the tumultuous milieu of mid-20th century Europe, is characterized by its commitment to grounding economic life in a strong legal and institutional framework. Founding figures such as Walter Eucken argued that a well-ordered economy cannot merely be left to the vicissitudes of market forces; rather, it must be shaped and stabilized through deliberate and principled governance. In this respect, ordo-liberalism offers a distinctive synthesis of law and economy, where juridical norms are transmuted into economic regulations that steer market processes towards socially beneficial outcomes.

The operationalization of ordo-liberalism necessitated the metamorphosis of abstract legal principles into concrete economic policies. Eucken, with his notion of a '*Wirtschaftsverfassung*', or economic constitution, enfleshed this transformative process. This economic constitution was not a static document but an evolving corpus of laws and regulations aimed at safeguarding the competitive order. This order, identified by the term '*Wettbewerbsordnung*', stipulates that competition is not natural but must be actively maintained and defended through policy measures that prevent monopolies and other market distortions that threaten the liberal economic order.

Ordo-liberals postulated that the State's role is not to manage the economy directly but to establish the conditions under which a market economy can operate optimally. Therein lies the ordo-liberal approach to the State's regulatory functions – what Eucken referred to as the 'policy of order', or '*Ordnungspolitik*'. This approach entails delineating clear, long-term rules of engagement for economic actors, rather than specific interventions or prescriptions that might arise from 'process policies', or '*Ablaufspolitik*'. Essentially, ordo-liberalism privileges the establishment of a robust regulatory regime that provides stability and predictability, which, in turn, stimulates economic activities and innovation within the constraints of the rule of law.

The ordo-liberal economic model identifies a key set of principles that underlie their vision of a competitive social market economy. First is the principle of monetary stability, highlighting the centrality of a sound currency to a functioning market. The ordo-liberals recognized that rampant inflation or deflation can erode the faith in a currency, leading to destabilizing speculative activities. Hence, they advocated for an independent central bank with a mandate to prioritize price stability, viewing this as the economic bedrock upon which other market activities could be safely built.

Next, ordo-liberals placed great emphasis on open markets as a realm of freedom and innovation. They argued that open and competitive markets, both domestically and internationally, foster efficiency and specialization, which drive productivity and economic growth. For such markets to thrive, however, ordo-liberals admonished about the need for active antitrust legislation and the prohibition of cartels and collusion that could distort competition and harm consumers.

The economic constitution advocated by ordo-liberals also entailed the protection of private property rights and the enforcement of contracts. Without clear rules determining ownership and ensuring contract adherence, the market's function as an effective coordinator of economic activity is compromised, engendering uncertainty and subverting the confidence that underpins economic transactions.

In articulating the social dimension of their market economy, ordo-liberals maintained that economic policies must also be attuned to social goals. This involves a commitment to a social safety net that buffers individuals against the hardships of unemployment, illness, and poverty, and to educational policies that promote a skilled workforce capable of adapting to technological and economic shifts. Such social policies are not merely altruistic but are seen as essential investments in human capital, which in turn sustain a vigorous and resilient economy.

Lastly, the ordo-liberal economic theory is grounded in the notion that a competitive order requires subsidiarity – the idea that matters ought to be handled by the smallest, lowest, or least centralized competent authority. Ordo-liberals contend that economic and social problems should be resolved at the level closest to their occurrence, with State intervention as a last resort and only if market solutions prove insufficient.

This mosaic of principles reveals a holistic view of the economic landscape where the State, market, and society are engaged in a dynamic equilibrium. Through the economic constitution, the ordo-liberal framework maintains a vigilant sentinel over market operations, safeguarding against the transgressions of private power while also restraining the State from overreach and preserving the individual's freedom to participate, innovate, and prosper within the economic sphere.

Although critiques of ordo-liberalism posit that its strict maintenance of competition can seem stringent and overly regulatory, this philosophy maintains that regulation should not stifle but rather sustain the vitality of the market. Regulation is seen as a precondition for competitive markets and therefore, as an essential spur to economic dynamism.

The ordoliberals therefore require the State to construct the framework of the economy. Framework surrounding the private domain, the process. This process works all the better if the framework is well laid out. 'It is up to the State [...] to act on all the exogenous data determining the process so that the results of the process are the most desirable on a human level.'[5]

In summary, the economic theory of ordo-liberalism stands out for its unwavering commitment to constructing a competitive order through a legal-intellectual apparatus serving as the bulwark against economic disorder. The model strives for a delicate balance between freedom and regulation, and individual initiative and social responsibility, with the aim of carving out a realm where both the market and human dignity can flourish in tandem. In this rigorous alignment of juridical norms with economic rules, ordo-liberalism remains a distinctive and influential voice in the discourse on the State's regulatory role and the market's driving forces.

ORDO-LIBERALISM IN CONTEMPORARY APPLICATIONS: A DIALOGUE ON SOCIAL MARKET ECONOMIES AND MOURIDISM IN SENEGAL

This section assesses how ordo-liberalism coheres with present-day economic practices, propelling a dialogue on the German perspective on social market economies and their relation to newer economic paradigms like mouridism of Amadou Bamba in Senegal, which focussed on freedom and human dignity.

As the global economy has evolved into an intricate web of interconnected markets and as political-economic ideologies continue to pivot and shift, the application of ordo-liberalism beyond its origins merits focused examination. In contemporary economic practices, the principles of ordo-liberalism interact with multifarious market models and ideologies, among them mouridism, to advance a discourse that remains pertinent amid global financial flux and the quest for sustainable development models.

The essence of ordo-liberalism, with its core emphasis on structuring the economy around the strictures of law, regulation, and human dignity, becomes a crucial touchstone for assessing economic progress and policy effectiveness in modern Germany. The German approach to social market economies has been influential, advocating for an economic system that upholds the competitiveness of the market while ensuring a broad safety net and equitable social policies. Central to this belief is that markets should serve societal needs rather than dominate them, a principle that extends an echo of ordo-liberal thought.

Ordo-liberalism's resonance with contemporary challenges is visible in the European Union (EU)'s economic governance. The focus on competitive markets, fiscal discipline, and economic coordination among member States can be traced back to ordo-liberal tenets. The continuous shaping of EU policies around competition law and the prevention of State aid that distorts the market are embodiments of its enduring influence. Moreover, the ordo-liberal advocacy for monetary stability is mirrored in the European Central Bank's priority of price stability and the vigilant monitoring of inflation across the eurozone.

Given the global reach of economic policies, ordo-liberalism also intersects with economic paradigms particular to the developing world. The African continent, with its diverse economic landscapes and cultural wealth, offers a compelling canvas for the investigation of economic structures that resonate with dignity and freedom, epitomized by the philosophy of mouridism in Senegal.

Mouridism, the socio-religious movement founded by Cheikh Amadou Bamba, shares with ordo-liberalism a central concern for human dignity and a certain reticence towards unrestrained market operation.[6] The model emphasizes moral economies rooted in ethical trading practices, community solidarity, and the dignified labour of its adherents. Although arising independently of ordo-liberal thought, the similarities are striking, as both systems push for an economic life that is respectful of human dignity and not exclusively driven by profit.

The mouride approach to economics, much like the ordo-liberal model, argues for a balance between individual liberty and community well-being – a balance that permits entrepreneurial success while fostering social cohesion. In Senegal, this is exemplified by the Dahiras, mouride-based community groups that act to support members socio-economically, embodying the ordo-liberal idea of a socionomy where the economic process is tied to social structures and cultural norms.

In bridging this connection between German ordo-liberalism and Senegalese mouridism, the common ground lies in the primacy accorded to human agency in the economic process. Both philosophies hold that the economy should not be an autonomous force but one that is capable of being directed in a way that reinforces human dignity, which in turn strengthens the overall social fabric.

The challenge that confronts modern advocates of ordo-liberalism is its application within economies that are increasingly dominated by digitization, global capitalism, and shifting centres of economic power. In responding to contemporary economic crises, ordo-liberal principles can guide policy responses that are geared towards creating conditions for market correction and competition without lapsing into protectionism or authoritarian control. The dynamic between expanding tech giants and traditional industry sectors illustrates the need for vigilant competition policies – another core aspect of ordo-liberalism – to prevent monopolizing tendencies and ensure market access for new entrants.

The quest for policy models that can sustain an equitable economy in the digital age leads back to the wisdom embedded in ordo-liberalism. Its principles uphold a competitive market as the engine of innovation, but one that requires regulation and State supervision to assure that such innovation is not detrimental to the societal good. The inclusion of social policy within the economic order ensures that the advancements brought about by technology translate to broad-based benefits rather than exacerbating inequality.

In sum, ordo-liberalism in contemporary application remains a critical framework through which to view and shape economic policy. Its call for a regulated market economy that respects human dignity and prioritizes social welfare is as pressing today as it was in the post-war period. The ongoing dialogue between ordo-liberalism and new economic paradigms, such as mouridism, enriches the understanding of how diverse cultural and economic landscapes can coalesce around shared values of liberty, dignity, and societal well-being. As the world grapples with complex economic issues and pursues sustainable growth models, the ordo-liberal philosophy continues to provide insight and direction for forging an economic order that serves humanity rather than subjugating it to market dictates.

CONCLUSION

Ordo-liberalism offers a framework where the state and the market are interdependent yet preserve a social aspect of economic activity. It is a testament to the mission of embedding human dignity at the centre of economic systems. This aspect can be revealed, for example, by a meticulous comparison between analysis of ordo-liberal philosophy (and its applied economic theory) and the theory of human dignity of economic mouridism of Amadou Bamba.

Ordo-liberalism, as an economic doctrine, represents an enduring commitment to a vision where the market and state mechanisms are interwoven in such a way that neither eclipses the critical social dimension of economic activity. It stands as a philosophical and practical edifice constructed upon the notion that economic endeavours are not merely pursuits of wealth, but are deeply integral to the preservation and promotion of human dignity and societal well-being.

At the heart of ordo-liberal thought is the conviction that the purpose of economic systems should be to secure a life of dignity for all individuals. This precept is not only a theoretical orientation but advocates for an applied economic theory with tangible policy implications. The resonance of this principle extends far beyond the historic confines of post-war Germany to engage with global economic paradigms that prioritize these very values, as seen in the theory of human dignity central to the Senegalese economic model of mouridism. A rigorous comparison between ordo-liberal philosophy and the economic teachings of Cheikh Amadou Bamba offers us profound insights into how differing contexts can yield similar commitments to human-centric economies.

In analyzing both models, one notes the shared emphasis on establishing an economy that serves the collective good while ensuring individual freedoms. Like the ordo-liberal model, mouridism constructs a socio-economic framework that resists the pitfalls of unchecked capitalism and the disempowering dependencies of State-dictated economics. Both philosophies conceive of an economic space where value is not just extracted but is created through the ethical engagement of individuals within their communities.

It becomes evident that the goal of a well-ordered economic system transcends culture and geography, speaking to a universal aspiration for systems that uphold the dignity of labour, the fairness of opportunity, and the equitable distribution of resources. As we grapple with the ethical implications of economic globalization, the dissipating borders of digital commerce, and the imperative for sustainable development, the ideals of ordo-liberalism offer a compass by which we might navigate these uncharted territories.

In conclusion, ordo-liberalism, with its disciplined approach to integrating economic functionality with social imperatives, continues to be relevant and instructive. Its core concept of human dignity resonates across different economic and cultural landscapes, challenging contemporary economic paradigms to adapt and adhere to this fundamental value. Whether it is in the bustling markets of Germany or the industrious communities following the legacy of Amadou Bamba in Senegal, the ordo-liberal commitment to human dignity in economics stands as an enduring testament to the belief that economies should serve the holistic advancement of humanity. We are therefore in the presence of a market economy which would synthesize, unlike planned or strictly liberal economies, between efficiency, equity and freedom.

NOTES

1. This article is taken from a conference given at the 'Séminaire Marx au 21e siècle' of the University of Paris 1 Panthéon–Sorbonne on June 2022 and intitled *L'ordo–libéralisme: l'économie sociale de marché et la pensée libérale en Allemagne*. Also see: Latournald (2016).

2. To present the ordo-liberal theory, we rely on: Bilger (1964, pp. 170–203), Weisz (1994, pp. 16–27); we also use these articles: (a) Böhm et al. (1989); (b) Barry (1989); and (c) Schmidt (1989); (d) Eucken (1950, 1971, 1989); (e) Hamm (1989); (f) Böhm; these articles come from: *Germany's Social Market Economy*, edited by Peacock and Willgerodt in 1989. Our argument is also based, to a large extent, on the analysis of the book: Eucken (1975). Finally, the objections on the principles of economic policies are made from: (a) Grossekettler (1989, p. 48); (b) Möschel (1989, pp. 142–159); (c) Tumlir (1989, pp. 125–141); (d) Wiseman (1989, pp. 160–177). These articles come from *Perspectives on the History of Economic Thought. Vol. II. Twentieth-Century Economic Thought*, Edited by Walker in 1989. To avoid any dogmatic a priori, we will retain the language of Walter Eucken and the other authors cited. We will pose the problems as he posed them. The references used refer to the English and German editions.

3. Only a construction of thought, a discourse allows reality to be perceived; and therefore, the observation and understanding of reality involves the development of concepts which are articulated in theories. This is Eucken's opinion, which implements an original approach composed of isolating abstraction [*isolierende Abstraktion*] or pointillism [*Pointiernd hervorhebende*] and economic morphology. Eucken starts from a principle: the reconstitution of the whole is not incompatible, quite the contrary, with the analysis and anatomical dissection of this whole. On the other hand, nothing replaces contact with the object, the grasp of its reality. So, the scientist must seek to reach the elements, and, to do this, he must, in some way, release abstractions. It must reach elements by abstraction; and to do this, separate them, isolate them. However, this analysis only separates the elements to find their connections, the internal relationships in the whole. Method by which research appropriates in detail the object studied. But for Eucken, to study scientifically is to analyze economic life. And to analyze economic life is to discover in economic and social formation a process.

4. The importance of the theory of the State in the mind of Walter Eucken, the lessons that the ordoliberals deduced from it, the developments that it received from his intellectual posterity (social market economy), demand that we stop somewhat to examine it. For the Friborg school, the state game is essential. It is focused on the organization of economic life. Two features emerge: (a) the State is regulated; (b) the State is subsidiary. The State is regulated, in the sense that its action must obey the prescriptions and rules decreed by the Economic Constitution. However, it must put in place the basic conditions guiding economic activity. In light of the distinction between two domains, the framework and the

process, the places and modalities of the game of the State become clearer. The process is the field of activity of individuals, it is coordinated by the price mechanism. This is the domain reserved for free individual initiative. The process is limited by the framework, which is organized by the State (it is the domain reserved for the State). In summary, said trivially, the process represents the private domain; and the framework the public domain. The State can intervene in the process when its action on the framework is unsatisfactory. As such, its action on the frame is said to be ordering; and that on the process is called regulatory. Orderly since he must constantly intervene on the frame. Regulatory since it must regulate and, so to speak, condition individual activity. And this, with a view to cleaning up economic life in such a way that it can always 'manifest its beneficial economic and social effects'. In this sense, the State preserves democracy.

5. Bilger (1964, p. 180).

6. See here: Villalón (1995), Grégoire (2001), Bava (2002), Babou (2007), Glover (2007), and Kane (2011).

REFERENCES

Babou, C. A. (2007). *Fighting the Greater Jihad: Amadu Bamba and the founding of the Muridiyya of Senegal, 1853–1913*. Ohio University Press.

Barry, N. P. (1989). Political and economic thought of German neo-liberals. In A. Peacock & H. Willgerodt (Eds.), *Germany's social market economy: Origins and evolution* (pp. 105–124). Macmillan.

Bava, S. (2002). Les Migrants musulmans sénégalais et la banque de l'informel à Marseille: une économie entre ici et là-bas. *Cahiers d'Études Africaines*, *42*(167), 505–531.

Bilger, F. (1964). *La pensée économique libérale dans l'Allemagne contemporaine*. Librairie Générale de Droit et de Jurisprudence.

Böhm, F. (1989). Rule of law in a market economy. In A. Peacock & H. Willgerodt (Eds.), *Germany's social market economy: Origins and evolution* (pp. 46–67). Macmillan.

Böhm, F., Grossman-Doerth, H., & Eucken, W. (1989). The ordo manifesto of 1936. In A. Peacock & H. Willgerodt (Eds.), *Germany's social market economy: Origins and evolution* (pp. 15–26). Macmillan.

Eucken, W. (1950). *The foundations of economics: History and theory in the analysis of economic reality*. Hodge.

Eucken, W. (1971). *Unser Zeitalter der Mißerfolge. Fünf Vorträge zur Wirtschaftspolitik*. J.C.B. Mohr (Paul Siebeck).

Eucken, W. (1975). *Grundsätze der Wirtschaftspolitik*. J.C.B. Mohr (Paul Siebeck).

Eucken, W. (1989). What kind of economic and social system? In A. Peacock & H. Willgerodt (Eds.), *Germany's social market economy: Origins and evolution* (pp. 27–45). Macmillan.

Glover, J. (2007). *Sufism and Jihad in modern Senegal: The Murid order*. University of Rochester Press.

Grégoire, E. (2001). Touba: la Capitale économique des Mourides du Sénégal. *Cahiers d'Outre Mer*, *54*(215), 369–393.

Grossekettler, H. G. (1989). On designing an economic order: The contributions of the Freiburg school. In D. A. Walker (Ed.), *Perspectives on the history of economic thought* (Vol. 2: Twentieth Century Economic Thought, pp. 38–78). Edward Elgar.

Hamm, W. (1989). The welfare state at its limit. In A. Peacock & H. Willgerodt (Eds.), *Germany's social market economy: Origins and evolution* (pp. 171–194). Macmillan.

Kane, O. (2011). *The homeland is the arena: Religion, transnationalism, and the integration of Senegalese immigrants in America*. Oxford University Press.

Latournald, A. G. (2016). *Une Allégorie du marché: la fiction néolibérale*. Éditions Universitaires.

Möschel, W. (1989). Competition policy from an ordo point of view. In D. A. Walker (Ed.), *Perspectives on the history of economic thought* (Vol. 2: Twentieth Century Economic Thought, pp. 142–159). Edward Elgar.

Peacock, A., & Willgerodt, H. (Eds.). (1989). *Germany's social market economy: Origins and evolution*. Trade Policy Research Center, Macmillan.

Schmidt, K. (1989). The public sector in a market economy. In A. Peacock & H. Willgerodt (Eds.), *Germany's social market economy: Origins and evolution* (pp. 195–207). Macmillan.

Tumlir, J. (1989). Franz Böhm and the development of economic-constitutionnal analysis. In D. A. Walker (Ed.), *Perspectives on the history of economic thought* (Vol. 2: Twentieth Century Economic Thought, pp. 125–141). Edward Elgar.

Villalón, L. A. (1995). *Islamic society and state power in Senegal: Disciples and citizens in Fatick.* Cambridge University Press.

Weisz, J. D. (1994). *L'Ordolibéralisme et la complexité modélisée.* Dossier DEA. Université Paris 13.

Wiseman, J. (1989). Social policy and the social market economy. In D. A. Walker (Ed.), *Perspectives on the history of economic thought* (Vol. 2: Twentieth Century Economic Thought, pp. 160–177). Edward Elgar.

ALONG THE BRITISH ROAD TO OLIGARCHY: DEATHS OF DISPAIR AND MOMENTS OF DANGER

Thierry Madjid Labica

University Paris Nanterre, France

ABSTRACT

This chapter begins with a brief discussion of the political alignments and trends that have defined the historical sequence inaugurated in the late 1970s. Next, it provides an overview of the resulting social polarization, between endemic forms of social insecurity and consolidation of oligarchic class power. These initial descriptions aim to offer a general picture of the type of social domination which capitalist politics have been struggling to generate, reproduce, and further entrench: what particular patterns of power relations capitalist politics have been trying to sustain? By what means? And in response to which particular moments of danger has capitalist resistance from above been strategized?

Keywords: United Kingdom; Thatcherism; capitalism; neoliberalism; Labour Party; trade-unions; strikes; Brexit

INTRODUCTION

One could reasonably argue that the distance stretching between our own historical moment in mid-2020s and the turn of the 1980s might require nothing short of intergalactic voyaging; the end of the Cold War, the resumption of war in Europe, protracted wars across the Middle-east and in central Asia, a global financial crisis of unprecedented magnitude, the now near-universally shared awareness of multiple ongoing environmental disasters, years of chaotic United Kingdom (UK) withdrawal from the European Union (EU) and of rising electoral strength of pro-independence (or reunification) parties in Northern Ireland and in Scotland, while in London as many UK Prime Ministers succeeded each

Trajectories of Declining and Destructive Capitalism
Research in Political Economy, Volume 40, 81–97

ISSN: 0161-7230/doi:10.1108/S0161-723020250000040006

other in the space of a mere 6 years (2016–2022) as in the course of the preceding two generations or so (1979–2016), all of these – and the list stretches on – all appear to have largely reconfigured the gravitational field of British society and politics, its vocabulary and expectations.

THE TURN OF THE 1980S: TRANSITION AND ENTRENCHMENT

For all the studious consideration which such departures require, being such singular developments in each case, one initial emphasis needs to be clarified from the outset: far from reflecting the variations and vicissitudes inherent in competing reform agendas within the arena of parliamentary democracy, much in this dynamic of change, rather, has pointed to a renewed and deeper drive towards entrenchment and sanctuarization of class power, capitalist relations becoming purer, or more absolute, and increasingly kleptomaniac in the process.[1] The story of the transition away from the postwar social democratic order has been a largely familiar one for some time. Central to this narrative, one '–ism' – 'Thatcher-ism' – has come to represent an effective and lasting condensation of such related notions as neoliberalism, financialization, and 'denationalization,' and entrepreneurialism, all of them signalling an agenda of now both declared and unrelenting hostility to two historic pillars of the earlier consensus: the welfare provisions of the 'nanny State' now deemed responsible for individual de-moralization (in a remarkable echo of much older themes of degenerative 'effeminacy') and the loss of the spirit of free enterprise, and a conventional pattern of industrial relations with its governing ethos of trade-union recognition, tripartism, collectivism, industrial democracy, and, N.B. State *non*-interventionism ('running along').

The 'turn to neoliberalization [which] entailed breaking every possible barrier to the profitable deployment of the surplus' (as David Harvey [2006, p. xxv] writes) spoke in the idiom of libertarian statophobia. Further, for the radical right, this was a transition *from* socialism narrowly equated with State interventionism and ownership, post-war collectivism, and mass trade-unionism.

New Labour and Tony Blair's long spell in power were the surest expression and vehicles of subsequent ideological entrenchment, receiving as they did the support of right wing media mogul Rupert Murdoch, now turned 'patron saint' of a bespoke pro-market, anti-union, pro-rich 'left.'[2] Five years into New Labour in power, Margaret Thatcher herself was quoted declaring that her 'greatest achievement' was 'Tony Blair and New Labour. We forced our opponents to change their minds.' As for Blair, former PM Thatcher

> ...was immensely kind and generous to me when I was Prime Minister [...]. Politicly, certain reforms she made, for example in Trade Union Law [...], we kept the basic legal framework [...]. We didn't renationalise many of state industries that she privatised [...]. I always thought my job was to build on some of the things she had done rather than reverse them.[3]

Mutual loyalties remained strong in later years: in 2016, it was revealed that Conservative PM 'David [Cameron] and George Osborne [Cameron's Chancellor of the Exchequer] were huge admirers of Tony Blair's style of government and often referred to him as "The Master".'[4]

Such marks of esteem and affection translated into lasting patterns and signals of renewed capitalist class assertiveness with, first, the maintenance of UK anti-union legislation (described by Tony Blair himself, in 1997, as 'the most restrictive on trade unions in the Western world') and the continued erosion of employment norms; secondly, the upward distribution and oligarchic wealth formation through tax cuts, further assisted by a highly effective tax avoidance and evasion industry; thirdly, the all-pervasive process of debt-formation and financialization, particularly notable with regard to the exponential growth of household indebtedness during Tony Blair's second and third mandate to 2008; fourthly, the long-term contraction of public services and the systematization of the drive to privatization notably resulting in the proliferation of Private Finance Initiatives (over 600 of them during New Labour's tenure) and outsourcing, whereby a logic of parasitical rentierism has been embedded in the administration of key services infrastructures and logistics through the formation long-term debt burdens; and fifthly, the new phase of the 'special relationship', itself amounting to stricter alignments of UK-US post-Cold War militaristic agendas, and ever greater British subservience to the American empire as a vehicle for the maintenance of Britain's global role.[5] This, coincidentally, developed at the very moment American power was seized by the more fanatical representatives of US capitalism.[6]

A sixth, slightly more counter-intuitive aspect may deserve to enter this all-too restrictive list, namely, statism. The massive State bailout in response to the 2008 financial crisis may have invited renewed acknowledgements of the role of the State under neoliberalism. Just as surely as class did not disappear with deindustrialization, or imperialism vanish after withdrawing from 'east of Suez', State interventionism and centralization never were in question under neoliberalism. As historian David Edgerton writes,

> Thatcherism was not so much the release of entrepreneurial power, but rather the creation of a brutally activist state, directly and powerfully transforming society, ideas, as well as the economy [. . .], there had never been state intervention this strong until Thatcher. Indeed, there was a strong bureaucratisation and an extension of central controls, of planning and of the State.[7]

Beyond the 2008 bailout, State responses to the Covid-crisis, or London's post-Brexit corrosion of devolved powers to Scotland, Northern Ireland and Wales (notably following the termination of EU structural funds programmes) have been unmistakable signs of these persisting trends.

OUTCOMES: 'AUSTERITY'-DRIVEN INEQUALITY AND ITS MORTAL REWARDS

Far from inviting careful reconsiderations of these and related priorities and their premises and already known implications, the response – 'disaster capitalism' style – to the 2008 financial crisis, Brexit at the hands of the Conservatives, and the pandemic, have been allowed to further exacerbate their disintegrative power. When it comes to exemplifying the contemporary outcomes of restoration and entrenchment one is spoilt for choice while being left with no option but to paint a rather dark picture of wealth polarization possibly lending itself to suspicions of exaggeration. The declining and destructive trajectory of capitalism in the UK – still the fifth largest economy – arguably finds one of its more potent illustrations in the situation of child income poverty rates which in the UK, according to UNICEF in 2023,

> ...were the highest among the world's richest countries, [...] When measuring percentage changes in child income poverty rates in 2012–2014 and 2019–2021, the United Kingdom lay bottom of the table of 39 high – and upper middle–income countries, with a 20% rise in child poverty rates.[8]

Crucially, two-thirds of the children growing in poverty grew in households in which at least one parent was in employment.

Research carried out by the Joseph Rowntree Foundation in 2020 showed that 'more than a million households were destitute in the UK at some point in 2019, with these households containing 2.4 million people, of whom 550,000 were children. On this basis, the number of households experiencing destitution in the UK had increased by 35% since 2017.'[9] According to the same organisation, in October 2023, '2.8 million of the poorest fifth of households (47%) were in arrears with their household bills or behind on scheduled lending repayments, 4.2 million households (72%) were going without essentials, 3.4 million households (58%) reported not having enough money for food.'[10] Meanwhile, in its June 2023 report, the Trussell Trust charity, which manages over 1,200 foodbanks across the UK, revealed that '14 percent of all UK adults (or their household) have experienced food insecurity in the twelve months to mid-2022', which 'translates into an estimated 11.3M people.'[11]

This minimal account would be fatally inadequate without at least a mention of what to many has been the sheer callousness presiding over the administration of ever greater inequality and class oppression in the name of 'austerity'. These policies invariably rested on familiar assumptions as to the work disincentivizing effects of social benefits and allowances. In the present case, however, old beliefs in the sinful overgenerosity inherent in the very notion of social protection reached fanatical heights in 2015 with a Department of Work and Pensions' 'Welfare Reform and Work Bill' aiming to achieve a further 12 billion budget cut by 2019.

A shining example was the new twist given to the Work Capability Assessment or WCA (introduced in 2008 by the labour government) to determine entitlement to employment and support allowance. The implementation of the WCA was entrusted to the care of French procurement agency Atos. Research has shown that

> In total, across England as a whole, the WCA disability reassessment process during this period was associated with an additional 590 suicides [...], 279 000 additional cases of self-reported mental health problems [...] and the prescribing of an additional 725 000 antidepressant items. (Citizen Network, n.d.)

The consequences of the WCA under DWP-Atos management has been one salient manifestation of the wider, deadly consequences of the exacerbation of inequality in the name of 'austerity', first signalled by the stalling of life expectancy improvement from 2012 onwards. According to a co-authored study in public health published in 2022 earlier estimations of austerity-related mortality needed to be revised upwards:

> ...across Great Britain, the authors note, almost 335 000 more deaths occurred in the period 2012–2019 than would have been predicted on the basis of previous trends between 1981 and 2011.[12]

Hence the currency acquired by the concept of 'deaths of despair' (DoD) – deaths related to drug and alcohol misuse, and suicide – in the UK as well as elsewhere (most notably in the US). Research published in *The Lancet* in 2023 noted for instance that 'an estimated 46,200 people lost their lives due to DoD between January 1, 2019, and December 31, 2021.'[13]

Restoration and entrenchment of class power has also been about revived, fully militarized imperialism involving long-term operations as well as displays of capabilities (as with the deployment of Royal Navy warships on Operation Fortis from May to December 2021). Recent engagements in war have inflicted immense destruction and have mainly ended in failure and self-inflicted humiliation (Iraq, Afghanistan), and at the time of writing, possible complicity in genocide (Gaza). By this means, however, the prime beneficiaries and representatives of British capitalist power have exhibited the sort of loyalty to US full spectrum dominance which the maintenance of their roles as global players requires.

Social brutalization at home thus converges with military devastation abroad, both in the service of the reproduction of increasingly fragile patterns of social and political domination. DoD – Deaths of Dispair, and Department of Defence (i.e., the US Pentagon on which Britain's neo-imperial reach so much depends) – offers a convenient reminder of a certain unity of purpose driving both the carnages and mayhem of militarized imperialism, and the more muted liquidations of the poor in the metropole literally in their hundreds of thousands; a certain unity of purpose, then, served by a long ethical tradition of indifference to human life, from Ireland to Gaza via Bengal and Iraq.

Which takes us to the other, ever receding end of the social spectrum. What has restoration of class power meant for the class doing the restoring? While the UK was emerging from two years of a devastating Covid-crisis only to now find itself faced with inflation hitting a 40 year high in 2022 and soaring energy bills, research by the Unite union has revealed 'profit margins for the UK's biggest listed companies were 73% higher in 2021 than pre-pandemic levels in 2019'. According to the same report, and against PM Sunak's argument that inflation was caused by a 1970s style wage-price spiral,

> ...data from the Office for National Statistics (ONS) shows that company profits jumped 11.74% in the six months from October 2021 to March 2022. Over the same period labour costs fell by 0.8%, accounting for inflation. This jump in UK-wide company profits is responsible for 58.7% of inflation in the last half year – as opposed to just 8.3% due to labour costs.[14]

Unsurprisingly, the Unite investigation further showed that between 2020 and 2021 – years of Covid decimation hitting the most deprived groups hardest – 'average pay for the highest paid directors of the UK's biggest listed companies leapt a colossal 29% from £2.01 million in 2020 to £2.59 million in 2021.'[15,16]

Between 1990 and 2022, according to the Equality Trust's December 2022 report based on just over 30 years of the *Sunday Times Rich List*, the wealth of the UK's billionaires had increased by more than 1,112.31%, from £53,874bn in 1990 to £653,120bn in 2022. Over that same period, the number of billionaires went from 15 to 177, with particularly prosperous Covid years since 'between 2020 and 2022 alone, billionaire wealth increased by almost £150bn.'[17]

Research for the Wealth Tax Commission has envisaged alternative fiscal estimations, noting that

> . . .a one–off wealth tax can raise substantial revenue. After accounting for non-compliance and administration costs, a one–off wealth tax payable on all individual wealth above £500,000 and charged at 1% a year for five years would raise £260 billion; at a threshold of £2 million it would raise £80 billion.[18]

None of this, however, prevented the Conservative government from announcing, in November 2022, the new round of 'austerity' cuts, resorting to a mix of tax rises (£24bn) and budget cuts (£30bn) to plug its £54bn 'fiscal black hole'.

CAPITALISM'S 'OVERDOSE OF ITSELF'?

My description so far has tended to concentrate on some of the tensions, contradictions and disorders induced by ideological alignment, consensus and consolidation rather than effective political and ideological challenges. Deindustrialization, deepening and deeply perilous financialization, continued labour market casualization and wage repression, depleted institutions of social cohesion in a country scarred by among the greatest inter-regional disparities in the developed world, have appeared to have been left to generate their own dynamic of crisis formation and transition to more of the worsening same. In other words, beyond those processes of restoration of class power and accumulation by dispossession described years ago by David Harvey (2005), this account may appear to fall within Wolf Streeck's terminally pessimistic vision of 'capitalism passing away as a result of having destroyed its opposition – dying, as it were, from an overdose of itself.'[19] To the question: 'Is capitalism coming to an end?,' Streeck's answer advances the following diagnosis:

> The problem is, while we see it disintegrating before our eyes, we see no successor approaching. [. . .] Capitalist society [. . .] disintegrates from within, from the success of capitalism and the internal contradictions intensified by that success, and from capitalism having overrun its opponents and in the process become more capitalist than is good for it.[20]

Although the power of Streeck's dark and damning insight seems impossible to evade, it cannot be fully abstracted from the time when the contributions collected in *How Will Capitalism End?*, were written and published, between 2011 and 2015. The UK unprecedented £850 billions bank bailout must certainly have created the sense of a whole historical time sequence coming to a crashing end, suddenly relegating to a world of yesteryear the not so distant jubilation of the post-Cold War transition to democracy, free-markets, and whatever millenarian *Schwärmerei* (enthusiasm) had become attached to 'globalization.'[21] And Streeck's overdose metaphor seems bound to gain further resonance in times of empty pledges and persisting official disregard for climate and environmental emergencies. Wolf Streeck's account, however, immersed as it is in the immediate post 2008 years, might invite notions of a capitalism now so absolute and solipsistic as to no longer suscitate any form of significant opposition to itself whatsoever, let alone its own 'gravediggers'.

But if so, if the very idea of anti-capitalist opposition were to have become so irredeemably irrelevant, then what are we to make of the sleepless activism with which militant capitalist politics ceaselessly rebuilds defences, digs new trenches, and deploys new psyops? What for? And against whom? While we need to recognize, as I have done from the outset, that no organized force in Britain has managed to impose significant non-, or anti-capitalist redirections, not even to mention anything like a socialist agenda, it remains that capitalism, capitalist politics and its handlers, in the course of time, have resurrected, and keep resurrecting social forces with which they have to contend on a variety of fronts. There being no such thing as capitalism on autopilot, it is to this embattled resistance from above – in the absence of which the trajectory of violent appropriation described so far would have been hardly able to proceed – that I wish to turn now.

REACTION TO WORKING CLASS MILITANCY AND ASSERTIVENESS: THE LAW, UNEMPLOYMENT, AND STATE VIOLENCE

The turn of the 1980s and the mid-2010s form two distinct phases, or political conjunctures, in the struggle for the maintenance of the patterns of capital accumulation which emerged from the later 1970s onwards. The former was a time of reactionary utopianism driving belligerent disruptions and departures. The latter was one of defensive preservation feeding on increasingly 'illiberal' nostalgia. Both were moments of danger for the capitalist class then deploying strategies of coercion in the face of major counter-hegemonic challenges.

The story of the 1980s remains a familiar one, as noted above, and in which the confrontation between the Conservatives in power and the trade union movement was centre stage, with the year-long miners' strike figuring the most emblematic episode of that whole decade. The following reminders may suffice here.

First, the anti-union offensive was itself key to the wider project to challenge and depart from the already ailing post-war consensus. The historic compromise between big State, big unions and big capital, for instance, had turned Trades Union Congress (TUC) conferences into the main political and industrial policy event of the year, and industrial correspondents into the elite of political journalism.[22] Back in power in 1979 after a long decade of trade union militancy and developing projects and experiences of workers' control, Conservative governments proceeded to ensnare trade union organizations (and their 13,289 million members by 1979) in an intricate web of legislations designed to restrict, prevent and deter much of their traditional practices and activities. The 1980, 1982, 1988, 1989, 1990, Employment Acts, and 1984, 1992, 1993 Trade Union Acts, inaugurated a whole new age of 'neo-liberal' State interventionism, in stark contrast with those not so far distant days when, quite uncontroversially,[23]

> [M]ost workers want nothing more of the law than that it should leave them alone. In this they can be said to display an instinct that is fundamental to British industrial relations. So marked is the characteristic that on some occasions the foreign observer looks in vain for what he would recognise as 'labour law' in Britain.[24]

Ending the priority given to full employment, with unemployment going from 5% in 1979 to 12.4 by 1983 – the 'shock and awe' strategy of deindustrialization could demand no less – was another, more indirect lever against organized labour. The whole strategy, however, carefully elaborated as it was in the 1978 Ridley Plan, eventuated in the unprecedented deployment, militarization and sheer ostentation of State violence, as spectacularly exemplified by the massive, mounted police assaults on the picketing miners at Orgreave near Sheffield in June 1984, or the print workers at Rupert Murdoch's News International in Wapping (London) in 1987.[25] This approach to industrial disputes as well as urban rebellions had its antecedents. There was first an element of revenge vis-a-vis the National Union of Mineworkers (NUM) who had played a critical role in defeating the Conservative politically and then electorally only 10 years earlier. Secondly, and as many observers have noted, the considerable powers given to the police at the time brought to the surface older and deeper links connecting the metropole with its silent legacy of racist and violent colonial militarized policing.[26] Expertise tried and tested during the multiple counter-insurrectional colonial campaigns of Malaya, Kenya, Cyprus, Oman, and elsewhere, never was restricted to the apparently remote world of the empire, especially when the empire next-door, i.e., Northern Ireland, had been a favoured testing ground since 1969 under Operation Banner. A third antecedent was the liquidation of the left in Latin America, from which key strategists behind the first Thatcher government derived much inspiration.[27] Incidentally, M. Thatcher showed herself keen to support the Pinochet regime from the moment she became Prime Minister, and never refrained from publicizing her high esteem and affection for the General, being 'very much aware that is you who brought democracy to Chile.'[28] A fourth coordinate of that conjuncture was the close partnership and community of views between the UK government and a Reagan administration then fully engaged in assisting terrorism and extermination across central America. 'Dear Margaret' went a private presidential message of loving support to the British PM in the midst of the 1984 strike, 'In recent recent weeks I have thought often of you [. . .] I'm confident as ever that you and your government will come out of this well. Warm regards. Ron.'[29]

The language of *war*, therefore, repeatedly mobilized in the Ridley Plan, by a vast array of anti-National Union of Mineworkers (NUM) media, and by the Prime Minister herself, was no mere passing exaggeration in the heat of the confrontation. It reflected deeper ambitions, not only to defeat the more militant sections of the trade union movement but beyond, to nullify the very notion of *class* itself ('a communist concept', M. Thatcher once declared) and class-based understandings of social justice. This was to a significant extent achieved through the developments briefly evoked here: the flood of anti-union legislation, the social disintegrations resulting from the sudden rise of mass unemployment, the new deployments of State coercion.

But there has been at least two more layers to this process. One concerns the media contribution to the disqualification and ultimate occultation of class. Although this cannot be discussed at any length here, it is worth pointing out how, from the miners' strike onwards, ordinary representations of the working class were increasingly associated with antisocial and criminal 'underclass' behaviours now available for a blooming poverty-porn media industry. Four years on from the miners' strike, the exuberantly opprobrious coverage of the Hillsborough football stadium disaster in April 1989, arguably constituted a critical moment in this symbolic reconfiguration. The other ultimately concerns what arguably consisted in the ideological capture by the right of the already ongoing democratic socialist-critique of the bureaucratic paternalism of the post-war State. The 1970s experiences of work-ins and workers' control, the elaborations of the Institute for Worker's Control, and their limited and yet visible incarnation at government level (through the personality of Tony Benn and his Alternative Economic Strategy agenda), all represented yet another plausible moment of socialist possibility, critical of – and beyond a post-war state persistently unable, or more likely, plain unwilling to allow the radical potential inherent in the project of *industrial democracy* to ever materialize.[30] And incidentally, M Thatcher's famous pronouncement, 'there is no alternative' (1980) deserves to be understood in this critical moment of bifurcations away from the post-war framework, and in which a credible socialist *alternative* had already gained currency over the course of the preceding decade. For capitalists and statesmen mourning their lost imperial prestige, confronted as they had been, or still were, with US defeat in Vietnam and revolution in Portugal, armed struggles and radical popular demands and aspirations across much of globe, from Derry (Northern Ireland) to the Dhofar (Oman), the moment was one of danger which the sobered hindsight would be mistaken to deride; the continued demonization of the 1970s 50 years on in Britain still speaks to that political fear.

SEPTEMBER 2015, SOCIALISM RESURGENT

What with consistently ebbing trade-union membership figures, steadily declining strike activity, receding numbers of workers covered by free collective bargaining and rising figures of individual complaints to industrial tribunals, disappearing industrial correspondents across the world of journalism, once-Marxist academics now 'retreating from class', and the world sailing towards a new millennium of globalized free-market relations, it certainly seemed that a lasting ideological victory had been secured.[31]

> For more than ten years, wrote Andrew Murray in 2003 in the context of the 2002–2003 firefighters' dispute, assertive trade unionism was off the public radar. The war against organised labour, which dominated British politics for a generation, until around the late 1980s, appeared to be over, at least to the self–satisfied victors. The media and the Conservative party regarded the unions as more–or–less finished business.[32]

In response to Prime Minister Tony Blair's alliance with the *fine fleur* of European pro-flexibility, Atlanticist pro-war leaders – Spain's Aznar, Italy's Berlusconi – the 'contentious link' between the trade union movement and the labour party entered a new phase of particularly fraught relations. The Fire Brigade Union (FBU) disaffiliated from Labour in 2004 and The Rail, Maritime and Transport workers Union (RMT) was expelled that same year for its support for socialist candidates in Scotland.[33] Such developments, along with the mass protests of the anti-war movement, gave clear signs of a consensus being ruptured, preparing the ground for the next stage.

A second moment of danger emerged in the wake of the 2008 crisis, when large-scale opposition to the coalition austerity agenda eventually achieved political articulation with the large and yet surprize victory of a democratic socialist candidate in the September 2015 labour leadership elections. The years of unabating virulence directed at Jeremy Corbyn's leadership of the main opposition party reflected the deep sense of panic experienced by a mainstream political and media establishment now confronted with a young, enthusiastic, and greatly expanded political force craving for radical, progressive redirections.[34] The more remarkable expressions of fear and exuberant hatred came from the Parliamentary Labour Party itself. Blairite MP John Woodcock, only a few weeks ahead of the leadership election set the general tone when he recommanded that 'we must be passionately intolerant' with the newly assertive left within the party. Conservative leaders wasted no time framing Corbyn as a 'security risk' to the nation, the economy and 'to your family.'[35] And remarkably, a few months ahead of the 2019 general election, D. Trump's Secretary of State Mike Pompeo himself waded in with the pledge to 'push back' and prevent Corbyn from winning.

The most clear-minded assessment, however, came from PM Theresa May after Corbyn's Labour near win (and biggest vote share increase since 1945) in the June 2017 general elections. During the 2017 Conservative party conference, Ms. May declared:

> . . .we have a job to do to ensure that people understand the importance of some of those issues that we thought we had won the argument about over the years -free market economics, the importance of fiscal prudence, wealth creation. [. . .] We thought there was a political consensus. Jeremy Corbyn has changed that. It's our job to go out and make those arguments all over again.[36]

May was not alone in this frank admission. According to the *Wall Street Journal* (WSJ) in 2018, in the US itself, 'Socialism has moved from being a taboo because of its associations with the Cold War to something that has found rising appeal'. Elsewhere along the political spectrum, Pankaj Mishra, commenting on the WSJ's analysis, observed that

> The fortunes of socialism have yet again risen as the structural malaise of capitalism is diagnosed more and more clearly by its victims, and conscious collective intervention rather than the invisible hand appears to be the only viable solution to an unfolding environmental catastrophe.

For Mishra, 'unquestionably, that curious global conjuncture in which neoliberal capitalism and technological leaps forward guaranteed endless progress, and a tiny elite passed off its interests as universal norms, has passed.'[37]

Regardless of PM May's insight, however, the whole point was to avoid confronting reform agendas and arguments within democratic forums. For after all, as a matter of principle, and as moderate Conservative Ian Gilmour once stated:

> Conservatives do not worship democracy. For them, majority rule is a device [. . .] and if it is leading to an end that is undesirable or inconsistent with itself then there is a theoretical case for ending it.[38]

This second moment of danger has unfolded in two stages. The searing electoral defeat of December 2019 was followed by the return of a labour leadership team determined to resume earlier alignments and to that end, silence and expel the left from the party. Political normalization remained relatively short-lived, though, first in the face of a variety of anti-racist and environmental campaigns, then with the resumption from late June 2022 onwards of trade-union militancy of unseen magnitude since the 1980s, across a vast array of sectors. Although each of a different nature, both these conjunctures speak to the same dynamic of social and environmental degradation and extreme polarization whose continuation can now only be secured through increasingly blatant 'illiberal' attacks on fundamental norms and democratic rights.

Although unsatisfactory for its lack of details, the following recapitulation of recent dispositions (2013–2023) aims to give an overall idea of the intensity and breadth of the effort to further shore up and prolong the prevailing modalities of political power in the face of gathering opposition to austerity, inequality, climate inaction, racism, and war.

Anti-union/Anti-strike Laws

- Trade Union Act 2016 (multiple new restrictions; see analysis by the Institute of Employment Right: https://www.ier.org.uk).
- The Conduct of Employment Agencies and Employment Businesses (Amendment) Regulations 2022; allows employers to resort to agency staff to cover for striking employees; was ruled unlawful a year later when the High Court

upheld the challenge by 11 trade union organizations. The government was attempting to resurrect the plan in January 2024.

- Strikes (Minimum Service Levels) Act, December 2023.

> The Strikes (Minimum Service Levels) Act allows employers to serve "work notices" on trade unions calling strike action in "relevant services." Work notices identify which workers are required to work during the period industrial action is due to take place and what work they must undertake. If a union does not take "all reasonable steps" to ensure members identified in the work notice comply, it will lose its legal immunity in respect of the industrial action, meaning an employer can apply for an injunction to stop the strike and can make a claim in damages from the union; non–complying workers will lose automatic protection from dismissal.[39]

- 2014 'Gagging Bill', and 2021 'Spycop Bill', see below.

Further Empowering of Employers

- Cuts to the Health and Safety Executive (HSE) funding, at £239 million in 2009–2010, and £135,6 million in 2017–2018; 1311 HSE inspectors in 2010, and 980 in 2016. In 2016, Professor Steve Tombs remarked that 'between 2003/04 (which marked the rolling out of the "better regulation agenda" in Great Britain) and 2014/15 [. . .], we find, at national level, that HSE inspections fell by 69% and HSE prosecutions fell by 35%; meanwhile, at local level, EHO [Environmental Health Officers] total inspections fell by 69%, EHO preventative inspections fell by 96% and local EHO prosecutions fell by 60%', and 'in some local authorities there are now no dedicated health and safety inspectors.'[40] A 'light touch approach' had been advocated by Gordon Brown addressing the Confederation of British Industry (CBI) in 2005.
- 2013: introduction of Employment Tribunal fees of up to £1,200 for bringing claims. The numbers of claims fell by over 70% within the following months. In 2017, the UK Supreme Court scrapped the tribunal fees, considering the paying system violated the right of access to justice. The Conservative government resumed its attempt to introduce Employment Tribunal and Employment Appeal Tribunal fees in January 2024.

Restrictions on Freedom of Speech

- 2014 Transparency of Lobbying, Non-Party Campaigning and Trade Union Administration Act. More commonly known as the 'Gagging Bill', the Lobbying Act aims to criminalize the engagement of non-party organizations (charities, non-governmental organizations [NGOs], Trade Unions) in public debates and was widely condemned as a direct attack on democracy. In-house corporate lobbyists, who represent the vast majority of lobbying activity, have been exempted from the bulk of the law's provisions.[41]

- (Third reading in 2024) The Economic Activity of Public Bodies (Overseas Matters) Bill. Known as the 'Anti-Boycott Bill' – with explicit reference to Israel and the Boycott, Divestment, Sanctions (BDS) movement – aims to stop councils and other publicly funded bodies (local authorities, universities), from pursuing their own foreign policy agendas.

Police Powers and Restrictions on Civil Liberties[42]

- Police, Crime, Sentencing and Courts Act 2022 (England and Wales): gives the police new powers to impose conditions on a protest, for instance, on the basis of the 'serious unease' it may cause; gives also the Home Secretary the power to determine what 'serious disruption to the life of the community' means.
- Public order Act 2023 (England and Wales): prolongs and gives further draconians powers to restrict the right to peaceful protest, including, for instance, the power to shut down a protest considered too noisy or likely to be a nuisance; the Memorendum accompanying the Bill contains explicit reference to three climate groups and campaign organizations: Extinction Rebellion, Insulate Britain and Just Stop Oil.[43]

Police, Soldiers' Immunity

- Covert Human Intelligence Sources (Criminal Conduct) Act 2021: known as the 'Spycop Bill,' the new law authorizes criminal conduct by the security and intelligence services and the police with no express limits on the types of criminal conduct which may be authorized. Amendments to exclude trade unions from the scope of the law were defeated.[44]
- Overseas Operations (Service Personnel and Veterans) Act 2021: protects UK soldiers from prosecution for crimes, including war crimes and torture, committed abroad after five years; follows the covering-up of evidence by the government and the military, of war crimes, murder, torture, and abuse of detainees during the occupation of Iraq (2004–2009).
- The Northern Ireland Troubles Legacy Act 2023: passed in the face of near universal opposition, the law ends proceedings and grants conditional immunity to perpetrators of violence over the period 1966 to 1998. The United Nations and the Council of Europe have been concerned that the new law may be in violation of the European Convention on Human Rights and other international obligations of the UK.

Immigration Acts

The recent spate of anti-immigrant legislation arguably represents the more relentless version of the overall drive to disempower, exclude, and deny the 'right to have rights'. Immigration Act 2014; Immigration Act 2016; Immigration, Nationality, and Asylum (EU exit) Regulations 2019; Nationality and Borders

Bill 2021; Illegal Immigration 2023; The Safety of Rwanda (Asylum and Immigration) 2024, against the UK Supreme Court's decision that the policy of deporting asylum seekers to Rwanda was unlawful.

CONCLUSION

Capitalism and capitalist politics in Britain have been in the process of openly dispensing with those 'values' and institutions which had once been so central to their historical development and legitimacy, i.e., democratic norms and expectations, the rule of law and human rights. The ongoing celebration of post-democratic and post-national oligarchic wealth and power demands corresponding degrees of nakedness, and something like the recreation at home of a colonial playground for a resurrected master race. This has been further reflected in the notable degree of weariness and disillusionment with forms of institutional power which have displayed open contempt for popular demands and aspirations. Hence, the ever greater disconnects between the decorous outwardness of elected chambers and the inward truth of capital's inexorable prerogatives, a situation familiar to much of the world where incidentally, such connections, however imperfect and inadequate in the polities of imperial metropoles, never were on offer in the first place. An alternate moral universe is being created in the process, itself open to various feudal and fascistic resurrections as well as revived forms of exterminist and genocidal 'common sense'. For popular movements, bipartisan bankruptcy and senilism may also be the chance – at a dear, violent price, no doubt – for new emancipatory beginnings.

NOTES

1. Borrowing from, respectively (and among many others), economist Husson (2008), philosopher Balibar (2020), and Amin (2003).
2. Newsinger (2013, p. 239).
3. See: https://www.bbc.com/news/av/uk-politics-22073434
4. See: https://www.newsweek.com/david-cameron-brexit-ken-clarke-tony-blair-control-freak-management-coalition-505421
5. Cited in McGaughey (2023). https://blogs.lse.ac.uk/politicsandpolicy/the-governments-anti-strike-bill-violates-international-law/
6. See Newsinger (2013, p. 238).
7. Edgerton (2019, pp. 455–456).
8. Reuters (2023).
9. Fitzpatrick et al. (2020).
10. UK poverty 2024: The essential guide to understanding poverty in the UK. *JRF*. https://www.jrf.org.uk
11. Hunger in the UK. The Trussell Trust (2023).
12. Walsh et al. (2022).
13. Camacho et al. (2023).
14. Unite the Union (2022, p. 7). https://www.unitetheunion.org
15. Office of National Statistics (2021). https://www.ons.gov.uk/
16. Unite the Union (2022, pp. 7–9). https://www.unitetheunion.org
17. The Equality Trust (2022). https://equalitytrust.org.uk/

18. Advani et al. (2020, p. 26). https://www.wealthandpolicy.com/wp/WealthTaxFinalReport_ExecSummary.pdf
19. Streeck (2013, p. 65).
20. Streeck (2013, p. 35).
21. National Audit Office (2009).
22. See: Jones (2011).
23. For detailed accounts, see: McIlroy (1995 [1988], pp. 245–253), Jackson (1990, pp. 317–327).
24. Wedderburn (1971, p. 13).
25. Nicholas Ridley was a conservative M.P. In 1977, Ridley authored a 28 page 'confidential' report for the Conservative Party Economic Reconstruction Group. The document was detailing plans for the future fragmentation and privatization of nationalized industries and a public sector that is not 'commercially orientated' and subject to 'a mixture of political pressures and union pressures'. The report's final annex, *Countering the Political Threat*, anticipated and made further recommendations as to how

> ...we might try to provoke a battle in a non-vulnerable industry, where we can win [...] A victory on ground of our choosing would discourage an attack on more vulnerable ground [...]. The most likely area is coal.

26. For instance, see: the 2022 Campaign Against Arms Trade and Netpol Report, *A very British Problem: The Evolution of Britain's Militarised Policing Industrial Complex*, and the references provided there.
27. See: Coulter et al. (1984, pp. 9–10).
28. Associated Press Archive (1999). https://www.youtube.com
29. Quoted in Jones (2024). https://www.nicholasjones.org.uk
30. See: Medhurst (2014).
31. Meiksins Wood (1999).
32. Murray (2003, p. 10).
33. Murray (2003, p. 10).
34. The membership of the Labour Party went from approximately 200,000 in 2015 on the eve of Corbyn's election to over 560,000 two years later.
35. British Broadcasting Corporation (2015). https://www.bbc.com/news/av/uk-politics-34231727
36. HuffPost (2017). https://www.huffingtonpost.co.uk
37. Mishra (2020, p. 178) (and *The Wall Street Journal* quote).
38. Quoted in Medhurst (2014, pp. 78–79).
39. Fire Brigades Union (2023). The new anti-strike legislation was repealed by the labour government which came to power in July 2024. The government also removed the ballot threshold that required 50% turnout contained in the Trade Union Act 2016. However, the bulk of anti-union legislation accumulated over several decades appears set to remain intact. https://www.fbu.org.uk.
40. Tombs (2016).
41. See: Parvin (2021). https://theconversation.com
42. Between 1997 and 2008, the various Blair governments created more than 3,600 new criminal offences.
43. See: Amnesty International (2023). https://www.amnesty.org.uk
44. Moretta and Ewing (2020, November 16). https://www.ier.org.uk

REFERENCES

Advani, A., Chamberlain, E., & Summers, A. (2020, December). *A wealth tax for the UK: Final report.* Wealth Tax Commission, London School of Economics/University of Warwick.

Amin, S. (2003). *Le Virus libéral.* Le Temps des Cerises.

Amnesty International. (2023, April 6). The public order bill explained. https://www.amnesty.org.uk/blogs/campaigns-blog/public-order-bill-explained

Associated Press Archive. (1999, March). *UK: Augusto Pinochet meets lady Thatcher*. AP Arcive.

Balibar, E. (2020). Bifurcation dans la 'fin' du capitalisme. In *Histoire interminable – D'un Siècle l'autre*. La Découverte.

British Broadcasting Corporation. (2015, September 12). Defence secretary Michael Fallon: Corbyn 'A Risk to Security'. *BBC*. https://www.bbc.com/news/av/uk-politics-34231727

Camacho, C., Webb, R. T., Bower, P., & Munford, L. (2023, November). Deaths of despair in England: An observational study of local authority mortality data. *The Lancet, 402*, S31. https://www.thelancet.com/pdfs/journals/lancet/PIIS0140-6736(23)02124-4.pdf

Campaign Against Arms Trade and Netpol. (2022, August). *A very British problem: The evolution of Britain's militarised policing industrial complex*. Report (p. 56). https://caat.org.uk/publications/a-very-british-problem-the-evolution-of-britains-militarised-policing-industrial-complex/

Citizen Network. (n.d.). Government disability policy increases suicide rate. https://citizen-network.org/news/government-disability-policy-increases-suicide-rate

Coulter, J., Miller, S., & Walker, M. (1984). *State of siege. Miners' strike 1984: Politics and policing in the coal fields*. Canary Press.

Edgerton, D. (2019). *The rise and fall of the British nation: A twentieth century history*. Penguin Books.

Fire Brigades Union. (2023/2024, December–January). *What does the strikes (minimum service levels) act mean for members?* FBU.

Fitzpatrick, S., Bramley, G., Blenkinsopp, J., Wood, J., Sosenko, F., Littlewood, M., Johnsen, S., Watts, B., Treanor, M., & McIntyre, J. (2020, December). *Destitution in the UK*. Joseph Rowntree Foundation.

Harvey, D. (2005). *A brief history of neoliberalism*. Oxford University Press.

Harvey, D. (2006). *The limits to capital*. Verso.

HuffPost (2017, October 2). Theresa may concedes Jeremy Corbyn 'changed the consensus' in Britain. https://www.huffingtonpost.co.uk/entry/theresa-may-concedes-jeremy-corbyn-changed-the-political-consensus-in-britain_uk_59d14972e4b05f005d34fbd4

Husson, M. (2008). *Un Pur Capitalisme*. Éditions Page 2.

Jackson, S. P. (1990). *An introduction to industrial relations*. Routledge.

Jones, N. (2011, March). The lost tribe of Fleet Street. Whatever happened to the labour and industrial correspondents? *Nicholas Jones Archives & Blog*. https//:www.nicholasjones.org.uk

Jones, N. (2024, January 3). Thatcher's promise to fight the enemy within: Cabinet secrets reveal her 'War of Attrition' against scargill. *Nicholas Jones Archives & Blog*. https//:www.nicholasjones.org.uk

Joseph Rowntree Foundation. (2024). *UK poverty 2024: The essential guide to understanding poverty in the UK*. Joseph Rowntree Foundation. https://www.jrf.org.uk/uk-poverty-2024-the-essential-guide-to-understanding-poverty-in-the-uk

McGaughey, E. (2023, January 16). *The government's anti-strike bill violates international law*. London School of Economics.

McIlroy, J. (1995 [1988]). *Trade union in Britain today*. Manchester University Press.

Medhurst, J. (2014). *That option no longer exists: Britain 1974-1976*. Zero Books.

Meiksins Wood, E. (1999). *The retreat from class*. Verso.

Mishra, P. (2020). *Bland fanatics: Liberals, race and empire*. Verso.

Moretta, A., & Ewing, K. (2020, November 16). The Bill that gives MI5 Carte Blanche to spy on trade unions. *Institute of Employment rights*. https://www.ier.org.uk/comments/the-bill-that-will-give-mi5-carte-blanche-to-spy-on-trade-unions/

Murray, A. (2003). *A new labour nightmare – The return of the awkward squad*. Verso.

National Audit Office. (2009, December 9). *Maintaining financial stability across the United Kingdom's banking system*. https://www.nao.org.uk/wp-content/uploads/2009/12/091091.pdf

Newsinger, J. (2013). *The blood never dried: A people's history of the British empire*. Bookmarks.

Office of National Statistics. (2021). *Deaths due to COVID-19, registered in England and Wales: 2021*. Census 2021.

Parvin, P. (2021, April). UK lobbying rules explained: Why no one seems to be in legal trouble. *The Conversation*. https://theconversation.com/uk-lobbying-rules-explained-why-no-one-seems-to-be-in-legal-trouble-159741

Reuters. (2023, December 7). *Child poverty levels in the UK worst among world's richest nations, UNICEF report finds.*

Streeck, W. (2013). *How will capitalism end?* Verso.

The Equality Trust. (2022, December 19). *Billionaire wealth 2022.* https://equalitytrust.org.uk/?s=billionaire%20wealth%202022&filter__tag=272

The Trussell Trust. (2023, June). Hunger in the UK. https://www.trussell.org.uk/

Tombs, S. (2016). *The degradation of labour inspection in the UK.* Autumn–Winter, Hesamag #14, Special report 18/34.

Unite the Union. (2022, June). *Unite investigates: Corporate profiteering and the cost of living crisis.* Unite the Union. https://www.unitetheunion.org/media/4757/unite-investigates-corporate-profiteering-and-the-col-crisis.pdf

Walsh, D., Dundas, R., McCartney, G., Gibson, M., & Seaman, R. (2022). Bearing the burden of austerity: How do changing mortality rates in the UK compare between men and women? *Journal of Epidemiology and Community Health, 76*, 1027–1033. https://jech.bmj.com/content/76/12/1027

Wedderburn, K. W. (1971). *The worker and the law* (2nd ed.). Pelican.

MITTERRANDIAN REFORMISM, OR THE GREAT TRANSFORMATION OF DECLINING FRENCH CAPITALISM

Zhiming Long[a] and Rémy Herrera[b]

[a]*Tsinghua University, China*
[b]*CNRS (National Center of Scientific Research), France*

ABSTRACT

We analyze how the French left led by F. Mitterrand and the Socialist Party failed to 'change the lives' of the French. We describe the difficulties encountered by the 'relaunch' policy of 1981 and the change of course carried out, first with the inflection to austerity in 1982–1983, accompanied by devaluations of the franc, then the turn to neoliberalism and financial markets in 1984–1985, with the emphasis placed on business recovery and European integration. This betrayal of the left's programme, leading to social inequalities and 'new poverty', partly explains the return of the right to power as early as 1986.

Keywords: France; capitalism; socialism; reformism; financial markets; currency devaluation; economic rigour; European integration

INTRODUCTION

It was on the evening of May 10, 1981 that the victory in the presidential election of François Mitterrand – then first secretary of the Socialist Party for 10 years – was proclaimed in France. The political programme that brought him to power announced structural changes for the French economy and society. However, in the epicentre of the capitalist world system, the time for the reconquest of globally dominant financial capital had come. As a matter of fact, the neoliberal era opened, under the figure of Reaganism – accompanied by Thatcherism. Question: were the convictions of Mitterrandian reformism going to resist this ideological groundswell coming from across the Atlantic – and from across the

Trajectories of Declining and Destructive Capitalism
Research in Political Economy, Volume 40, 99–105

Published under exclusive licence by Emerald Publishing Limited
ISSN: 0161-7230/doi:10.1108/S0161-723020250000040007

Channel –? One had already been able to measure the brutality of the reaction of the US Federal Reserve (Fed) to the capitalist crisis of the 1970s. For, the United States had imposed on the world its choice of dismantling the Bretton Woods system from 1971 onwards, and, at the end of the year 1979, to sharply raise its interest rates.

STAGE 1: THE POLICY OF 'RELAUNCHING' THE ECONOMY, DESPITE MONETARY TENSIONS

F. Mitterrand's mandate began with the entry into office, at the end of May 1981, of the government led by Pierre Mauroy, who immediately initiated a policy of 'relaunch'. The State nationalized the 39 largest banks, plus 2 financial companies, as well as 2 steel enterprises, 5 industrial groups, and took a majority stake in the capital of several high-tech companies, and also in that of some subsidiaries of foreign transnational firms. These nationalizations were motivated by economic reasons, in the service of a development strategy which was intended to be proactive.

From the start, priority was given to employment, by increasing its volume, encouraging older employees to withdraw from professional activity and postponing the entry of young people into the labour market. Many positions were created in administrations, local authorities or social security organizations; and public enterprises were invited to hire. Added to this are the reduction in the legal weekly working time, the lowering of the retirement age and the emphasis placed on the training of young people. Employment benefited above all from the revival of production driven by public deficits and the boost in consumption of the working classes, thanks to the improvement in purchasing power.

The government provided the State with reinforced action tools, in particular through an industrial policy combining general aid and sectoral support. Public enterprises were seen as 'spearheads' of an industrial development structured in plans by sectors; hence the increase in operating subsidies and capital allocations directed towards them. Efforts intensified in order to fill the deficits and to diversify productive investment support schemes.

The budgetary activation decided by the Mauroy government, in the form of aid measures for industry, job creations and social transfers, increased public spending. This made it necessary to find new revenues: a tax on large fortunes, another on the lavish expenses of businesses, and a third on the 'exceptional' profits of banks and oil companies. These measures, although positive, were not up to par; the State budget deficit widened. Faced with the financing needs of public administrations, compulsory contributions had to increase further and the State debt swelled. Public sector accounts continued to deteriorate.

During the year 1982, the policy of relaunch allowed the maintenance of a stronger growth in France than in other industrialized countries. However, the boost in household consumption saw its effects mitigated by the depressive impact it had on investment and foreign trade. So the worsening of unemployment was only slightly slowed down. The savings rate fell, and investment suffered from this. The weight of interest charges deteriorated the profitability and competitiveness of companies.

Pressures on the foreign exchange market persisted, accentuated by movements of speculative capital. Since February 1981, uncertainty over the outcome of the vote had caused the franc to gradually slide towards its floor rate against the German mark. The attacks against the national currency caused a haemorrhage of foreign currencies due to capital flight and the purchase of foreign securities by French residents. Nevertheless, they were going to be unleashed the day after the electoral victory of the left, consuming a good part of the official foreign exchange reserves.

Faced with these tensions, the position adopted by the Prime Minister, P. Mauroy, was initially to defend the franc, without leaving the concerted floating margins of the European Monetary System (EMS). This choice required firm measures from the monetary authorities to keep it close to its pivot rate. First, it was necessary to raise interest rates, which were already very high. The *Banque de France*'s intervention rate on the monetary market had to be increased – as long as the franc was attacked, and the Fed did not lower its rates. Exchange controls then had to be strengthened. Finally, the availability of official reserves was increased to be able to intervene to defend the national currency (Herrera, 2022).

The room for maneuver for this exchange rate policy was further limited by the fact that the economy was experiencing a current account deficit. Capital outflows and this current account deficit widened the balance to be financed. The State debt and its interest burden were becoming worrying. Ultimately, France had to depreciate its currency. Outlined at the end of 1981, applied in 1982, consolidated in 1983, the turnaround in austerity was definitive in 1984. The adjustment aimed to correct imbalances by now prioritizing the fight against inflation, the restoration of current accounts and the recovery of businesses. The franc was devalued three times, its effective exchange rate losing more than 20% of its value between 1981 and 1984.

STAGE 2: FROM RESISTANCE TO SUBMISSION TO FINANCIAL MARKETS

The measures associated with the first monetary readjustment (October 1981) were restricted, but foreshadowed what was to come: setting aside expenditures, experimenting with new pay rules in the public service, price recommendations, beginning of reforms to social systems, etc. The anti-inflationary device put in place with the second devaluation (June 1982), heavier and more effective, included the general blocking, between June and October, of public remunerations and private wages (except the minimum wage) and prices, as well as an increase in value added tax and spending cuts in social security.

The policy of 'relaunch' was thus halted from mid-1982. Then, the rigour tightened with the third change in parity (March 1983), breaking domestic demand through the deindexation of wages on prices. Expenditures declined, the burden on households as well as compulsory contributions increased. This policy lowered consumption and, indirectly, investment, but helped to reduce external deficits.

These three monetary readjustments made it possible to increase competitiveness gains, as well as exports, and therefore, often, corporate profits. The external balance recovered. Supported by record high interest rates, the so-called 'strong franc' strategy began. The Mauroy government embarked on the path of monetary orthodoxy, seeking a virtuous circle through the sequence of currency appreciation – disinflation – new appreciation, according to a logic of weak growth enhanced by a strong currency, intended to change the internal structures and external exchanges of French capitalism.

Standards for the evolution of the money supply were strictly set, with all liquidity henceforth being monitored. The use of money creation to finance the budget deficit was reduced. The supervision of bank credits remained strong, with banks being required to finance their additional outstanding amounts by increasing their own funds or their required reserves. The device made it possible to use interest rates as the main instrument of monetary control and to pass on their variations to the accounts of banking establishments.

Since 1981, the Fed had reduced its interest rates; the Bank of France could lower its own on the monetary market, as the decline observed in the United States. French interventionism was also to manifest itself through strengthened exchange controls, in order to kerb the capital flight which did not stop. However, the State had to commit to the European Community to relax this framework, as well as to eliminate distortions of competition between deposit collection networks. From 1983, French interest rates remained higher than the inflation rate, and this gap, greater than in Germany, helped to reduce tensions on the foreign exchange market due to an inflationary differential continually unfavourable to France. Disinflation and 'strong franc' tightened liquidity control, replacing traditional intervention instruments with market mechanisms.

In France, the State was the agent of the boom in financial markets, taking the initiative to 'modernize' the system of financing the economy – and the management of public debt. The model followed was that of the process of deregulation and decompartmentalization of the monetary and financial market launched during the 1970s in the United States, from Chicago to New York, and the 'Big Bang' of the City in London.

These 'reforms' pushed France into the neoliberal era and placed the country under the domination of finance. On the Paris stock exchange, the stock market was unified, the bond market perfected, in turn making it possible to better regulate Treasury issues. The monetary market was opened to non-bank operators, connected to the bond market, then supplemented by the creation of new negotiable investment tools favouring the raising of short-term capital; including to meet the financing needs of the State.

The aim was to reduce 'distortions of competition' within the financial sector. If the field of its application still remained restricted, its principle was affirmed. The accelerated expansion of the markets was favoured by a series of innovations encouraged by this new regulatory environment, starting in 1983. The provisions taken in 1982 in favour of savings were reinforced. The modernization of the stock and bond markets was deepening. Derivatives were entering the stock market.

The privileges granted to the owners of capital by the favourable tax regime for shares and bonds were not contested, and the interest rates paid were always maintained at sufficiently high levels, in real terms, to guarantee comfortable returns on capital to savings. The influence of market interest rate mechanisms extended into the financing of the economy. Nevertheless, at the same time as speculators prospered, the idea that financial markets, rather than banking intermediation, would offer optimal financing conditions to economic agents prevailed among the leadership of the French Socialist Party (Herrera, 2020).

STAGE 3: CONSEQUENCES OF THE FAILURE OF MITTERRANDIAN REFORMISM

The 'Socialists' managed to stem inflation and restore profits (Ding et al., 2023) by blocking wages (in 1982), breaking their price indexation (in 1983) and modifying expectations (in 1984). If imported disinflation had seen its effects offset by the appreciation of the US dollar, that correlated with the slowdown in economic growth observed in France was strong, linked to the contraction in domestic demand, caused by the rise in unemployment, and also by remuneration evolving independently of price dynamics.

To the instruments habitually used by monetary and budgetary policies in a capitalist market economy, the Socialists added in the conduct of activity those of dirigisme in order to break the inflationary spiral, with governmental objectives very close to the restrictive recommendations of employers.

Taking action in July 1984, the new government of Laurent Fabius confirmed this shift to the right, by deciding budget cuts and a reduction in allocations to public enterprises. As early as mid-1984, it announced that it wanted to both contain the budget deficit and reduce compulsory contributions. In the end, neither of these two objectives set was achieved in 1985. The budget deficit remained worrying, and the State debt even more so. But what was the most serious? Public administration indebtedness? Or neoliberalism called to the rescue by Socialists inspired by the dogmas of the supply-side economy dominant in the United States?

The 'regulatory' role of financial markets was no longer contested by the government, which complied with the 'need to free companies from administrative supervision', relaxed surveillance after the blockages (in 1984), liberalized prices in the competitive public sector (in 1985), lifted exchange controls (in 1986), and pushed for autonomization of local enterprises, flexibilization of their management and the broadening of competition legislation.

On the economic field, the nationalized groups retained their previous independence. They were even provided with new financial tools intended to increase their capital, and everyone was invited to recover their accounting balance. The nationalized banking sector has never been used to redirect available financing towards sectors deemed strategic for national sovereignty. In practice, its management autonomy remained total. Moreover, constraints applied to the functioning of the labour market, such as administrative authorizations for dismissals, were relaxed. State interventions were always limited by the promotion of market mechanisms.

From 1984 onwards, as disinflation was self-sustaining, the share of wages in value added was reduced. These evolutions, with a slowed progression of tax charges and the stabilization of financial charges, had the effect that the financial situation of companies recovered. However, all this was costly in terms of gross domestic product (GDP) growth – lower in France than that of other G7 countries.

The weakening of economic growth affected employment. Although the evolution of the active population remained dynamic, that of the volumes of jobs occupied continued to contract in agriculture, to decline significantly in industry and to slow down in services. Accentuating these trends, the impact of the reduction in the duration of work proved modest, and, quickly, to save money, work sharing saw the scale of its measures limited. The 'Socialist' government did not succeed in stopping the increase in unemployment, only slightly reversing its upward slope. The purchasing power of French households was contracting.

The French government remained prisoner of neoliberalism and applied a 'model' of low-intensity growth whose most certain consequences were the deterioration of unemployment and the explosion of social inequalities. The constraints squeezing social budgets only made poverty even worse. French-style neoliberalism mobilized the capitalist State in order to develop market mechanisms to the maximum, consolidate financial oligopolies and satisfy one of the key objectives of the neoliberal programme: curbing inflation – in a context of high interest rates. At the cost of frustrating social demands, reducing income and accepting mass unemployment, priorities were given to the recovery of corporate profits.

The choice was not to question the play of market mechanisms, nor the neoliberal straitjacket of European integration. A break with the capitalist system was never seriously imagined, nor especially desired, by the 'Socialist' governments. The ruling Socialist Party nationalized to recapitalize and restructure enterprises in difficulty. It did not use the public sector as a lever for structural change, nor did it alter its management methods. It supported capitalist owners incapable of understanding and undertaking the changes required in the neoliberal era (Herrera, 2010).

CONCLUSION

This 'Mitterrandian left' had no alternative social project, and even less the desire to overcome capitalism. Having sold its soul, 'French-style socialism' logically lost the legislative elections in 1986. The chosen direction had turned its back on the policy for which a majority of French people had brought Mitterrand to power in 1981. By 1985, corporate profitability had recovered, inflation was under control, while dollar rates and oil prices fell. Rigour left an economy with restored internal and external accounts, but weakened by the weight of external debt. The structures of capitalism were in fact affected by this 'Mitterrandian reformism' only to be modernized on behalf of archaic local employers, stuck in the inability to adapt to changes of capitalism.

REFERENCES

Ding, W., Long, Z., & Herrera, R. (2023). Elements for a study of the profit rate: France, 1896-2018. *Research in Political Economy*, *39*, 189–195.

Herrera, R. (2010). *Un Autre Capitalisme n'est pas possible*. Éditions Syllepse.

Herrera, R. (2020). *En Lutte: les résistances populaires en France de 1981 à nos jours*. Éditions Critiques.

Herrera, R. (2022). *Money – From the power of finance to the sovereignty of the peoples*. Palgrave Macmillan.

THE SPANISH FINANCIAL–REAL ESTATE CAPITALISM AND ITS SOCIO-POLITICAL IMPLICATIONS

Juan Pablo Mateo

Complutense University of Madrid, Spain

ABSTRACT

This chapter offers a materialist critique of capitalism in Spain, integrating the patterns of capital accumulation, the divisions it engenders, and its influence on movements advocating social change. For this purpose, it scrutinizes the financial-real estate model – consistently bolstered by State intervention – from the labour theory of value. The analysis reveals how this model distorts macroeconomic indicators and exacerbates social and geographic disparities, as well as fostering an urban design that profoundly impacts the living conditions of workers. Furthermore, these dynamics have facilitated the emergence of a postmodern left based on identity politics and self-determination, which has exposed deep rifts within the labour movement. More broadly, it reflects an assimilation of the values intrinsic to capitalism, signalling a departure from traditional class-based politics.

Keywords: Spain; capitalism; finance; real estate; housing boom; urbanism; historical materialism; labour theory of value

INTRODUCTION

One of the hallmarks of the Marxist approach is its holistic perspective of the economic system, grounded in historical materialism: the way specific structures within the mode of production influence the working class's living conditions, subjective experiences, configuration, and shape the modalities of social conflict. Thus, this chapter delves into the structure and dynamics of the financial–real estate sector within Spanish capitalism, exploring its enduring effects and the

Trajectories of Declining and Destructive Capitalism
Research in Political Economy, Volume 40, 107–121

ISSN: 0161-7230/doi:10.1108/S0161-72302025000040008

implications for both the physical landscape and the articulation of a subject for radical change. However, this claim requires some preliminary clarifications.

The term 'financial–real estate regime' encapsulates a tripartite process: (i) financial activities, which in Spain are closely tied to banking, and also encompass financialization – financial asset as the ideal form of capital – and the associated asset price bubble; (ii) the construction industry, not only in relation to housing but also infrastructure and tourism; and (iii) the public sector's role in fostering this rent-seeking model. While this focus does not dismiss the multifaceted nature of Spanish capitalism, as if it were solely defined by finance and construction, it does posit that these sectors play a pivotal role with wide-ranging and diverse consequences. In fact, the literature makes reference to an 'asset–price Keynesianism' (López & Rodríguez, 2011), the 'real estate–tourism–financial complex' (Ramiro & González, 2019), an 'urbanistic tsunami' (Gaja, 2003, 2008), or the 'financialization of real estate activities' (Méndez, 2021).

Another objective of this article is methodological: it aims to reassert the value of holistic analysis, grounded in historical materialism, although it cannot be systematic and in-depth due to space constraints. This is particularly pertinent in response to the rise of postmodern, identity-focused, and fragmentary movements within the left, and their academic counterparts, which have significant implications for political praxis.

This chapter commences with a theoretical exploration of the financial–real estate dimension, supplemented by an examination of its specific manifestations in Spain. It then scrutinizes the distortions in the process of capital accumulation and the interplay with State intervention. Following this, the discussion turns to the principal outcomes of this dynamic, including ecological impacts, characteristic urban development, and the resultant territorial divisions. This chapter concludes with a critical assessment of the Spanish left's turn.

THE FINANCIAL–REAL ESTATE MODEL: THEORY AND GENESIS

The asset price bubble in the construction sector, particularly within real estate, holds a pivotal position from the standpoint of the labour theory of value and the materialist approach to political economy. This phenomenon wields a profound influence across various economic sectors and social strata, primarily because it pertains to a durable consumer good, housing.[1]

The housing boom, in essence, distorts the conventional dynamics of the economy, inverting the relationship between appearance and essence, cause and effect, as well as content and form (Mateo, 2019). This inversion is not merely theoretical, as it sheds light as well on the underlying mechanisms that lead the working class to internalize and uphold the values promulgated by capitalist ideology. This internalization is critical to understanding the alignment of working-class aspirations with capitalist objectives, a phenomenon that has far-reaching implications for both economic behaviour and social policy.

The existence of speculative bubbles and the over-dimensioning of financial and construction activities are not anomalies or departures from a hypothetical ideal form of capitalism. Rather, they are manifestations that are integral to its functioning, both objectively and subjectively. Real estate price bubbles represent a divergence of price trajectories from the underlying economic fundamentals, abstract labour times. This divergence gives rise to a secondary capital circuit where causality seems inverted: investment drives up asset prices, which in turn enhances profitability and enables the appropriation of income by asset owners. The transaction's focus shifts to acquiring the right to future gains, essentially a claim on a portion of the surplus value produced (Harvey, 2006 [1982]).

However, these bubbles stem from the underlying difficulties in capital's ability to valorize itself, creating the objective conditions that fuel their growth. Thus, the inherent contradictions of capital are temporally and spatially deferred, the 'spatio-temporal fix'. This is a social phenomenon, deeply entwined with the social relations of production, and stands in stark contrast to orthodox economic models that fail to move beyond the simplistic interplay of supply and demand, demographics, and individual decisions of owners and tenants.

The accumulation patterns in Spain have been significantly influenced by recurring speculative bubbles in residential assets, beginning with the industrialization period of the 1960s and early 1970s, through the economic upswing following the industrial restructuring of the 1980s (1985–1992), and notably during the bubble period (1999–2007) that led to the Great Recession of 2008–2013. These patterns have persisted in various forms to the present day. Over 70% of Spain's wealth accumulation since the 1950s is concentrated in the real estate and construction sectors (Ramiro & González, 2019), while 70% of household assets are residential properties, 11% points higher than the Eurozone average (Alves et al., 2023). During the housing boom that preceded the crisis of 2008–2013, nearly two-thirds of the apartments constructed were not aimed at satisfying the need for primary residences but were instead built for luxury consumption or speculative investment, often remaining unoccupied to capitalize on potential value appreciation (Carpintero & Bellver, 2013).

On one hand, socio-political dynamics intertwined with social unrest have played a role. While rental housing was prevalent during the Second Republic (1931–1936), the Franco dictatorship (1939–1975) shifted the focus towards home ownership starting in the 1940s.[2] Consequently, Spain has maintained one of the highest rates of homeownership in recent decades, laying the groundwork for the prevailing economic model. This political landscape is further enriched by Spain's unique orography and climate, which position it as a premier global tourist destination. These factors combined with the country's delayed industrialization and the resulting rural-to-urban migration in the second half of the 20th century, later augmented by international immigration from the 1990s.

On the other hand, structural economic factors are at play. Firstly, there are underlying problems within the accumulation process, such as diminished profitability. The profit rate in the mid-1990s was nearly a third less than the average between 1965 and 1974. Following a decline during the growth phase of 1995–2008, by the latter year, it had fallen by −49%, and by the end of the recession, it was 60% lower.

Excluding unproductive sectors, the profit rate drop from 1995 to 2013 would stand at −60%, with only a modest recovery thereafter.[3] This diminished capacity to generate surplus has led capital to seek alternative investment opportunities, with construction emerging as a viable sector to channel idle resources.

Secondly, entering a monetary union from a subordinate or peripheral position, as was the case with Spain adopting the euro, results in a relatively overvalued currency. This situation tends to exacerbate economic, territorial, and social divisions. Consequently, non-tradable sectors are favoured, lacking the balancing mechanisms typically provided by a sovereign nation-State, which will be further discussed.

A DISTORTED PROCESS OF CAPITAL ACCUMULATION

The economic landscape of Spain is distinguished by the prominent role of the sectors within the Finance, Insurance, Real Estate (FIRE), construction, and tourism industries. Analyzing the Gross Value Added (GVA) reveals that the combined contribution of FIRE and construction escalated from 19% in the latter half of the 1990s to a zenith of 26% during the years 2007–2008, before stabilizing around 21–23%. In the lead-up to the Great Recession, the construction sector saw its share of total GVA climb from 9% to 12%. Despite not regaining these heights post-recession, the Real Estate segment has shown a marked relative increase, doubling from 6% in the early 2000s to a consistent 11–12% since 2011 (INE, 2023a).

The housing boom has been a significant driver of financial sector growth, as the surge in prices has led to increased credit and higher levels of debt among non-financial corporations and households. This trend is further exacerbated by the substantial leverage of commercial banks, in order to offset their diminished relative profitability (Sánchez, 2021). This reliance on debt has subsequently been used to justify the implementation of wage adjustment measures.

The flip side is a pronounced deindustrialization process in Spain, more severe than that of its European neighbours (Casaú, 2023; Fariñas et al., 2015). This trend has its roots in the economic crisis of the 1970s and the subsequent restructuring before Spain's accession to the European Economic Community (EEC) in 1986.[4] Additionally, the housing boom has led to inflated land and asset prices, further undermining the industrial sector.[5] Moreover, a significant portion of industrial activity in Spain is conducted by foreign-owned subsidiaries, and the Spanish economy exhibits less than half the elasticity to changes in industrial sector demand compared to these countries. As a result, the industry's ability to stimulate economic growth is considerably constrained (Cabrero & Tiana, 2012).

Moreover, the Spanish countryside has been significantly impacted by the European Union (EU)'s regulatory framework. The transition from traditional, extensive livestock farming to more intensive methods, as mandated by the EEC/EU, has played a critical role in the depopulation of rural areas, what is called 'Empty Spain' (Melchor & Armesilla, 2022).

These issues have contributed to a distinctive business dualism. A mere 0.36% of business units employ more than 100 people (INE, 2023c), with a high degree of shareholding polarization, a significant decline in public sector participation due to the privatization wave that began in the late 1980s, coupled with an increasing presence of foreign capital (Santos, 2022). The prevalence of small businesses is stark: 56% of units operate without any salaried employees, and approximately a quarter employ just one or two people. This results in 83% of companies having fewer than three workers, and 92% having fewer than six (INE, 2023c). Such fragmentation within the business sector leads to a dispersed working class, which poses challenges for collective bargaining and union organization.

The persistence of this economic structure has given rise to an accumulation model that defies the norms of a 'healthy' or 'normal' economy. Instead of dynamic growth in sectors with high technological sophistication, the real estate asset bubble generates a kind of growth in which, through intersectoral linkages, the most vigorous activities are those with minimal mechanization, lower productivity, and in the cases of tourism and construction, a high degree of labour instability marked by temporary and seasonal employment.[6]

Despite substantial investment, with the net stock of non-residential productive capital at constant prices (K^*) growing by an average of 4.6% annually from 1995 to 2007, the capital-to-labour ratio ($K^*/L_{w,}$ wage-earner) saw a negligible annual increase of just 0.2% during the same period, or 0.6% from 1999 onwards. Paradoxically, the capital–output ratio (K/Y) experienced a slightly more pronounced increase. However, when economic growth picked up again from 2014, this ratio declined by an average of 1.7% annually until 2017.

The key factor is the high rate of job creation during periods of economic expansion. From 1995 to 2007, employment surged by two-thirds of the economically active population, rising from 12.3 million to over 20 million between 2006 Q4 and the end of 2008, similar to wage employment in the productive sectors, when measured in full-time equivalents, resulting in an annual job creation rate of 3.4% over 12 years. Remarkably, during the period from 2000 to 2006, Spain accounted for half of the employment growth in Europe (Steinko, 2010), which bolstered governmental and societal support for the prevailing economic model.

However, this rapid job creation had implications for labour productivity, which exhibited a countercyclical pattern. Prior to the Great Recession, it grew at a meagre annual rate of 0.16% – excluding unproductive activities – which was less than the total GDP per worker at 0.38% per year. The picture becomes even bleaker when the productivity index excludes mixed income earners, with productivity actually declining by 0.36% annually. Fortunately, these indicators showed some improvement during the post-crisis recovery, with average annual increases ranging from 0.3% to 0.7%.

Dissecting the data by sector reveals that construction, trade, professional and other services had K^*/L_w ratios between 45% and 70% of the economy's average, with the exception of construction, which anyway decreased from 81% to 74% between 1999 and 2007. Despite this, these sectors attracted nearly three-quarters of gross investment and were responsible for creating three-quarters of the total employment during that period, even though they only contributed 58% of the total GVA. Labour productivity indices in these sectors, except for 'Other services', declined in absolute terms, in stark contrast to the 2% increases seen in industrial sectors, mining, or information and communications, with the financial sector exhibiting the best (apparent) productivity performance.

The Great Recession, however, led to a significant spike in unemployment, with one in every five employees losing their job, resulting in an unemployment rate that remained above 20% until 2016. Consequently, the capital–labour ratio grew by 6% annually during the prolonged recession from 2008 to 2013, which in turn led to increases in labour productivity indices ranging from 1.7% (output per wage-earning worker in the productive sphere) to 3% annually (excluding mixed income earners).

Spain's economic growth has not been driven by labour-saving technological advancements that typically enhance productivity and reduce production costs, which has undermined the foundation for real wage increases. As a result, average real wages saw little or no growth from 1995 to 2007.[7] But during the crisis years from 2007 to 2015, real wages did increase by 7%, a rise partly attributed to the composition effect, including the elimination of lower-paying jobs (Mateo, 2019). Additionally, the cost of housing has eroded purchasing power more than statistics reveal, while some workers receive supplementary income from rental properties or inherited homes, further complicating the economic picture.

A STATE SUBORDINATED TO THE SPECULATIVE MODEL

The sustainability of this accumulation model has been heavily reliant on State intervention. First, the banking sector's dominance in Spanish capitalism can be traced back to the protectionist policies of Franco's regime (1939–1975), which shielded national banks from foreign competition. In more recent times, the European Central Bank has served as a critical lifeline. Domestically, the Spanish State has played a pivotal role in bolstering banks with both explicit and implicit support, and it established the so-called 'bad bank' (SAREB, i.e., *Sociedad de gestión de activos procedentes de la reestructuración bancaria*, or Asset Management Company from Bank Restructuring) to consolidate devalued residential assets.[8]

Secondly, major construction firms have flourished due to the lucrative opportunities afforded by the State through public works concessions. This trend, which began during the dictatorship and continues to this day, has been significantly fuelled by the surge in tourism, and it has shaped the infrastructure that supports Spain's thriving tourist industry.[9]

Furthermore, legislative measures have been instrumental in facilitating the establishment and operation of the financial–real estate regime. As Vives and Rullán (2014) aptly point out, financial liberalization reforms have been pivotal in steering the Spanish urban development along market-oriented lines. The intersection of finance and urban planning is evident in mortgage legislation, which has allowed financial activity to be integrated into global capital circuits through mortgage securitization. Thus, the neoliberal regulation of the mortgage system began with the 1981 law and was further entrenched by the advent of securitization in 1992. This legislative shift preceded the first studies and reports advocating for urban liberalization, and the enactment of the Valencian Urban Activity Regulation Law (LRAU) in 1994, which marked a significant turning point (Gaja, 2003; Vives & Rullán, 2014).[10] The urban legislative framework has since adhered to a neoliberal rationale, under the premise – ratified by the Competition Defense Court in 2013 – that all land is urbanizable unless expressly protected for public interest reasons. This stance implicitly attributes the escalation of housing prices to land availability.

Following the prolonged recession that began in late 2008, Spain saw an economic resurgence from 2013 to 2014 until the onset of the COVID-19 pandemic in early 2020. The recovery period of 2013–2019 witnessed a revival of the real estate market, despite a substantial stock of vacant housing (Méndez, 2021). Banks, burdened with 'toxic assets' from falling housing prices and non-performing loans (NPLs), found themselves in a challenging position, unable to meet the Basel III Accord requirements. In this adverse climate, global investment funds emerged as the new drivers of the real estate sector, having accumulated extensive residential asset portfolios internationally (Gil & Martínez, 2023).

The regulation of Real Estate Investment Trusts (REITs), known in Spain as Socimis, dates back to 2009. However, they did not become prominent until 2013, when, under the influence of the European Property Real Estate Association, a legislative environment conducive to attracting international capital was established (Gabarre, 2019). Changes included amendments to the Urban Leases Law, reducing the mandatory duration of rental contracts to facilitate property sales upon revaluation, and the deregulation of rent increases, regardless of the evolution of the consumer price index. Taxation for Socimis was also significantly reduced, granting them various privileges (Méndez, 2021; Vives & Rullán, 2014). As Gil and Martínez (2023) note, these reforms enabled rapid returns by enhancing the liquidity of the rental sector and linking it more closely to global capital markets.

If that were not enough, some municipalities and regions with neoliberal leanings privatized portions of the public housing stock.[11] Consequently, the price of housing grew by 32% in 2014–2019, which in Madrid and Catalonia reached 56% and 45%, respectively (Bank of Spain, 2020), and rental prices by 45.3% in 2015–2019 (Méndez, 2021), particularly in large cities and tourist destinations with beach.[12] In essence, there was a swift and substantial transfer of wealth from bailed-out banks and State-owned housing to global financial investors (Gil & Martínez, 2023), accompanied by the eviction of families, exorbitant rent hikes, and systematic legal violations.[13]

This economic shift has led to an increase in the proportion of households living in rental accommodation, from 13.6% just before the Great Recession in 2007, to 15.4% in 2013, and 17.5% in 2018, surpassing 20% in regions like Madrid, Catalonia, and the Balearic Islands in the Mediterranean Sea (OVS, 2019). This trend towards renting is a direct result of extreme labor precariousness and the inability of many to afford home ownership. Renting is particularly prevalent among lower-income groups, the youth – with the proportion of renters under 35 years old jumping from 24% to 43% between 2011 and 2017, whose wages fell after the Great Recession – and non-EU immigrants (Bank of Spain, 2020; Méndez, 2021). The rental market is predominantly at market rates, with a decline in subsidized rentals, which has contributed to the rise in evictions for non-payment of rent.

SOCIO-POLITICAL IMPLICATIONS

Environment and Urban Planning

The territorial implications of the prevailing economic accumulation regime are profound, particularly in terms of their environmental impact. The construction sector, encompassing both housing and infrastructure, exerts considerable pressure on the natural environment through its substantial demand for materials, its reliance on predominantly non-renewable energy sources, and the emissions it generates.[14]

These activities contribute to an ecological footprint that far exceeds the sustainable capacity of the land, with the average footprint per inhabitant in Spain surpassing 5 hectares – more than triple the ecologically productive surface available per capita (1.4 hectare per capita). This imbalance requires imports of resources to maintain current consumption levels. Since the mid-1980s the amount of energy required to produce a unit of value added has been on the rise despite its tertiary productive transformation, bucking the trend of other European economies. This divergence is partly due to the expansive nature of Spain's productive geography, which demands more land, covers greater distances, and involves a larger number of work centres.

The physical manifestation of this economic model is evident in the extensive urban development patterns that have reshaped the living conditions of the working class. The urban expression of this regime is the Urban Action Programme (PAU), as described by Dioni (2021), which has led to the creation of neighborhoods characterized by large blocks of flats within gated communities or rows of semi-detached houses. The large avenues are designed for vehicles, but pedestrian movement is limited, reducing social interactions on the street.[15] This form of urbanism contrasts sharply with the more integrated and community-oriented design of historic neighborhoods, with plenty of small businesses. As a result, daily life is often centred around distant shopping centres, accessible primarily by car, which are typically situated adjacent to major highways, exacerbating traffic congestion and lengthening commutes.

Urban planning, as Dioni (2021) emphasizes, is far from a neutral technical issue; it profoundly influences how people live, interact, or with whom their children will study and form communities. In other words, it contributes to creating ideology. Thus, the prevailing model of urban development promotes individualism and competition over communal living, as people retreat into the insular comfort of gated communities, driven by a desire to avoid perceived external threats. This trend promotes individual solutions, and marks a departure from the neighbourhood movement, which was a significant form of political activism during the late Francoist era in Spain.[16]

In summary, the financial–real estate model not only has an ecologically predatory nature but also contributes to the territorial polarization of economic activity and population distribution. This reality highlights the subversive potential of environmental defence movements and the critical importance of addressing territorial disparities as part of any comprehensive post-capitalist transformation initiative.

Territorial Fractures

In Spain, Madrid, along with the traditionally industrial regions of Catalonia and the Basque Country–Navarre – which benefit from a favourable economic agreement, a privilege to the detriment of poorer regions – stand out economically, as do the Balearic Islands in the Mediterranean. At the dawn of this century, these areas boasted a GDP per capita that was 30–50% higher than the national average. Since 2020, despite the economic downturn affecting the Islands, they have reached levels of 40–65% above the average. This disparity indicates that provinces in less developed areas have a GDP per capita that is approximately 55% of that of the Community of Madrid (INE, 2023b).

The construction bubble has therefore exacerbated inequality, leading to an increasing territorial dualism. This model predominantly benefits urban centres, especially those in the most developed regions and those with tourist attractions. Within the urban hierarchy, cities like Madrid and Barcelona are vying for positions in the *Global League of Cities* – which alludes to a de facto separatism of an elitist nature, as thoroughly claimed by Slobodian (2023) – engaging in a transnational dynamic that encompasses the flow of finance, investment, international talent, and luxury tourism.

In stark contrast lies what has been previously termed the 'Empty Spain', regions surrounding the Community of Madrid that have suffered from the adverse effects of globalization. These areas have experienced pronounced and premature deindustrialization (see Barandiaran et al., 2019; Myro, 2021), leading to economic decline, job scarcity, and a consequent lack of social services, which in turn has resulted in depopulation. Paradoxically, these regions tend to be ideologically conservative, often voting for right-wing parties that traditionally advocate for less State intervention. Yet, these communities frequently demand State support, revealing a contradiction with the liberal principles of such parties.

Yet another territorial issue, the national question, represents the more significant fissure within the Spanish working class. Historically, there have been strong separatist movements in the Basque Country and Catalonia, with their influence extending to Navarre and the French Iparralde (*Euskal Herria*), as well as to the Mediterranean Levant and the Balearic Islands (*Catalan countries*). To a lesser extent, similar sentiments are present in Galicia, while regionalist expressions in the South (Andalusia) and the Canary Islands – closer to West Africa – tend to have more cultural than political overtones, with 'folkloric' elements also found in areas like León and Asturias.

However, the underlying political economy of these movements varies greatly. While ethnic or cultural arguments, often rooted in a mythologized historical narrative, are commonly presented – far away from any materialist approach, as extensively analysed by Polo (2021) – the economic rationale cannot be overlooked. For some Basque and Catalan separatists, the rest of Spain is seen as an economic burden, a region perceived to be less advanced and thus hindering their own economic progress. Consequently, a segment of the working class in these wealthier regions paradoxically supports the notion of 'national liberation', driven by a reluctance to engage in the income redistribution across the country. This stance contributes to the territorial fragmentation of the working class, rather than uniting it in pursuit of common class interests.

FINAL REMARKS FROM THE LEFT: THE SUBJECTIVE-IDENTITY LOGIC UNDER THE FINANCIAL–REAL ESTATE REGIME

More than a decade after the eruption of the 15M movement (anti-austerity movement in Spain) in 2011 – showcasing the political naivety and immaturity of a great part of the participants – the Spanish left finds itself on a road to nowhere. The involvement in government (the trees) should not obscure how the left undermines the possibilities to build a sustainable alternative in the medium to long term (the forest). The connection with the financial–real estate model may not be direct, nor is Spain's situation entirely unique, but it does warrant thoughtful consideration.

Historically, the left has concentrated on objective elements, those pertaining to the fundamental structures of society. However, there has been a noticeable shift towards emphasizing subjective elements, which prioritize individual identities (the differences) over social class (what unites us). This shift is evident in the rise of the so-called 'aspirational middle class' (Hernández, 2023) and what Bernabé (2018) describes as 'The diversity trap'. The postmodern inclination towards identity politics, subjectivism, individualism, and micro-narratives has gradually supplanted the materialist perspective with universal aspirations, once centred on the working class. Owing to the particular nature of the national question in Spain, this is reflected in a pronounced emphasis on the distinct national or regional sentiments (identities). Hence, the proliferation of regionalist or separatist leftist movements, which draw inspiration from the German romantic idealism of the 19th century, as Polo (2021) correctly elucidates.

The economic structure's dualism manifests in a reduced concentration of workers within individual corporations, a trend linked to deindustrialization and the prevalence of small businesses, a deterioration of labour relations and an increase in the number of false self-employed workers (Arrizabalo et al., 2023). Besides, regions where this accumulation regime is deeply entrenched tend to exhibit more conservative tendencies (Steinko, 2010), and the above-mentioned PAUs epitomize the typical habitat for the emergent aspirational middle class.[17]

Yet, the financial–real estate model's perniciousness extends beyond its territorial impact; it exacerbates the classic dichotomy between essence and appearance, particularly in the context of labour and income. Steinko (2010, p. 23) incisively notes that

> ...when wealth appears to emanate from reclassified land, effortlessly and without productivity, and when the stock market seemingly dispenses dividends to small shareholders, it becomes facile to argue that the struggle for a just society, founded on labour rather than rental income, is outdated.

Indeed, the asset bubble undermines the tangible nature of labour activity, the arena where socialization occurs, subjective bonds are formed, and transformative movements take shape.

The appreciation of assets also creates a divide within the working class, distinguishing between winners and losers: those who inherit real estate or possess land that increases in value, become fortunate, fostering a mindset that treats housing as an object of speculation. Notably, despite the presence of powerful international investors, the majority of these rentier landlords are still private individuals with medium incomes (Carmona, 2023), which further complicates the socio-economic landscape.

Subjective identity politics align with the financial–real estate model for several interconnected reasons. Firstly, they offer a subjective and individualistic approach that, as Steinko (2010, p. 23) articulates, is 'not supported by comprehensive projects of global transformation but fits comfortably within a culture of private battles against the world's evils'. This is fertile ground for right-wing rhetoric that criticizes wealth and inheritance taxes as unjust, and perpetuates the narrative that workers lived beyond their means during the housing boom – idea permanently repeated in the media during the Great Recession. Such subjectivism is reflected microeconomically in the focus on individual gender self-identification and macroeconomically in a liberal cosmopolitanism that overlooks geopolitical realities. This latter aspect leads to support for the self-determination of Spain's regions, even for the wealthiest (Mateo, 2018).

Secondly, the Spanish left exhibits a peculiar inclination towards localism or municipalism, extolling decentralization – centralism is associated with Franco's dictatorship, even in areas such as education and health – and an odd affinity for small businesses. Within this context, the prospects for radical transformation are bleak, particularly under the constraints of the Eurozone. The left seems to overlook how capital erodes national sovereignty both from above, through supranational agreements that entrench neoliberal economic policies (the EU), and from below, via the very decentralization it paradoxically champions (Monereo, 2020) or special zones (Slobodian, 2023).

Thirdly, and as a consequence, there is a tendency to prioritize short-term, piecemeal solutions. Various groups, feeling marginalized, vie for tax exemptions, quotas for subsidies, or public sector employment opportunities – essentially, any form of advantage (Mateo, 2020). This approach often results in a fragmented struggle for immediate gains, rather than a unified effort towards systemic change. Briefly, instead the materiality of exploitation (surplus value), the intangibility of the feeling of grievance.

In this context, the traditional capital–labour conflict loses its centrality, diminishing the focus on transforming the mode of production. Identity politics becomes the primary concern for the left, relegating class struggle to just one among many conflicts. To counteract this trend, the left should adopt an internationalist strategy rooted in a national project: the nation-State must be reaffirmed as the labour movement's frame of reference, yet with an internationalist outlook that, for the Spanish case, extends across the Mediterranean, including the European and African peripheries, and strengthens bonds with Latin America. This approach represents the sole geopolitical counterbalance to Anglo–Saxon imperialism and the neoliberal agenda championed by Europe's most developed nations. As previously discussed, the European capital project risks relegating Spain to a role of providing Northern countries with low-technology services, such as tourism, which underpins the financial–real estate model and contributes to both the material and subjective weakening of the labour movement.[18]

CONCLUSION

From this analysis, I would like to briefly highlight the following reflections.

First, an approach based on historical materialism must be holistic, incorporating the mode of production in the ecosystem, geopolitics, and with a class perspective in which the objective basis is related to the formation of class consciousness. In short, it is a matter of vindicating the explanatory potential of Marxism, not only to explain the present but also to make proposals for economic, social and political transformation.

In turn, the concrete analysis of the Spanish economy requires considering the productive specialization in the framework of the Eurozone, as well as the foundations of a speculative bubble that incorporates, as has been shown, multiple implications. The critique of the 'financial–real estate regime' has thus a rupturist component in social and environmental terms and, in general, with the aim of shaping of a democratic society that cannot be capitalist.

As a consequence, to forge a socialist future, a shift in the economic structure is imperative, favouring large enterprises and a centralized approach to economic planning. The right to self-determination must be redefined, focussing on what is produced and how it is produced. This reorientation is crucial for democratizing the productive regime and establishing a foundation for long-term, environmentally sustainable welfare.

NOTES

1. With much more intense implications than other asset bubbles, such as the case of the stock market (see Case et al., 2001).

2. For reasons of space, I refer to Chapter 6 of Mateo (2019).

3. On the evolution of the rate of profit and its determinants, see Mateo (2019), and a shortened version can be found in Mateo (2022). The unproductive sectors would be Finance, Insurance, and Real Estate (FIRE), and Government (GOV).

4. Indeed, it was a pivotal moment that significantly influenced its financial–real estate dimension. After the long industrial recession, absent a developmental state, and certainly without any move towards productive democratization, the welfare state found itself reliant on financing from international financial markets using global surpluses. This was complemented by the redirection of EEC funds into Spain, which were earmarked for the modernization of transport infrastructure in a manner that aligned with the interests of large capitals. However, this came with strings attached, such as the requirement to implement monetarist policies that maintained high interest rates to uphold an overvalued currency, thereby enhancing corporate profits – a harbinger of the trends that would intensify in the 1990s. This scenario represents the financialization of the welfare state (Steinko, 2010), which, although still incomplete and relatively underdeveloped following the protracted era of Francoism, proved to be functional for the financial–real estate accumulation model, albeit at the expense of eroding much of the domestic productive base.

5. However, as a decline in industry's share of GDP can mask an outsourcing of activities, the recent study by Casaú (2023) identifies a deindustrialization of the vertically integrated 'industrial subsystem', occurring from the late 1990s – with the adoption of fixed exchange rates – through to the Great Recession, and relatively more pronounced in terms of relative GVA. On the positive side, Myro (2021) underscores the export capacity in the pharmaceutical and drug sectors, which boasts a high technological component, as well as in the production of automobiles (medium-high level) and transport materials.

6. Arrizabalo et al. (2023, p. 324) conclude that 'Real estate, construction, hotels, restaurants, tourism, and entertainment are the sectors in which the presence of false self-employment is highest'. In relation to the variables of capital accumulation, I follow Mateo (2019, 2022).

7. The calculation makes reference to the wage per equivalent (full-time) wage earner. When using the GDP deflator, there is no increase of average wage, but if the CPI is considered, the rise would be 0.3% annually from 1995 to 2007.

8. Sánchez's outstanding PhD research (Sánchez, 2021) calculates explicit aid (recapitalization, asset purchases in various formats, loans, costs associated with the bank bailout, etc.) at 352 billion euros, representing 2.67% of the Spanish GDP from 2008 to 2019; and implicit public aid to obtain financing at more favorable conditions than market rates, amounting 1.24 trillion euros, the 9.46% of the cumulative GDP for the period. Thus, 'implicit public aids are essential for a banking sector that structurally depends on them' (Sánchez, 2021, p. 759).

9. The other large corporations exist due to State support (protectionism, privileged access to contracts) or through privatizations, as evidenced in the telecommunications, construction, and energy sectors.

10. Beginning in the 1990s, legislative changes – initially on the Mediterranean coast – shifted towards a *disaggregated* or *dualistic* approach, aligning more closely with neoliberal ideology. In this framework, the property developer is celebrated as the dynamic force, the 'Schumpeterian entrepreneur', while the landowner is often perceived as a barrier to entrepreneurial initiative (Gaja, 2003).

11. In the Madrid region, the sale of thousands of residential units to international private equity firms, including Blackstone and Goldman Sachs, sparked significant controversy. These transactions were criticized for being executed at below-market prices, adversely affecting numerous low-income families. Following complaints from social movements, in 2020 the Supreme Court invalidated the entire sale in a landmark ruling (Gil & Martínez, 2023).

12. Nevertheless, it is important to clarify that a large portion of landlords in the rental housing market are small-scale property owners, as will be mentioned thereafter.

13. The US investment firm Blackstone, initiating its investment ventures in 2012, emerged as the largest private homeowner in Spain through various Socimis, with a staggering 95% of its portfolio focused in the Madrid metropolitan area (Gabarre, 2019; Ramiro & González, 2019). Remarkably, Spain houses up to one-fifth of Blackstone's global real estate assets (Gil & Martínez, 2023).

14. Each square meter of a house requires an average of one ton of energy and materials (Carpintero & Bellver, 2013).

15. This trend signifies a pivot toward the North American paradigm of dispersed, low-density urban sprawl, characterized by urban planning that caters solely to automobile use. Emphasis is placed on flow (car movement) rather than stock (utilization of public spaces, pedestrian activities). In this context, consider the increase of common urban areas devoid of seating options – Madrid being a notable example in recent years. This design shapes social interactions in a mercantilist way: sharing a moment with friends is contingent upon participating in the circuit of accumulation (pay for a drink in a café to be seated).

16. In environments where street life is diminished, as traditionally promoted by small businesses and local services, public concerns over safety can be easily stoked. The persistent media focus on squatting in Spain has contributed to a collective anxiety that security companies have capitalized on. As a result, Spain, with its population of 47 million, has become the fourth-largest market in the world for security alarm systems, despite having a significantly smaller population than the leading countries: United States, Japan, and China. This explains that Securitas Direct, the market leader in the sector, invested as much in advertising in 2022 as an international behemoth like Amazon (Delgado, 2023).

17. Dioni (2021) explains that in these new neighborhoods, there has generally been an increase in votes for parties representing neoliberalism and identity politics, including the (liberal) far-right party Vox.

18. A clarifying data is the evolution of the average real wage since the establishment of fixed exchange rates (1999–2022). Del Rosal and Murillo (2023) show that in Spain, there was a decrease of −4.91%, similar to countries like Italy (−5.2%) and Greece (−4.5%), in stark contrast to the 'winner' economies of Central and Northern EU, with an increase of around 10% (the Netherlands, Finland, Germany), 20% (France, Denmark), or even more (Luxembourg, Ireland, Sweden).

REFERENCES

Alves, P., Broto, C., Gil, M., & Lamas, M. (2023). *Indicadores de riesgos y vulnerabilidades en el mercado de la vivienda en España*. Documentos Ocasionales 2314. Bank of Spain.

Arrizabalo, X., del Rosal, M., & Murillo, F. J. (2023). False self-employment and Bogus internships in Spain. *Economic and Labour Relations Review*, *34*(2), 314–327.

Bank of Spain. (2020). *El Mercado de la vivienda en España entre 2014 y 2019*. Documentos Ocasionales 2013. https://www.bde.es/f/webbde/SES/Secciones/Publicaciones/PublicacionesSeriadas/DocumentosOcasionales/20/Fich/do2013.pdf

Barandiaran, J., Cardoso, M., & Díez, L. (2019, March 5). *Desindustrialización prematura en España*. BBVA Research. https://www.bbvaresearch.com/wp-content/uploads/2019/03/Observatorio_Desindustrializacion_Prematura_BCD_v1.pdf

Bernabé, D. (2018). *La Trampa de la diversidad*. Akal.

Cabrero, A., & Tiana, M. A. (2012). El Contenido importador de las ramas de actividad en España. *Boletín Económico*, *2*, 45–57.

Carmona, P. (2023, November 7) *Mapa del Madrid rentista*. El Salto Diario. https://www.elsaltodiario.com/vivienda/mapa-del-madrid-rentista

Carpintero, Ó., & Bellver, J. (2013). ¿Es Posible la sostenibilidad ambiental de la economía española? In E. Assadourian & T. Prugh (Eds.), *¿Es Aún la ? La Situación del mundo 2013* (pp. 557–579). Worldwatch institute's annual sustainability report. Icaria-FUHEM Ecosocial.

Casaú, M. A. (2023). *El Proceso de desindustrialización española en un contexto de fragmentación productiva internacional. Un enfoque de subsistemas*. Unpublished document. Autonomous University of Madrid.

Case, K. E., Quigley, J., & Shiller, R. (2001). Comparing wealth effects, stock market versus housing market. NBER Working Paper 8606. http://www.nber.org/papers/w8606

Del Rosal, M., & Murillo, F. J. (2023, January 7). La Creciente divergencia territorial y de clase en la Unión Europea. *Rebelión*. https://rebelion.org/la-creciente-divergencia-territorial-y-de-clase-en-la-union-europea/

Delgado, D. (2023, February 14). Alarmas de ultraderecha y violencia rentable. https://ctxt.es/es/20230201/Politica/42108/reportaje-alarmas-desokupa-nazis-ultraderecha-violencia-negocio.htm

Dioni, J. (2021). *La España de las piscinas*. Arpa.

Fariñas, J. C., Martín, A. M., & Velázquez, F. J. (2015). La Desindustrialización de España en el contexto europeo. *Papeles de Economía Española*, *44*, 92–104.

Gabarre, M. (2019). *Tocar fondo. La mano invisible detrás de la subida del alquiler*. Traficantes de Sueños.

Gaja, F. (2003). El Suelo como excusa: el desarrollismo rampante. *Papeles de la FIM*, *20*, 55–66.

Gaja, F. (2008). El 'tsunami urbanizador' en el litoral mediterráneo: el ciclo de hiperproducción inmobiliaria 1996-2006. *Scripta Nova*, *XII*(270), 66.

Gil, J., & Martínez, M. A. (2023). State-led actions reigniting the financialization of housing in Spain. *Housing, Theory and Society*, *40*(1), 1–21.

Harvey, D. (2006 [1982]). *Limits to capital*. Verso.

Hernández, E. (2023, January 21). Qué Vota la gente que se compra el móvil más caro y luego no llega a fin de mes. *El Confidencial*. https://www.elconfidencial.com/cultura/2023-01-21/voto-elecciones-clase-media-aspiracional-movil-gasto_3561650/

INE. (2023a). *Annual Spanish national accounts: Aggregates by industry*. National Statistics Institute.

INE. (2023b). *Spanish regional accounts*. National Statistics Institute.

INE. (2023c). *Statistical Use of the central business register*. CBR. National Statistics Institute.

López, I., & Rodríguez, E. (2011). The Spanish model. *New Left Review*, *69*, 5–28.

Mateo, J. P. (2018). La Cuestión nacional en España y el materialismo histórico: el caso de Cataluña. In *International Congress Pensar Marx hoy*, October 2–6, Complutense University of Madrid.

Mateo, J. P. (2019). *The theory of crisis and the great recession in Spain*. Palgrave Macmillan.

Mateo, J. P. (2020, March 23). Las Reivindicaciones en la etapa de las políticas de la identidad. *Crónica popular*.

Mateo, J. P. (2022). Theory and practice of crisis in political economy: The case of the great recession in Spain. *Review of Radical Political Economics*, *54*(1), 83–105.

Melchor, A., & Armesilla, S. J. (2022). La Inserción de España en la división internacional del trabajo a través de la Unión Europea: desindustrialización, destrucción del mundo rural y subordinación capitalista. *Nuestra Bandera*, *257*, 29–42.

Méndez, R. (2021). Financiarización urbana y burbuja del alquiler en España: tendencias y contrastes en perspectiva multiescalar. *Documents d'Anàlisi Geogràfica*, *67*(3), 441–463.

Monereo, M. (2020). *Oligarquía o democracia. España, nuestro futuro*. El Viejo Topo.

Myro, R. (2021). El Futuro de la industria Española. *Revista de Economía Mundial*, *59*, 139–162.

Observatorio de Vivienda y Suelo (OVS). (2019). *Boletín especial. Alquiler, 2019*. Ministerio de Fomento.

Polo, J. (2021). *Románticos y racistas. Orígenes ideológicos de los etnonacionalismos españoles*. El Viejo Topo.

Ramiro, P., & González, E. (2019). *¿A Dónde va el español?* Traficantes de Sueños.

Sánchez, C. (2021). *El Papel de las ayudas públicas en el funcionamiento del sector bancario privado: ¿Medidas excepcionales o dependencia estructural? Estudio del caso español (1980-2019)*. PhD. Complutense University of Madrid.

Santos, I. (2022). Las Redes y estructuras del poder político-económico en España. *Nuestra Bandera*, *257*, 43–62.

Slobodian, Q. (2023). *Crack-up capitalism. Market radicals and the dream of a world without democracy*. Metropolitan Books.

Steinko, A. (2010). *Izquierda y republicanismo. El salto a la refundación*. Akal.

Vives, S., & Rullán, O. (2014). La Apropiación de las rentas del suelo en la ciudad neoliberal Española. *Boletín de la Asociación de Geógrafos Españoles*, *65*, 387–408.

PART III

PRESENT, SOUTH

SENEGAL: THE DESCENT INTO THE ABYSS WITH THE IMF AND WORLD BANK STRUCTURAL ADJUSTMENT PROGRAMS

Demba Moussa Dembele

Council for the Development of Social Science Research in Africa (CODESRIA), Senegal

ABSTRACT

This chapter argues that the crisis of the neocolonial economic model in Senegal opened the door to the neoliberal agenda of the International Monetary Fund (IMF) and the World Bank. Their policies literally destroyed the gains accumulated during the first two decades of independence, through the dismantling of the public sector and the weakening of the State through the drastic restriction of its intervention in economic and social areas. As a result, after more than 20 years of implementing these policies, Senegal ended up joining the list of the 'least developed countries' (LDCs), considered as the 'poorest' countries in the world, according to the United Nations. However, Senegal is not alone. It is just one example of the destructive agenda of the IMF and World Bank imposed on many other countries in Africa and beyond. One major lesson to be learnt from the experience of Senegal and other African countries is the huge economic, social and even political costs associated with neoliberal prescriptions. The other major lesson is the collapse of market fundamentalism, which was already exposed during the 2007–2008 international financial crisis. A collapse made more glaring during the COVID-19 pandemic. In light of this, this chapter calls for a paradigm shift for Senegal and other African countries, by reclaiming their right to development and moving away from failed policies and models. A goal made easier by the new international context characterized by the shift of economic power to the Global South.

Trajectories of Declining and Destructive Capitalism
Research in Political Economy, Volume 40, 125–140

Published under exclusive licence by Emerald Publishing Limited
ISSN: 0161-7230/doi:10.1108/S0161-723020250000040009

Keywords: Senegal; Africa; neoliberalism; liberalization; state; structural adjustment programs (SAPs); development; global south

INTRODUCTION

In his masterwork, *Capital*, Karl Marx (1974) had indicated that Africa had contributed to the 'primitive accumulation of capital'. Indeed, according to Samir Amin (1990), Africa and the Global South have contributed to the permanent accumulation of capital of imperialist countries ever since the dawn of the capitalist system. In fact, Africa has paid a heavy price to the birth and expansion of the capitalist system on a world scale. The colonization and plunder of Africa's resources was the primary source for the industrialization and development of Europe (Rodney, 2018).

After colonization, most African countries inherited from a neocolonial model of development, which kept African economies under the control of former colonial powers. This model came crashing in the late 1970s, opening the way to the International Monetary Fund (IMF) and the World Bank, which imposed Structural Adjustment Programs (SAPs) literally destroying the African economies as we will show later, with the example of Senegal.

THE CRISIS OF THE NEOCOLONIAL MODEL IN SENEGAL

The economic and social policies in post-independence Senegal were part of what is called the 'Neocolonial Pact'. It is a continuation of the Colonial Pact which shaped the relationships between France and its colonies during the colonial period. The post-independence economic model had several key features. First, it was entirely controlled by the former colonial power, which was the main trading partner. The currency used in Senegal, the CFA franc (or franc of the *Colonies Françaises d'Afrique* [African French Colonies]), was one of the symbols of that control and an instrument of plunder of the country's resources. Indeed, the CFA franc has almost exclusively served the interests of French companies and the geopolitical standing of France in the world. The nature and monetary policies associated with the CFA franc are among the major obstacles to African countries' development (Dembele, 2023).

Another key feature of the Senegalese economy was its dependence on the exports of raw materials, which were the main sources of foreign exchange earnings. A third characteristic of the Senegalese economy was an active intervention of the State and the leading role of the public sector. This was illustrated by the control of key economic sectors by the State and the development of a large public sector.

However, the poor management of State-owned companies and growing public spending resulted in the accumulation of deficits, covered by external borrowing. This was compounded by the fall in commodity prices, the main sources of foreign exchange. This exacerbated the financial difficulties of the State and led to the crisis of the neocolonial model. Senegal turned to the IMF and the World Bank to find solutions to its economic and financial crises.

THE IMF AND WORLD BANK IN SENEGAL

These two institutions came to African countries with a single and simplistic agenda: attack and discredit State intervention, dismantle the public sector in order to promote the interests of the private sector, especially foreign investors. The blueprint of their policies was contained in a Report commissioned by the World Bank, familiarly known as the 'Berg Report', conducted by Elliot Berg (World Bank, 1981). This Berg Report was in response to the Lagos Plan of Action (LPA) issued a few months earlier in 1980 by the Organization of African Unity (OAU) and the United Nations Economic Commission for Africa (UNECA).

The Lagos Action Plan (LPA)

The Lagos Plan of Action was an attempt by African countries to propose endogenous solutions to the continent's crisis. The LPA was the result of several months of debates among African experts and policymakers. It proposed a path to Africa's industrialization by using its immense natural resources and by mobilizing domestic financial resources.

The LPA was the first attempt to develop an African-designed road map to promote the industrialization of the continent. It resulted from the realization that development policies of the first two decades of 'independence' had failed.

In its Preamble, the LPA emphasizes the following: 'In their development plans, Member States should give a primary role to industrialization, keeping in mind its impact in meeting the essential needs of their populations'. Industrialization was considered essential to 'liberate Africa from underdevelopment and economic dependence', adds the LPA. African States made the decade 1980–1990 that of industrial development in Africa.

The strengths of the LPA resided in the fact it was entirely designed by Africans. It was an attempt to regain sovereignty over Africa's development policies. The Plan was an attempt to put Africa on a path to economic independence and self-sufficiency in several key areas. Most of all, the Plan put the State at the centre of the development process.

This is why the LPA was not acceptable to Western powers and to the international institutions under their control, like the IMF and the World Bank. This explains why the Berg Report was issued with the objective to counter the Lagos Plan of Action and push African countries deeper into external dependence and perpetuate their underdevelopment. The LPA agenda was replaced by the notorious Structural Adjustment Programs (SAPs), promoted by the Berg Report. With the catastrophic economic and social consequences observed in almost all African countries ever since the intervention of the IMF and the World Bank.

The Berg Report

The prescriptions of the Berg Report were accepted by almost all African governments, without thinking about their devastating economic and social consequences.

One can summarize the prescriptions as follows:

- fiscal austerity through the reduction in public spending, especially in the social sectors;
- drastic cuts in personnel and hiring freeze in the public administration;
- dismantling the public sector through restructuring, privatization and dissolution;
- liberalization of external trade in order to open the domestic market to foreign goods;
- deregulation of domestic prices, with the removal of subsidies and price controls;
- weakening the State and restricting its economic and social role.

These prescriptions were imposed on Senegal for over two decades.

THE RECORD OF SAPS IN SENEGAL

It was in the late 1970s and early 1980s that the IMF and World Bank began their intervention in Senegal. In exchange of loans, they imposed their prescriptions with the goal of radically changing the economic and social policies implemented in the 1960s and 1970s.

Dismantling the Public Sector

One of their main targets was the public sector for two reasons. First, for ideological reasons, because the IMF and World aimed to impose capitalism in Senegal against what they perceived as 'socialist policies'. Second, these two institutions accused the public sector as the main cause of the country's financial woes due to the accumulation of deficits because of its poor management.

Therefore, the IMF and World Bank imposed draconian measures to reorganize the public sector. State-owned companies as well as parastatal companies went through restructuring, privatization or closure. Even State-owned companies assisting farmers in rural areas were closed, leaving farmers with little technical and financial assistance. This contributed to the aggravation of the crisis of the agricultural sector.

Weakening the State

The dismantling of the public sector, especially of State-owned companies deprived the State of some of its main economic instruments and resulted in the weakening of its social functions. In addition, the IMF and World Bank subjected the State to harsh critique in order to discredit it as agent of economic development (World Bank, 1994). According to these institutions, the African State was 'at the heart of the continent's economic crisis'. It was considered as 'wasteful', 'corrupt', 'rent-seeking' and 'inefficient'. All these epithets were intended to discredit the State and put in doubt its capacity to elaborate and implement efficient economic policies.

The campaign against the State was both economic and ideological. In the eyes of the IMF and World Bank, a strong involvement of the State in economic activities was seen as an illustration of 'socialism'. As such as, they must be banned or strongly restricted. This explains why even services and subsidies for farmers provided by the government in the rural areas were reduced or eliminated.

The imposition of austerity measures further deprived the State of most of economic and financial resources, making it even weaker in the face of strong pressure from the IMF and the World Bank. It is in the context that the two international institutions decided to propose a drastic reduction in the personnel of the public administration through the so-called 'voluntary leaves'. If the objective was to make the administration more 'efficient', the opposite was achieved. In fact, the result was the disruption and degradation of the public service in several sectors.

Furthermore, public institutions, like the Parliament, were marginalized in the definition and control of public policies. For instance, the National Assembly was bypassed in implementing policies and agreements that normally need its approval.

Wholesale Privatization

Faced with a weak resistance from the State and even from trade unions, the IMF and World Bank embarked on a series of large-scale privatization of public and State assets, primarily for the benefit of foreign investors. In fact, in the name of 'strategic partners', the priority was given to foreign investors at the expense of the national private sector. No sector was spared: even basic social services, such as electricity and water distribution, were privatized.

In fact, one of the most controversial decisions was the privatization of the State-owned electricity company, SENELEC. The State and trade unions at the company resisted against this privatization. But in the end, under heavy pressure, even blackmail, from the IMF and World Bank, the State backed down and sold the company to a Canadian entity. After a few years, it turned out that the Canadian investors did not keep their promises to invest in SENELEC and improve its operations. So, the State had to take it back, with a huge cost!

Banks and insurances were not spared either. Most of State-owned banks, which were not closed, were privatized, including development banks providing investments in the agricultural sector or in the housing sector. By the end of the 1990s, there was no publicly owned bank in Senegal. The State was left without any financial instrument to mobilize long-term savings and invest in key sectors of the economy. Therefore, in implementing the prescriptions of the IMF and World Bank, the State lost almost all the public sector it had put together during the first two decades of independence.

Trade Liberalization

The goal of the privatization of State assets was to expand the activities of foreign investors. Trade liberalization aims to achieve the same objective, in addition to further weakening the State by challenging its policies in the area of external trade. Trade liberalization was imposed in order to remove most of the restrictions and measures aimed at protecting the domestic market. Many tariffs and non-tariff barriers were eliminated, exposing most domestic companies to competition from subsided exports from developed countries. In fact, several State-owned and public companies in key sectors could not sustain foreign competition.

As a result, trade liberalization contributed to the collapse of Senegal's promising industrial sector. The case in point is the textile industry. Senegal used to have a vibrant textile sector which was one of the leading sectors in West Africa. Due to trade liberalization, local production fell sharply and secondhand clothing has inundated the Senegalese market.

The other consequence of trade liberalization is the financial losses for the public finances since taxation on imports of goods and services was an important source of revenues for the government. Therefore, trade liberalization further exacerbated the country's economic and financial crisis.

Senegal was not alone in this case. Trade liberalization imposed by the IMF and World Bank have incurred staggering financial and economic losses for Africa and other countries of the Global South. The British non-governmental organization (NGO) Christian Aid has estimated those losses at more than 270 billion dollars over a 20-year period (Christian Aid, 2005).

'Good Governance'

The failure of the above prescriptions and the huge costs associated to them, not only in Senegal but also elsewhere in Africa, led the World Bank to come up with the concept of 'good governance' (World Bank, 1989). According to this international institution, the catastrophic record of its neoliberal prescriptions was the result of poor implementation by African States, which lack 'good governance'. Indeed, 'good governance' was a tool to further weaken the State. Its goal was to compel the State to put in place policies and measures aimed at facilitating the activities of the private sector, at securing and protecting private property and preventing strikes. This also means that the State should take strong measures against corruption and nepotism, all of which should help reduce the costs of transactions and make business more profitable. In short, 'good governance' means a State to the service of foreign investors.

LESSONS FROM A FAILED MODEL

In Senegal, the prescriptions of the Berg Report for more than two decades plunged the country into deeper economic and social crisis it is going through even today.

Deterioration of Human Development Indicators (HDIs)

The IMF and World Bank succeeded in literally destroying the Senegalese economy and State. Through closures and privatization and trade liberalization, the painstaking gains made during the first two decades of independence were almost wiped out. The private takeover of key sectors did not give the expected results. In addition to losing its economic role, the State was further weakened by fiscal austerity, hiring freeze in the public administration and 'voluntary leaves' in the public administration and the civil service. Privatization allowed foreign companies to take control of key economic sector, including the provision of water, electricity, transportation, banks, etc.

The State lost most of its economic functions, transferred to new entities controlled by consultants hired by the IMF and World Bank. One should keep in mind that the State was the main employer in the so-called 'modern' sector. Therefore, the drastic reduction in public spending, hiring freeze in the public administration and large-scale privatization of public assets resulted in an unprecedented level of unemployment, the deterioration of public services and worsening living conditions. This translated into the deterioration of the country's Human Development Indicators (HDIs) (UNDP, 2022).

The deterioration of its HDIs landed Senegal in January 2001 in the category of the Least Developed Countries (LDCs), the 'poorest' countries in the world, according to the United Nations. This is the outcome of two decades or so of strict implementation of the notorious SAPs. The category of LDCs was recognized in 1971 by the United Nations. These countries are seen as very disadvantaged in their development process for historical, structural and geographic reasons. The LDCs are characterized by low human resources, low productive capacities and vulnerability to external shocks.

Senegal is still in this category ever since. The LDCs were hard hit by the COVID-19 pandemic which has reversed for several decades of painstaking gains made by these countries, according to the United Nations Conference on Trade and Development (UNCTAD, 2020).

The fall into the category of the least developed countries (LDCs) has accentuated the external economic and financial dependence of Senegal. This has contributed to the erosion of its sovereignty over development policies.

One of the most dramatic consequences of the SAPs in Senegal is mass unemployment of the youth, especially in the rage of 25–35 years of age. The solution to this problem has eluded successive governments. The high unemployment rate and the dim prospects for short-term solutions explain the tragedy of irregular migration. Thousands of young Senegalese, including former students, have tried to go to Europe through dangerous means. Hundreds of them have perished in the Sahara Desert or in the Mediterranean Sea.

Another outcome of SAPs in Senegal and elsewhere in Africa is the weakening of the State. The narrative about 'failed States' in Africa tends to put the blame on 'corruption', 'nepotism', and 'patrimonialism', among other derogatory epithets. But this narrative fails to name the true culprits of State failure in Africa: the IMF, World Bank and their destructive neoliberal agenda! During the heyday of SAPs, even spending on security was drastically scaled down in the national budgets in the name of budget austerity. The outcome has been the weakening of national defence, in particular the military. The spread of terrorism in the Sahel region is a direct consequence of the weakening of the State and the low spending on defence and security.

After two decades of SAPs, one can see that Senegal has descended into the brink of collapse, like other countries which came under the control of the IMF and World Bank. The country has become weaker and more dependent on its so-called 'development partners'. The IMF and World Bank still dictate macroeconomic policies. In May 2023, an agreement was signed with the IMF, with the usual neoliberal prescriptions analyzed throughout this paper.

The Failure of Capitalism in the Periphery

Senegal descent into the abyss is also a reflection of the failure of capitalism in the periphery. As indicated earlier, the primary objective of the SAPs imposed by the IMF and the World Bank was to wean Senegal from 'socialism', assimilated to State intervention and a large public sector, and promote capitalism and 'free market'. For sure, they succeeded in dismantling what the State had built over two decades after independence. But after more than three decades and so, the promotion of capitalism has been a big failure. Indeed, the crisis of the neocolonial model and the consequences of the SAPs illustrate the failure of capitalism in the periphery.

Senegal has lost some tangible gains it had made during the first two decades of independence. As we mentioned, its HDIs have deteriorated. Its prospects at industrialization were destroyed by the SAPs. In fact, its promising and burgeoning industrial sector was destroyed under the combined effect of State retrenchment and large-scale trade liberalization. Due to trade liberalization, secondhand clothing has inundated the Senegalese market at the expense of a dynamic textile sector which was one of the leading sectors in West Africa.

THE COLLAPSE OF MARKET FUNDAMENTALISM

The neoliberal failed model analyzed above is a symptom of the deep crisis of market fundamentalism. It was already revealed by the 2007–2008 international financial crisis. The collapse of market fundamentalism has been even acknowledged by mainstream circles.

The former World Bank President, Robert B. Zoellick (2010) made one of the most damning critiques of market fundamentalism, after the 2008 financial crisis. He said:

> Even before the crisis there was a questioning of prevailing paradigms and a sense that development economics needed rethinking. The crisis has only made that more compelling.

Zoellick's critique against mathematic models found a strong echo with Paul R. Krugman (2009), from Princeton University and a Nobel Laureate, who also slammed those economists fascinated with models and 'mistook beauty, clad in impressive-looking mathematics, for truth'. Their certitude about the strength of their models prevented them from foreseeing the crisis:

> Few economists saw our current crisis coming, but this predictive failure was the least of the field's problems. More important was the profession's blindness to the very possibility of catastrophic failures in a market economy.

The critique was particularly harsh for the monetarist school, considered as the 'product of a Dark Age of macroeconomics' (Krugman, 2009).

Moreover, in his piece, Krugman quoted Mister Allan Greenspan, former Fed Chairman for nearly 20 years, as 'admitting that he was in a state of 'shocked disbelief,' because 'the whole intellectual edifice had collapsed'. Krugman added that 'since this collapse of the intellectual edifice was also a collapse of real-world markets, the result was a severe recession – the worst, by many measures, since the Great Depression' (Krugman, 2009).

The COVID-19 pandemic has accentuated the crisis of market fundamentalism. It is in this context that *The Economist*, one of the strongest vehicles of neoliberal thinking, came up with a lengthy analysis calling into question the current state of macroeconomics:

> But now, in the wreckage left behind by the coronavirus pandemic, a new era is beginning. What does the future hold? (...) What is clear is that the old economic paradigm is looking tired. One way or another, change is coming. (The Economist, 2020)

Of course, the words 'looking tired' simply mean 'discredited'. Indeed, the market fundamentalism is completely discredited after leading the world to the brink of collapse. Therefore, Senegal and African countries should move away from neoliberalism and look for other development paradigms.

FOR A PARADIGM SHIFT

In Senegal, and in Africa in general, numerous voices have called for a paradigm shift in light of the failed neoliberal policies, made more glaring with the COVID-19 pandemic. Indeed, the trajectory of Senegal and most African countries analyzed above clearly shows that they cannot experience development within the neoliberal paradigm. Therefore, they need to shift to a new paradigm by reclaiming their right to development.

Reclaiming the Right to Development

The right to development refers to the historic declaration adopted by the United Nations General Assembly in December 1986 (Owoeye, 2021). It is worth recalling that Africa made a significant contribution to the process that led to the adoption of that landmark declaration. In fact, the right to development was first recognized in 1981 in Article 22 of the African Charter on Human and Peoples' Rights as a definitive individual and collective right. Article 22–(1) states that:

'All peoples shall have the right to their economic, social and cultural development with due regard to their freedom and identity and to the equal enjoyment of the common heritage of mankind'.

The Preamble of the Declaration on the Right to Development claims that:

> ...development is a comprehensive economic, social, cultural and political process, which aims at the constant improvement of the well–being of the entire population and of all individuals on the basis of their active, free and meaningful participation in development and in the fair distribution of benefits resulting therefrom.

This claim provided the legal and political basis for nations and governments to adopt policies aimed at fulfiling the objectives of the declaration. These include (Owoeye, 2021):

- adoption of progressive economic and social policies at national levels;
- full sovereignty over natural resources;
- ownership of development policies;
- recognition of peoples' economic, social and cultural rights.

This declaration has been obliterated by the neoliberal onslaught at the beginning of the 1990s. Now, with the abject failure of the neoliberal paradigm, Africa should consider the implementation of Agenda 2063 within the framework of the right to development.

Implementing Agenda 2063: Building 'The Africa We Want'

Indeed, the crisis of the neoliberal paradigm, exacerbated by the COVID-19 pandemic, has prompted calls for Africa to look for alternative development policies. Even before the pandemic, a consensus was building that Africa should move away from past models imposed from abroad and which have all failed with a heavy cost to the continent (UNECA, 2011).

It is in light of these changes in the world and of its own experience of the several decades of 'independence' and failed development that the African Union adopted in 2013 the Agenda 2063, titled *The Africa We Want*. This means building the Africa that the African people want for themselves. Not the Africa that bilateral and multilateral 'development partners' want for the African people. Therefore, the new Africa cannot be built with the same discredited failed neoliberal policies.

It must be built with a new paradigm. According to the African Union Commission, Agenda 2063 is seen as 'a manifestation of the Panafrican drive for unity, self-determination, freedom, progress and collective prosperity pursued under Panafricanism and African Renaissance'. To reach this, the declaration aims to build 'an integrated, prosperous and peaceful Africa, driven by its own citizens, representing a dynamic force in the international arena'.

To achieve the objectives of Agenda 2063 requires a complete change in policies from both national governments and regional and continental institutions. The Lagos Plan of Action (LPA) has certainly inspired Agenda 2063. In fact, the spirit of the LPA and its core policies were rehabilitated by Carlos Lopes during his mandate as head of the UNECA. Under his leadership, several annual reports from UNECA (2013, 2014, 2015) focused on the industrialization of the continent based on the domestic transformation of its natural resources. Lopes and his colleagues influenced the content of Agenda 2063 since the African Union and the UNECA, both based in Addis Ababa (Ethiopia), work hand in hand on economic issues.

Achieving Self-sufficiency in Basic Needs

The COVID-19 pandemic has exposed the extent of Africa's dependence on food, health, pharmaceutical products and energy. Indeed, the pandemic has shown that sovereignty on health, pharmaceutical production and food production is a fundamental security issue, which should not be left to the whims of the markets nor to the hands of external forces. Therefore, Africa needs to build a sovereign and resilient health sector and promote food sovereignty.

It is estimated that 90% of Africa's needs in medicine come from abroad, with spending worth dozens of billions of dollars in hard currency each year. After the traumatic experience of the COVID-19 pandemic, there are growing calls from policymakers, health specialists and institutions for Africa to move towards self-sufficiency in pharmaceutical production. To achieve that goal, African countries should work together and set up regional pharmaceutical production facilities in the different regional economic communities. Otherwise, foreign pharmaceutical companies will build those facilities and make even more profits on the back of the African people.

Regarding food sovereignty, it is useful to remind African leaders that the agricultural sector is key to Africa's development. This is why that agriculture should be a priority sector to provide the continent's needs in food and as the main engine for economic growth and development. This is one of the reasons why African heads of State adopted the Maputo Directive, during the African Union Summit in Mozambique in 2003, urging the countries to allocate at least 10% of the national budget to the agricultural sector.

However, at their Summit in Malabo (Equatorial Guinea) in 2014, the leaders realized that only a handful of countries complied with the Maputo Directive. Africa's great dependence on food imports as illustrated by the Russia–Ukraine war should be a strong wakeup call for African leaders to understand, once for all, that food sovereignty is not only an economic goal but a fundamental national security issue.

Beyond sovereignty in health and food production, there is need for recovering peoples' sovereignty over natural resources by putting an end to the new scramble for Africa's natural resources, which are being given away to multinational corporations, especially in the extractive sector, which is the main source of illicit financial flows (UNCTAD, 2020).

All of the above requires rebuilding developmental States and the public sector.

Rebuilding Developmental States

One of the main objectives of neoliberalism has been to weaken and even destroy the State so that multinational corporations can plunder Africa's resources without a strong resistance. This explains why one of the main targets of SAPs was the State, which was accused of being an obstacle to Africa's development (Mkandawire, 2001)! Yet, the Declaration on the Right to Development stressed that the State has the right and obligation to formulate appropriate national policies and measures in promoting development and fair distribution of the benefits resulting from economic growth for achieving and protecting human rights, according to Article 2–(3) of the Declaration (Owoeye, 2021).

As a matter of fact, one of the important lessons learnt from the experience of SAPs is the indispensable role of the State in economic development. In 2011, the UNECA published a report on Africa, which claims that the weakening of the State has been one of the main factors behind the widespread poverty and the deterioration in the continent's HDIs (UNECA, 2011).

The Declaration on the Right to Development gives a strong legitimacy to the State as a key factor in the development process. Indeed, Africa, like other continents, needs the intervention of an active and competent State as well as efficient public institutions to implement the Agenda 2063. This is why several calls were made on the necessity to rebuild developmental States in Africa (Mkandawire, 2001; UNCTAD, 2007; UNECA, 2011). The collapse of market fundamentalism and lessons from the COVID-19 pandemic have made those calls more relevant and even an imperative.

Already, in several countries, including Senegal, the State is reasserting itself in several areas. Development planning has been reinstated in Senegal and elsewhere (Lopes, 2013). In Senegal, the Ministry of Economic Planning has been restored. The State has nationalized some key sectors that were privatized, and created financial institutions for small- and medium-sized enterprises (SMEs).

With developmental States, there will be possibilities to rebuild a strong and competitive public sector and the return of development planning which is indispensable in building an industrial base (Chang, 2016) in order to transform domestically, create jobs and retain wealth.

Accelerate Regional and Continental Integration

Regional and continental integration is also key to Africa's growth and industrialization. Regional economic communities (RECs) have an important role to play in advancing the continental agenda, in terms of trade, investments and economic transformation. For instance, in the Economic Community of West African States (ECOWAS), any progress made towards a common currency would have a positive effect on other regional communities and give a big boost to the continental monetary projects, such as the African Monetary Fund and the African Central Bank, whose ultimate goal is to prepare the advent of an African common currency.

The African Continental Free Trade Area (AfCFTA), launched in January 2021, is supposed to accelerate the integration of the continent. However, so far, this has not been the case. According to statistics unveiled by a senior official from UNECA, intra-African trade, as a share of global trade, declined from 14.5% in 2021 to 13.7% in 2022. The average intra-African trade is estimated at 13%, compared to 55% in Asia and 70% in Europe.[1]

These figures show that Africa has a long way to go in terms of economic integration. Yet, regional and continental integration is an important tool in strengthening Africa's voice in the international arena, especially in South–South cooperation.

Developing South–South Cooperation

There have been several manifestations of solidarity between African countries and other countries of the Global South during the COVID-19 pandemic. Beyond the solidarity on health issues, South–South cooperation has been expanding on economic and financial issues. According to United Nations Trade and Development (UNCTAD), South–South exports have increased on average by 13% between 1995 and 2016, compared to an average growth rate of 8% for world exports during the same period. The value of South–South exports has increased from 600 million dollars in 1995 to 4 trillion dollars in 2016. The share of South–South exports in world exports rose from 42% to 57% during this same period. In 2016, 25% of world trade was between countries of the South (UNCTAD, 2018). One can observe a similar trend in investments. Foreign direct investments (FDIs) from the South rose from 110 billion in 2005 to 381 billion dollars in 2017. Investments in the South from other countries of the South increased from 1,700 billion dollars in 2010 to 4,100 billion dollars in 2016 (UNCTAD, 2018).

In fact, South–South trade has surpassed North–North trade. For instance, UNCTAD recognized the changed structure of international trade over the past 25 years. It claimed that the share of trade between developed economies had declined by nearly 15% since 1995, while the growth of South–South trade was up by 14.1%, during the same period (UNCTAD, 2022). In the early 1990s, there was observed a period of sharp decline in the North–North share of international trade. Around the time of the global financial crisis of 2007–2008, South–South trade overtook North–North trade for the first time. Today, it is believed that South–South merchandise trade accounts for 35% of global trade, compared to 25% for North–North trade. South–South trade tends to be more beneficial to African countries because it is more diversified, it brings greater technology transfer, and more development-friendly than North–South trade (Mold, 2023).

Building Strong Ties With the BRICS+ Group

Still in the area of South–South cooperation, Africa can have powerful partners to turn to. The group of BRICS (Brazil, Russia, India, China and South Africa) has been reinforced by new members in 2004, with the addition of two African countries (Egypt and Ethiopia), Iran, Saudi Arabia and the United Arab Emirates. The cumulative gross domestic products (GDPs) of the new BRICS group have surpassed the G7 countries in terms of purchasing power parity. Several African countries have already applied to join the group. In the next few years, more African countries will likely become members of this group. This will help strengthen the ties between the BRICS and the continent. This prospect will give Africa more space, economically and politically, to push for more sovereignty and autonomy in the definition and implementation of its policies. The move towards de-dollarization spearheaded by the BRICS will help African countries against the dictatorship of Western currencies in their external trade.

The BRICS+, China, Russia and India, in particular, can provide huge markets for African exports as well as investments and technologies adapted to African countries' needs. In fact, China and Russia, as well as India, have signed currency swaps with several African countries, in order to facilitate trade and investments and reduce the needs for dollars and euros.

China, one of the leading members of the BRICS+; is Africa's main trading partner for more than a decade or so. It is also one of the main sources of investments in Africa, especially through the Africa–China Cooperation Forum and the Bridge and Road Initiative (BRI).

A report indicates that capital equipment supplied to Tanzania, Kenya, and Uganda by China is more economically accessible, profitable to users, and demonstrably more appropriate to the operating conditions in these three economies. These features made them distinct from capital goods coming from Western countries (Hanlin & Kaplinsky, 2016).

Financing Africa's Development

In addition to trade, South–South cooperation is an important source of investments and loans for African countries. However, Africa needs to mobilize more domestic resources for its development and depend less on external sources. Indeed, one of Africa's perennial problems has been its dependence on external sources of financing, whether through official development assistance (ODA), loans from multilateral institutions or private lenders. These sources of financing always come with political and economic conditions.

Yet, Africa's dependence on external sources is paradoxical. Several studies have indicated that in reality Africa is a net creditor to the world (AfDB, 2013; UNECA, 2015; UNCTAD, 2020). Illicit financial flows, through tax evasions and transfer pricing, are robbing Africa of staggering financial resources. For instance, between February and May 2020, Africa had lost five billion dollars as capital flight (AfDB, 2021). Between 2015 and 2020, UNCTAD has estimated illicit financial flows from Africa at 88.6 billion dollars, accounting for 3.7% of the continent's cumulative GDPs (UNCTAD, 2020). During the same period, the inflow from ODA was 48 billion dollars and FDIs 54 billion dollars. Each of these inflows was lower than the illicit outflows.

Therefore, Africa has the potential to raise substantial resources domestically with different fiscal and monetary policies and more cooperation inside and outside the continent. African countries need efficient public institutions, among them an active developmental State. Domestic resource mobilization would require stemming the flows of capital flight. UNCTAD has indicated that the continent retains the 88.6 billion dollars it is losing annually, if there are important changes in Africa and at the international level. Closer cooperation among African countries, like automatic exchange of tax information among them, could effectively help curtail illicit financial flows. This would also require international tax cooperation on the part of Western countries, the United Nations system, countries in the Global South as well as international institutions.

CONCLUSION

After the crisis of the neocolonial model, Senegal, like most African countries, was subjected to the most destructive economic policies, known as SAPs, imposed by the IMF and the World Bank. They literally destroyed the State and other public institutions. Under these policies many gains made during the first two decades of independence were lost. As a result, Senegal made a leap backward and fell into the category of the LDCs in 2001.

But Senegal is just one example. Other African countries and several countries of the Global South had been subjected to the same or similar policies. The SAPs were part of the neoliberal paradigm, which led the world to the brink of collapse in 2008 with the international financial crisis. The COVID-19 pandemic further exposed the failure of neoliberal policies, which are now largely discredited even in developed countries. This prompted growing calls in Africa on the necessity to look for alternative development policies. In this regard, as strongly argued by the late Professor Samir Amin, Africa and the Global South need to delink from global capitalism and reclaim their right to development (Amin, 1990). This recommendation is more relevant than ever, in light of the deep transformation of the international context characterized by the shift in economic and political power to the Global South, with the BRICS+ group as the leading force. Already several African countries have joined the group and others are on the way. Therefore, Senegal and the African continent are in better conditions to move away from failed policies and models and shift to a people-centred development paradigm. For that to happen, African leaders and policymakers must have the courage to think outside the orthodox/neoliberal economic framework (Tandon, 2009).

NOTE

1. These figures were given during the 2024 Conference of Ministers of Finance, Planning and Economic Development (COM24), held in Zimbabwe, February 28–March 5, 2024.

REFERENCES

AfDB. (2021, March). *African economic outlook 2021.* African Development Bank.

African Development Bank and Global Financial Integrity. (2013, May). *Illicit financial flows and the problem of net resource transfers from Africa.* Joint Report by the AfDB and GFI.

African Union Commission. (2014, May). *Agenda 2063: The Africa we want*. African Union.

Amin, S. (1990). *Delinking: Towards a polycentric world*. Zed Press.

Chang, H.-J. (2016, April). *The industrialisation imperative: Why does Africa (still) have to industrialise? Professor Adedeji annual lecture*. United Nations Economic Commission for Africa.

Christian Aid. (2005). *The economics of failure: The true costs of trade liberalization to poor countries*. A Christian Aid Briefing Paper.

Dembele, D. M. (2023). Colonial legacy, monetary policy and resource mobilization for development in Africa. *Research in Political Economy*, *39*, 53–71.

Hanlin, R., & Kaplinsky, R. (2016). South–South trade in capital goods: The market–driven diffusion of appropriate technology. *European Journal of Development Research*, *16*, 361–378.

Krugman, P. R. (2009, September 2). How did economists get it so wrong? *New York Times*.

Lopes, C. (2013, August 8). 50 years of development planning in Africa: Retrospect and prospects. *South Views*, *75*. South Centre.

Marx, K. (1974). *Capital*. Progress Publishers.

Mkandawire, T. (2001). Thinking about developmental states in Africa. *Cambridge Journal of Economics*, *25*(3), 289–293.

Mold, A. (2023). Why south-south trade is already greater than north-north trade, and what it means for Africa. In *Global economy and development*. Brookings Institution.

Owoeye, O. (2021, January 28). The right to development and its role in international economic law. *South Views*, *212*. South Centre.

Rodney, W. (2018 [1972]). *How Europe underdeveloped Africa*. Verso.

Tandon, Y. (2009). *Reflections and foresight on development and globalization: Daring to think different*. South Centre.

The Economist. (2020, July 24). The COVID–19 pandemic is forcing a rethink in macroeconomics.

UNCTAD. (2007). *Economic development in Africa. Recovering political space: Domestic resource mobilization and developmental state*. United Nations Trade and Development.

UNCTAD. (2018). *Forging a path beyond borders: The global south*. United Nations Trade and Development.

UNCTAD. (2020). *Economic development in africa report 2020: Tackling illicit financial flows for sustainable development in Africa*. United Nations Trade and Development.

UNCTAD. (2022). *Trade and development report 2022*. United Nations Trade and Development.

UNDP. (2022). *Human development report*. United Nations Development Programme.

UNECA. (2011). *Economic report on Africa. Governing development: Role of the state in economic transformation*. United Nations Economic Commission for Africa.

UNECA. (2013). *Economic report on Africa. Getting the most out of the African commodities: Industrialization for growth, employment and economic transformation*. United Nations Economic Commission for Africa.

UNECA. (2014). *Economic report on Africa: Dynamic industrial policy in Africa*. United Nations Economic Commission for Africa.

UNECA. (2015). *Illicit financial flows: Report of the high level panel on illicit financial flows from Africa*. Mbeki Panel. United Nations Economic Commission for Africa.

World Bank. (1981). *Accelerated development in Africa. An agenda for action*. Berg Report. The World Bank.

World Bank. (1989). *Sub–Saharan Africa: From crisis to sustainable development*. The World Bank.

Zoellick, R. B. (2010, September 29). *Democratizing development economics*. Speech at Georgetown University in Washington D.C.

POST-APARTHEID SOUTH AFRICA: A NEOLIBERAL DISASTER MADE AND IN THE MAKING

Seeraj Mohamed[a] and Ben Fine[b]

[a]*University of the Western Cape, South Africa*
[b]*SOAS University of London, UK*

ABSTRACT

In absolute terms, and relative to both hopes and potential, post-apartheid economic and social reproduction has been a disaster. A key element in explaining this is to situate it within an extraordinarily rapid and full adjustment, albeit with peculiar South African features in light of the heritage of apartheid, to neoliberal imperatives, properly understood. These do not involve the withdrawal of the State, as suggested by neoliberal ideology, but do include extensive State intervention to bring about globalization of production (and commodity relations more generally) and, in particular, the financialization of the economy. In a South African context, this has been associated with the unbundling of its (Mineral–Energy Complex) conglomerates, their integration with global capital, extensive expansion of the financial sector (together with capital flight, much of it illegal), the formation of new black elites, and State capture and centralized control for these purposes at the cost of economic and social functioning for the vast majority of those sections of the population already extremely disadvantaged under the apartheid system. The result more broadly has been to deliver what we term the five lows (of investment, productivity, wages, employment and provision of social and economic infrastructure). These evolving conditions, across their various aspects, and their association with the unravelling of effective progressive opposition for alternatives, are documented.

Keywords: Post-apartheid; South Africa; financialization; neoliberalism; Minerals-Energy Complex; black economic empowerment; state capture; conglomerate unbundling; globalization

Trajectories of Declining and Destructive Capitalism
Research in Political Economy, Volume 40, 141–167

Published under exclusive licence by Emerald Publishing Limited
ISSN: 0161-7230/doi:10.1108/S0161-723020250000040010

INTRODUCTION

Any new visitor to South Africa with an ounce of interest in its history is almost inevitably struck by its peculiarities, especially those inherited from the spatial segregation that remains an enduring legacy of apartheid with at most occasional fractures for a new black elite and burgeoning middle class. Otherwise, racial inequality is extreme but by no means unique to South Africa. This begs a question that deserves to be brought to the fore. Is it better to see 30 years of political liberation as the period of post-apartheid South Africa or as the period of neoliberalized South Africa? The pendulum of judgement has increasingly swung towards the latter. Indeed, it could be argued that referring back to the legacy of apartheid in explaining South Africa's trajectory over the past three decades obscures rather than illuminates the determining role played by its neoliberalization.

Such is argued in what follows beginning by laying out what exactly we mean by neoliberalism as the basis on which to explain the form it has taken in post-apartheid South Africa, which has left the legacy of the (economic and social) inequities of apartheid largely untouched if transformed in how they are ameliorated, if at all. The enduring role of South Africa's Minerals–Energy Complex (MEC) is vital, not least as it has been transformed by globalization, corporate restructuring (unbundling) and financialization. This has all given rise more broadly to what we term the five lows (of investment, productivity, wages, employment and provision of social and economic infrastructure) with government policy conforming to the dictates of neoliberalization at the expense of any coherent strategy for economic and social development other than to get by against the economic and social dysfunctions that it only serves itself to intensify. As Marx might have amended his quip, when it comes to South Africa, history repeats itself under each of apartheid and post-apartheid – the first time as tragedy and the second time as farce and disaster.

THE NEOLIBERAL CONDITION

It is 30 years since the post-apartheid era began. It has been disastrous in both absolute terms, as will be documented, and relative to aspirations and potential. The transition witnessed the most progressive of constitutions in terms of the people's rights and expectations. It also drew upon a dream ticket of alliance of trade unions and political parties, a vibrant civil society, their combination and unity in the struggle against apartheid, universal support and prestige on an international scale, and the most charismatic and lauded of leaders on the world stage. The South African transition, following upon that of the Soviet Union and the tragedy to which this has now led with the war with Ukraine/NATO (*North Atlantic Treaty Organisation*), has rapidly degenerated into a farce.

It is apt to recall the fears expressed by the lawyer, radical sociologist and anti-apartheid activist Harold Wolpe before his untimely death in 1996, that the ANC (African National Congress)'s embrace of social democracy might preclude the struggle for socialism unless the capitalist state were radically transformed.[1] Instead of degenerating into social democracy – we should be so lucky – the present take on South Africa is widely understood in terms of state capture and rampant corruption, with neoliberal postures already being embraced prior to the ANC assuming (national unity) government. Unity within and across the tripartite alliance of ANC, COSATU (*Congress of South African Trade Unions*) and the CPSA (*Communist Party of South Africa*) has subsequently acceleratingly unravelled. The extraordinary prestige of the ANC, as the bearer of liberation and as reflected in electoral success, has evaporated with failure at lower levels of government and the growing prospects of the need for a coalition government at national level, following those at lower tiers.

Whilst the speed of this degeneration is startling, it has not occurred in a vacuum. Globalization and neoliberalization long preceded the transition, and the Asian crisis of 1997–1998 and the Global Financial Crisis (GFC) of 2007–2008 marked instabilities that would necessarily impact upon, and be internalized within, South Africa to a greater or lesser extent, as would the continuing rise of China. The transition has in part been sandwiched between the HIV/AIDS and COVID-19 pandemics, accompanied by increasing and unavoidable, if reluctant, attention to environmental crises. Nor has our conceptual world stood still. Postmodernisms and their progenies have more than left their mark, but they have become displaced by a material turn, albeit married with, not marred by, an integral cultural content, with attention to 'financialization' experiencing a meteoric rise across the social sciences (with the notable exception of mainstream economics where it ill fits but is most needed) alongside attention to economic and social reproduction and intersectionalities.

To get our heads around these developments, and their application to South Africa, is as challenging as it is liable to be contested. As an entry point, not least because many see it as the original sin that marked the disastrous post-apartheid trajectory, we begin with neoliberalism. This has been subject to a vast and rewarding literature across many of its aspects (Fine & Saad-Filho, 2016). But these often have three drawbacks.

First is in pointing, for example, to assaults on working people, austerity and other aspects of capitalism that are not unique to the current period but are continual and even endemic across the history of capitalism. Second, they do not stand up to empirical scrutiny especially in the relationship between neoliberal ideology and policy practices (in our view, neoliberalism is profoundly interventionist). Third, neoliberalism does not tend to be grounded in its understanding as a stage of capitalism with its own unique features of economic and social reproduction.

Our own take on these conundrums is to understand neoliberalism as the contemporary stage of capitalism underpinned by, but not reducible to, financialization. Economic and social reproduction has been increasingly marked, and remarked, by the role of finance. In retrospect, given the burgeoning literature on financialization across the social sciences and corresponding topics, this is to push against an open analytical door. Everything from globalization to everyday life has been reconstructed in terms of 'financialization'. By the same token, the term has taken on multiple empirical and analytical meanings, from the mere presence of monetary motives even in the absence of money to the speculative activities of trading in carbon futures.[2] Especially popular is the idea of making profit without making anything. Our own understanding of financialization (as opposed to its consequences and implications with which it is often conflated) is that it involves the securitization of prospective streams of revenues that can then be traded as financial assets and also form the basis for the creation of further financial assets. As such, this is not a new point of departure for capitalism but its intensive and extensive expansion (in terms of assets and the activities to which they are attached) is a defining feature of the current period – with mortgages representing a most prominent but far from unique example. Or, to give another example, it is not the expansion of credit (cards) as such that is financialization but the speculation in the debt obligations to which such credit arrangements give rise. And so the examples could go on and on.

But we also find it useful, if not imperative, to understand neoliberalism as having gone through three phases, each of which has implicitly been acknowledged. The first is the shock therapies of the Thatcher–Reagan period, in which privatization, commercialization and austerity were to the fore as well as liberalization in the functioning of financial markets. The second, neatly misrepresented by the notion of Third Wayism, has in part been focused upon addressing, if not redressing, the dysfunctions attached to shock therapy, but with the state continuing to underpin the promotion of financialization. And the third, and current phase, has been marked by increasingly overt collaboration between the state, private capital and finance to forge policies to renew and sustain accumulation, preceding but especially in response to the GFC. It has, for example, given rise to what is termed the new, or revival of industrial policy, and it is reflected in the increasing role of private capital in social provision through access to state funding, as with Public–Private Partnerships.[3]

While these phases of neoliberalism have a sequential history, they are equally logically sequential: the first phase involves an enhanced role of financialization in accumulation and the restructuring of capital, its economic reproduction, most notably through privatization; the second extends it to new areas of social provision through commercialization; and the third phase integrates it across economic and social reproduction. The first two phases tend to be perceived as involving state withdrawal in line with neoliberal ideology, but this is incorrect not least because the state's interventions remain extensive if attuned to the needs of private capital in general and of finance in particular. The third phase, because the state's interventions in liaison with capital are more overt, especially in wake of crises and support to private capital and, usually temporarily, social assistance, are even perceived to signal the end of neoliberalism as opposed to its intensification with extensive support for, and renewal of, financialization.

Given the scale and scope of presence and influence of financialization in practice, it is hardly surprizing that the literature on it has become conceptually amorphous and increasingly extensive.[4] The single most important conclusion from the heavy weight of empirical studies is to point unambiguously to its dysfunctional effects.[5] Financialization means lower investment, productivity, wages, employment (and higher unemployment), more and deeper crises, greater inequality, lower social services, more austerity, lesser democracy, and so on. Such generalizations are, however, unwarranted, otherwise we are unable to explain what has been termed the political economy of excesses, beginning with the financial sector itself. But, for sequences of revenues to be securitized and to provide the foundation for profit and interest, production must take place as is most obvious in the realm of energy and environmental crises – if also for food in which the world is now characterized by as many malnourished through over-eating as nutritional deprivation (Bayliss & Fine, 2021).

Unsurprisingly, the dependence of neoliberalism upon financialization has effects far beyond economic reproduction. In brief:

- First and foremost is the rise or strengthening of financial interests.
- Second is that the imperatives of financial interests lead to the marginalization, other than for incorporation and control, of other interests. This not only is especially so of labour movement representation but also extends to other (progressive) civil society organizations.
- Third, separately but closely related, policy itself is increasingly centralized and concentrated (although responsibilities for delivery can be devolved/ decentralized without the resources and powers to deliver).
- Fourth, with the rise and corporate control of popular and social media, in the context of both variegated and volatile vulnerabilities and limited means through which otherwise to express let alone engage in remedial activism for much of the population, politics has a tendency itself to be volatile, subject to swings and open to capture, primarily in populist and authoritarian forms but also with significant if generally temporary gains for progressive movements depending upon the extent of their own organizational strengths and stabilities.

THE MEC IS DEAD, LONG LIVE THE MEFC

There is tendency in scholarship and popular discourse to designate a policy, policies and national orientations as becoming more, or possibly less, neoliberal. This has some descriptive validity but it can also be misleading insofar as neoliberalism, as a stage of capitalism, situates the formation and implementation of policy rather than offering a set of standards against which it is judged. A striking example is the massive increases in housing benefit across Europe for those who have become unable to afford private rents, let alone, become homeowners through mortgaging.[6] Such safety nets (an apparent breach with neoliberalism through increase in welfare expenditure) is the condition for sustaining the financialization of housing provision, and mortgages, in which the net effect is to transfer the benefits to landlords, builders and mortgage providers.

A similar situation, with the extending of safety nets to the unemployed and impoverished to maintain financialization of the economy, has played out in South Africa. The maintenance and grudging extension of social grants has been shown to be necessary for the government and big businesses to maintain the highly unequal financialized economy. The ability of big business to continue extracting wealth and rents from an economy unable to address massive structural unemployment has required the extension of social grants, including a Social Relief of Distress (SRD) grant introduced in 2020 during the COVID-19 pandemic. The SRD grant is the first social grant to be introduced to working age South Africans (other than disability grants).

The government has pursued an 'austerity' approach to fiscal policy since the adoption of the Growth Employment and Redistribution (GEAR) programme in 1996.[7] Frustration is continually expressed with regard to the level of government expenditure on basic services, the child support grant and the old age grants. During the pandemic, the Minister of Finance emphasized that the fiscal policy framework would pursue a budget surplus through continuing with a fiscal consolidation approach that had been implemented since 2012. When the SRD grant was introduced, he stressed that the ZAR350 (rands) SRD grant would be temporary. However, due to the very high and increasing levels of structural unemployment, poverty and inequality, the government has been forced to extend the SRD grant (doing so in one-year periods) since 2021, despite not intending to do so.

Indeed, the government hastily reintroduced the SRD grant in 2021 after the violent protests and social unrest (including rioting and looting) in KwaZulu–Natal and Gauteng Provinces from 9 to 18 July 2021. The spark for the unrest was the arrest of former President Jacob Zuma on contempt of court charges on July 7. This triggered massive levels of social unrest at a time when the pandemic had increased suffering and hardship in already food insecure, impoverished communities. The official (narrow) unemployment rate in KwaZulu–Natal Province increased from 26.9% in the first-quarter of 2020 to 30.5% in the first-quarter of 2021 and, for the non-metro areas of the Province, the annual increase was from 30.4% to 37.2%. The official (narrow) unemployment rate for Gauteng Province increased from 31.4% in the first-quarter of 2020 to 34.4% in the first-quarter of 2021 and for the non-metro areas of the Province the annual increase was from 30.0% in to 30.2%.[8]

The unrest led to communal violence and vigilantism with racial profiling by some business owners and residents of more affluent suburbs that had set up self-defence units. It is estimated that 337 people died during the unrest and 3,400 were arrested on allegations of inciting public violence, murder, arson and looting, Gounden (2021). The latter also reports from the South African Property Association estimates that the damage to property and businesses during the nine days of unrest exceeded ZAR50 billion. One hundred and sixty-one Malls were damaged, 3,000 stores were looted, including 161 liquor outlets, and 11 warehouses and 8 factories were considerably damaged. Manufacturing, mining, agriculture and transport (including rail and ports) sectors were also affected by looting, damage, arson and disruption of businesses and traffic.[9]

The unrest was a devastating blow to the messaging by South African government and big business that South Africa had become a rainbow nation that had unified behind efforts to eradicate the pandemic and rebuild the economy. It showed the depths of the intersecting class and racial divisions caused by levels of inequality that are the highest in the world and that Palma (2019, p. 23) classifies as 'obscene'. The reinstatement of the SRD grant in 2021 showed up differences within the Cabinet (for example, between the Social Security and the Finance Ministries). These differences remain evident with the Department of Social Development publicly making the case for a basic income grant (BIG), a proposal the ANC-led government rejected in 2002, and the reluctance of the National Treasury to expand further public expenditure and the social security system.

Against this vignette of social provisioning, and there could be many more with their idiosyncrasies, how is South Africa situated in terms of neoliberalism as a stage of capitalism, and with what consequences? First, as argued at the time of transition, the South African economy had long been dominated by what has been termed its MEC (Fine & Rustomjee, 1997). The MEC system of accumulation was based on large mining finance houses coordinating the extraction of mineral wealth while maintaining a system of cheap black migrant labour with support from the apartheid government. In a breathtaking nutshell, the MEC arose historically out of the development of a core set of sectors in and around mining but was dominated by foreign as opposed to Afrikaner capital whose interests commanded political power. Large Afrikaner business groups had largely been built with government support and access to retirement savings of Afrikaner workers.

However, a two-fold process brought about the integration of English and Afrikaner South African corporate interests around the MEC by the end of the 1960s. On the one hand, large-scale Afrikaner capital in and around mining was created, increasingly cooperating with its erstwhile counterpart. On the other hand, this involved the creation of large-scale state enterprises to serve their needs, not least for electricity, steel and transport. These developments were also accompanied by the extensive reliance upon both foreign sources of finance but also those that were home-grown.

During the 1970s, the MEC across both its private- and State-owned wings grew prodigiously, not least as a result of the meteoric rise in the prices of gold, energy and other minerals. It led to the strengthening of what were dubbed mining houses although a handful came to dominate ownership of productive capacity across the entire economy. The mineral boom, followed by the growing crisis of apartheid itself, meant that diversification out of the productive strengths of the economy, into capital, intermediate and consumption goods remained constrained just as it had been during the earlier disjuncture between economic and political power. In addition, economic controls during the apartheid crisis tended to insulate the South African economy from its globalized, neoliberal integration.

In this sense, the idea that the post-apartheid economy became neoliberal, as a result of the policies adopted, has some purchase. It informs criticism as well as defence of the policies adopted (as a necessity in light of the power of international capital). Moreover, the original sin of succumbing to neoliberalism is then seen to be compounded by what is now referred to as state capture, brought on by the Zuma Presidency.

We see things differently, with the neoliberalization of South Africa involving making up for lost time through the speed of adoption of the features of the three phases of neoliberalism in overlapping tandem with one another, alongside particular South African features. In a sense, insofar as it was ever free to be captured, state capture to the imperatives and forms of all three phases of neoliberalism were embraced almost immediately upon the ANC assuming power even if they took a more extreme turn under Zuma (something that is itself typical of, if not unique to, neoliberalism).

In these terms:

- First of all, it has been the global restructuring of the MEC. The former conglomerates have been unbundled into their constituent sectoral activities and integrated into globally organized productive enterprises.
- Second, this has been part and parcel of the financialization of the economy, appropriately renaming the MEC as the Mineral–Energy–Finance Complex (MEFC) (not least as finance has been the fastest growing sector in the economy, putatively contributing 20% of GDP).
- Third, at most, developmental plans for economic and social development have been renewed again and again, generally with limited ambition and neoliberal tinges, never implemented nor reviewed, with the Treasury and the Presidency centralizing policy control and authority.[10]
- Fourth, what has been ambitious and, in a sense, successful has been so-called Black Economic Empowerment (BEE), the creation of a fraction of elite black capitalists primarily drawing their wealth out of the global, financialized restructuring of the MEC and/or favourable access to state contracts.
- Last, and by no means least, South Africa has been particularly marked by (illegal) capital flight. At times, it has been estimated to be as reaching more than 20% of GDP, higher than levels of investment, Ashman et al. (2013).[11] This has created a dynamic in which long-term outflows are sustained through high interest rate flows of short-term capital, conducive both to financial instability and costly credit.

These features indicate why the legion dysfunctions associated with neoliberalism should have been intensified in the South African context through BEE and capital flight. It also explains why the favourable aspects prevailing at the outset of the transition should have been so rapidly wasted. In what follows, we focus in particular and in turn on what might be designated as the five lows characterizing the South African economy:

- There is low investment as a result of financialization in general and capital flight in particular, falling as much as 50% below what is essential for economic and social development and despite a sophisticated financial system and high levels of financial activity.
- Second is a correspondingly low level of productivity increase with
- Third, knock-on implications for levels of wages.

- Fourth is low levels of employment (and high unemployment).
- Fifth are low levels of investment and provisioning in economic and social infrastructure, ranging over housing, health and education to meeting the requirements of a just energy transition across the most unequal and (fossil fuel) energy-intensive economy in the world.

First Is Low Investment[12]

There is low investment as a result of financialization in general and capital flight. The negative impact of finance on South Africa's industrial development and building a deeper and more diversified manufacturing sector existed before the neoliberal era, underpinned by financialization. The sophisticated financial sector developed from the imperial banks aligned with the English mining finance houses, the Afrikaner financial corporations that developed as part of the Afrikaner nationalist movement and state development finance institutions. The English financial institutions had close ties to English and US financial institutions and the Afrikaner financial sector had close ties to European finance.

The financial system that developed during the 20th century was one where the banks generally were little involved in financing productive investment. A market-based financial sector developed where the stock market was the major source of investment finance for big businesses. This type of financial sector placed much power in the hands of pension funds and other institutional investors, which owned a large portion of the shares listed and traded on the Johannesburg Stock Exchange (JSE) (Mohamed, 2014). The privately owned financial institutions, which were part of, or aligned to, larger diversified corporations (many of which were family-owned groups) played a large role in the allocation of capital, including extraction of capital offshore.[13] Lewis (1991) found evidence of collusions amongst the conglomerates that dominated most of the markets of the economy. He asserted that by the 1990s, the life assurance corporations were playing an outsized role in allocating capital in the South African economy, with their conservative investment criteria favouring blue chip stocks of the conglomerates.[14] Mondliwa and Roberts (2019) explain that maintenance of long-term rights and regulatory access during the post-apartheid period explains why the subsidiaries of conglomerates that dominated the economy during the 1980s (and unbundled during the 1990s) continue to dominate most subsectors of the economy. This is particularly true of financial corporations. Ashman et al. (2013) provide an overview of how different sectors of the South African economy, including households, have become increasingly financialized since the 1990s through more intensive and extensive use of financial activities and instruments.

South Africa has had low average gross fixed capital formation (GFCF) as a percentage of GDP throughout the post-apartheid period (Fig. 1). It was 16.5% from 1990 to 2021 compared to the average GFCF as percentages of GDP from 1990 to 2021 for the world of 24.2%, 27.3% for middle-income countries and 27.7% for upper middle-income countries.[15] The average level of investment as a percentage of GDP provides a strong indicator of inadequate investment.

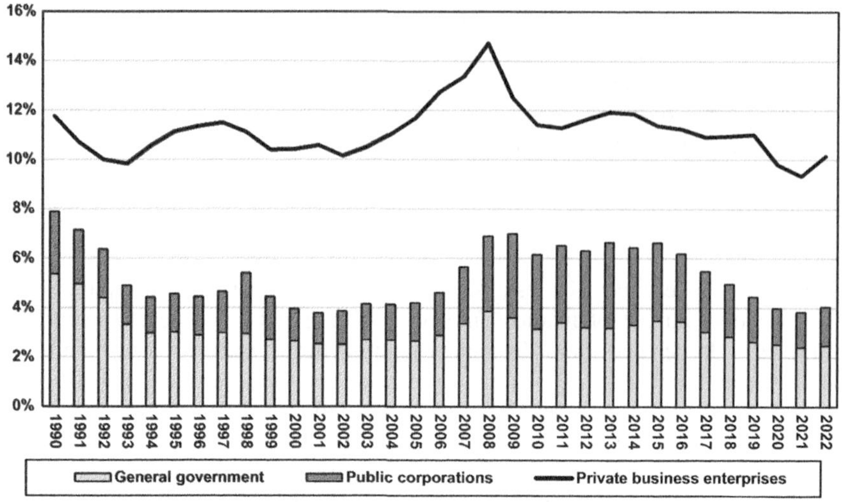

Fig. 1. Gross Fixed Capital Formation by Government, Public Corporations and Private Business Enterprises (as Percentages of GDP). *Source:* Authors' calculations on South African Reserve Bank (SARB) data. https://www.resbank.co.za/en/home/what-we-do/statistics/releases/online-statistical-query. Accessed on November 26, 2023.

Consideration of where investment occurred taking into account the MEFC provides deeper insight into the structural problems of the South African economy. The restructuring of these large private- and state-owned corporations, and their financialization, is evident in the pattern of investment and the formation of capital stock in the economy.

Zalk (2021, pp. 32–33) shows that profitability of South African corporations has not been low and, therefore, does not explain the relatively low levels of investment in South Africa. He does find that relative sectoral profitability has been an important factor affecting relative investment levels across different economic sectors. He examines the period from 1994 to 2019 and concludes that the sectors with the highest net industry markups were service sectors with limited tradability. He also finds that heavy industries performed better and invested more during the period when mineral prices boomed. Diversified and higher value-adding manufacturing sectors had the lowest net industry markups.

Fig. 2 shows real GFCF by sector and supports Zalk's views. Real investment by the services sectors and investment by MEC-related industrial sectors have been higher than GFCF for non-MEC non-services sectors. Real GFCF in services sectors, which is much larger than real GFCF for non-services sectors, increased from ZAR 240 bn in 2002 to peak at ZAR 488 bn in 2008 (Fig. 3). This period is notable because it leads up to the GFC, when there were surges of short-term foreign capital (particularly portfolio flows) into the South African economy and (to some extent and associated) marked increases in domestic credit extension to the private sector, see below for details.

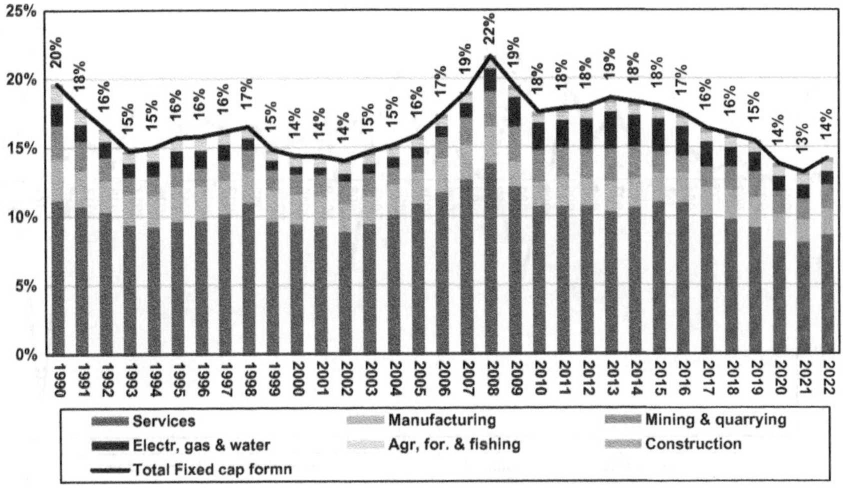

Fig. 2. Gross Fixed Capital Formation by Sector (as Percentages of GDP). *Source:* Authors' calculations on Quantec's South African Industry Indicators (QSAII). https://www.quantec.co.za/easydata/. Accessed on August 26, 2024, similarly for later tables.

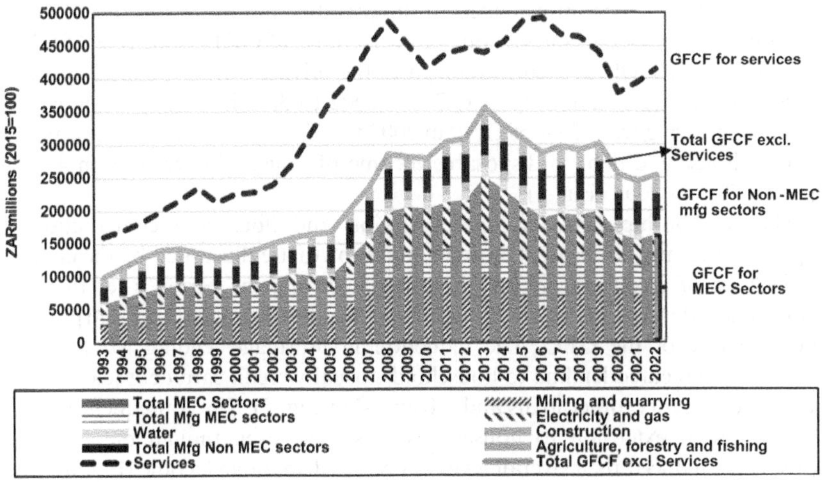

Fig. 3. Real Gross Fixed Capital Formation by Sector Showing MEC and Non-MEC Industrial Sectors (ZAR Millions, 2015 = 100). *Source:* Authors' calculations. See Fig. 2.

Net portfolio flows as a percentage of GDP were −0.2% in 2002; 2 years later it was 2.4%; by 2006 it reached 6.3%; and in 2008 as a result of the GFC it had collapsed to −5.2%.[16] The total credit extended by all monetary institutions to

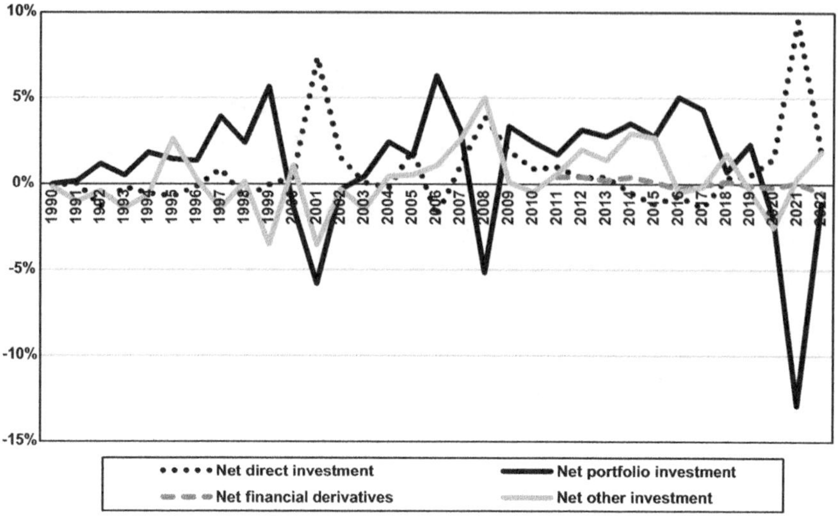

Fig. 4. Net Foreign Capital Flows (as Percentages of GDP). *Source:* Authors' calculations. See Fig. 1.

the private sector exploded from 53% of GDP in 2002 to 76% in 2008. During 2002 to 2008, when credit extended to the private sector grew by 24% of GDP, investment by private businesses only grew by 4.5% of GDP, from 10.2% in 2002 to 14.7% in 2008. Of the credit extended to the private sector, the total extended to households grew from 25% of GDP in 2002 to 38% in 2008, with mortgage advances growing from 25% of GDP in 2002 to 37% in 2008.[17] During this period average household debt to disposable income of households grew from 47% in 2002 to 78% in 2008 (Fig. 4).

The relationship between financialization and household contribution to aggregate demand, levels of investment and growth are illustrated by the changes in the type of credit extended to households during the period after the 2008 GFC. The extension of credit through mortgage lending decreased sharply after 2008 because of the GFC. The reduction in mortgage lending led to banks increasing unsecured lending to households, usually credit card debt (categorized under the category 'other loans and advances' in Fig. 5). The consequence of this shift in credit extension to households was that, even though on aggregate households reduced their overall level of debt to disposable income (Fig. 6), their debt service costs to disposable income did not decrease and their savings to disposable income generally remained close to 0% (South African Reserve Bank [SARB] data from 2008 to 2023).

On average, South African households that do have access to credit seemed to be paying off their debt, which constrained their consumption expenditure. Given that household consumption has generally been around 60% (and investment and government expenditure has been low), one can see why GDP growth per capita

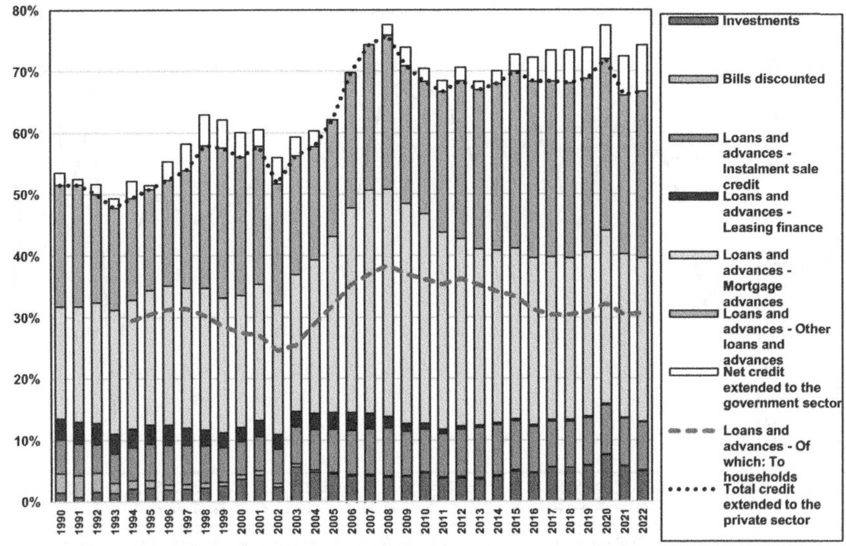

Fig. 5. Credit Extension by all Monetary Institutions (as Percentages of GDP). *Source:* Authors' calculations. See Fig. 1.

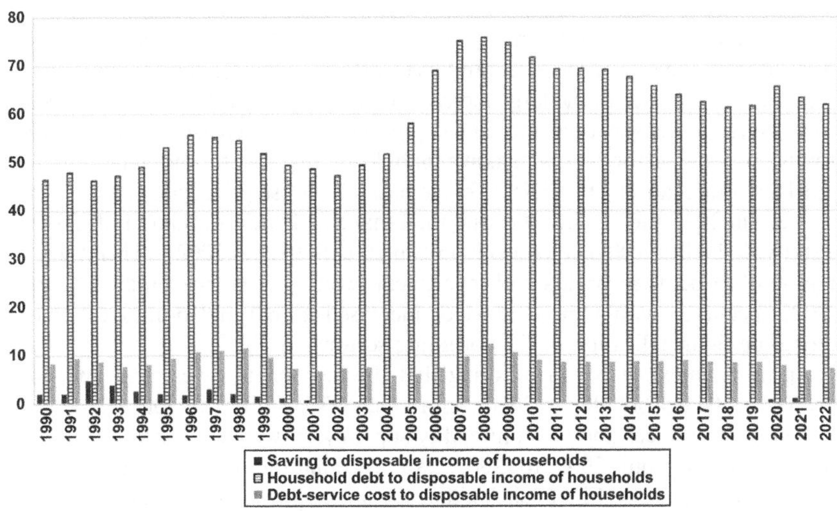

Fig. 6. Household Debt, Savings and Debt Service Costs (as Percentages of Household Disposable Income). *Source:* Authors' calculations. See Fig. 1.

has declined every year since 2013 (except for the bounce back in 2021 from the large decline caused by the pandemic in 2020). Real GDP per capital in 2022 was lower than it was in 2008 (Fig. 7).

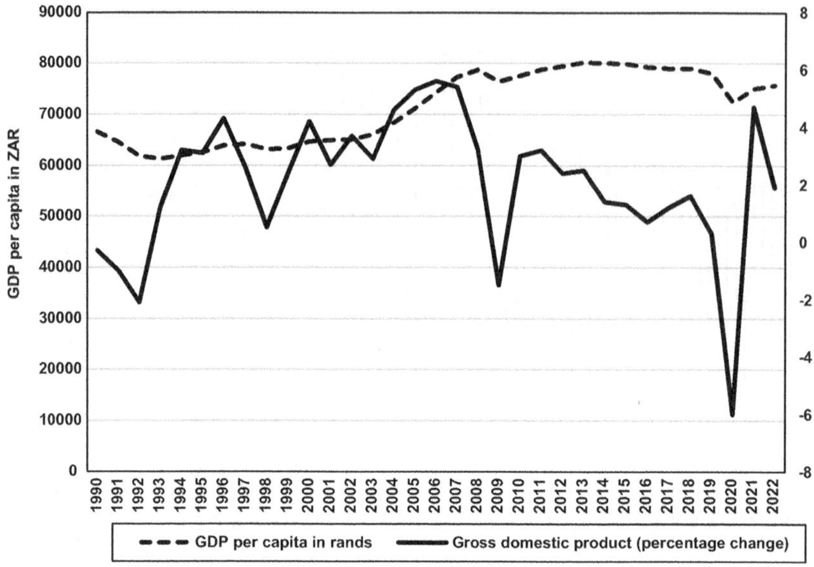

Fig. 7. Real GDP per Capita in Rands and Percentage Change in Real GDP. *Source:* Authors' calculations. See Fig. 1.

Our analysis links investment performance to the structural weaknesses derived from the role of the MEC and its transformation into the MEFC. We find that the consequence of the large increase in liquidity in the financial markets due to the surge in net short-term foreign capital flows and increased credit extension to the private sector was a massive bubble in real estate and financial asset markets. For example, the FNB average national house price index (2000 = 100) was 119 in 2002 and 323 in 2008, and the Financial Times All Share Index for the JSE (with 2010 = 100) surged from 36.1 in 2002 to 98.9 in 2008.[18] Therefore, the relationship between profits and investment levels in sectors identified by Zalk (2021) occurred within the context of increased global and domestic liquidity alongside financialization of the corporate sector.

In this context, it is worth noting that the increase in investment and GDP growth in the period 2002 to 2008, before the GFC, is often attributed to the rise in commodity prices and the commodity super cycle, which is generally accepted to have been from 2003 to 2007. An examination of the South African value-added data (see Fig. 8) shows that the larger growth in value added was in the service sectors, with their share of total value added growing from 50.9% in 2002 to 53.8% in 2007, while the share of value added by mining as a percentage of total value added was 5.9% in 2002, declining to 5.0% in 2003 and 2004 and recovering to 6.0% by 2007 (real value added for mining and quarrying was ZAR 230 bn in 2023 and peaked at ZAR 236 bn in 2007) (Fig. 8).

The combined share of total exports of mineral products, precious metals and products of iron and steel increased from 55.9% in 2003 to 60.9% in 2007 (Fig. 9).

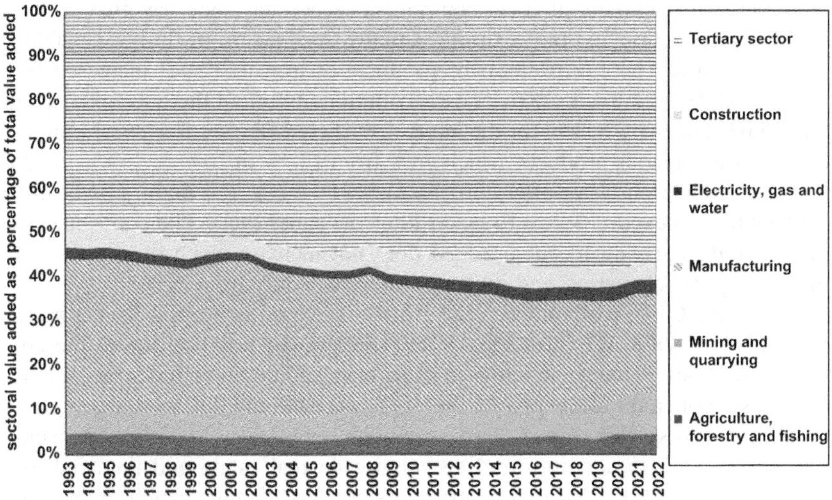

Fig. 8. Contributions to Total Value Added of Different Economic Sectors (Percentages). *Source:* Authors' calculations. See Fig. 2.

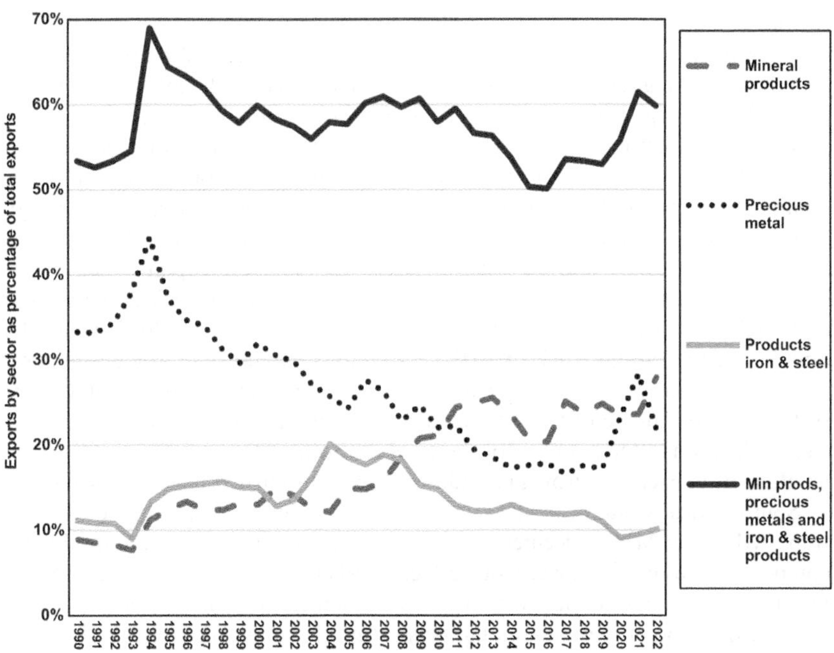

Fig. 9. Mining and Minerals Exports as Percentages of Total Exports (Percentages). *Source:* Authors' calculation. See Fig. 2.

However, when looking at these components separately, one sees that precious metal's contribution to total exports actually declined from 27.1% in 2003 to 26.3% in 2007. The contribution of products of iron and steel increased from 16.2% in 2003 to 18.8% in 2007. The contribution of both of these sectors declined after 2007. The main reason for the increase of these MEC sectors' contribution to exports was minerals products, which grew from 12.3% in 2003 to 15.8% in 2007, and then grew even faster after 2007 to 25.5% by 2013. The main growth in the contribution to exports seems to occur after the super-cycle. The contribution of mining and quarrying to value added does not increase much during the commodity super-cycle period and increases above 6% only from 2008.

Before the GFC, real annual GDP growth increased to around 5% per annum from 2004 to 2007. We have shown that this growth was not due to the commodity super-cycle but to increases in short-term capital flows and large increases in extension of credit to the private sector. The growth in GDP was largely due to value added in service sectors, associated with debt-driven household consumption and growth in activities and speculation in real estate and financial asset markets. But the GFC led to a reversal in short-term foreign capital inflows and large reductions in credit extension. The earlier economic growth was not sustainable, was brought up short, and the overall trajectory of growth, investment and employment has been negative since the GFC. The main impact of the downturn was on non-services sectors, particularly the non-MEC manufacturing sectors.

Overall, the poor levels of investment on the structure and capacity of the economy can be gauged by comparing capital stocks of different sectors in 1993 and 2022 (see Fig. 10). Over 85% of the change in capital stock for that period was from five sectors: the financial intermediation, insurance and business services sector, general government, electricity gas and water, transport, storage and communications, and community, social and personal services. The largest increase in capital stock was from the FIIREBS sector (financial intermediation, insurance, real estate and business services). In 1993, the capital stock of real estate activities was 77% and in 2023 it was 74%. The capital stock of the FII part of FIIREBS (financial intermediation, insurance) was 19% in 2023, which left only 7% of the capital stock of FIIREBS sector's capital stock for business services. The share of the increase in capital stock for the entire manufacturing sector as a percentage of the total change in capital stock was a miserly 3.4%, a clear indication of the poor performance of the South African economy in general let alone its capacity to grow and industrialize on its current manufacturing base.

South Africa is often classified with countries suffering from a 'middle-income trap' (MIT). An MIT is deemed to occur when a country's wages are too high to compete in markets for lower value-added goods but is also unable to compete in producing goods and services with higher value added. If applicable in general, this begs the question of why this should be so. And the application of this characterization to South Africa in particular usually fails to discuss the country's economic structure, the levels of market concentration, (illegal) capital flight and the impacts of financialization. The South African conglomerates began unbundling and restructuring during the 1990s. The Anglo America Corporation (AAC), which during the

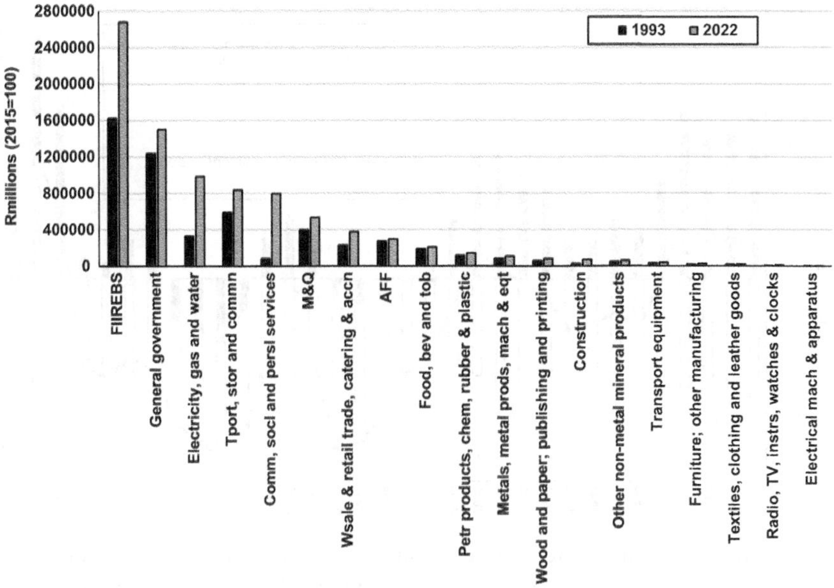

Fig. 10. Comparison of Real Value of Capital Stock for Economic Sectors for 1993 and 2022 (ZAR Millions, 2016 = 100). *Source:* Authors' calculation. See Fig. 2.

1980s controlled over 50% of the market capitalization of the JSE, was a highly diversified conglomerate with interests across almost every sector of the South African economy, including finance, agriculture, forestry, mining, manufacturing, retailing and media. The South African government allowed AAC and some of the other largest South African corporations to move their primary listings abroad, including Old Mutual, Billiton and South African Breweries. The impact of these offshore listings has been felt in the growth of the contribution of outward financial transfers on the current account of the balance of payments.

As a result, the South African economy is in a vulnerable situation given the payments of dividends and repatriation of profits by foreign owners of South African companies, and stocks and bonds are important drivers of the current account balance. Fig. 9 shows that while the country has had a positive trade balance for most of the period 1990 to 2003, the balance on the current account overall has been positive only during the early 1990s (1990–1994) and during 2001 and 2002 (at the time of the Dotcom crash in the United States), and during the Covid-19 pandemic and associated economic crisis.

The consequences are that, first, South Africa has to attract financial flows into the country. Since most of these have been in the form of short-term capital flows, classified as portfolio and other flows, policy has been to raise interest rates (particularly when outflows have resulted in a weaker rand to dollar exchange

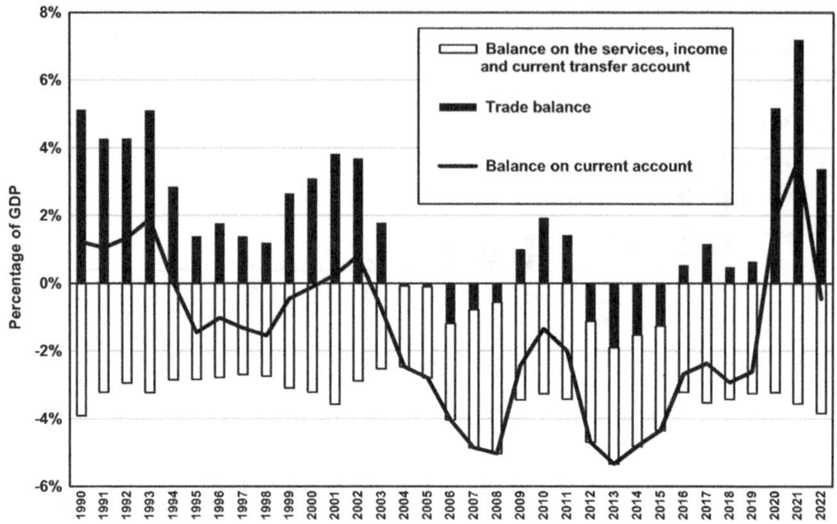

Fig. 11. Current Account: Comparing Trade Balance and Financial Transfers on Current Account (Percentages of GDP). *Source:* Authors' calculation. See Fig. 2.

rate) so that inflows of short-term capital can offset the outward financial transfers on the current account (Fig. 11) (on top of longer-term capital outflows).

Second, South African manufacturing relies on imported capital equipment and intermediate goods. The balance of payments has been identified (including within the government's GEAR document) as a constraint on economic growth and expansion of the manufacturing sector because increased demand for manufactured goods leads to trade deficits and increased pressure on the balance of payments. The scale of financial transfers out of the country is, therefore, a binding constraint on the balance of payments and expansion of investment, consolidating what are already structural weaknesses in diversifying out of increasing dependence on mining and low value-added minerals exports. The dysfunctional model of using short-term capital inflows to fund capital flight, and the adoption of policies in a pinch to allow for it through austerity and higher interest rates, reinforces low levels of investment and corresponding consequences for economic and social performance more generally.

Second Is Low Levels of Productivity Increase With, Third, Knock-On Implications for Levels of Wages

The structure of the economy has been skewed towards services with more output from lower productivity sectors. Manufacturing capital stock is concentrated in energy and capital-intensive sectors with strong linkages that export relatively low value-added products. This situation has been exacerbated by financialization, and the misallocation of capital to services sectors that benefited from

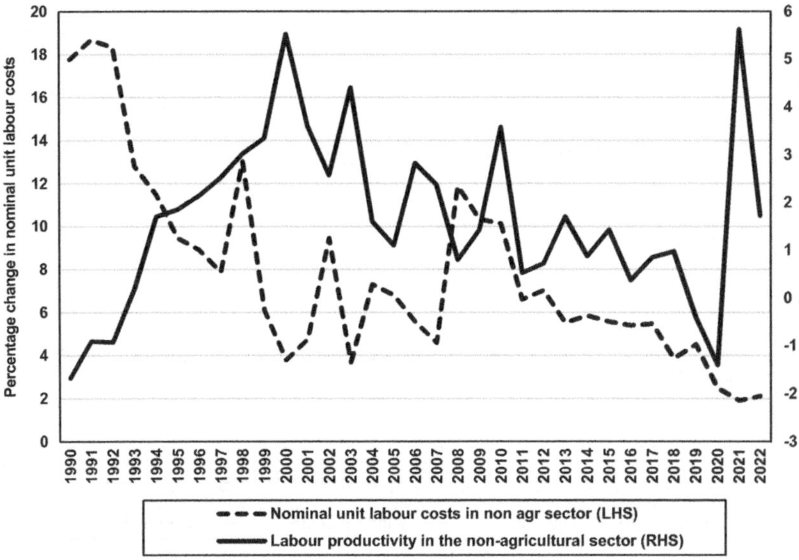

Fig. 12. Annual Percent Change in Labour Productivity and Nominal Unit Labour Cost in the Non-agricultural Sector. *Source:* Authors' calculations. See Fig. 2.

increased debt-driven consumption and speculation in real estate and financial assets before the GFC. The unsurprising result has been declining productivity growth and associated decline in unit labour costs (Fig. 12).

Fourth Is Low Levels of Employment (and High Unemployment)

South Africa's rate of unemployment is so high it is an outlier when compared to the rest of the world (Fig. 13).

Employment in the services sector has grown but much of this growth has been in precarious employment and has been due to outsourcing, casualization and informalization of the South African labour market.[19] The increase in employment that was not precarious in services was growth in government employment. This mainly occurred after 2002 when the government mistakenly attributed the rising economic growth in South Africa to their neoliberal economic policies. They were able to increase government spending while maintaining low deficit and debt to GDP ratios because of economic growth. The expansion in government employment, which had been constrained for almost a decade after the democratic elections, indicated an expectation that increased growth (and corresponding levels of government revenue) was more or less automatic. Such blind optimism continued to prevail after the GFC, with the presumption that growth would bounce back, even though growth had been debt-driven, with bubbles in

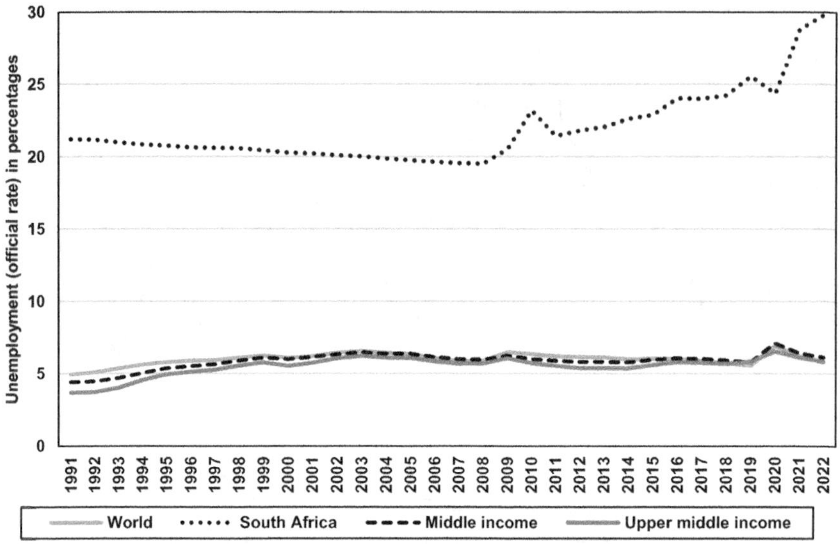

Fig. 13. Unemployment Rates for the World, Middle-Income, Upper-Middle Income Countries and South Africa (Percentages). *Source:* Authors' calculations on World Development Indicators (WDI), World Bank (1991–2022). https://databank.worldbank.org/source/world-development-indicators. Accessed on August 26, 2023.

real estate and financial asset prices. The government, then, implemented fiscal consolidation, i.e., austerity, halting its own increases in employees.

The increase in employment from 2003 meant a large increase in more secure jobs for black South Africans in government and a large addition to the growth of the black middle class (Fig. 14). It is worth remembering that these workers would have been part of the debt-driven consumption frenzy (including homes and cars) that occurred in South Africa in the few years before the GFC. By 2016 the government was blaming the public sector wage bill for low government expenditure on social and economic investments and provision of basic services.

The corresponding rhetoric of cutting public sector wages and salaries, with fears of retrenchments, has created uncertainty and instability in a relatively powerful group of workers. These workers have been rounded up under the broad brush of accusations of corruption, the beneficiaries of state capture, and the reason for the failures of Eskom and other SOEs even though much of the problems related to corruption and state capture can be dated back to the transition and early days of the post-apartheid government. The early adoption of neoliberal fiscal policies and austerity led to inadequate investment in state capacity and maintenance and expansion of infrastructure. Overall, though, it is the failure to create employment other than in government, and not in manufacturing in particular, that is so striking within South Africa, intensifying the extraordinarily high levels of unemployment (see Fig. 15).

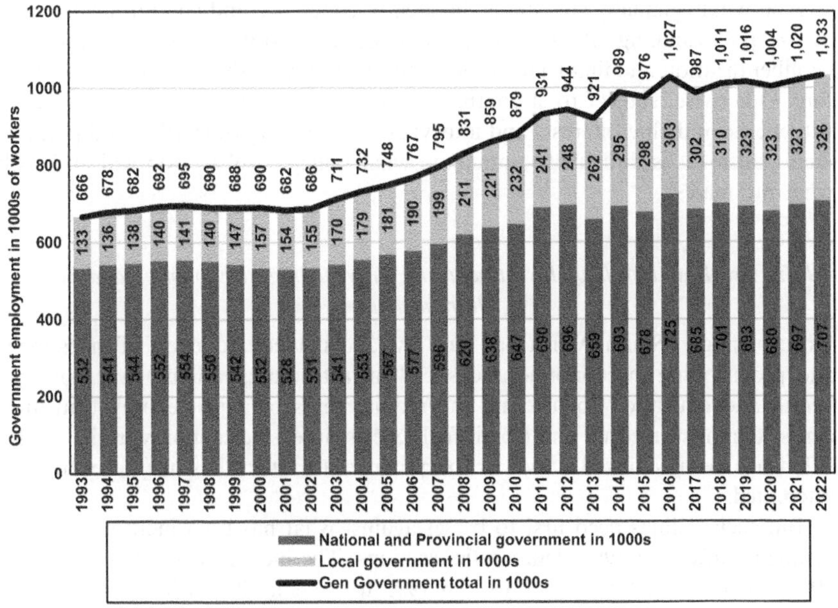

Fig. 14. General Government Employment. *Source:* Authors' calculations. See Fig. 2.

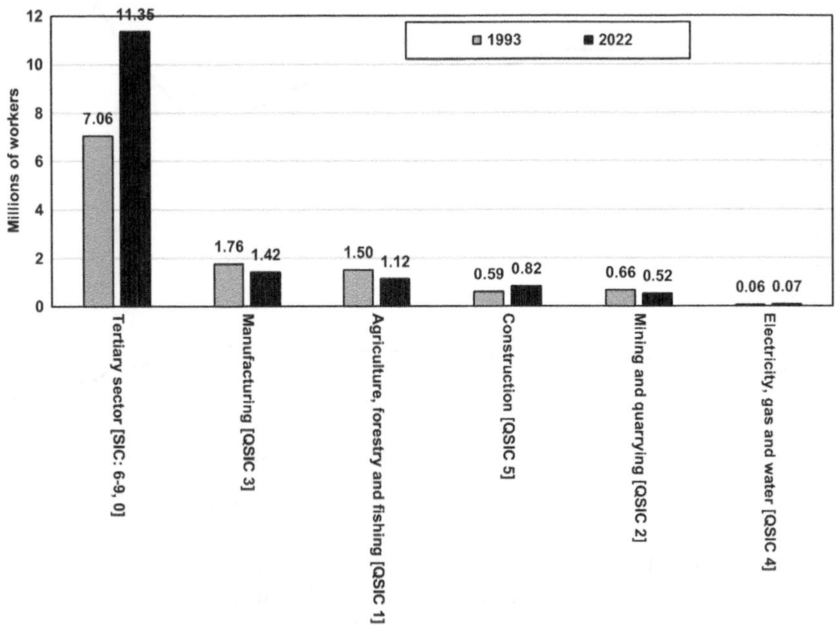

Fig. 15. Employment Across Economic Sectors (Millions of Workers). *Source:* Authors' calculations. See Fig. 2.

And what is equally striking is the lack of coherence and commitment in and across policymaking other than to manage and prioritize the globalization, neoliberalization and financialization of the economy, with its MEFC core to the fore. Otherwise, subject to strength, organization and leverage of political constituencies, and elite interests and idiosyncrasies deriving from BEE and political factionalism, it is difficult to anticipate what policies will be adopted and with what rationales.

Fifth Are Low Levels of Investment and Provisioning in Economic and Social Infrastructure

Unsurprisingly, South Africa has had low and inadequate levels of investment and provisioning in economic and social infrastructure, ranging over housing, health and education to meeting the requirements of a just energy transition across the most unequal and (fossil fuel) energy-intensive economy in the world. What has been achieved stands in sharp contrast to what has not, or even been attempted.

But such failings need first to be set against what has been increased income inequality after the 1993 democratic elections. The income share of the bottom 50% of earners declined from 13% in 1993 to 5.3% in 2021 while for the same period that of the top 10% grew from 46.3% to 66.5% (Figs. 15 and 16). According to the 2022 World Inequality Report, the top 10% owned 86% of the wealth (the

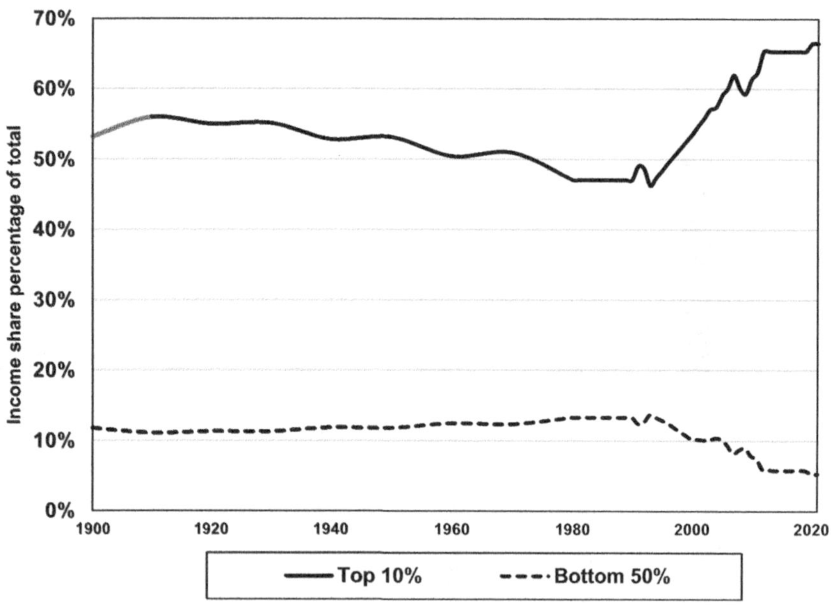

Fig. 16. Top 10% and Bottom 50% Income Shares in South Africa, 1900–2021. *Source:* Authors' calculations on World Inequality Report (2022), see Chancel et al. (2022).

top 1% owned 55%) while the bottom 50% had a negative 2% share of the wealth because of debt (Chancel et al., 2022). Statistics South Africa (StatsSA) estimated that 55.5% of the population lived in poverty (below the upper-bound poverty line) in 2015. Statistics South Africa (2022) reported that grants were the second most important South African household source of income (51%) after salaries, wages and commissions (59%) with 52% of households having reported salaries, wages and commissions as their main source of income and 24% social grants as their main source of income. It also reported that 15% of households had inadequate access to food and a further 6% severely so.

The South African National Treasury (NT) in their 2023 Medium Term Budget Policy Statement presented data on social assistance as a percentage of GDP for South Africa and the countries in Table 1, last column, as a way to showcase that South Africa spends more than other developing countries on social assistance. It also argued that, even though pursuing fiscal consolidation that requires constraints on social expenditure, the needs of the poor are being addressed. In its other columns, Table 1 reveals a different truth to the NT's selective use of data by providing additional columns of data to contextualize the level of South African expenditure on social grants. It also displays unemployment, poverty and inequality data for the countries that the NT chose for comparison. On average, South Africa has five times the average level of unemployment and three times the level of poverty, with its Gini (like the other indices) in another league than the others. As a result, its proportion of GDP spent on social assistance at less than three times the average for others is far from generous (and hardly rectifying levels of unemployment, poverty and inequality).

The government's austerity approach has constrained economic and industrial development, helped to maintain the power and ownership of the economy by wealthy elites and big businesses, supported financialization and wealth

Table 1. Comparing South Africa's Unemployment, Poverty, Inequality and Social Assistance Expenditure (as a Percentage of GDP) With Various Countries.

	Unemployment (%)	Poverty (% Below Poverty Line)	Gini Index	Social Assistance Expenditure (as a % of GDP)
South Africa	**32.8**	**55.5**	**63.0**	**4.61**
Chile	8.8	6.5	44.9	3.53
Argentina	7.4	39.2	42.0	3.25
India	7.9	21.9	34.2	1.43
China	5.3	0.0	37.1	1.05
Peru	7.6	27.5	40.2	1.23
Indonesia	5.3	9.4	37.9	0.54
Thailand	1.3	6.3	35.1	1.60
Simple average excluding South Africa	**6.2**	**15.8**	—	**1.80**

Source: Author's calculations on 2023 Medium Term Budget Policy Statement for social assistance expenditure as percentages of GDP for various countries, StatsSA (2019; 2021) for other South African data World Bank (1991–2022) WDI for rest of data from other countries (various years, most recent data).

extraction from South Africa and provided an environment for worsening unemployment and inequality. The shift to neoliberal posturing at the early stages of the democratic era meant that the government has failed to address the apartheid legacy of deprivation of the majority nor targeted the capacity to tackle industrial economic transformation to challenge the MEC/MEFC system of accumulation. However, in order to maintain an economic system that benefits a small percentage of the population while fostering higher levels of structural unemployment, poverty and inequality, there has been pressure on the government from factions within the ruling party and the elites to keep providing basic services and social grants. The result of these tensions and contradictions in South Africa has been an approach to public finances and budgeting that has repeatedly undervalued the potential contribution of the majority of the population towards the socio-economic development of South Africa.

CONCLUSION

A 2023 report for the South African Government Department of Social Development states that, while the government's Child Support Grant (CSG) effectively reaches 13 of the 20 million children in South Africa every month, the amount of ZAR 500 per month from the CSG in 2023 'is too small to protect the poorest children from hunger, malnutrition and stunting'. They report that seven million children, 37%, continue to live below the food poverty line (ZAR 663 per person per month in 2022) and that 27% of children under five are stunted. On top of the AIDS/HIV and COVID-19 pandemics, the consequences for (child) mortality rates have been both tragic and disastrous, all the more so for having been preventable at almost every level of economic and social policy if only departing from those policies too readily adopted by the few for the few, Sender (2025). These are the children with a generation between them and the end of apartheid. They have never known apartheid but they have only known neoliberalism.

NOTES

1. See discussions in Reynolds et al. (2019).
2. See Mader et al. (2020) for wide-ranging contributions on financialization.
3. For all of this in greater detail, see Fine (2020a, 2020b).
4. See Fine (2022) for an attempt to sort this out.
5. So much so that even the World Bank and IMF now acknowledge threshold effects above which it is unwise for an economy's share of financial services to grow, Itaman (2022), hardly a startling conclusion in wake of the GFC.
6. See National Housing Federation (2019).
7. We are mindful of not seeing 'austerity' policy as permanent since it implies cuts that cannot go on indefinitely.
8. See Statistics South Africa (2021).
9. National Treasury (Government of South Africa) (2021).
10. See Fine (2012a, 2012b) and Ashman et al. (2014).
11. For an update, see Fine (2024).

12. This is the first and longest account of a 'low', being the most important in and of itself and in conditioning the other lows. It addresses the levels and forms taken by the accumulation of capital. It allows us both to engage with, and depart from, traditional macroeconomic analyses (although this is not addressed at length and made explicit as such).

13. A progressive and critical literature on understanding the large corporations and business groups seemed to be taking off during the 1980s but was not sustained after the end of apartheid albeit with some occasional notable exceptions.

14. See also Lewis (1995). He shows evidence of widespread collusion in South Africa's oligopolistic markets and that single firm dominance was ubiquitous. He concludes that oligopolies colluded in sharing South Africa's markets amongst themselves and engaged in what he terms 'corporate forbearance' where conglomerates would deter their subsidiaries from entering markets dominated by subsidiaries of other conglomerates (pp. 141–144).

15. Calculated using the World Bank's (1991–2022) World Development Indicators (WDI).

16. South African Reserve Bank (SARB) data.

17. Using SARB data on Credit extension by All Monetary Institutions.

18. House price growth in South Africa during the period before the GFC was larger than in the USA and other countries that had a housing bubble. However, house prices did not crash in South Africa after the GFC and even benefited from lower interest rates after the introduction of quantitative easing in the USA and Europe. The FNB index grew from 331 in 2010 to 572 in 2022 (an increase of 1.6 times over 12 years versus the 2.7 times increase during the housing bubble during 2002–2008).

19. See Tregenna (2010) and Mohamed (2010).

REFERENCES

Ashman, S., Fine, B., Padayachee, V., & Sender, J. (2014). The political economy of restructuring in South Africa. In H. Bhorat, A. Hirsch, & R. Kanbur (Eds.), *The oxford companion to the economics of post-apartheid South Africa* (pp. 67–74). Oxford University Press.

Ashman, S., Mohamed, S., & Newman, S. (2013). The financialization of the South African economy and its impact on economic growth and employment. In *Paper prepared for United Nations Department of Economic and Social Affairs (UNDESA) Project: Strengthening National Capacities to Design and Implement Development Strategies for Inclusive, Equitable Growth and Sustainable Development Project*, 1st January, New York.

Bayliss, K., & Fine, B. (2021). *A guide to the systems of provision approach: Who gets what, how and why*. Palgrave MacMillan.

Chancel, L., Piketty, T., Saez, E., & Zucman, G. (2022). *World inequality report*. World Inequality Lab. https://wir2022.wid.world/www-site/uploads/2021/12/WorldInequalityReport2022_Full_Report.pdf

Fine, B. (2012a). Assessing South Africa's new growth path: Framework for change? *Review of African Political Economy*, *39*(134), 551–568.

Fine, B. (2012b). Chronicle of a developmental transformation foretold: South Africa's national development plan in hindsight. *Transformation*, *78*, 115–132.

Fine, B. (2013). Beyond the developmental state. *African Communist*, *186*, 40–54.

Fine, B. (2020a). Situating PPPs. In J. Gideon & E. Unterhalter (Eds.), *Critical reflections on public private partnerships* (pp. 26–38). Routledge.

Fine, B. (2020b). Framing social reproduction in the age of financialisation. In A. Santos & N. Teles (Eds.), *Financialisation in the European periphery: Work and social reproduction in Portugal* (pp. 257–272). Routledge.

Fine, B. (2022). From Marxist political economy to financialisation or is it the other way about? In D. Fasenfest (Ed.), *Marx matters* (pp. 43–66). Brill.

Fine, B. (2024). Financialisation and illegal capital flight. In J. Wiegratz (Ed.), *Capitalism and crime in Africa: The neoliberal period* (pp. 169–177). Routledge.

Fine, B., & Rustomjee, Z. (1997). *South Africa's political economy: From minerals-energy complex to industrialisation*. Wits University Press.

Fine, B., & Saad-Filho, A. (2016). Thirteen things you need to know about neoliberalism. *Critical Sociology*, *43*(4–5), 685–706.

Gounden, V. (2021). The July 2021 protests and socio-political unrest in South Africa. https://www.accord.org.za/conflict-trends/the-july-2021-protests-and-socio-political-unrest-in-south-africa/. Accessed on August 31, 2023.

Hall, K., Proudlock, P., & Budlender, D. (2023). *Reducing child poverty: A review of child poverty and the value of the child support grant*. Children's Institute and University of Cape Town for the National Department of Social Development. https://ci.uct.ac.za/sites/default/files/media/documents/ci_uct_ac_za/533/CSG%20Review_Full%20report_web.pdf. Accessed on October 30, 2023.

Innes, D. (1984). *Anglo American and the rise of modern South Africa*. Heinemann.

Itaman, R. (2022). The finance-growth nexus enigma: Bringing in institutional context and the productiveness debate. *Journal of Economic Surveys*, *36*(2), 504–527.

Lewis, D. (1991). The character and consequences of conglomeration in the South African economy. *Transformation*, *16*, 29–48.

Lewis, D. (1995). Markets, ownership and manufacturing performance. In A. Joffe, D. Kaplan, R. Kaplinsky, & D. Lewis (Eds.), *Improving manufacturing performance in South Africa: The report of the industrial strategy project* (pp. 133–148). University of Cape Town Press.

Mader, P., Mertens, D., & van der Zwan, N. (Eds.). (2020). *The Routledge international handbook of financialization*. Routledge.

Mohamed, S. (2010). The state of the South African economy. In R. Southall, D. Pillay, P. Naidoo, & J. Daniel (Eds.), *New South African review 1: Development or decline* (pp. 39–64). Wits University Press.

Mohamed, S. (2014). Banking and credit markets. In H. Bhorat, A. Hirsch, & R. Kanbur (Eds.), *The Oxford companion of South African economics*. Oxford University Press.

Mohamed, S. (2017). Financialization of the South African economy. *Development*, *59*(1–2), 137–142.

Mondliwa, P., & Roberts, S. (2019). From a developmental to a regulatory state? Sasol and the conundrum of continued state support. *International Review of Applied Economics*, *33*(1), 11–29.

National Housing Federation. (2019). Public expenditure on housing: The shift from capital spend to housing allowances – A European trend? *Research Briefing*. http://s3-eu-west-1.amazonaws.com/pub.housing.org.uk/public_spending_housing_europe_uk_briefing.pdf. Accessed on August 26, 2023.

National Treasury. (2021, August). Economic impact of the recent unrest. In *Presentation to the Select Committee on Finance, Government of South Africa*. https://static.pmg.org.za/210824NT_invitation_on_economic_impact_of_the_recent_unrest.pdf. Accessed on August 31, 2023.

Palma, G. (2019). Behind the seven veils of inequality: What if it's all about the struggle within just one half of the population over just one half of the national income? *Development and Change*, *50*(5), 1133–1213.

Quantec. (1990–2022). Quantec South African industry indicators. https://www.quantec.co.za/easydata/. Accessed on August 26, 2023.

Reynolds, J., Fine, B., & Van Niekerk, R. (Eds.). (2019). *Race, class and the post-apartheid democratic state*. University of KwaZulu –Natal Press.

Sender, J. (2025). Accounting for some recent deaths in South Africa: Zombie economics blues. In R. Mesthrie, R. Van Niekerk, & I. Valodia (Eds.), *Political economy and critical engagement in South Africa: Essays in honour of Vishnu Padayachee* (pp. 217–237). UKZN Press.

South African Reserve Bank. (1990–2022). Quarterly bulletin data. https://www.resbank.co.za/en/home/what-we-do/statistics/releases/online-statistical-query. Accessed on August 26, 2023.

Statistics South Africa. (2019). Inequality trends in South Africa: A multidimensional diagnostic of inequality. https://www.statssa.gov.za/publications/Report-03-10-19/Report-03-10-192017.pdf. Accessed on August 26, 2023.

Statistics South Africa. (2021). Quarterly labour force survey. *Quarter*, *1*. https://www.statssa.gov.za/publications/P0211/P02111stQuarter2021.pdf. Accessed on August 21, 2023.

Statistics South Africa. (2022). General household survey 2021. https://www.statssa.gov.za/publications/P0318/P03182022.pdf. Accessed on August 31, 2023.

Tregenna, F. (2010). How significant is the intersectoral outsourcing of employment in South Africa? *Industrial and Corporate Change*, *19*(5), 1427–1457.

Zalk, N. (2021). Structural change in South Africa: A sectoral historical perspective. In A. Andreoni, P. Mondliwa, S. Roberts, & F. Tregenna (Eds.), *Structural transformation in South Africa: The challenges of inclusive industrial development in a middle–income country* (pp. 28–52). Oxford University Press.

A BROKEN HISTORY: CONTEMPORARY LEBANON (1958–2018) – HOW THE LURE FOR PROFIT DESTROYED A NATION

Frédéric Farah[a] and Jérôme Maucourant[b]

[a]*University of Paris 1 Panthéon–Sorbonne, France*
[b]*Jean Monnet University in Saint-Etienne, France*

ABSTRACT

The crisis in the Lebanese economy, unique in contemporary economic history, is the result of a choice made by the ruling elite. Refusing to rebuild the State after the civil war, it set out to divide the nation in order to reign over it. This economic crisis is political in nature, and the lessons we can learn from it are important for the Arab world, where 'political capitalism' is rife.

Keywords: Lebanon; political capitalism; crisis; economic history; ruling elite; State; nation; predatory system; Dutch disease; civil war; Arab world

This small country, which is so important, Klemens Wenzel von Metternich (Kamal Salibi, *Histoire du Liban*, Naufal, 1997)

INTRODUCTION: AN UNPRECEDENTED CRISIS

The Lebanese crisis has no equivalent in the economic history of the last two centuries.[1] In addition to the massive and rapid collapse of the national economy from 2019 onwards, one specific feature should be noted: the depth of the depression is attributable to the State itself, in particular via one of its eminent institutions, the central bank. It is as if the ruling elite preferred to throw the country into chaos, for fear that its grip on the nation would loosen. This reading is informed by the concept of *political neo-capitalism* (Maucourant, 2013, pp. 995–1017), which can be deduced

Trajectories of Declining and Destructive Capitalism
Research in Political Economy, Volume 40, 169–182

Published under exclusive licence by Emerald Publishing Limited
ISSN: 0161-7230/doi:10.1108/S0161-72302025000004001l

from the work of Max Weber for the present day, and by the conceptual framework of the *wealth defence* (Winters, 2018, pp. 158–225). Bringing these issues together is an interesting way of understanding why today's parliamentary-democratic societies are also, historically, the most unequal in economic terms. With this hypothesis, the class dimension is integrated into the analysis. Our aim is to illustrate the thesis that there are no economic ills that are not *ultimately* political.

In this respect, the Lebanese case simply represents an extreme case of the self-destructive tendencies of capitalism, because the country's history over the last few decades and the geopolitical context have put no brake on this hubristic system.[2] This is how we will develop our argument: (1) a reminder of what Lebanon could have become, i.e., a broken history; (2) assumptions about the nature of the crisis; (3) criticism of the fixed exchange rate; (4) and on the *Dutch disease* in this specific context; and (5) conclusion on the crisis process.

FROM NATIONAL PROJECT TO PREDATORY STATE

Before the present phase of predatory State, it is worth looking back at an episode in the history of the Lebanon which will show us that the question of the country's development is a recurring one. The Lebanese State is presented as historically weak or, in a less negative version, as being committed to a certain liberalism that has made it prosper, whereas the Arab States in the aftermath of the Second World War were quick to embrace socialist paths, such as Iraq, Syria and Egypt. After a serious political crisis in 1958, the country embarked on a sort of *Golden Age* as is being said more and more often, which was then shattered by the Civil War (1975–1990). But the geopolitical environment shattered the fragile evolution towards a modern et social State, as we will see. The period opened by General Fouad Chehab from 1958 – after the Camille Chamoun presidency and continued by Charles Helou – is rich in lessons for the rest of contemporary Lebanese history.

Before assuming the office of President of the Republic, Chehab led the troops from 1943 to 1958, and it was during his time as head of the army that he was able to observe the many economic and social disparities in Lebanon.[3] His social instincts led him to take an interest in economic disparities. What's more, he was aware that perpetuating such inequalities between regions would make Lebanon more vulnerable to outside interference and could not ensure the country's stability. He called on an organization, the International Institute for Research and Training – Education and Development (*Institut international de recherche et de formation – Éducation et développement*, IRFED), founded in 1958 by Father Lebret, a Dominican priest and economist (Berthelot, 2014; Labaki, 1998). The IRFED was tasked with diagnosing the country's situation and working towards an economic development plan. During the 1960–1964 mission, Lebret carried out an in-depth study of the situation in the country's various sectors and regions. During this mission, Lebret came to the indisputable conclusion that the Lebanese economy was unbalanced because it had neglected the productive sectors since independence and favoured a hyper tertiary sector and certain regions such as Beirut and the nearby mountains.

The 1961 IRFED report indicated that 18% of the population accounted for 60% of the country's income (Verdeil, 2010). The aim was to develop an integrating State first and foremost. In his study, he states:

> What Lebanon lacks most, more than water, more than roads, more than electricity, are teams of people totally dedicated to the public good and working together, at all levels, to solve the multitude of problems of economic development and human upliftment. (Lebret, 1960–1961, vol. 2, pp. 476–477)

He proposed an economic plan to the government in 1964. The work was extensive and involved many local players in order to get to know the country and its needs as well as possible. This work continued from 1964 to 1970 with surveys by Raymond Delpart to identify living standards by region. A series of actions were then taken to train civil servants and numerous equipment plans were implemented (water, electricity, roads), not to mention the creation of public institutions (central bank [Banque du Liban], civil service council, central inspectorate).

Chehab wanted a balanced and fair modernization of the country. The Lebret mission represented a hope for the affirmation of a more solid State, and also for the advent of a fairer society. The Lebanese elites of the time opposed this plan and set about reducing its scope. The reforms have been partly emptied of their content, but it should be noted that, at the end of his presidency, public spending 'represented a third of the national product, i.e., almost the same proportion as in Syria – a country where the economy was administered', as Samir Kassir (1994, p. 37) observes.

Kassir therefore reminds us that there was an overall increase in living standards and – drawing on the work of Boutros Labaki – with a narrowing of the gap between communities, something that is now forgotten (Kassir, 1994, p. 43). However,

> ...at the time this evolution was not measured (...). Finally, and this was the essential point, the disparities were magnified in the immediate perception of things, in the contrast between the ostentatious luxury of the upper classes and the less ostentatious misery of the most deprived. The fact that there were wealthy Muslims did not detract from the general impression that this contrast was a community divide. (Kassir, 1994, p. 44)

So, admittedly, the Lebanon of the 1960s was not a *Golden Age*, but in many respects, it was a period of remarkable progress, and it's no coincidence that Chehab was popular among Muslims. For a quarter of a century after 1950, Lebanon experienced a GDP per capita growth of 3–4%! The underlying reason for this success, despite its limitations, was the construction of a modern State – which implied a progressive logic of State autonomy from the economic elite – coupled with an emerging social State, whose public spending was productive in many respects.

But during the explosive end of the 1960s, and the no less volcanic beginning of the 1970s, this trend was thwarted by the logic of going to extremes in the

Middle East. Lebanon, at once a buffer State and too weak to assert its sovereignty, became a sounding board for regional conflict. It is therefore with great relevance that Georges Corm (1986) has raised the issue of the *Géopolitique du conflit libanais* (*Geopolitics of the Lebanese Conflict*), because half a century after the genesis of the tragedy, it can be forcefully asserted that this dimension was the critical ingredient of the civil war. The promising evolution that was to take shape after the six years of Chehab's 1964 term of office was thus shattered. However, in the post-war Lebanon of the 1990s, Lebret's concerns seemed to find renewed interest. But it has to be said that the development model proposed in the aftermath of the Lebanese civil war has not been concerned with reviving the Chehabist inspiration and that of Lebret, quite the contrary. The model adopted has been one of aggravating imbalances and has given rise to worrying clientelism, an institutional vacuum and worrying inequalities in development.

ON THE NATURE OF THE PRESENT CRISIS

Introduced by private banks in 2019, an astonishing informal capital control system signals Lebanon's slide into a crisis from which it has yet to emerge. Three types of interpretation have been proposed. The first is that the country is a victim of *crony capitalism*, with Western complicity, in which a veritable 'bancocracy' (Corm, 2020) has tested the limits of its power of predation over the economy.[4] There are many ways of describing this type of economic system (*crony capitalism* or *political capitalism*) to describe a system that is *essentially* focused on capturing wealth rather than creating it. The driving force behind such a principle is therefore political or even military, unlike 'rational capitalism', which has an endogenous dynamic.[5] In the Lebanese case, the freezing of dollar deposits is simply the expression of a savage repudiation of debts, the only way to avoid the total collapse of the banking system. As well as being a *buffer State* (Corm, 2006, pp. 99–108), the patrimonial nature of the political structures plays a harmful role. Moreover, instead of a State, should we not be talking about the *governance of factions*, given that Lebanon is the only country in the world whose army receives military aid from the United States and Iran (Nahas, 2020). At this point, we understand that the civil war in 1975–1990 not only destroyed many human lives and the country's productive forces but also broke the momentum that, at the turn of the 1960s, had laid the foundations of a modern State.

Indeed, what has been called the reconstruction of the country under the leadership of Rafik Hariri has been nothing more than a process of destroying the pre-war institutional structure (Dagher, 2022). Transforming the State into a purely predatory system (Salhab & Maucourant, 2016) with no regard for any form of general interest, reducing public action to a coalition of players seeking to maximize their interests in the short term, rendering the *rule of law* meaningless so that illicit or even criminal activities can continue, had a first consequence: budget deficits that are as extravagant as they are recurrent.[6] Such amounts maintain a high risk premium on national debt securities: this can only encourage the rent-seeking economy to the detriment of productive forces. It is interesting to note that interest rates of 10% in the year 2009 fell steadily during the decade to 2010 and began to rise again in the middle of the following decade before returning to the 2009 level at the end of 2018, the year before the collapse (Obeid, 2020). Note the very high level of return required for this type of investment in financial capital, relative to the low level of interest rates prevailing in the world at the time. Admittedly, it could be said that things were not much better in the Middle East than in Lebanon. Think of Egypt, where liquidity rationing, very high interest rates, a foreign exchange crisis, etc. were rife. But Egypt is experiencing another form of the same *political neo-capitalism*, which is fuelling revolts, frustration and migration.

This type of *short-term* capitalism is perfectly rational in this type of situation, but is a factor of stagnation in the long term. Growth factors are external, dictated by the vagaries of global capital flows or politics. Disinterest in productive activities prevails, i.e., a preference for rentier capitalism in vogue among the many Lebanese allies of rentier States. Such practices would have been doomed to failure in a hurry, were it not for the money of the diaspora, Lebanon's role as a place of refuge for earnings with a problematic status (which 'banking secrecy' makes it possible to conceal discreetly), clientelist spending fed from outside and, lastly, the misfortunes of globalized capitalism in search of small niches to fall back on when the wind blows. In this respect, it is important to bear in mind the extreme smallness of this country, which is easily turned upside down in one direction or another by money flows preoccupied with immediate profitability or in the service of electoral corruption.

This type of capitalism, which deliberately neglects industry and handicrafts in favour of service activities or property speculation, exposes the country to growing trade deficits, which quickly turn into a serious balance of payments problem due to the geopolitical hazards specific to the region. In 2019, the Lebanese trade balance recorded a trade deficit of $8.4 billion in the first half of the year, representing a year-on-year increase of 4.9% (L'Orient–Le Jour, 2019). This neglect by the ruling elite of the internal structure of the country's economy is all the more remarkable given that these hazards have been perfectly identified for a long time. After 1992, there was no serious prospect of peace with Israel, and the failure of the *Pax Americana* in Iraq was obvious by the mid-2000s. Moreover, at the very moment of the 'reconstruction' led by Rafik Hariri in the 1990s, the Gulf States were already offering alternatives that did not exist in the 1950s.

The *structural preferences* (Weiller, 1972, pp. 68–71) of the national economy that is dictated by the ruling elite imply low average productivity in the economy, making it increasingly dependent on the international market despite its astonishing human and natural wealth.[7] This is where the paradox arises: counter-productive policies, preoccupied first and foremost with ensuring a good return on property and financial rents (itself a consequence of ever-increasing public debt due to the inertia of the rulers), are fuelling a flight of talent which, in turn, allows another form of rent, the emigrant remittance, which seems to ensure a certain durability of the *predatory system*.[8,9] Worse still, those who have remained in the country, the most fragile and the most deprived, are obviously very receptive to sectarian ideologies and their clientelist practices. There is a deleterious socio-political lock-in here that only a social State, however modest, would be able to loosen.

From an ideological point of view, a certain vision justifies this uprooting of young graduates so that they go and develop their 'human capital' where the return is the best. This line of thinking, encouraged for a time by the World Bank, is not specific to Lebanon. However, it is in the name of globalization that we are allowing a proliferation of higher education courses to develop, bordering on chaos, while at the same time neglecting the national economy, which allows us to avoid upsetting the status quo. As a result, 'investment in human capital' feeds a quasi-rentier economy, with remittances from emigrants accounting for up to 20% of national income (according to estimates) and certain prominent elements of this emigration – back home – playing a disproportionate role.[10] A member of the government in 2005 refused to worry about this migratory phenomenon, explaining that the Lebanese labour market was normally part of that of the Arabian Peninsula...[11] This shows that Lebanese-style liberalism is not so much *laissez-faire*, *laissez-passer* as *ne-rien-faire-du-tout* (do nothing at all), allowing the business as usual and industrial inaction.

The constant deterioration in the external accounts, whether we are talking about the trade balance or current transactions (a deficit of 25% of GDP! [Fonds monétaire international, 2019]), a consequence of structural weaknesses, implies a decline in the employment of the national workforce and drives spending to absorb the flow of labour that does not spontaneously leave the country.[12] As Charles Abdallah, an economist who works as project manager for the Delegation of the European Union and teaches at the University Saint-Joseph in Beirut, rightly points out, *the trade deficit thus feeds the budget deficit*.[13] This is a requirement for the continuity of the clientelist system that is characteristic of the Lebanese *para-State*. Obviously, recruitment does not follow any logic of administrative efficiency and very often concerns poorly qualified people (Dagher, 2002). It is in these conditions that there are indeed *twin deficits*, which never have the mechanical evidence that the usual theory lends them. Rather, the dialectical link between these deficits must be emphasized for this particular structure in which public spending has no economic rationality but essentially a political rationality.

THE FATAL CONCEIT: THE ERROR OF HARD CURRENCY

At this stage of the reasoning, it is obvious that the choice of a fixed exchange rate, de facto since 1992 and *de jure* since 1997, is perfectly logical. One refused to listen to the clear-sighted voices that announced the coming bankruptcy of the country.[14] It is true that this option was part of the global dynamic of financialization and globalization, the illusion of the time, i.e., the preference for financial and land rents and the transformation of Lebanon into a simple appendage of the global system (particularly regional). The question is not whether the Lebanese economy should be open or not, but this one: should the State be deprived of the ability to develop national resources? However, the desire for total *laissez-faire* and a minimal State[15] forms a coherent whole with the fixed exchange rate regime: the State, in addition to its predatory function on the common people, becomes a simple instrument of attraction for transnational capital and its Lebanese component, often expatriated. The fixed exchange rate is a necessary guarantee because of the risks specific to this country: recurrent budget and external deficits, linked to low productivity in the economy and problematic tax yields. That this implies a financial cavalry is obvious to any serious financier or economic historian. But who was serious among the decision-makers or the 'experts' who wanted to be mood of the 'new economy' and 'happy globalization'?

However, as early as 2001, the Paris conference on Lebanon was already designed to protect the fixed exchange rate and the parasitic architecture that it implies, to the detriment of all long-term economic considerations. It was not stressed enough at the time that the country was heading straight for default.[16] This is not to deny that, in certain circumstances, the fixed exchange rate regime can be interesting. Our point lies elsewhere: in order to rebuild a productive economic base, which is possible given the value of the country's human and natural potential, it was necessary to have a degree of exchange rate flexibility, for example via a *stability* regime (i.e., a fixed exchange rate allowing for adjustments if necessary, relative to a basket of currencies) or even a pure floating regime. It is precisely because the political system does not allow for budgetary rationality that the monetary tool must be given flexibility.

In other words, monetary flexibility can reflect the essential forces of the economy. This is a guarantee that the dangerous decisions of the elite will not seriously handicap the future of the nation. Fiscal folly and industrial neglect would soon have been halted by a currency crisis. Fixed exchange rate is the essential mechanism for locking in a predatory economy. It must be rejected despite all the immediate conveniences it can offer. The same applies to dollarization, the dogma of reconstruction. It is obvious that a monopoly of the national currency would have dampened the ardour of a certain number of depositors. Actually, experience shows that it is preferable to have more modest and more stable flows of capital which can be invested more harmoniously in the national economy. It is surprizing, moreover, that the Governor of the central bank and his economists (who might have been expected to be familiar with the old Eurodollar multiplication mechanism) were not even aware of the consequences of authorizing the clearing of dollar cheques in Lebanon in 1994. It goes without saying that the equivalence between *real dollars* and these *fictitious dollars* was to become increasingly impossible over time. Facilitating dollarization was an ingredient in the disaster.

A simple review of the chronicle of events reinforces this argument. In 2017, the economist and financier Shadi Karam said of the Governor of the central bank, Riad Salamé (still in office in 2023, 30 years into his reign):

> On several occasions, he could have let the system collapse. But no one knows the financial, political and security costs of cleaning it up. He could perhaps be criticised for not putting enough pressure on the political class, but he always considered that the stability of the pound and the banking sector were in the country's interest, no matter how irresponsible the behaviour of the political class. (Al-Attar, 2017)

We now know that the Governor was probably making extraordinary and illicit profits from his position.[17] This is the only reason for his obsession with keeping his job and his lack of any real pressure on the political class: he could have threatened to resign as a warning, or even left office to create a salutary shock for the nation. There is no abstract reference to 'the country's interest' for this type of individualistic, predatory and rational social agent. Riad Salamé has known perfectly well for a very long time that the fortresses of the Lebanese central bank were nothing but illusions thrown at those, many in the financial and academic world, who wanted to believe the unbelievable. Some even gave lessons in moral and civics to the young people of the *Thaoura* (the popular revolt that began on October 17, 2019).

The peg to the national currency which has been in effect for almost a quarter of a century (during the successive terms of office of Riad Salamé) has been accompanied by a continuous rise in the real exchange rate that other monetary regimes could have prevented.[18] Under these conditions, many activities are only profitable because of the importance of 'work without rights' or ridiculously low taxation.[19] Overall, economic development has been hampered and the de facto subsidy of popular consumption has been achieved at increasing social cost over time.[20] This (temporary and relative) safeguarding of the purchasing power of the 'common man' is the strongest argument put forward by the ruling elite and its intellectual and media relays. In reality, only this elite has made any real profit from artificially fixing the exchange rate at the cost of draining society as a whole. When the time came to pay the cost of these expedients, they simply refused to honour their debts by blocking deposits (deposits are only bank debts, remember).

'DUTCH DISEASE' OR POLITICAL DISEASE?

At this stage, the issue of 'Dutch Disease' needs to be discussed for Lebanon. This concept, originally developed to account for the perverse effects of the discovery of gas fields, is relevant to the Lebanese economy.[21,22] External monetary flows (large remittances from the diaspora, among others) are effectively disproportionate to the country's national wealth and thus play the same role in the overall economic circuit as the extraction of raw materials. Traditionally, a distinction is made between a *spending effect* (due to these external revenues) and *a resource movement effect* (which first increases the level of real wages in the resource-exporting sector), causing *indirect deindustrialization*: '*the non-rents sectors contract. The economy becomes highly polarised to the benefit of the rentier sector*' (Nahas, 2020, p. 98). The recurrence of these capital inflows, because they rapidly fuel demand for consumer goods – increasing the relative price of goods and services in the sheltered sector – tends to reduce the overall efficiency of the economy over time.[23]

Despite the indisputable nature of the economic mechanism described above, there is no *resource curse* but rather economic policies that are inappropriate or simply absent because of the very structure of the State. It is perfectly possible, in absolute terms, to implement fiscal policies that encourage economic diversification, particularly through the construction of infrastructure. In fact, Talal F. Salman (2019), economist, project director for the United Nations Development Programme (UNDP), argues as much at: there is even an urgent need to ward off the resource curse just as oil fields are being discovered (L'Orient–Le Jour, 2022) so as not to add *Dutch disease* to *Dutch disease*! There are never economic ills that are not ultimately political ills. The *diaspora economy* could well have fuelled Lebanese prosperity.

Alongside public policies aimed at countering the resource curse, which experts may agree on, there is the essential question of the appropriate monetary policy and regime.[24] Should we retain, as Salman argued, the principle of a fixed exchange rate regime in this configuration of the 2020s, which will probably see the possible extraction of oil and gas in Lebanon? We believe that the exchange rate regime in force in Lebanon for the past 30 years has, on the contrary, aggravated the problems of the Lebanese economy.[25] Despite his awareness of the seriousness of *Dutch disease*, Salman, like many economists and financiers, believed in 2019 that Riad Salamé, the master manipulator at the head of the central bank, had plenty of reserves to defend the national currency![26] There is something fundamental in this error: the belief in the effectiveness of a fixed exchange rate regime, whatever the circumstances. There is an element of truth, inherited from good traditional theory, when Salman writes:

> When Lebanon decided to peg its currency in the early– to mid–1990s, it was a wise choice economically for a small open economy with free movement of capital.

But such an assertion overlooks the singularity of the Lebanese institutional complex, which is quite surprizing for such an author. This blindness (typical of a certain mainstream thought) makes money the sole guarantor of the economic system's durability. Yet, as Thorstein Veblen explains, the central bank is a part *Big Union of Vested Interests* which knows perfectly well how to exploit the 'routine credulity' of the business community (Maucourant, 2016).[27]

However, the long-term value of the exchange rate is essentially endogenous; the economy cannot be saved by monetary decree, an illusory idea shared by neo-liberals (advocates of *hard currency*) and ultra-interventionist economists (in favour of strict capital controls and a multitude of exchange rates). Pegging the currency to the US dollar will not therefore have ensured financial stability, prevented dollar prices from drifting out of line, or even dollarization. But what is at stake now is the very survival of the Lebanese lira as the national currency. Many advocate dollarization, which is probably irreversible, according to Jean-François Ponsot. Certainly, following Siham Rizallah, we can even think that this monetary regime is the least bad at the heart of the disaster (Rizkallah & Ponsot, 2023). Nevertheless, it does undermine the effectiveness of future policies by depriving us of an essential attribute of sovereignty.

CONCLUSION: ECONOMICS OF NEGATIVE DESTRUCTION

As a result of the structures we have described, Lebanon is accumulating a debt of nearly 86 billion dollars, 1.7 times the size of its GDP, on the eve of the *Thaoura* in October 2019. With the agreement of many experts, the fixed exchange rate functioned like a monetary 'Maginot Line'. The demand for an inordinate financial return, which we mentioned earlier, could not be met by the tax or banking system, hence the implementation of the old *principle of cavalry*, which allows the interest of old investors to be paid with the money of new investors. It was in March 2020 that one of the largest debtors, the State, precipitated the collapse of the system, failing to obtain the loans it needed to pay off previous debts. From the Paris agreements in 2002 to the start of the Syrian conflict, various events linked to politics and the global economy have led to an influx of capital capable of delaying the fatal deadline.

In 2016, however, the prospect of a resolution to the Syrian conflict receded. To attract new capital, Riad Salamé was taking the foolish gamble of delaying the deadline even further, by offering extravagant returns to commercial banks in return for the dollars incorporated into the State/central bank/commercial bank system. There is no need to speculate about a 'Western conspiracy' to join the IMF in worrying about the consequences of this 'financial engineering' (Le Commerce du Levant, 2017). However, without these expedients, it would have been difficult for the central bank to pay $4 billion in interest in return for the $60 billion in bank deposits in its accounts, an astonishing and untenable amount (Halabi & Boswall, 2019, p. 2)! In 2020, the elite resigned itself to the bankruptcy of the State, but not of the banking system, precipitating the collapse of the economy. The World Bank could then write: '*Lebanon's GDP fell from $52 billion in 2019* to $21.8 billion in 2021, a decline of 58.1% – *the sharpest contraction recorded among 193 countries*' (Banque mondiale, 2022). The explosion of the port of Beirut in August 2020, the result of the State's failure to act, and the coronavirus epidemic, finally put an end to all forms of protest and ushered in the tragedies of the Lebanese and Syrian *boat people*.

NOTES

1. The present work is an extensively revised and updated version of an article entitled *The Lebanese Collapse: Some Hypotheses* and published in *Maghreb-Mashrek International* in 2023. Discussions with Charles Abdallah (economist and project officer at the *European Union Delegation*, Beirut) were invaluable in the preparation of this text. All the quotations and extracts from French books or articles have been translated by the authors.
2. This a system that knows no limits and that finds its limit only in collapse.
3. Indeed, In November 1956, Chehab was appointed Minister of Defence by President Chamoun, in addition to his responsibilities as Army Commander. See: https://fouadchehab.org/biography/?lang=fr
4. Georges Corm wrote this:

> First of all, it is important to remember that the Lebanese economy is heavily predated on by the political class. The country has been transformed into a veritable bancocracy, with citizens' bank deposits confiscated by decision of the Banking Association.

5. We prefer to speak of political neo-capitalism, insofar as Max Weber thought of the ancient and medieval forms of capitalism using the syntagm 'political capitalism'. What is at stake, whether in ancient or modern forms, is that sovereignty is not substantially distinct from property.

6. Before the crisis in 2019, deficits fluctuated between 29.5% and 34.2% of current expenditure between 2012 and 2018 and deficits as a percentage of GDP rose from 8.88% in 2016 to 8.65% in 2017 and 11.30% in 2018. See:https://fr.countryeconomy.com/gouvernement/deficit/liban?year=2018

7. See Hariri et al. (2021):

> The post-war growth model was based on a gradual but systematic collapse in agricultural and industrial productivity through a process of crowding out productive work, with a dual dependence on the work of foreigners in Lebanon and the work of Lebanese abroad (...) This atrophy of agriculture and industry has been accompanied by a fall in industrial productivity (with added value per worker falling from more than $15,000 per year in 2010 to $11,600 in 2018) and agricultural productivity (from $8,500 to $6,600 per year between 2000 and 2018). (our translation)

8. Public debt will rise from 131.05% of GDP to 172.27% between 2012 and 2019.

9. Lebanon's indebtedness has gone through four phases: (1) an initial phase of rapid increase in public debt, between 1993 and 2002, during which the public debt/GDP ratio rose from 46% of GDP to 163% of GDP; (2) a second phase of slow rise in public debt, between 2002 and 2006, peaking at 183% of GDP at the end of 2006; (3) a third phase of fall in the debt ratio between 2006 and 2012, reaching 130.4% at the end of 2012; (4) a final phase of slow rise in the public debt ratio (Antonin, 2020).

10. Lebanon's macroeconomic figures are sometimes doubtful, especially those relating to international issues, such as the 'errors and omissions' in the balance of payments, as Charles Abdallah points out.

11. Personal interview with Ahmad Fatfat (who was Minister of the Interior during the 2000s), Tripoli, 2005. This interview was conducted in the wake of the upheavals following many assassinations (notably intellectuals) during this year.

12. Trade deficits fluctuated between $17 billion and $15 billion between 2012 and 2019 (L'Orient–Le Jour, 2023).

13. Seehttps://www.pseau.org/outils/organismes/organisme_detail.php?org_organisme_id=27313

14. Like the future President of the Republic, Michel Aoun (then in exile), in 1997. Insofar as a tripartite executive dissolves responsibilities and inhibits action, his policy was bound to be thwarted. Great hopes were raised in civil society and in all confessional communities during 1988–1989, before the West authorized Syria to oust him on October 13, 1990, in return for the participation of the Bassist regime in Damascus in the war against Iraq in 1991. But would it have been possible for them not to have been disappointed? Is a political *alternative* (and not just an *alternation of* factions) conceivable within the present Lebanese institutions?

15. See the privatization of town planning (thanks to the expropriation of ordinary people, a 'masterpiece' of Rafik à Hariri and his company Solidere). They even went so far as to privatize the service for collecting garbage, resulting in the 2015 garbage crisis.

16. See Al-Attar (2017):

> The public debt, which was 2.3 billion dollars at the end of 1992, rose to 35 billion dollars at the end of 2004, including 26 billion in interest, i.e. three times the amount of the initial debt (...) In 2002, on the edge of bankruptcy, the country asked for international aid at the so-called Paris 2 conference, during which the government undertook to stop the haemorrhaging and to reform the country, but these commitments were not followed up with action.

17. According to French public service radio: '*Prosecutors suspect Riad Salamé, the Governor of the* Banque du Liban, *of embezzling more than US$300 million in public funds, some of which was used to buy properties in Europe*'. *Source: Radio France International* (Liban: le Gouverneur de la Banque centrale va-t-il éviter la justice française?, May 16, 2023). https://www.rfi.fr/fr/moyen-orient/20230515-liban-accus%C3%A9-de-d%C3%A9tournements-de-fonds-riad-salam%C3%A9-attendu-par-la-justice-fran%C3%A7aise.

18. Probably very corrupt, as evidenced by the investigations (Maucourant Atallah, 2021). In order to cover up its own excesses, the ruling elite has concealed the governor's immense misdeeds. All in all, a highly profitable exchange of opacity. It's no coincidence that the *Banque du Liban* has become an empire of opacity and manipulation.

19. See Hariri et al. (2021):

> The eviction of productive work and the generalisation of low or unprotected work have until now been determining features of the collapse of the country's productivity. Even before the crisis of 2019, recruitment and wage policies in both the private and public sectors gradually led to a massification of unskilled and low-protected work. As a result, it is work 'without rights,' i.e., work that is excluded de jure or de facto from access to rights and social protection, that dominates the overall employment balance, with the so-called 'informal' sector accounting for 36% of GDP and 'informal' employment for 66% of the working population.

20. From a base of 100 in 1970, the real exchange rate rose to 250 before the crisis. The trend in deposits in millions of dollars was almost identical! See Nahas (2020, p. 100). To the economists and politicians still defending the principle of the *peg*, we might point out this comment by the author:

> The policy of stabilising the exchange rate has not succeeded in reducing dollar inflation; on the contrary, it has been accompanied by a steady rise in the index, from 220 to 460, i.e. more than double. The injection of resources from outside the country has led to high demand-led inflation that is completely disconnected from the exchange rate, despite the almost total dollarisation of the economy. (our translation)

21. In terms of an appreciation of the real exchange rate and, subsequently, among other things, of a sub-optimal allocation of factors of production reducing long-term global productivity. For a fairly recent summary, see in particular: Arzelier, 2016, pp. 96–97.

22. The thesis is also defended by Nahas (2020):

> The 'Dutch disease' favoured activities producing non-tradable goods and services, reducing to nothing or almost nothing the companies exporting service goods which existed before the war and which even survived during the war (public works, air transport) (p. 104).

The circle of misfortune is closing: bad government over the past 30 years has encouraged emigration ('*half a cohort emigrating*!'), which generates income flows that structure an economy of disaster. The economic, human and cultural losses of this economy based on the export of labour cannot be underestimated.

23. In the early days of political economy, Richard Cantillon discovered that money is not neutral and that its additional circulation increases the price of relative resources located closest to the spillover of flows. This leads to a cumulative phenomenon which comes to an end at the end of a cycle exhausting the effects of the initial spill. We can see the problem in our case study: the price system is disturbed in a systemic way by the quasi-rentier structure of the economy (Maucourant, 2020, pp. 5–32).

24. Let's look at the specific ways in which this syndrome operates in Lebanon:

> The influx of capital is not linked to the export of non-renewable resources, but to remittances from Lebanese emigrants who are constantly leaving the country. Unlike in oil-exporting countries where, when resources are exhausted, no one has a claim on them, in Lebanon, the capital attracted accumulates in the form of bank deposits and financial claims whose holders

remain convinced of their right to claim them back, at any time, with interest. This is precisely what is happening today. (Nahas, 2020, p. 35) And:

(...) The distortion of prices due to the intense Dutch disease that characterises Lebanon has simultaneously produced: a specialisation in non-tradable goods, small, low-productivity, labour-intensive businesses, and a massive double movement of Lebanese emigration and imports of cheap foreign labour. (p. 117)

25. Nahas' remarks on the real exchange rate and dollar inflation seem sufficiently convincing in this respect.

26. See Salman (2019): 'It is true that Banque du Liban (BDL), Lebanon's central bank, has ample ammunition to defend the lira'.

27. This a fine lesson for Lebanon in 2019 – indeed! – and the European Central Bank in 2023, whose funny leader explained that 'inflation comes almost from "nowhere"' (Dalton, 2023).

REFERENCES

Al-Attar, S. (2017, June 2). Riad Salamé: l'ingénieur du système. *Le Commerce de Levant*. https://www.lecommercedulevant.com/article/27421-riad-salam-lingnieur-du-systme

Antonin, C. (2020, September 9). Liban: Sortir de la spirale de l'endettement. *OFCE Le Blog*. https://www.ofce.sciences-po.fr/blog/liban-sortir-de-la-spirale-de-lendettement/

Arzelier, M.-P. (2016). Les Modèles de syndrome hollandais. Analyse et perspectives de recherche. In M. Salhab & J. Maucourant (Eds.), *État, rente et predation - L'actualité de Veblen*. Presses de l'Ifpo-Université de Technologie et de Sciences appliquées libano-française.

Banque Mondiale. (2022, January 25). La Crise libanaise: un grand déni sur fond de dépression délibérée. https://www.banquemondiale.org/fr/news/press-release/2022/01/24/lebanon-s-crisis-great-denial-in-the-deliberate-depression

Berthelot, Y. (2014). Louis-Joseph Lebret (1897-1966), acteur d'une économie plus humaine. In L. Loty, J.-L. Perrault, & R. Tortajada (Eds.), *Vers une Économie "humaine"?* (pp. 57–78). Éditions Hermann.

Corm, G. (1986). Géopolitique du Conflit libanais - Étude historique et sociologique. *La Découverte*.

Corm, G. (2006). Sortir du cercle vicieux et du statut d'État tampon ? *Confluences Méditerranée*, *56*(1), 99–108.

Corm, G. (2020, October 2). Il faut que Macron défende fermement la solution d'un Etat laïc. Interviewed by S. Aubouard. *Marianne*. https://www.marianne.net/monde/georges-corm-il-faut-que-macron-defende-fermement-la-solution-dun-etat-laic

Dagher, A. (2002, February 15–16). *L'Administration libanaise après 1990*. Colloquium Le modèle de l'État développemental et les défis pour le Liban.

Dagher, A. (2022). *Comment une élite prédatrice a détruit le Liban*. Le Bord de l'Eau.

Dalton, E. (2023, March 27). Lagarde says inflation crisis came from 'Nowhere', describes Putin as 'a Terrifying Man'. *The Journal*. https://www.thejournal.ie/lagarde-inflation-5905973-Oct2022/

Fonds Monétaire International. (2019, July 10). Liban: Conclusions de la mission de consultation de 2019 au titre de l' article IV. https://www.imf.org/fr/News/Articles/2019/07/02/mcs070219-lebanon-staff-concluding-statement-of-the-2019-article-iv-mission

Halabi, S., & Boswall, J. (2019, November). Lebanon's financial house of cards. *Triangle Working Paper*. https://www.thinktriangle.net/wp-content/uploads/2019/11/Extend_Pretend_Lebanons_Financial_House_of_Cards_2019.pdf

Hariri, N., Scala, M., & Dirani, A. (2021, June 26). La Crise libanaise ravage un marché du travail déjà dysfonctionnel. *L'Orient–Le Jour*. https://www.lorientlejour.com/article/1266367/la-crise-libanaise-ravage-un-marche-du-travail-deja-dysfonctionnel.html

Kassir, S. (1994). *La Guerre du Liban de la distension nationale au conflit régional*. Karthala-Cermoc.

L'Orient–Le Jour (2019, August 23). Le Déficit commercial en hausse de 5% à fin juin. https://www.lorientlejour.com/article/1183647/le-deficit-commercial-en-hausse-de-5-a-fin-juin.html

L'Orient–Le Jour (2022, November 24). Fonds souverain: les discussions ont commencé. https://www.lorientlejour.com/article/1319163/fonds-souverain-les-discussions-ont-commence.html

L'Orient–Le Jour (2023, January 9). Le Déficit commercial libanais a augmenté de 60,2%. https://www.lorientlejour.com/article/1323838/le-chiffre-de-la-semaine-602-.html

Labaki, B. (1998, December 28). La Mission Lebret au Liban (1959-1964) - Qu'en est-il après plus d'un tiers de siècle ? *L'Orient–Le Jour*. https://www.lorientlejour.com/article/272954/La_mission_Lebret_au_Liban_%25281959-1964%2529_Quen_est-il_apres_plus_dun_tiers_de_siecle_.html

Le Commerce du Levant. (2017, February 1). Ingénierie de la BDL: le FMI chiffre à 10% du PIB l'injection de capitaux dans les banques. https://www.lecommercedulevant.com/article/27028-ingnierie-de-la-bdl-le-fmi-chiffre-10-du-pib-linjection-de-capitaux-dans-les-banques

Lebret, L.-J. (1960–1961). *Besoins et possibilités de développement du Liban. Étude préliminaire* 2 vol, Mission Irfed – Liban. Ministère du Plan.

Maucourant, J. (2013). Un Retour des capitalismes politiques? *Économies et sociétés (Cahiers de l'ISMEA), Histoire de la pensée économique, 6*, 995–1017.

Maucourant, J. (2016). Théorie du système prédateur (une lecture de Thorstein Veblen). In M. Salhab & J. Maucourant (Eds.), *État, rente et prédation – L'actualité de Veblen* (pp. 43–64). Presses de l'Ifpo–Université de Technologie et de Sciences appliquées libano-française.

Maucourant, J. (2020). Sovereignty and economy according to Montchrestien and Cantillon. *Economic Alternatives, 1*, 5–32.

Maucourant Atallah, N. (2021, April 13). Les Questions soulevées par l'enquête visant Riad Salamé en Suisse. *Le Commerce du Levant*. https://www.lecommercedulevant.com/article/30324-les-questions-soulevees-par-lenquete-visant-riad-salame-en-suisse

Nahas, C. (2020). Un État et une économie pour le Liban. *Cercle des économistes arabes* [Youtube]. https://www.youtube.com/watch?v=Phe5uxnV7YA

Obeid, H. (2020, June 21). L'Envol de la dette publique à l'origine de la crise libanaise. *The Conversation*. https://theconversation.com/lenvol-de-la-dette-publique-a-lorigine-de-la-crise-libanaise-140805

Rizkallah, S., & Ponsot, J.-F. (2023, March 3). La Dollarisation au Liban - Les défis de la BDL dans ses choix monétaires et de régime de change face à une crise économique multidimensionnelle sans précédent. https://doi.org/10.58079/u6ew

Salhab, M., & Maucourant, J. (Eds.). (2016). *État, rente et prédation – L'actualité de Veblen*. Presses de l'Ifpo-Université de Technologie et de Sciences appliquées libano-française.

Salibi, K. (1997). *Histoire du Liban du XVIIe siècle à nos jours*. Naufal.

Salman, T. F. (2019, February 19). Currency conundrum - The Libanase lira and the Dutch disease. *Executive – Independent Thinking for a Discerning Mind*. https://www.executive-magazine.com/economics-policy/currency-conundrum

Verdeil, E. (2010). Beyrouth dans les plans de l'IRFED et d'Écochard. In *Beyrouth et ses urbanistes: Une ville en plans (1946-1975)*. Institut français du Proche-Orient. https://www.ifporient.org/

Weiller, J. (1972). Note Complémentaire - Les préférences de structure. In R. Bastide (Ed.), *Sens et usages du terme structure dans les sciences humaines et sociales*. De Gruyter Mouton.

Winters, J. (2018). Wealth defense and the complicity of liberal democracy. In J. Knight & M. Schwartzberg (Eds.), *Wealth: NOMOS - American society for political and legal philosophy* (Vol. 58, pp. 158–225). NYU Press.

THE CRISIS OF LEGITIMACY IN IRAN AND THE ONGOING STRUGGLE FOR FREEDOM

Farhang Morady

University of Westminster, UK

ABSTRACT

Ongoing protests are challenging the legitimacy of the Islamic Republic of Iran. In 2022, the tragic death of a young Iranian woman continues to affect the Islamic Republic's foundation. Her death led to a massive protest movement that brought together people from different social classes, including some of the regime's staunch supporters. These protests have sparked discussions about the Islamic Republic's legitimacy and complicated relationship with the state, politics, and society. This chapter delves into the protest movement's underlying causes, examining local and global factors contributing to its emergence.

Keywords: Islam; resistance; legitimacy; freedom; capitalism; social classes; imperialism; nationalism; protests; revolution

INTRODUCTION

In 1979, the Islamic Republic of Iran emerged as a powerful force driven by radicalism, Islamism, and anti-imperialism. The Revolution galvanized and mobilized the underprivileged, inciting them to revolt against the wealthy and oppressive establishment. It emboldened those with limited financial means to challenge the corrupt monarchy and global powers. The Revolution pledged to address the needs of the marginalized and offer them the support they deserve.

The Revolution took many by surprize, as modernization was expected to result in more secular and progressive societies. Instead, religious forces advocating for a more conservative society gained power. This was evident in the strict

Trajectories of Declining and Destructive Capitalism
Research in Political Economy, Volume 40, 183–198

Published under exclusive licence by Emerald Publishing Limited
ISSN: 0161-7230/doi:10.1108/S0161-723020250000040012

enforcement of wearing the hijab for women, which restricted their freedom and opportunities in an evolving world (Morady, 2020a, b).

Since 1979, diverse social groups have grown, including bureaucrats, high-ranking military officials, and industrialists. Consequently, the political terrain has become more varied. The state now represents not just the merchant class but also modern industrialists, bureaucrats, and top military commanders, each with unique class interests.

Despite the far-reaching effects of the Revolution, it failed to transform fundamentally the essence of the modern State, the structural framework of society, or Iran's relationship with the global capitalist system. While the Revolution brought about significant changes and disruptions to the political and social landscape in Iran and beyond, it did not uproot the class society that was in place before 1979.

In the early stages of the Iranian Revolution, the leaders of the newly formed Islamic Republic were faced with a complex challenge. They had to balance the need to govern a modern country that was part of the global capitalist system with the enforcement of their religious values, particularly the mandatory hijab for women.

To navigate this difficult situation, the Islamists developed a range of interpretations of religion (Bayat, 2013). Various government administrations with different political affiliations, including those described as 'right-wing', 'radical', 'reformist', and 'moderate', all used religious ideology to promise progress in the country's economic, political, and social conditions.

Just like many 'Third World' leaders, the Iranian Islamists used populist deceptive language to appear supportive of press freedom, multi-party elections, and opposition to powerful nations like the US. Although they claim to support press freedom and multi-party democracy, they have repeatedly suppressed social movements, such as those of 2009 and 2022, by casting them as enemies of Islam and supporters of imperialism (Morady, 2020a, b).

Under significant pressure from the Revolutionary movement, the new clerical rulers challenged the interference of the major powers in Iran. In response, the US and other Western powers viewed the Iranian Revolution as a threat to their interests in the energy-rich and financially important region.

Yet, the genuinely anti-imperialist character of the 1979 Revolution long confused many Iranians on both the left and the right. So did the reactions of the US and other great powers. Since the Revolution, the US and its allies have imposed sanctions on Iran for various reasons, beginning with the hostage crisis in 1980.

As a result, some perceive Islamist movements as progressive and anti-imperialist, representing the oppressed, while others criticize Islamists in power as being backward and dictatorial, arguing that they struggle to effectively manage domestic and international affairs.

This chapter explores the Islamic Republic's relationship with capital, the state, and imperialism from a historical perspective. It will analyze the current crisis of legitimacy faced by the Islamic Republic in light of recent political and social movements, particularly the protests in 2022.

ISLAM AND ISLAMISM IN IRAN

Describing the meaning of 'religion' can be a complex undertaking. At its core, religion encompasses a shared set of beliefs that transcend social boundaries. As a social construct, it is adaptable to changes in societal conditions, as evidenced by the significant influence of Islamic concepts and institutions throughout Iran's history (Harman, 2010; Morady, 2020a, b; Roy, 2004; Voll, 1982; Zubaida, 1989). In Iran, the role of Islamism has been twofold. It has both offered social protections to the poor and legitimized the position of the wealthy in society.

Religion's ambiguous nature has led to various interpretations and appeals among different groups, especially during times of social upheaval (Engineer, 1984, 1987). Throughout Iranian history, Islamist leaders have received financial backing from merchants, landowners, and, more recently, industrialists and bureaucrats. This has given the leaders significant social and political influence to consolidate their positions. By inspiring hope among those facing adversity, they have motivated people to overcome challenges. However, their claim to religious authority requires obedience to both divine and earthly powers.

Religion has historically played a significant role in maintaining social order in Iran. However, it has also been a driving force behind opposition to governing authorities in Iran. Furthermore, it has evolved into a strategy for mobilizing political forces against regional competitors and establishing the Islamic Republic's hegemony in the Middle East.

Ayatollah Ruhollah Khomeini, the leader of the 1979 Revolution, partially Islamized the concept of the working class. To rally the poor to his movement, Khomeini spoke of the need for the *mustazafin* (the poor and oppressed) to rise up against the *mustakbirin* (the rich and oppressors). He urged the poor to become the 'vanguard' of the Islamic Republic, 'leading society' in fighting 'the corrupt powers of the world'. Khomeini promised that the new State would 'build houses for workers [and] provide free water and electricity for the needy' (Khomeini, 1979).

Over time, some *mustazafin* were given political positions in the regime, particularly as part of the Islamic Revolutionary Corps (IRGC) and the *Basij*, a volunteer morality police. Following the Revolution, the IRGC and the Basij attacked leftist groups and imposed 'Islamic morality' on women, refusing to wear the hijab. Indeed, the extensive protests of 2022 began with the death in detention of a young woman, Mahsa Amini, after the Basij arrested her for not wearing a hijab (De Hoog & Morresi, 2022). However, their wider role is to maintain social and religious protection of the State and capital.

The IRGC and the Basij have gained significant importance and have become a dominant economic force in the country. They have also become a means of upward mobility. Some of their members have risen to positions of power and wealth, including those who have become industrialists and members of Parliament (Murphy, 2007). This has made them crucial to the ruling elite of the country.

One of the most influential figures in the IRGC was Qassem Soleimani, a prominent commander. He played a crucial role in advancing Iran's political objectives not only in Iraq and Syria, Lebanon, but in Yemen and some countries in Africa and Latin America. Soleimani and other notable figures in the IRGC emphasized nationalist interpretations of Islam, which helped to develop a stronger connection to the nation-state and encouraged a realistic approach to geopolitics.

STATE, NATIONALISM AND ANTI-IMPERIALISM

Islam and its followers are not confined to the borders of a modern nation State. Rather, they belong to the *umma*, the global Islamic community. The Islamic Revolution recognized the importance of the nation State through religious means, but it also diminished the significance of the *umma*.

After the Revolution, Islamists acknowledged the significance of the modern state and its institutions, such as the parliament and the Constitutional Assembly. Khomeini stated that 'Islamic government is not dictatorial or absolute, but rather constitutional'. He went on to explain that he meant 'constitutional in the sense that the rulers are bound by specific conditions when governing and administering the country'. He did not mean that laws should be approved based on the majority's opinion (Khomeini, 1981, p. 51).

Khomeini insisted that the clerical establishment must wield greater authority in the judicial system and must possess the power to make constitutional decisions. These 'conditions' were enforced under the Supreme Leader's guidance. A referendum in March 1979 led to the approval of a new constitution. The constitution granted ultimate authority to a supreme religious jurist (*faqih*) for judging economic, political, and social issues.

The aim was to establish a distinct and authoritative presence while simultaneously appearing supportive of a particular class's interests. However, this ambiguous language of religion generated opposition from some who saw it as portending a retreat from modernity, from capitalism, or from both. Indeed, some observers thought it was incompatible with Islam (Arjomand, 1989; Rodinson, 1981).

Interestingly, some Islamist leaders who believed in 'essentialism' also rejected Western secular culture and promoted an idea of Islamic purity (Algar, 1983). Khomeini's statement in 1979 affirmed that 'the recent religious movement was one hundred per cent Islamic and was founded by clerics alone' (Khomeini, 1981, p. 33).

Others viewed this as a triumphant return to the past and a rejection of rationalism, secularism, pluralism, modernization, and capitalist development (Ayubi, 1991; Gellner, 1981; Keddie, 1994; Lewis, 1993; Morady, 2020a, b). The anti-Western rhetoric of the Islamist leaders encouraged some to stress the supposedly 'anti-imperialist' character of the Islamic Republic. According to them, the state came to power through a revolution in which the working class and poor rose up. In line with this, they held the West responsible for the protest movements in 2009 and 2022 (Petras, 2009).

To counter the Western threat, Iran formed alliances with opposition groups and anti-imperialist forces in the Middle East and globally. These alliances included the Palestine Liberation Organization (PLO), the Houthi in Yemen, Hezbollah in Lebanon, as well as Cuba and Venezuela (Morady, 2024).

Iran's motivations for intervening in the region were a mix of altruistic goals and political considerations influenced by the actions of Western powers and regional competitors. Its profound ambition to establish itself as a dominant power in the region, combined with a sense of isolation exacerbated by sanctions and the looming spectre of invasion, compelled the nation to actively seek an alternative approach aimed at countering Western influence and asserting its own dominance within the region.

The Islamic Republic has seamlessly integrated modern capitalism into its system, blending Western political frameworks with Islamic principles. This fusion has laid the groundwork for their institutions and objectives, with Islam serving as a religious and governance model. As a result, Islamists consistently interpret and apply their religious beliefs across various spheres, including economics, politics, and society.

ISLAMISING A MODERN POLITICAL SYSTEM

The revolutionary Iranian state emerged from a complex interplay of social, political, economic, and religious forces. In response to the revolutionary situation and increasing demands, the Islamic Republic crafted a hybrid political system. Several institutions were founded following the Revolution, including the Assembly of Experts (*Majles-e Khobregan or Majles-e Khebregan-e Rahbari*) in 1979. Its primary responsibility was to oversee the government. The Guardian Council (*Shora-ye Negahban*) was then established in 1980, tasked with accepting or rejecting candidates for parliament and presidency. Further, the Expediency Council (*Majma Tashkise Maslahate Nezam*) was created in 1988 to resolve any disputes between the Guardian Council and Parliament.

Alongside the traditional army and intelligence service, the Revolutionary Guards have their own security agency. In practice, there are two intelligence branches in Iran. The Ministry of Intelligence and Security reports to the executive, and the Revolutionary Guards' Intelligence Organization is under the military. The Revolutionary Guards played a crucial role in supporting the Islamists in maintaining power during the early years of the Revolution, countering the internal threat from the army, which remained loyal to the Shah.

The fusion of religious and secular systems in this distinctive amalgam poses an obstacle for both the authorities and those in actual control. The struggle to harmonize theocracy and democracy has led to strife and bewilderment, with the religious hierarchy assuming a preeminent position in the government.

What sets the Islamic Republic apart is that it doesn't just rely on religious ideology or laws to establish authority but it also has a religious leader who holds a central role in governance. The most important aspect is that the Supreme Leader, *Velayat-e Faqih,* has a responsibility to recognize and communicate

God's intentions.[1] This gives him significant power. Since 1989, the Supreme Leader's office has been transformed into a collection of complex branches and advisors with a large budget. This office operated independently from the government and lacked transparency and accountability (Murphy, 2007). To gain insight into the power dynamics in Iran, it is crucial to comprehend the functioning of various political institutions that connect the religious and secular spheres. However, it is important to avoid oversimplifying the concept of religious and democratic legitimacy.

Iran's written constitution outlines the Supreme Leader's position and includes references to certain democratic principles. It reflects the delicate balance between religious authority and secularism in the Iranian government as it seeks approval from both democratic and ministerial bodies (Constitution of the Islamic Republic of Iran, 2022).

As per the constitution, the president is directly chosen by the citizens and acts as the head of government, not the head of State. The president can appoint ministers who are answerable to the parliament. The parliament holds the right to summon any minister for inquiry and dismiss them from their position if deemed necessary.

The Guardian Council comprises 12 clerics who serve for a 6-year term. It is noteworthy that half of the members are appointed directly by the supreme leader, while the remaining members are nominated by the Supreme Judicial Council, which Parliament then appoints. The Council of Guardians is responsible for reviewing all legislation passed by the Majles, ensuring that it aligns with the Constitution (Morady, 2020a, b).

In the Islamic Republic system, multiparty representation is not permitted. However, different interpretations and class differences are evident in various factions usually labelled 'moderate', 'reformist', 'radical', and 'conservative'. Abdul Karim Soroush serves as an excellent illustration. He is a distinguished reformist who ultimately developed a critical perspective towards the *Velayat-e Faqih* principle. Immediately after the Revolution, Soroush played an important role in the Council of the Cultural Revolution, the body that formulated the ideology of the Islamic Republic in its early days. Soroush's perspective caught the interest of Islamist scholars who sought to reconcile Islam with modern concepts of freedom and rationality. Soroush articulated this viewpoint when he stated that 'religious morality would be the guarantor of a democracy, where the rights of the faithful to adopt religion would not vitiate the democratic, earthly, and rational nature of the religious government' (Soroush et al., 2000, p. 154).

Soroush and the reformists advocated for a government chosen by the people. The conservatives, by contrast, argued that the people's rule must align with the will of God as communicated by the Supreme Leader.

The competition between different individuals and factions reflects power struggles between social classes. For example, there were three candidates in the 2009 presidential election. Mahmoud Ahmadinejad was both conservative and radical. The reformist candidate was Mir-Hussein Mousavi. The third was Mehdi Karroubi, a former Prime Minister (1981–1989) and previous speaker of the

Parliament from 2000 to 2004, leading to a political conflict known as the Green Movement or *Jonbesh–e Sabz*.

The Movement was a coalition of forces led by Karroubi and Mousavi during and after the 2009 presidential elections. It comprised interest groups from different social backgrounds, including the modern middle class and a section of the working class with varying ideals and aspirations. The core leadership consisted of reformists, clergy, and academics who championed a non-violent civil rights movement, repeatedly emphasizing that theirs was not revolutionary. They remained committed to the Islamic Republic and its Constitution, broadly accepting the framework of capitalism.

The Movement was a coalition of forces comprised of interest groups from different social backgrounds, including the modern middle class and a section of the working class with varying ideals and aspirations. The core leadership consisted of reformists, clergy, and academics who championed a non-violent civil rights movement, repeatedly emphasizing that theirs was not revolutionary. They remained committed to the Islamic Republic and its Constitution, broadly accepting the framework of capitalism.

Although the movement's leadership expressed frustration with electoral fraud and the transfer of political power to other groups, they failed to recognize the crucial role of the working class and their potential for instigating real change, as they did back in 1979 when they played a fundamental role in paralyzing the Shah's regime.

However, the Green Movement significantly affected the legitimacy of the Islamic Republic, which continues to search for its authority.

MANAGING CAPITALISM

This historical context was important during the Revolution in 1979. The memories of invasion and constant intervention by global powers, especially in the 19th and the 20th centuries, had left a lasting impact. The military coup organized by Britain and the US in 1953, and their support of the Shah until 1979, contributed to this impact (Abrahamian, 2013). As a result, the Islamic Republic had to strike a balance between operating within the system, promoting its radical message, and guarding against external powers that could challenge its authority.

Amidst the turmoil of revolutionary times, numerous affluent individuals and professionals left Iran, necessitating the leadership to nationalize significant industries as per Article 44 of the Constitution of the Islamic Republic. Nevertheless, it was an inescapable reality that the government would ultimately have to manage the country's economy within a capitalist system.

The political turmoil escalated when Iranian students took control of the US Embassy, holding 98 hostages for over a year in 1979. In response, the US imposed sanctions on Iran. Not long after, the perceived threat of the Iranian Revolution encouraged Iraq, with support from the US and neighbouring countries, to invade Iran in 1980.

Despite the transnational nature of Islamism, the Islamic Republic has paradoxically used nationalism in various political situations, taking a pragmatic approach towards the nation's behaviour in the global community. Initially, the leaders called on Muslims from around the world to join them, but this changed during the 8-year war with Iraq from 1980 to 1988.

During the conflict with Iraq, the Islamic Republic saw the war as an opportunity to shift citizens' attention away from internal issues and towards a common enemy: Saddam Hussein, the leader of Iraq. By framing the war as a religious crusade against infidels and their Western allies, they were able to exploit divisions between secular and Islamist factions, and to rally the nation around a nationalistic and religious message. This strategy allowed the regime to suppress dissent and consolidate support for their cause. As Rafsanjani put it in 1985:

> ...we have been able to use the war to awaken the people and address the challenges threatening the revolution. (Chubin & Tripp, 1988, p. 71)

In 1986, Iran experienced a decline in productivity and an increase in urban poverty due to Western sanctions and the war. This made it hard for Iran to continue the war. The price of oil plummeted from roughly \$30 to as low as \$10 per barrel, settling at approximately \$18 the following year (Statistical Centre of Iran, 1991). This was predominantly because Saudi Arabia, a close ally of both the US and Iraq, exported substantial quantities of oil, thus flooding the market. Consequently, Iran's oil revenues in the first-half of 1986 decreased by 59% compared to the first half of 1985 (Renner, 1988, p. 194). Adding to the country's difficulties was the challenge of mobilizing individuals for the war front, as many young Iranians lacked the motivation to participate in a seemingly endless war that was justified by an empty ideological motive.

Finally, Iran accepted UN Resolution 598, calling for a complete ceasefire, which went into effect on July 18, 1988. The war ended with no success for either country but huge financial consequences. Over 33% of Iran's national budget went into the war, and it involved \$450 billion in damages to cities, ports, oil facilities and other infrastructure (Lob, 2020, p. 129).

After the war ended, Khomeini passed away, and Khamenei, who was not a Grand Ayatollah, succeeded him. The Islamic Republic leaders had to amend the constitution to allow for his assumption of power in order to assume leadership. This move showed how political pragmatism once again took precedence over religious codes in the country's leadership transition.

REFORMISM, HOPE, AND DESPAIR

After the war, rebuilding and ending isolation led to better relationships with Western and Eastern nations. This included welcoming and promoting involvement from global financial organizations like the International Monetary Fund (IMF) and the World Bank (WB). Two distinct approaches emerged for the direction of the economy. One was a call for normalizing development along capitalist lines, with a free market and collaboration with the West. The second position called for greater state control over the economy, including import substitution industrialization. During the early days of the Revolution in Iran, there were three main factions. The Islamist right consisted of conservative clergy and bazaar traders. The radical wing, led by Mousavi, had its social base among the poor. And the pragmatic right, led by Rafsanjani, represented big business interests and advocated for free market neoliberalism.

Despite their changing fortunes over time, all three groups have continued to play a significant role in Iran's politics. The pragmatic right emerged as the dominant force and succeeded in the face of competition from the radical Islamists. However, depending on economic and political interests, some representatives have changed their positions over time. For example, Mousavi switched sides and ran as a reformist candidate in the 2009 presidential election.

During the early part of the Revolution, State-led development played a critical role in achieving the goals of national independence and economic self-sufficiency stated in the Constitution. For the past 35 years successive presidents – Rafsanjani (1989–1997), Khatami (1997–2005), Ahmadinejad (2005–2013), Rouhani (2013–2021), and Ebrahim Raisi (2021–2024) – have all implemented variations of market reforms by embarking on a privatization strategy.

In 1994, the Iranian parliament approved a law that allowed the government to sell State-owned industries. This move aimed to attract foreign capital to invest in Iran, which would provide the necessary funds for restructuring.

The introduction of a Structural Adjustment Programme (SAP) under Rafsanjani immediately led to currency devaluation, price liberalization and privatization. In 1991, the World Bank provided Iran with a loan of $250 million, and pledged another $850 million in 1994 if Iran met the assigned conditions. By 1993, the rial's value was allowed to float. The electricity, transport and telephone prices increased by nearly 100% (Behdad, 2000, p. 115). Hence, the economic reforms increased inequality, with the top 10% of the population receiving 34% of the national income and the bottom 10% receiving only 2% (Rakel, 2008, p. 91).

After the presidencies of Rafsanjani and Khatami, Ahmadinejad implemented a policy of reducing subsidies and replacing them with targeted social assistance. Initially, many poor people supported this approach. The money saved from ending subsidies was used to provide cash handouts to every family, regardless of income. However, the end of food subsidies and the imposition of Western sanctions led to a decline in living standards, which affected the poorest people in the country the most. Basic goods such as bread, meat, sugar and eggs became more expensive. By the end of Ahmadinejad's term, unemployment had reached 4 million, with 39% of people aged 14 to 29 out of work. Inflation had also risen to over 40% (Mohammadi, 2013; Taghavi, 2010).

In 2013, Rouhani became President and made the promotion of an open market his top priority. His approach was based on two main factors. The first was managing Iran's relationship with the US, which had posed a significant obstacle to the country's progress. The second was the conviction that economic reforms should be expedited. He was optimistic that the Iranian economy would improve with the betterment of relations with Western and neighbouring countries, and with the eventual lifting of international sanctions. He emphasized the importance of constructive interaction with other nations based on moderate policies and described his government as one of prudence and hope (Mohammadi, 2013).

In July 2015, Rouhani reached an agreement with Barack Obama's government to stop Iran's nuclear processing. This renewed hope that Iran's economy would improve by attracting foreign investments. However, the US government still did not completely lift sanctions and kept a close eye on companies trading with Iran.

In May 2018, President Donald Trump announced that the US was leaving the 2015 nuclear deal and would be reinstating sanctions on Iran. This decision had an immediate and negative effect on Iran's economy, leading to a 300% fuel price increase in November 2019. This price hike triggered a protest movement in over 100 cities across Iran. The state responded with brutal repression. Amnesty International reported that 321 people were killed and 3,000 wounded (Amnesty International, 2019).

The 2019 protest movement was mainly led by the working and poor classes, who were demanding equality and justice. The movement served as a warning to the Islamist leaders in power, highlighting their inability to fulfil their promises. The economic difficulties and COVID-19 pandemic further worsened Iran's situation, forcing Rouhani's government to request a $50 billion loan from the IMF. However, the Trump administration opposed this request. And then Iran's efforts to deal with the pandemic failed both domestically and internationally, leading to a sense of despair.

A NEW TWIST ON AN OLD PROBLEM

By 2020 Iran's per capita GDP had dropped to $2,300 from $7,800 in 2011. The top 20% of the population owned a staggering 47% of the wealth, with the bottom 20% holding only a measly 0.5%. The reinstatement of sanctions by the US after its withdrawal from the nuclear deal in 2018 has severely damaged the Iranian economy. The brunt of the impact has been borne by ordinary citizens, especially those with lower incomes.

Despite ordinary citizens' economic difficulties, the government insisted on upholding traditional values that limited personal freedom. The Islamic Republic disregarded the increasing dissatisfaction, particularly among the youth, in a nation that has undergone significant social change. In 1976, the adult literacy rate was only 37%. By 1986 it had increased to 52%, and reached an impressive 89% in 2021. The female adult literacy rate was at 24% in 1976, increasing to 41% by 1986 and a remarkable 85% in 2021. The percentage of people using mobile phones has also increased from just 1% in 2000 to 79% in 2021 (World Bank Monitor Report, 2022).

The 2022 protest movement in Iran was largely driven by the persistent social oppression faced by the Iranian people, with a particular focus on gender inequality and the imposition of religious values. The movement also highlighted the economic inequalities prevalent in the country. The State's use of violent tactics in response to the protests only served to further inflame public anger towards the immoral actions of the morality police.

This widespread unrest has brought to light a growing crisis of legitimacy for the Islamic Republic. A notable difference from earlier protests is the absence of support from the clergy. This shift in the power dynamic may have far-reaching effects on Iranian politics and society, with the potential for significant changes in the coming years. The protests have galvanized a large section of the population, who demanded greater justice, equality, and representation in the country.

It exposed the actions of the morality and security police, which have fuelled an unparalleled level of rage. This represents a colossal challenge for the Islamic Republic. Nevertheless, some Islamist leaders persist in their draconian approach, displaying no indications of acknowledging the demands of the majority of the Iranian people. As a result of having few alternatives, Iranians have turned to public demonstrations as a means of expressing their dissatisfaction with the oppressive social and political structures, compulsory hijab and systemic corruption.

The ongoing protests have vividly portrayed the formidable challenge confronting the Islamic Republic. Widespread discontent among the population, particularly among the poor and the middle class, has underscored the depth of the societal unrest. Even the most ardent supporters of the regime showed disillusionment. This was evident in the 2024 parliamentary election, where there was a significant decrease in voter turnout despite the regime's efforts to increase participation. The turnout plummeted to as low as 41%; in the capital Tehran, it was even lower at only 24%. This decline in participation was observed in the aftermath of the 2023 protest movement (Ghaffari, 2024).

The sudden death of Iranian President Ebrahim Raisi in a helicopter crash in May 2024 came as a shock, given his careful selection as president in 2021 by the Islamic Republic. The 63-year-old hardline cleric was widely seen as a protege of Khamenei and a leading contender to succeed him in the future. The passing of Raisi is not expected to lead to significant changes in major domestic and foreign policy decisions, as these are ultimately decided by Khamenei.

However, the regime is likely to be cautious in showing any signs of weakness or political instability, especially amid discontent against the regime and increased tensions with the West and Israel, exacerbated by the ongoing Israel–Hamas conflict.

GLOBAL AND REGIONAL CHALLENGES

The Western powers, particularly the US, have sought to exploit legitimate grievances among Iranians, as they have done in the past. In addition to imposing sanctions, Western leaders have collaborated with the Iranian opposition to influence political movements. It is unlikely that the Iranian people would seek to reinstate a monarch or another dictator through mass protests. Their ideal scenario involves establishing a new government that truly represents their needs and aspirations.

A sequence of major international political events in the region has provided the Islamic Republic with strategic advantages, enabling it to establish relative legitimacy over its adversaries in the Middle East.

In 2010, the Arab Spring marked a series of interconnected political uprisings and protests across several countries in the Middle East. This included significant events in Yemen, Iraq, Lebanon, and Syria, with involvement from Iran, Saudi Arabia, and the United Arab Emirates (UAE).

Saudi Arabia and the UAE supported the President of the Republic of Yemen, Ali Abdullah Saleh, while Iran backed a rival opposition group led by the Houthis. During the Syrian Civil War, Iran supported Bashar al-Assad against opposition from Saudi Arabia. Furthermore, the US withdrawal from Iraq and Afghanistan has positioned Iran as a significant player in the region, extending its influence from Yemen to Iraq, Syria, Palestine and Lebanon (Morady, 2024).

Due to Iran's increasing influence in the region, the US became involved, ultimately leading to the signing of the Abraham Accords by Israel and the Gulf countries in September 2020. As a result, Bahrain and the UAE formally recognized Israel. However, in 2023, China mediated between Iran and Saudi Arabia to reduce tension and ensure regional stability (Mahdavi & Keskin, 2022).

During the BRICS Summit in August 2023, Iran made a significant geopolitical move by forging a strategic alliance with Brazil, Russia, India, China, and South Africa. This alignment brought together countries with diverse geopolitical interests, including traditional adversaries such as Iran, Saudi Arabia, and the UAE. The implications of this development are far-reaching, impacting not only regional power dynamics but also global politics, trade, and security considerations. This strategic realignment has the potential to reshape alliances and influence decision-making processes on the world stage.

Tensions in the region flared up again on October 7, 2023, when Hamas launched an attack on southern Israel, resulting in profound global implications. Despite not engaging directly, Iran provided support to Hamas. The Israeli military's offencive in Gaza led to the loss of over 40,000 lives so far, including children, and sparked widespread condemnation and significant protests across the globe (Knell et al., 2024).

On April 1, 2024, the conflict escalated when Israel carried out an airstrike on the Iranian consulate in Damascus, Syria, resulting in the deaths of 18 Iranians (Gritten, 2024). Iran, reluctant to engage in an all-out war, considered the attack in Damascus a significant violation and raised the issue with UN authorities. However, when a resolution was presented to the Security Council to address the issue, it was vetoed by the US, Britain, and France, leaving Iran feeling compelled to respond.

On April 13th, 2024, Iran launched a major missile and drone attack directly against Israel. Over 300 missiles and drones were fired from Iran, including Syria, Iraq, Yemen, and Lebanon (Staff, 2024). Despite receiving security and military support from the US, Britain, France, Jordan, and other Arab states, some of the Iranian missiles landed in Israeli army bases.

By late 2024, escalating regional tensions have significantly reshaped the geopolitical dynamics of the Middle East. Israeli military operations targeting

Hezbollah resulted in the elimination of several key leaders. Shortly thereafter, the collapse of Bashar al-Assad's regime in Syria – driven by the Islamist group Hayat Tahrir al-Sham (HTS), a coalition of rebel forces supported by Turkey – added a new layer of complexity to the unfolding crisis. Meanwhile, the Islamic Republic has struggled with severe domestic economic challenges, including soaring inflation, widespread unemployment, and a sharp decline in currency value. These economic hardships have further eroded its already declining regional influence.

CONCLUSION

This chapter sets out to assess the root causes of the legitimacy crisis currently confronting the Islamic Republic of Iran. The crisis holds great significance as it reflects the Islamic Republic's ability to navigate the challenges of capitalism since coming to power. This marks a significant departure from the original goals of the Iranian Revolution, which initially aimed to overthrow the dictatorial regime, alleviate poverty, and usher in a new era of democracy. Regrettably, the revolution deviated from its intended path as the new leaders used religion to legitimize their authority and embraced capitalism to consolidate their power.

The protest movement that has emerged in the last two decades reflects the class struggle within the Islamic Republic. The existing economic and social challenges, including but not limited to poverty, inequality, and social unrest, stem largely from the disparity in wealth distribution. Economic challenges have led to many Iranians joining the movement to address these inequalities. Official records show that the inflation rate in Iran surged to 48% in 2022. With 60 million people, 75% of the population lives in poverty, and the overall unemployment rate is 12%, while the youth unemployment rate has surged to almost 30% (Morady, 2023).

The leaders in the Islamic Republic of Iran have employed diverse religious interpretations to legitimize class stratification and uphold societal structure. Despite their efforts, they have been unable to establish stability and have, as a result, turned to endorsing oppressive ideologies, particularly targeting women.

With the growing generational gap in Iran, conflicting values and expectations have created complex contradictions in society. For instance, the use of contraceptive pills has led to a significant decrease in the annual population growth rate, which has remained under 2% since 1991. According to Izadi's (2014) report, more women are now opting for birth control. The divorce rate rose from 12% in 2007 to 21% in 2014. And as of 2020, for every 100 registered marriages, there were 32.9 divorces.

There exists a notable divide among women that is primarily based on their respective social classes. Those from more affluent backgrounds often prioritize their careers, while those from less privileged backgrounds may view homemaking as a more viable option. This division has led to tensions, particularly among Islamist women who strive for greater equity and fairness in society. This division has resulted in heated debates and ideological conflicts, creating a loss of legitimacy and growing disillusionment among Islamist followers. Many women feel that their voices are not being heard, and the current leadership is not adequately addressing their needs. This sense of disenfranchisement has caused many to lose faith in the ability of their leaders to create a society that is truly just and equitable.

Whoever succeeds Raisi, the Islamic Republic will continue to grapple with the significant challenge of managing the new generation of Iranians with diverse economic, political, and social demands. Navigating complex societal dynamics to ensure equal opportunities and access to resources for all members of society necessitates a nuanced understanding of the social and economic factors contributing to this divide and a commitment to crafting policies that address these inequalities.

Despite a decline in the frequency and scale of the protest movement in Iran, the underlying discontent and grievances within the country continue to present a significant risk of prolonged political unrest. This ongoing instability could further undermine the legitimacy and authority of the leaders of the Islamic Republic, potentially leading to heightened internal tensions and challenges to the current political establishment.

All indications point to a potential 'war of attrition', in which opposing groups gradually gain or lose political power over time, leading to far-reaching consequences for the entire area. Certain events may act as the catalyst for significant protests. It is uncertain how much the divide will escalate before significant political consequences occur, potentially bringing about radical changes in Iran.

NOTE

1. The Shia religion holds the belief that Imams are the rightful successors to Prophet Mohammed, which is a fundamental principle of their faith. They adhere to three core beliefs: the existence of One God, the prophethood of Mohammed, and the occurrence of a resurrection and judgement day. Furthermore, Shi'ites believe that only direct descendants of Ali (the cousin of the Prophet) have the right to be titled as Imam and rule on behalf of Allah. Unlike the Sunni denomination, who uses the term 'imam' more generally to refer to a cleric, Shi'ites consider Imams to be divinely guided and therefore infallible. Present-day responsibilities of Imams include the administration of infallible and divine justice.

REFERENCES

Abrahamian, E. (2013). *The coup: 1953, the CIA, and the roots of modern U.S.–Iranian relations*. The New Press.

Algar, H. (1983). *The roots of the revolution*. Open Press.

Amnesty International. (2019). Iran: Details of 321 deaths in crackdown on november 2019 protests. https://www.amnesty.org/en/documents/mde13/2308/2020/en/

Arjomand, S. (1989). *The turban for the crown: The Islamic revolution in Iran*. Oxford University Press.

Ayubi, N. (1991). *Political Islam: Religion and politics in the Arab world*. Routledge.

Bayat, A. (2013). *Post–Islamism: The changing faces of political Islam*. Oxford University Press.

Behdad, S. (2000). From populism to economic liberalism: The Iranian predicament. In P. Alizadeh (Ed.), *The economy of Iran: Dilemmas of an Islamic state* (pp. 100–145). I.B. Tauris.

Chubin, S., & Tripp, C. (1988). *Iran and Iraq at war*. I.B. Tauris.

The constitution of the Islamic Republic of Iran. (2022), Cambridge University Press.

De Hoog, N., & Morresi, E. (2022, October 3). Mapping Iran's unrest: How Mahsa Amini's death led to nationwide protests. *The Guardian*. https://www.theguardian.com/world/ng-interactive/2022/oct/31/mapping-irans-unrest-how-mahsa-aminis-death-led-to-nationwide-protests

Engineer, A. A. (Ed.). (1984). *Islam and revolution*. Ajanta.

Engineer, A. A. (1987). *The origin and development of Islam: An essay on its socio-economic growth*. Sangam.

Gellner, E. (1981). *Muslim society*. Cambridge University Press.

Ghaffari, B. (2024, April 3). Iran election turnout slumps as hardliners prevail. *Financial Times*. https://www.ft.com/content/c2e621aa-d5c3-498b-9e00-c114b2d31776

Gritten, D. (2024, September 9). Israeli strikes on Syria military sites kill 18, government says. *BBC News*. https://www.bbc.co.uk/news/articles/cy0nrd730jdo

Harman, C. (2010). *Selected writings*. Bookmarks.

Izadi, E. (2014, August 12). Iran bans vasectomies, wants more babies. *Washington Post*.

Keddie, N. (1994). The revolt of Islam, 1700 to 1993: Comparative considerations and relations to imperialism. *Comparative Studies in Society and History*, *36*(3), 463–487.

Khomeini, R. (1979). Khomeini's speeches. https://fararu.com/fa/amp/news/18520?fbclid=IwAR0eWOZbU2HHV6axYrsp4gBJrJjUsE8k5EEeSKzb9hegeIDFblufjS5qJQg

Khomeini, R. (1981). *Islam and revolution: Writings and declarations of Imam Khomeini*. H. Mizan Press.

Knell, Y., Thomas, M., & Brown, P. (2024, August 15). Israel-Gaza war: More than 40,000 killed in Gaza, Hamas-run health ministry says. *BBC News*. https://www.bbc.co.uk/news/articles/cn49v0nzv3ko?utm_source=chatgpt.com

Lewis, B. (1993). *Islam and the west*. Oxford University Press.

Lob, E. (2020). *Iran's reconstruction Jihad: Rural development and regime consolidation after 1979*. Cambridge University Press.

Mahdavi, M., & Keskin, T. (2022). *Rethinking China, the Middle East and Asia in a "Multiplex world"*. Brill.

Mohammadi, N. (2013). Four million Iranians looking for jobs: Ahmadinejad's promises of uprooting unemployment have not materialised. *Mehr News Agency*. www.mehrnews.com/detail/News/2046491

Morady, F. (2020a). *Contemporary Iran: Politics, economy, religion*. Bristol University Press.

Morady, F. (2020b). How Iran is battling with economic sanctions and COVID-19. *Transforming Society*. https://www.transformingsociety.co.uk/2020/11/03/how-iran-is-battling-with-economic-sanctions-and-covid-19/

Morady, F. (2023). Iran: One year on from the "Women, Life, Freedom" protests. *Rebel*. https://www.rebelnews.ie/2023/09/12/iran-one-year-on-from-the-women-life-freedom-protests/

Morady, F. (2024). Israel-Iran conflict: A battle for regional dominance. *Rebel*. https://www.rebelnews.ie/2024/05/09/israel-iran-conflict-a-battle-for-regional- dominance/

Murphy, F. (2007). *Ali Khamenei*. Chelsea House.

Petras, J. (2009). Iranian elections: The 'Stolen Elections' hoax. *Global Research*. www.globalresearch.ca

Rakel, P. E. (2008). *Power, Islam, and the political elite in Iran. A study on the Iranian political elite from Khomeini to Ahmadinejad*. Brill.

Renner, M. (1988). Determinants of the Islamic republic's oil policies: Iranian revenue needs, the Gulf war, and the transformation of the world oil market. In H. Amirahmadi & M. Parvin (Eds.), *Post-revolutionary Iran*. Westview Press.

Rodinson, M. (1981). *Marxism and the muslim world*. Zed Press.

Roy, O. (2004). *Globalised Islam: The search for a new ummah*. Hurst.

Soroush, A. (2000). Reason, freedom, and democracy. In M. Sadru & A. Sadri (Eds.), *Islam: Essential writings of Abdolkarim Soroush*. Oxford University Press.

Staff, A. J. (2024, April 15). Iran attacks Israel with over 300 drones, missiles: What you need to know. *Al Jazeera*. https://www.aljazeera.com/news/2024/4/14/iran-attacks-israel-with-over-300-drones-missiles-what-you-need-to-know

Statistical Centre of Iran. (1991). Statistical yearbooks. https://www.amar.org.ir/

Taghavi, R. (2010). Why Iran's Ahmadinejad is pushing to cut popular government subsidies. *Christian Science Monitor*. www.csmonitor.com/World/Middle-East/2010/0430/Why-Iran-s-Ahmadinejad-is-pushing-to-cut-popular-government-subsidies

Voll, J. O. (1982). *Islam: Continuity and change in the modern world*. Westview.

World Bank Monitor Report. (2022). Iran's economic outlook. Spring 2023. http://www.worldbank.org/en/region/mena/publication/mena-economic-monitor

Zubaida, S. (1989). *Islam, the people, and the state: Essay on political ideas and movements in the Middle East*. Routledge.

THE UGLY UNDERBELLY OF "EMERGENCE": INDIAN CAPITALISM IN THE ERA OF GLOBALIZATION

Surajit Mazumdar

Jawaharlal Nehru University, India

ABSTRACT

While India has been recognized as one of the prominent 'emerging' markets in the era of globalization, much less in focus has been the nature and basis of this emergence and the implications it has had for India's working people. This chapter argues that India's relatively high measured growth in the last three decades is not indicative of Indian capitalism's movement in the direction of becoming a core advanced capitalist economy. The accumulation process in India instead has been even more dependent than in the past on India's characteristic of being a cheap labour Third World capitalism. The conditions maintaining these, however, have also been reproduced precisely because they have also constrained that accumulation process and its ability to absorb the large labour reserve that exists. If India's big business class as well as foreign capital has flourished under globalization, extremely premature de-industrialization, arrested structural change, and mass unemployment have also marked the trajectory of the Indian economy. These have ultimately only created conditions for a crisis of accumulation and the transition to an extremely parasitic phase of Indian capitalism. Rising authoritarianism and the undermining of India's secular democracy has been the political expressions of the crisis and the sharpening contradictions underlying it.

Keywords: Accumulation; capitalism; crisis; de-industrialization; emerging market; globalization; India; third world; underdevelopment; unemployment

Trajectories of Declining and Destructive Capitalism
Research in Political Economy, Volume 40, 199–213

Published under exclusive licence by Emerald Publishing Limited
ISSN: 0161-7230/doi:10.1108/S0161-723020250000040013

INTRODUCTION

Seen in a longer-term perspective and set against even capitalism's own historical standards, the transformative impact of India's encounter with the capitalist mode of production stands out in many respects. This is true even when the comparison is made with other countries which like India are in the Third World.[1] Yet India is placed among the category of 'emerging' markets by international investors and organizations. One of the now famous BRICs group of countries, India's status as one of the world's major economies is also acknowledged by its membership of the G-20. This importance that India has attained over the course of the distinct phase of the capitalist world economy that has been called 'Globalization' is a reflection of a *specific* trajectory of capitalist development in an exceptionally large and populous country. India's capitalists have been able to grow rapidly, despite the constraints or limitations of a Third World capitalism, by leveraging the cheapness of the labour services of its vast population of working people. What is distinctive about the Indian trajectory of low wage-based insertion into the process of globalization is the absence of its association with a world market based, and foreign direct investment facilitated, acceleration of industrial capitalist development. Instead, the historical limits to capitalist accumulation have worked in different ways to continuously reinforce and reproduce the cheap labour conditions and the presence of a large labour reserve. This co-existence of intensive exploitation and mass unemployment or underemployment, and its implications for the working millions, has been the ugly underbelly of the Indian process of emergence. The contradictions inherent in such a dualistic trajectory have, however, eventually generalized the crisis and produced also a crisis of accumulation and of profits. This crisis has no tendency of self-correction, and instead is only generating forces intensifying the contradictions and unleasing even more destructive tendencies in Indian capitalism.

INDIAN CAPITALISM AND THE LIMITS TO 'EMERGENCE'[2]

The per capita production levels attained by India lag far behind much of the world. It was only in 2007 that India became a lower middle-income country in the World Bank's classification scheme, and here too it is below the average for that category. Its Gross National Income (GNI) per capita in current US dollars was less than a fifth of the world average before the COVID-19 pandemic. India's position appears better if GNIs are measured on a Purchasing Power Parity (PPP) basis, though for reasons that will be discussed later this is not the most appropriate measure in this instance. Even on this basis, however, India's GNI was below 40% of the world average and less than a 10th of that of the US. Relatively speaking, therefore, India's per capita income position in the world is not radically different from what it was in 1947, when India gained independence from almost two centuries of British colonial rule.

If we use per capita Manufacturing Value Added (MVA) and the highest share attained by the manufacturing sector in both GDP as well as employment as indices of the level of industrialization, India is also one of the least industrialized of the world's major economies. Despite this, it is also one of many countries experiencing de-industrialization, in its case of a particularly 'premature' variety (Rodrik, 2015). On the other hand, India has one of the most agrarian of employment structures – with agriculture accounting for 45% of the total employment. The ownership of agricultural land is highly concentrated, and there are as many if not more rural households without land than those with (Rawal & Bansal, 2022). There is a significant use of hired labour along with family labour, especially in larger holdings, and the income from wages of agricultural households now typically exceeds that from cultivation. The overwhelming chunk of agricultural produce is also marketed rather than being for self-use. Despite all these characteristics, however, India's is still primarily a peasant agriculture and large-scale corporate farming is virtually completely absent. The vast majority of over 90 million agricultural households cultivate relatively small holdings and also have very low earnings.

More generally, over 70% of the labour force in India remains in the countryside. Moreover, 'self-employment' rather than wage employment accounts for more than half the total employment in the economy. Self-employment in this case means working in an 'own-account enterprise' or as helper in such a household enterprise, often employing no, or very limited, hired labour. In addition, the size of the workforce in casual wage employment is also as large as those in regular employment. Another notable feature of the Indian economy is that the proportion of the population that is employed is itself also significantly lower than in other Asian countries, and even most advanced economies. On the other hand, the ratio among those employed of those deemed to be in 'informal' employment, which includes the majority of even those in regular wage employment, at almost nine-tenths, is perhaps unmatched in the world.

Going beyond purely economic criteria, pre-capitalist institutions like caste continue to play in India an important role in social life, including in the economic and political domains. From those who predominate in the propertyless to the composition of the propertied class, caste background clearly appears as an important determining factor. Property ownership largely in the name of men, and significantly lower labour-force participation rates of women as compared to men, are also long-term characteristic features of India's economy. The latter is in fact the main reason for the low employment to population ratio. It does not, however, mean that women are idle – only that they are engaged in unpaid work that is important to the sustenance and reproduction of their often low-income households.

Despite all the above, there are three important reasons for the importance that India enjoys in the contemporary capitalist world economy. One is the size of its still reasonably growing population, around 18% of the world total, which makes India one of the largest economies of the world despite the low per capita income. It also similarly means that even with a low per capita MVA, India has one of the world's largest industrial sectors – it is the second largest producer of steel and cement in the world, produces more electricity than all but two countries, ranks fourth in the world in terms of petroleum refining and passenger car production, and is among the top manufacturers of motorcycles.

A second reason is the fact that India has been part of the larger story of globalization – of a shift in the geography of world production towards lower wage locations in the Third World, especially those in Asia. India, like several other countries in Asia, has consistently grown at a pace faster than that of the rest of the world, and even in comparison to its pre-globalization growth trend. The growth has seen ups and downs, pales in comparison to the record of China over the same period, and has been dominated by services and construction rather than industry. Yet it has pushed up India's share in world production and therefore also its significance in the world market for both consumer and producer goods. From around 1.3% in the early 1990s, India's share in world GDP increased to over 3.2% on the eve of the COVID-19 pandemic. In terms of the increments to world production and the global market, and opportunities for capital investment, therefore, India's significance has been even greater. The importance of Indian financial markets as an outlet for globally operating financial capital has also correspondingly increased.

The third factor of importance has been India's standout export success in specific sectors like software services (outsourcing) and pharmaceuticals (generics). Indian growth has not been export-led by any means, and the general pattern of its insertion into global value chains has been import-intensive and domestic market oriented in character. Trade and current account deficits of a much higher order than in the past have been the norm, and India's significance in world trade is less than it is in production. Yet, specific historical factors that preceded India's insertion into globalization enabled some sectors to beat the general trend and make India the leading developing country in them (Chaudhuri, 2012; D'Costa, 2004). Even though enrolment in higher education had historically been very low relative to the large population in the relevant age-group, the availability of a significant number of potential white collar workers for performing different kinds of mental labour, including those with a technical education, were an outcome of the quest for 'self-reliance' that had accompanied the post-independence import-substitution strategy. In fact, there had already been a long history of a higher end flow of such labour from India to the West, specially the US, through migration (Hoffman & Batalova, 2022) – what used to be referred to as the 'brain drain'. The enactment of a patent law in 1970 that permitted only process and not product patenting, on the other, hand, had laid the foundation for the growth of an Indian pharmaceutical industry that could replicate successful drugs and offer them at lower prices, but without having the capacity to develop them.

Foreign capital does have a presence in Indian production which is by no means insignificant, though the use of India as a base for production for exports is minimal and half the exports by FDI firms are accounted for by the IT sector (Mazumdar, 2022). Foreign financial flows also play a very important role in Indian financial markets, though most of the blue chip companies whose securities are most commonly traded in Indian stock markets are Indian controlled firms, including some which are in the public sector. In fact, FDI firms are largely unlisted. India has been a net capital importer, and these mainly private capital flows have financed the current account deficits as well as the accumulation of foreign exchange reserves by India's central bank, the Reserve Bank of India (RBI). Though part of the foreign capital is from other Asian developing countries, and Indian firms too have investments abroad, foreign investments and linkages between Indian and foreign firms also serve as conduits for the flow of value created within India to the metropolitan countries. However, the Indian capitalist class oversees a significant part of the capitalist activity within India and remains the principal immediate exploiter of the country's working class. Further, its position cannot be described as being exclusively limited to occupying a subordinate position in value chains to apex global firms. It does have a significant autonomous sphere of profit-making.

At the top of the pyramid of India's capitalist class are large, mainly family controlled, business groups – who typically have many companies in their fold and whose operations can straddle several different sectors (Mazumdar, 2015). While these operations can include the use of fairly sophisticated methods of production, Indian firms are rarely the originators of any important innovations and remain largely dependent on sourcing technology from outside (Mani, 2020; Tyabji, 2000). Yet some of them are now big enough to be rubbing shoulders with the top corporations in the world – with the size of India's domestic economy providing an important basis for that. While they do also have international operations, including in the advanced economies, in comparison to FDI into India, her outward FDI is limited. The stock of the former is about two and a half times the latter. India's total foreign liabilities are over 40% of her GDP, while her foreign assets other than reserve assets are just over a fifth of her foreign liabilities.

The contemporary Indian economy thus continues to reflect the characteristics of capitalist underdevelopment in a dual sense. While commodity production is extensive and the web of commodity relations incorporates the entire economy, 'pure' capitalist production relations based on the division between propertyless sellers of labour-power and their property owning capitalist employers are very far from encompassing the entirety of Indian society. Even if modified under the impact of capitalism, the social conditions of production still reflect the pre-capitalist past to a great degree. On the other hand, the heights attained by the tendencies inherent in industrial capital – to accumulate and expand production without limits, and to continuously revolutionize the methods of production – remain extremely limited. The endogenous ability for the latter is particularly scarce and in this regard Indian capitalist development remains significantly dependent on the externalities emanating from advanced capitalism. India's status as an 'emerging' economy thus is not based on her shedding through her development the characteristic features of a Third World capitalism and 'converging' towards the advanced capitalist situation. Indeed, this is one of the reasons why its rise is not perceived by the hitherto dominant western capitalist powers as a threat in the same way as China's is. If the size of India's population has thereby mattered to a great extent during the era of globalization, it has done so with extremely divergent consequences for India's capitalists and the majority of those making up that population. The latter providing a large and highly elastic reserve of very cheap labour, at the expense of serving as a vast home market, is what has been the essential condition for the 'success' of the former.

THE HISTORICAL ORIGINS OF INDIA'S CHEAP LABOUR CAPITALISM

The historical roots of the backwardness and conservatism of Indian capitalism go back to the circumstances of its origin, in the shadow of capitalist colonialism. Its subsequent development was also such that the limitations inherited from the past always exerted a significant influence on its development in every phase. The balance between continuity and change in that development was thus exceptionally weighed in favour of continuity.

Indian capitalism did not emerge in the mid-19th century out of an internally generated transformation of a pre-capitalist socio-economic order. Instead it was linked to the enclave like development of a modern factory industry as an offshoot of the process of colonial exploitation of a pre-capitalist society by what was then the world's leading capitalist nation (Ray, 1994). This development of capitalist enterprise also failed to exert any decisive influence on the course of the Indian economy in the colonial era, and in counteracting the destructive and stagnationist tendencies generated by the context of India's subordination. The dominant component of this enterprise was in any case foreign and tied to the colonial set up. Even the native industrial capitalist class that took time to emerge out of the shadow of foreign dominance reflected a strong continuity with the past and with the colonial context. It was formed from within the existing mercantile communities, with sections of them using the accumulations from trade, and the access to machinery from the colonial master, to diversify their profit-making activities into mainly light manufacturing. The pauperization of sections of the Indian population ensured that this limited development was never constrained by the unavailability of wage-labour.

There was thus little in terms of 'revolutionary' elements in the emergence of Indian capitalism (Mazumdar, 2013). After almost a century of capitalist development, India's economy at the time of her independence in 1947 was one where a pre-capitalist agriculture dominated by a parasitic landed class produced more than half the output and employed three-quarters of the workforce. Modern factory industry on the other hand contributed a small share in production, not even a tenth, and even less in employment. This industrial sector was also still dominated by light industries, and its technological capacities were extremely limited. The transition to independence, and the emergence of an Indian capitalist State for the first time, while important in accelerating the process of capitalist development in India, was also similarly muted in character and failed to produce a radical break from the past.

India's position in the divide between an advanced core and an underdeveloped periphery in the capitalist world economy was in any case fixed by history as part of the initial conditions of her post-independence development. Any change in this position could only be the result of that development, not its starting point. The end of direct foreign rule only meant that India's international economic relations could be within limits reordered and reoriented, but offered no prospect of a capitalist development process that was completely delinked from the world economy. Where there was, however, potentially greater room for change was in the internal context, in particular the property ownership structure in Indian agriculture. Significant land reforms of one or the other kind were important changes that preceded the rapid industrialization and growth of Asian economies like South Korea, Taiwan and China. Nothing comparable happened in India as the balance of class forces worked towards ensuring that the property ownership structure – of capitalist enterprise, both Indian as well as foreign, as well as of landed property – remained largely untouched. While land reform laws were enacted, they remained largely on paper and produced no significant dent on the pattern of ownership and control over land (Appu, 1996).

The 'built-in-depressor' in India's agrarian structure, and the social relations and consciousness that went with it, were thus never decisively eliminated.[3] Instead, a more limited and slow process of agrarian change was initiated through the 'Green Revolution' strategy and putting in place of a system of State support to agriculture (Ramakumar, 2022). The primary objective of this was to induce the existing agrarian structure to produce shifts in production techniques – the use of high yielding varieties of seeds and intensive use of inputs like fertilizers – that would allow productivity and production to expand in a land constrained situation. This, however, left no scope for any transfer of a surplus from agriculture to industry and narrowed the initial base from which the capitalist accumulation process had to proceed. This failure of India's post-independence land reforms programme imparted to its subsequent process of capitalist development a distinct character, marked by the virtual absence of what Marx had described as an inherent feature of capitalism.

> It is in the nature of capitalist production to continually reduce the agricultural population as compared with the non-agricultural, because in industry (in the strict sense) the increase of constant capital in relation to variable capital goes hand in hand with an absolute increase, though relative decrease, in variable capital; on the other hand, in agriculture the variable capital required for the exploitation of a certain plot of land decreases absolutely; it can thus only increase to the extent that new land is taken into cultivation, but this again requires as a prerequisite a still greater growth of the non-agricultural population. (Marx, 1974, p. 637)

In absolute terms, the agriculture-dependent population in India continuously increased for almost the entire second-half of the 20th century, and in recent years appears once again to be on the rise. While a significant contribution to this was made by demographic growth, the land under cultivation did not increase as there was little scope for that by independence. Essentially non-agricultural employment grew too slowly. Though agriculture's share in GDP fell below half by the mid-1950s, it was only when this had reduced to less than a fifth, more than six decades after independence, that the combined employment in non-agricultural activities crossed that in agriculture. Moreover, manufacturing did not play a significant role in the expansion of non-agricultural employment. Manufacturing employment in fact started stagnating at the same time that agricultural employment began declining. Manufacturing's share in GDP itself virtually stopped increasing within roughly three decades of independence.

All the above have to be set against the fact that the growth of the total income or value added in agriculture barely kept pace with the growth of the Indian population, so that in per capita terms it increased very slowly, at a long-term rate below even one percent per annum. It then becomes clear that Indian agriculture served as the reservoir for a large amount of surplus labour. Capitalist development benefitted from this to the extent that this guaranteed highly elastic cheap labour conditions, and scope for intensive direct and indirect exploitation. This provided the structural basis that worked, along with a legal framework which limited the applicability of the term worker, to make 'informality' the norm in employment (Das Gupta, 2016). However, capitalist accumulation and growth prospects were also always constrained by other implications associated with those same conditions (Mazumdar, 2013). In addition to the lack of flow of a surplus from agriculture for capital accumulation in industry at any stage, the periodic scarcity of agricultural raw materials and wage-goods like food, were significant constraining factors in the earlier stages of post-independence industrial development. The limited development of the home market on the other hand was a long-term constraint that was continuously reproduced as the inevitable other side of the perpetuation of cheap labour conditions. The stunted industrialization that ensued did not, however, mean that the tendency for replacing living labour with dead labour was absent, especially in large-scale capitalist enterprise. However, the cheap labour conditions nevertheless reinforced the conservatism of the Indian capitalist class – a tendency to develop more its capabilities of extracting absolute surplus value while remaining reliant on foreign technology sources for generating relative surplus value.

CONTINUITY AND CHANGE IN THE TRANSITION TO GLOBALIZATION

A highly unstable process of accumulation and growth, which lurched between one crisis and the next, marked Indian capitalism's development over four decades between the adoption of an import–substitution strategy after independence and her insertion into the process of globalization. Symptomatic of the fact that import substitution did not mean India was outside the capitalist world economy were the foreign exchange constraints that dogged Indian capitalism during this period. The major part of the liberalization that paved the way for India's entry into globalization was itself triggered by an exchange crisis in 1991, and the imposition of stabilization and structural adjustment programmes as conditions for an IMF bailout. That crisis, however, was itself partly the result of a trade and investment liberalization, and increasing recourse to international commercial borrowing, that took place in the 1980s as part of the recovery of Indian capitalism from the decade and a half of industrial stagnation (Chandrasekhar & Ghosh, 2002).

The double 'dependence' which was a general characteristic of Indian capitalism – its heavy reliance on cheap labour and on sourcing technology from abroad – were only increased by the new competitive context created by its increased integration with global circuits of capital. The imperatives of seeking to be a competitive location, and the increased openness to volatile capital flows, also reinforced the fiscal crisis of the State. The inability of the State to discipline the propertied classes and mobilize resources from them had always served to constrain the State's ability to support the capitalist accumulation process. This constraint became even more severe in the globalization era.

Indian capitalism found, however, in the conditions emerging out of a crisis and in the face of severe constraints, an opportunity to flourish as it never had in the past, even if not on a long-term basis. Even if originally triggered by crisis, the neoliberal economic 'reforms' after 1991 came to be thus wholeheartedly embraced by India's capitalist class.

A two-sided process of reinforcement of the labour surplus situation was the direct result of the 'reforms', making the labour supply conditions even more elastic and setting the stage for a long period of extreme wage stagnation. The initial impact of economic policy changes, in the form of weakening of State support to agriculture, triggered an agrarian crisis from the mid-1990s (Ramakumar, 2022) – the erosion of agriculture's capacity to provide sustenance to a large proportion of the labour reserve. In the early 1990s, agriculture still accounted for nearly two-thirds of total employment but a significant number then started getting pushed out of the sector. The agrarian crisis and liberalization on the other hand also meant that over time food prices increased much faster than those of manufactured goods. Manufactured prices reflected most the gains of increases in labour productivity, the access of capitalists to the means for which only increased with the opening up of India's economy. The relative cheapening of manufactured commodities also encompassed capital goods. Food price movements, on the other hand, tended to push up the relative price of labour power despite real wage stagnation, food being a significant part of the wage basket in a low wage economy. These in combination meant a generalizing strengthening of the labour substituting tendency across all sectors of the Indian economy. Though population growth rates have slowed down in India, her demographic transition is still in its early stages, and the proportion of the working age population is likely to go on rising for a few more decades. As such, the reinforcement of the labour surplus situation and wage stagnation tended to push up profitability and the surplus share in capitalist production activities. The non-wage share in income thus increased with growth – the beneficiaries being the propertied classes and a relatively small stratum of white collar employees (Chancel & Piketty, 2018).

The era of globalization of course has been one in which the mobility of capital and of commodities has fostered a shift in world production in the direction of lower wage locations in the Third World, as part of the mechanism for intensified exploitation of the working class for the benefit of both international and domestic capital. Cheap labour alone, however, was not sufficient to enable Indian capitalism to insert itself into the evolving global production system along the lines of China or the East and South East Asian region in general (Mazumdar, 2022). Instead, it made Indian integration more import-intensive in character – though the sources of these imports increasingly shifted from the advanced capitalist economies towards Asia. Even sectors achieving export success were significantly dependent on imports of intermediates and capital goods. Trade, therefore, had a net adverse effect on manufacturing demand in India. This reinforced the squeezing of demand for manufactured consumption goods inherent in the income distribution trends.

Despite the rise in trade deficit, Indian capitalism managed to avoid any serious currency crisis for two reasons. One was the growth of its 'invisibles' earnings and the other was capital inflows. The two main sources of invisibles earnings have been IT services exports and remittances from Indians working abroad. Paradoxically, the IT services sector, where mental labour with significantly higher remuneration predominates, turned out to be one of the biggest beneficiaries of the cheap labour context of Indian capitalism. Almost entirely reliant on exports, its growth was least subject to home market constraints. On the other hand, the general low wage context of its location meant that the dollar could purchase much more in the Indian market than in the US if it was converted into rupees at the prevailing exchange rate. In international markets, the relatively high cost mental labour also was cheapened through this process which gave rise to the differences in the size of the Indian economy on current dollar and PPP bases. India's surpluses in goods and services trade with countries like the US, and foreign capital flows through a dollar-based western dominated financial system, became critically important in offsetting the large trade deficits in trade with countries like China.

Ultimately, however, the greater purchasing power of the dollar in India was the direct effect of cheap labour on prices of non-tradeables. Their non-tradeable character further meant that they provided domestic market-based growth opportunities which were not threatened by import competition, provided rising incomes of a narrow segment of the population could generate an expanding demand. Construction (real estate and infrastructure) and many services served precisely this role even as the manufacturing demand from this population tended to reach saturation levels. The spill-over effects of speculative capital inflows on asset prices, and the credit growth these also fuelled, reinforced such spending growth. The fiscally constrained State vacating or privatizing many of these activities where it had played the prominent role in the past also opened them up for exploitation by private capital. A shift in the State–capital relationship, or more accurately a closer unity of purpose the two, was important in many ways to the growth of Indian big business (Mazumdar, 2022). To the extent that all of these accelerated the pace of real capitalist accumulation, the expenditure on capital formation also spurred growth of manufacturing demand – for means of production rather than means of consumption.

The only circumstance which could have prevented the labour surplus of Indian capitalism from becoming endemic, and eventually enable a significant rise in wage levels, was if the capital accumulation process had been able to sustain a high rate of expansion for a long period. However, the very conditions which drove it also simultaneously reinforced the narrowness of the domestic base for realizing the value contained in non-agricultural commodities, which could not be sufficiently compensated by exports. On the other hand, the growth in expenditure on services and on asset or wealth accumulation by relatively higher income groups did not provide a sustainable basis for capital accumulation either – the fixed capital requirements in many of these activities being considerably lower than in manufacturing and industry. A problem of over-accumulation, therefore, was inbuilt into the unbalanced growth pattern of Indian capitalism. This surfaced soon enough – the 2008 global crisis brought to a rude halt an unprecedented investment (and foreign trade) boom that had begun in the early years of the 21st century (Mazumdar, 2019). In the decade and a half since then, accumulation has been unable to recover, paving the way for the industrial stagnation and de-industrialization that has marked this period. The growth of profits also slowed down considerably and these added to the fiscal pressures of the State.

CRISIS, PARASITISM AND AUTHORITARIANISM

The period between 2003 and 2008 was the high point of Indian capitalist development in the post-1991 period. Stimulated by high levels of capital inflows and the acceleration in growth in the world economy, this period saw both an unprecedented investment boom as well as growth of manufactured exports. Temporarily, the construction boom and industrial investment engineered growth of demand for manufacturing even as growth moved further in the direction of services, inequalities increased very sharply and manufactured imports grew even faster. Unlike many other Third World economies who generated growing export surpluses and became net 'capital exporters' during this period, India saw an adverse movement in her balance of payments as the growth of merchandise trade imbalances was only partially moderated by the rapid growth of services exports and remittances (Mazumdar, 2014).[4] The large inflows of speculative finance more than compensated for this, but the consequent appreciation of the Indian rupee did not quite help the cause of reducing the imbalance in trade. Rapid growth of corporate profits and rising inequality, however, did push up State tax revenues from corporate and income taxes. This initiated the onset of an era of growth of a faux redistribution process – not involving any fundamental redistribution but some stepping up of expenditure on different kinds of State income support to low-income households even while adhering to the tenets of fiscal conservatism. The basis for this lay in the fact that under conditions of rising inequality and wage stagnation, an unchanged share of the State in national income meant a decline relative to the share of the propertied classes but an increase relative to that of working people. In the period before 2008, this allowed some stepping up of public expenditures under 'schemes' of income support, even as the levels of State debt relative to GDP were also brought down.

The idyllic situation of Indian capitalism came to an end in the years after 2008 as the accumulation process floundered with the emergence of excess capacity, the fiscal situation came under stress, and banks came to be saddled with a large amount of bad debt. Even as capital flows and global trade growth slowed down, international commodity prices rose as did gold imports into India as asset seeking resources moved away from productive investments. By 2011–2012, Indian capitalism came well and truly in the grips of a crisis in which it stayed for the entire decade leading up to the COVID-19 pandemic. This also coincided with the retreat from the post-crisis 'stimulus' and the enduring shift towards 'fiscal consolidation' as the dominant logic of fiscal policy. Within that constraint, the State made repeated efforts to revive investment by trying to induce more private investment. Improving the 'Ease of Doing Business', the 'Make-in-India programme', pro-capital amendments in labour laws, 'Start-Up India', subsidization of private capital through the 'Production-Linked-Incentive Scheme', corporate tax concessions, and cleaning up the stressed balance sheets of commercial banks, and even redirecting public expenditure towards building transport and digital infrastructure, etc., have all been part of the attempts to kick-start the investment process. Private capitalist enterprises, however, have lapped up any benefits these offered to them, but have continued to hold back on investment. The depressed investment situation and the onset of industrial stagnation also underlay the declining significance of imports even as the crisis of globalization held down export levels. This is what prevented the external imbalances from running out of hand, which in turn also served the objective of attracting capital flows of a financial nature towards India. The forms of these flows, however, have tended to undergo some change. The relative importance of classic portfolio investment has declined while other forms formally designated as direct investment – like private equity, venture capital invested in start-ups, etc. – have become increasingly important.

The inherent class outlook of the Indian capitalist class has of course ruled out any possibility of real redistribution and stepping up of public expenditure being used as the means of resolving the crisis of accumulation. Instead, the crisis, and the preferred means of dealing with it, has sharpened the contradictions between its capitalist class and the working people. A politics built around faux redistribution has continued to have a basis because the crisis has only served to reduce the labour absorption capacity of capitalist accumulation and reinforced stagnation in earnings from labouring activity. It has thus become possible for the relative weight of State support in the means by which working households sustain themselves to increase. However, under the circumstances the scope to use this to tilt the balance of forces further in favour of the capitalist class has been limited, even as the need for such tilting has increased. As the crisis of accumulation has become prolonged, capitalists are increasingly seeking their way out of it by tilting the distribution even more in their favour at the expense of the labour share, to centralize capital further in the hands of their relatively more successful members, and to encroach increasingly upon the value creation and appropriation processes that remain outside the fold of the corporate sector (specially the large unorganized sector). Indian capitalism thus has been moving in the direction of increasing parasitism as the alternative to accumulation by expansion of production. On the other side, the pattern of Indian integration into globalized capitalism has tended to make for India acquiring a more pro-western orientation and fuelled rivalry with China, a country with whom it already had a long-standing border dispute. This has made for a relatively more ambivalent position in the emerging West vs. East geo-political tensions, and nurtured hopes that a shift of global production out of China will now favour India. This also plays its part in keeping Indian capitalism wedded to neoliberalism.

The political expression of Indian capitalism's response to the crisis and its increasing parasitism has been the steady reconstruction of India's long-standing constitutional secular democracy, and its gradual morphing into an autocracy over the last decade. The drumming up of religious nationalism that targets the largest religious minority, a systematic process of abusing the law and the law enforcement machinery to stifle all political opposition to the ruling regime, undermining the independence of the judiciary and the autonomy of public institutions, promoting a cult of personality centred around the persona of India's Prime Minister since 2014, the coercing and cajoling the media into becoming an instrument to advance these ends, the monopolization of political funding from the propertied and wealthy, the use of coercion or money power to split and win over sections of opposition political parties, etc. – these have all served as mutually reinforcing means for such a reconstruction. The politics of faux redistribution has also been turned to the same purpose, showcased as the 'benevolent' side of increasing despotism. While the shell of a formal constitutional democracy has been retained, it has been increasingly emaciated of any content. The real objective of this has been to effectively immobilize India's working people, and to prevent the emergent contradictions from impelling them in the direction of asserting their class interests even in the limited way permitted by a bourgeois democratic system. It does not always succeed and struggles of the working class and the peasantry continue. The most notable was the recent epic struggle waged by Indian farmers, which pushed back the attempts to introduce new legislations which were designed to strengthen corporate appropriation of the value generated in agriculture.

CONCLUSION

The hollowing out of Indian democracy was of course inherent in the trajectory of Indian capitalist development, and the inevitable contradiction between an electoral democracy based on universal suffrage and a growing economic polarization. Such a hollowing out has also taken place across the capitalist world, including the advanced capitalist countries, in the last few decades. To that extent, the rapid erosion of India's democracy in recent times is the acceleration of a larger and longer pattern. It is also not the first time that Indian democracy was seriously overtly imperilled – the 'Emergency' of 1975–1977 being an important previous occasion. However, based as it is on the solid backing of the capitalist class, and mobilization of a large section, though not majority, of the Indian population behind a poisonous reactionary ideology, the current phase of authoritarianism in India is distinct. It is nevertheless an attempt at imposing an 'order' over a state of disorder, which cannot resolve the fundamental conditions giving rise to that disorder. It can, and is, only adding new elements to it. In a large country with such great linguistic, cultural and religious diversity, this poses some exceptional dangers. In more senses than one, therefore, India's capitalist development may be now in a phase where it is threatening what may have been its most significant historical creations.

NOTES

1. The term Third World here encompasses all those regions which had typically been under the colonial domination of the original centres of capitalist development till the mid-20th century, and had generally been bypassed till then by the rapid economic expansion that followed the Industrial Revolution of the 18th century.
2. Underlying international data from United Nations, United Nations Industrial Development Organization (UNIDO), United Nations Trade and Development (UNCTAD), International Labour Organization (ILO), The World Bank, International Monetary Fund (IMF). Indian sources are Reserve Bank of India (RBI), *Handbook of Statistics on the Indian Economy, and Census of Foreign Liabilities & Assets of Direct Investment Entities*; National Statistical Office (NSO), National Accounts Statistics (NAS), and Periodic Labour Force Survey (PLFS).
3. This expression was used by Thorner (1956).
4. An analysis of this phenomenon termed as the 'capital flows paradox' can be found in UNCTAD (2008).

REFERENCES

Appu, P. S. (1996). *Land reforms in India: A survey of policy, legislation and implementation*. Vikas Publishing House.

Chancel, L., & Piketty, T. (2018). *Indian income inequality, 1922–2015: From British Raj to Billionaire Raj?* World Inequality Database Working Paper Series, 11. https://wid.world/www-site/uploads/2017/12/ChancelPiketty2017WIDworld.pdf

Chandrasekhar, C. P., & Ghosh, J. (2002). *The market that failed: Neoliberal economic reforms in India* (2nd ed.). Left Word Books.

Chaudhuri, S. (2012). Multinationals and monopolies: Pharmaceutical industry in India after TRIPS. *Economic and Political Weekly*, *47*(12), 46–54.

Das Gupta, C. (2016). *State and capital in independent India: Institutions and accumulation*. Cambridge University Press.

D'Costa, A. P. (2004). The Indian software industry in the global division of labor. In A. P. D'Costa & E. Sridharan (Eds.), *India in the global software industry: Innovation, firm strategies and development* (pp. 1–26). Palgrave Macmillan.

Hoffman, A., & Batalova, J. (2022). Indian immigrants in the United States. *Migration Policy Institute*. https://www.migrationpolicy.org/article/indian-immigrants-united-states

Mani, S. (2020). *India's quest for technological self-reliance: Analysis of her record with respect to patents in the post trips phase*. Centre for Development Studies. CDS Working Paper 496. https://cds.edu/wp-content/uploads/WP496.pdf

Marx, K. (1974). *Capital* (Vol. III). Progress Publishers.

Mazumdar, S. (2013). Continuity and change in Indian capitalism. In U. Becker (Ed.), *The BRICs and emerging economies in comparative perspective: Political economy, liberalization and institutional change* (pp. 81–102). Routledge.

Mazumdar, S. (2014). Globalisation and growth: The Indian case in perspective. In R. Khasnabis & I. Chakraborty (Eds.), *Market, regulations and finance: Global meltdown and the Indian economy* (pp. 213–230). Springer.

Mazumdar, S. (2015). Monopoly and Indian industry. In C. P. Chandrasekhar (Ed.), *Indian industrialization, ICSSR research surveys and explorations in economics* (Vol. I, pp. 94–125). Oxford University Press.

Mazumdar, S. (2019). The Indian economy in the second decade of the twentieth century: Signs of a crisis? In A. Bhatnagar & C. Saratchand (Eds.), *Analytical perspectives on the Indian economy* (pp. 17–36). Aakar Books.

Mazumdar, S. (2022). Globalization, big business and economic nationalism: The Indian case. In A. Pickel (Ed.), *Handbook on economic nationalism* (pp. 327–352). Elgar.

Ramakumar, R. (2022). Introduction. In R. Ramakumar (Ed.), *Distress in the fields: Indian agriculture after economic liberalization* (pp. 1–68). Tulika Books.

Rawal, V., & Bansal, V. (2022). The land question in contemporary India. In R. Ramakumar (Ed.), *Distress in the fields: Indian agriculture after economic liberalization* (pp. 90–116). Tulika Books.

Ray, R. K. (1994). Introduction. In R. K. Ray (Ed.), *Entrepreneurship and industry in India 1800-1947* (pp. 1–69). Oxford University Press.

Rodrik, D. (2015). *Premature deindustrialization*. NBER Working Paper Series, Working Paper 20935. https://www.nber.org/papers/w20935

Thorner, D. (1956). *The agrarian prospect in India*. Lectures on Land Reform delivered in 1955 at the Delhi School of Economics. University Press.

Tyabji, N. (2000). *Industrialisation and innovation: The Indian experience*. Sage Publications.

UNCTAD. (2008). *Trade and development report: Commodity prices, capital flows and the financing of investment*. United Nations.

PAPUA NEW GUINEA, IN THE TRAP OF AUSTRALIAN IMPERIALISM

Poeura Tetoe[a] and Rémy Herrera[b]

[a]*Ministry of Education of French Polynesia, France*
[b]*CNRS (National Center of Scientific Research), France*

ABSTRACT

This chapter shows the ambivalence of the relationships between Papua New Guinea and Australia, by successively analyzing the historical links which bind these two countries (Part I), their continuity after independence (Part II), and the mechanisms of this dependence, especially at the economic and political levels (Part III). The social structures of Australia's former colony are studied, in particular in relation to the issues of the access to land and the expansion of the mining sector penetrated by foreign capital, around which the interests of the States and the transnational firms, on the one hand, and those of the Papua New Guinean people, on the other hand, are clashing.

Keywords: Papua New Guinea; development; dependency; natural resources; land regime; law; debt; public aid; Australia

INTRODUCTION

Maintaining privileged relations with the United States, Australia is a major regional power – imperialist, or rather sub-imperialist, as it is always subservient to Washington – whose direct sphere of influence essentially covers Papua New Guinea (PNG), the south-western South Pacific (Solomon Islands, Vanuatu, Fiji, Tuvalu, Nauru, Kiribati, in addition to the Coral Sea, Norfolk and Lord Howe, and a few dependencies in the Indian Ocean) and, in South-East Asia, East Timor. However, its officially asserted 'national defence' interests extend over a wide triangle delimited between Pakistan/India, Russian Siberia/China and the Pacific, including Indonesia. The acceptance of this zone by its allies does not exclude certain rivalries and occasional tensions – notably with France, which retains possessions in this region, or Great Britain, which still has a relatively

Trajectories of Declining and Destructive Capitalism
Research in Political Economy, Volume 40, 215–224

Published under exclusive licence by Emerald Publishing Limited
ISSN: 0161-7230/doi:10.1108/S0161-723020250000040014

strong influence over its former colonies. Australia's mission of 'regional stabilization' is carried out in partnership with New Zealand, which is more interested in Polynesia; with the United States encircling the whole area in an immense arc, beyond Hawaii, the Johnston, Wake and Midway atolls under military administration and the Line Islands, thanks to the control it exercised over Palau, Guam, the Federation of Micronesia, the Commonwealth of the Northern Marianas and American Samoa. This is Australia's 'preserve', providing an outlet for its exports and allowing it to dominate key sectors of many of the region's economies (Herrera, 2007), particularly in mining. Nevertheless, this phenomenon is most visible in the case of PNG.

THE LINKS OF HISTORY

PNG's links with Australia were strengthened at the end of the 19th century, when the gold rushes began. In 1883, a few months before the Berlin Conference, settlers from Queensland annexed the eastern part of the island of New Guinea. It was not until German interests in the Pacific were affirmed that London officially took possession of these territories, which were handed over to Australia in 1905. At the time, the main export was copra, with coffee, cocoa and rubber being secondary crops for export. As soon as World War I broke out, the Australian army occupied the German territories of New Guinea and Bismarck, before the League of Nations handed over the mandate in 1921. Australia was beginning to build up its own 'empire', taking over from England and setting out to economically conquer colonies in the Pacific.

In Papua and New Guinea, the incentives granted by the colonial administration to mining companies, and to the banks that financed them, encouraged new explorations, from which Australia drew substantial revenues. During the 1920s, Australia's external copper supplies came mainly from the Laloki mine, near Port Moresby. New Guinea Goldfields, a company which operated at Edie Creek and then at Golden Ridges, was floated on the Australian Stock Exchange in 1927, raising a record amount of capital at the time. Gold was discovered at Bougainville in 1924, then, in large quantities, at Porgera in the Highlands in 1938... In terms of value, gold was becoming a major export.

During the depression of the 1930s, which forced many settlers into bankruptcy, large trading companies from southern Australia arrived in force, buying up plantations in difficulty. At the same time, gold discoveries had also attracted big Australian investors. Private economic interests were therefore advancing within the colonial political framework. At the end of World War II, the United Nations renewed Australian trusteeship and, through the PNG Act of 1949, allowed the reunification of Papua and New Guinea.

In 1973, this territory was granted self-governing status within the Australian federation and, 2 years later, independence, taking the official name of *Papua Niugini*. Nevertheless, in the meantime, PNG had been placed dependent on the Australian market, which only opened up to imported products to the extent that its own industries required. This is in the metropolis that profits were reinvested – not in the periphery. PNG's exclusive specialization in the production of primary goods was to be so in depth that it prevented any industrialization, including in the coconut sector. These relations of economic domination were guaranteed by a tight military control of the country, which was placed under colonial administration.

Until the early 1960s, the colony's production and trade structures remained dominated by copra, coffee and cocoa, which were imported by the Australian agri-food industry. In the second-half of the 1960s, with the support of the colonial State and in the wake of Australian mining cycles, the phase of intensive exploitation of PNG's deposits began. New investors appeared, such as Conzinc Rio Tinto of Australia, as one discovery followed another: at Panguna on the island of Bougainville (in 1964) by Bougainville Copper, the Australian subsidiary of the Conzinc Rio Tinto group; at Ok Tedi in the Star Mountains (in 1968) by Kennecott Cooper Corp., also part of Rio Tinto, etc. This same transnational firm extended its exploration to Porgera in the mid-1960s, joined by its compatriots Mount Isa Mines and New Guinea Goldfields, among others.

Still under colonial rule, PNG's economy was turned upside down: by 1975, gold and copper had become the country's leading exports. That same year, Bougainville Copper posted the highest profits ever made by an Australian company. The mining boom, supported by Canberra and international organizations, accentuated the country's primary specialization and worsened its dependence on Australia, whose capital controlled the bulk of its exports. The economy of the colony, disarticulated, limiting its role to serving as a reservoir of labour, a supplier of raw materials and a plantation zone, became interwoven with the productive and commercial structures of the Australian metropolis, being a kind of overseas extension of it. More than half of Australia's direct investment went there. On the eve of independence, taken as a whole, Australian companies and their US and UK subsidiaries in Australia (Conzinc Rio Tinto, BHP, Carpenter, Burns Philp, Westpac, National Australia Bank, Comalco, Thiess, Boral, Dunlop...) were making profits from PNG that were close to a quarter of this country's gross domestic product (GDP).

The legal foundations on which the colonial economy rested was based on land and mining laws, that were not without effect for the indigenous populations – access to and appropriation of land becoming a crucial issue. The registration of customary land and the establishment of land ownership cadastres then became a priority for the Australian colonial administration. The pressure exerted on inland communities led to frequent clashes with the indigenous peoples. Australian plantation and trading companies first entered the coastal plains and islands, then the Highlands, where opportunities for new conquests opened up. Plots of land were requisitioned and leased to settlers, who recruited indigenous labour, particularly for coffee growing, which was gaining ground – and, with it, monetization.

However, from the 1950s onwards, the most vigorous penetration of the territory was linked to mining exploration, supported by both Canberra and international organizations. In 1952, the Native Land Commission was given responsibility for registering customary land, while the Land Act of 1962 imposed controls on land transactions, prohibiting the sale or lease of land by individual indigenous people outside customary law and reserving such transactions to the colonial State. The limited effects of these systematic registrations led to a number of relaxations. The Land Tenure Conversion Act of 1963 was designed to encourage landowners to register their plots themselves. But once again, the results were inconclusive and the indigenous communities stubbornly resisted.

The colonial authorities, anxious to secure titles to the land they had already acquired in order to satisfy the demands of the settler-planters, launched a new offencive against collective ownership in 1969 with the adoption of the Land Titles Bills, followed by the Land Reform Bills in 1971. By tightening its control over customary land tenure and reinstating registration procedures as its exclusive prerogative, the Australian administration reverted to the land tenure system most suited to its interests, at a time when PNG's specialization was undergoing a profound transformation, moving from agriculture to the mining and oil sectors. Nevertheless, the numerous protests forced Australia to suspend the 'reform' a few months before the territory achieved self-governing status. Postponed *sine die*, the application of the land laws had to take other forms; all the more so as the new government (not yet independent) had expressed the wish to recover alienated land and to give constitutional recognition to customary land ownership.

DEPENDENCE DESPITE INDEPENDENCE

The 1972 elections brought to power a coalition led by Michael Somare's PNG Union Party, supporter of independence. Tensions soon flared, both within the alliance and with Australia. The stakes were so high, and the mining and oil profits so enormous, that Australia had carefully prepared for the independence of its colony. Other territories in the region had already been liberated, but PNG's key location for the United States and its Australian ally was accentuated, in the context of the Cold War, by the imperialist defeat in Vietnam. The Papua New Guinean independence movement had gained strength in the 1960s, marking a desire to break with the colonial system and, on the part of the elites, that to promote local production and a redistribution of profits that was more favourable to them.

Following independence, proclaimed on September 16, 1975, one of the Somare government's priorities was to implement a development plan which, thanks in particular to State control of key sectors, would lead to the takeover of the local economy by the Natives. This ambitious programme, aimed at strengthening the country's economic sovereignty, failed to achieve its objectives, despite occasional advances. The failure was linked to the weaknesses of the central State and of the sense of national identity, but above all to the strategy applied. For, beyond proclamations of principle, the measures actually adopted did not call into question the preponderance of primary export products inherited from colonization, and even put again improving the attractiveness of the institutional environment for foreign investors in the mining sectors at the top of the agenda: pressure to 'reform' the land tenure system and impose individual private ownership, guarantees for non-expropriation, abolition of customs duties, free repatriation of profits, construction of support infrastructure, etc.

The 'securitization' of foreign capital, encouraged by international organizations, was guaranteed by a policy of political stabilization of the territory – and by harsh social repression. The 1975 miners' strikes in Panguna resulted in massive waves of arrests, while the central government refused, in Bougainville, to meet the demands of landowners' community groups seeking to renegotiate the terms of their contract with Conzinc Rio Tinto. That same year, PNG joined the International Monetary Fund (IMF), the World Bank and the General Agreement on Tariffs and Trade (GATT). The continuation of Australian public aid ensured the continuity of privileged relations with the former metropolis.

Determined by international markets, mining cycles set the pace for the country's economic life (Herrera & Tetoe, 2011). At the end of the 1970s, mining focussed mainly on the Panguna and Wau deposits, then controlled by Bougainville Copper and New Guinea Goldfields, respectively. The surge in precious metal prices in the early 1980s revived exploration. By 1988, Panguna was the largest open-pit copper mine in the world, and one of the largest for gold. The Papua New Guinean government, as a minority shareholder, derived almost a fifth of its budgetary revenue from it. However, the mine had to cease operations in May 1989 following the outbreak of the bloody conflict with the people of Bougainville – close to those of the Solomon Islands, but separated from them by colonization; a conflict that descended into civil war for almost a decade and in which a large part of the local population perished (in the complicit silence of dominant media). From 1990 onwards, the relay for gold was going to be taken by the mines of Ok Tedi, Porgera and Lihir, to which 80% of foreign investment was directed, boosted by generous tax breaks. The dynamism of gold exports (and other strategic minerals such as silver, copper, nickel, etc.), followed by oil, had nothing in common with the changes in those of coffee or palm oil.

Since the 1980s, internal events (closure of the Panguna mine, mounting public debt) and external shocks (higher cost of imported energy, falling prices for exported raw materials) have combined to worsen the country's financial situation. The internal and external accounts deteriorated with simultaneous widening of the State budget and current account deficits, while foreign exchange reserves melted away. These difficulties forced the government to go further into debt to international lenders. In the end, the attempt at self-centred development was so short-lived that the country seems to have gone straight from colonialism to neoliberalism.

The structural adjustment programmes (SAPs) successively applied in 1989, 1995 and 1999 marked PNG's entry into the neoliberal era. Prime Minister from 1988 to 1992, Rabbie Namaliu, the leader of the political party called Pangu Pati, launched the first SAP, disguised as 'restructuring reforms' for the economy: privatization of State-owned enterprises, liberalization of foreign trade, deregulation of investment, tax gifts for businesses, a more flexible labour market, etc. The aim was to re-establish the 'stability' of macroeconomic indicators, to be achieved at the cost of a contraction in public spending, a restrictive monetary policy and a devaluation of the currency (kina). The results were very mixed:

although the GDP growth rate recovered and the various imbalances in the components of balance of payments were contained, the constraints imposed by this strategy were asphyxiating. The structural causes of dependence were in no way eradicated.

The illusion could not last: by 1994, the deterioration in public finances meant that the country had to turn again to the IMF for loans. The counterpart was a second SAP, launched in 1995 by Julius Chan's government. The reality of this so-called 'structural reform' programme was that it accentuated the country's economic subjugation by continuing to dismantle State regulations on foreign investment, foreign trade, prices and the labour market. The measures taken were in line with neoliberal dogmas: renewed privatizations, a floating exchange rate, further abolition of customs duties, price liberalisation, wage cuts and freezes, increase in household costs for education and health, and so on. In 1996, the country joined the World Trade Organization (WTO) – after entering the Asia Pacific Economic Cooperation (APEC) in 1993 and obtaining observer status within the Association of South-East Asian Nations (ASEAN).

Drastic and unpopular, these decisions did not prevent the country's situation from deteriorating. Faced with exogenous shocks (the effects of the Asian crisis, falling export prices, drought, etc.), the government of Prime Minister Mekere Morauta (1999–2002), then that of the historic leader M. Somare (Prime Minister from 2002 to 2010, and leader of the National Alliance Party), adopted a third SAP, dictated jointly by Australia and international institutions, including the Asian Development Bank. Still under the banner of 'stabilization', they further accelerated liberalization and the opening up to foreign capital – in an economy now dominated by hydrocarbon and gold exports.

One of the most decisive reforms of the 2000s was that of the financial sector, which consolidated the independence of the Central Bank and transferred to private ownership several credit institutions, insurance companies and pension funds that had previously been majority State-owned. In this 'modernized' system, controlled by foreign financial oligopolies and where pension funds were making their appearance, the profits generated by the accumulation of fictitious capital, here as elsewhere, exploded. Dependency persisted, albeit in a different context, that of financialized capitalism.

What distinguishes neoliberalism in PNG, a country where over 95% of land is now under customary law (Herrera & Tetoe, 2015), is the priority given to establishing land ownership cadastres in order to register community land. The justification for this strategy was the argument that the persistence of ancestral rights over the soils and subsoils would act as a brake on development. Hence the insistence – by foreign investors and international organizations – on the privatization of land and the establishment of institutions guaranteeing individualized property titles subject to modern capitalist laws.

The very specific relationship of this social formation to land and its attachment to collective ownership are reflected in the fact that land laws derive from two sources, both constitutionally recognized: the western capitalist tenure system, introduced by the colonial administration and currently managed by the modern State; and the customary system. Consequently, two forms of land organization coexist: one based on traditional systems and covering almost 97% of the soils; the other corresponding to other land, whether State-owned or private. Thus, in practice, so-called 'alienated' land administered by the State, and reserved for mining and hydrocarbon companies in particular, currently covers less than 3% of the national territory. It is therefore easy to understand why transnational firms are so keen to privatize indigenous communal properties. As a matter of fact, every SAP has included a 'land reform' component – i.e., privatization of land – as a condition of its loans.

Faced with pressure from investors and lenders, the position of the Papua New Guinean government remains ambiguous. In theory, land transactions should be carried out through the State, since it alone is authorized to buy and lease community land. The existence of use rights that foreign capital cannot ignore naturally poses a problem for the local authorities, particularly when allocating deposits to transnational firms or building infrastructure to support their activities. This requires the granting of resource exploitation rights to private investors and the alienation of customary land.

We observe, however, that this very particular land structure, still dominated by traditionally collective forms of social organization, has not prevented the growth of the export sectors of mining, hydrocarbons and agribusiness. It is true that some land transactions take place outside the sphere of State intervention. But we see that, if the State recognizes the customary property rights of community groups everywhere – even where the subsoil is rich, it only preserves the integrity of these rights in practice where the lands are of little interest to private investors. Elsewhere, it seizes the soils and transfers their use – including to foreign capital – along with everything that goes with it, both below (oilfields, mines) and above (plantations, forests).

A series of laws were enacted to this end, by sector of activity. Access to natural resources and their exploitation by foreign companies is thus achieved with the support of a State that knows how to articulate these appropriation processes and ancestral structures of collective ownership, without however establishing a 'free' land market. When a joint venture project is launched, the solution is generally for the investors to pay monetary compensation to the landholders. Clearly, 'every man for himself' attitudes are gaining ground, leading to tensions and even the break-up of clans. But, simultaneously, the groups recognized as landholders, or even as shareholders, have got money and prestige from it. Despite pressure exercised to divide and individualize land ownership, successive Papua New Guinean governments have been unable to challenge customary ownership because of the scale of the popular uprisings which made them retreat – at least until now.

THE MECHANISMS OF ECONOMIC DEPENDENCE

Today, three-quarters of the Papua New Guinean workforce is still engaged in subsistence food growing, whose products are consumed by farmers themselves or sold on local markets – and only marginally exported. However, it is the highly capital-intensive mining and energy sectors, which account for almost 20% of GDP, that are the engines of the economy's growth. At the start of the 2010s, the country's copper production ranked 13th in the world and its gold production 11th – with the world's third-largest gold reserves. Most of this gold is refined in Perth, and then re-exported from Australia. The largest mining systems in activity are concentrated in the Highlands and on the surrounding islands: Ok Tedi, Lihir, Porgera, or Morobe.

Australia is omnipresent in the capital ownership structure of the mining consortiums: until 2001, the Ok Tedi site was majority-owned by the world's leading mining group at the time, the Australian–British BHP–Billiton – which had to pull out after an environmental scandal; the Lihir site belongs to Newcrest Mining, the world's fifth-largest gold producer, located in Melbourne; this same group operates the Wafi–Golpu (gold and copper) and Hidden Valley–Hamata (gold, silver) joint-ventures in Morobe Province, etc. The same applies to control of the oil and gas consortiums in the Southern Highlands.

The Papua New Guinean economy, extremely dependent on the outside world, is therefore more particularly subordinate to Australia (Herrera & Tetoe, 2012). During the 2010s, its first commercial partner was still, by far, the former colonial authority. Nearly half of commodity imports came from Australia, which found a guaranteed outlet for its products in PNG. The importance of the Australian market, close, vast and dynamic, was also perceptible in terms of exports: more than a quarter of them were destined there, but for a much more limited range of merchandises.

This dependence is reflected in the composition of trade. At the aggregate level, the leading import items are fuels, capital goods and chemicals. A large part of imports is driven, not by the logic of accumulation of domestic capital, but by that of foreign investment in the oil and mining sectors, the engines of exports. Imports of consumer goods only arrive afterwards, reflecting the non-priority nature of satisfying the basic needs of the population, as well as luxury behaviours of the most privileged sections of society. The structure of exports includes almost exclusively primary products. More than two thirds of these are unprocessed mineral products (gold, crude oil, copper, silver, etc.) and around a quarter are unprocessed agricultural products (coffee, cocoa, palm and copra oils, wood, etc.). Furthermore, trade with Australia is also distorted by the weight of 'special transactions and confidential items', classified as 'defence secrets'.

Concerning trade with the United States, oil sales lead the way in exports, followed by gold; and, on the import side, machinery, capital goods and transport equipment come out on top. Since the start of the 2000s, trade has intensified with China, which has become PNG's third partner.

The strong dependence of the Papua New Guinean productive apparatus, inserted in a polarizing network of regional exchanges that do not meet the country's development needs, is visible in the dissymmetry existing between the trade balance surplus and the deficit in the balance of invisibles. The first is due to the expansion of external demand; and the second to payments of dividends on foreign direct investments (FDIs) and debt interest. However, profits leaving the country widen the chronic deficits in the current account balance and the financial balance. These surplus transfers are largely carried out for the benefit of Australian banks and companies. The bulk of dividends paid to foreign asset holders go to Australian capital owners. The equilibrium of payments balance is therefore essentially achieved, thanks to incoming flows of FDIs and external public aid. FDIs are predominantly Australian (followed by those from the United States), and mainly invested in mining and hydrocarbons. Public aid comes primarily from Australia (and secondarily from Japan).

The logic of these private and public flows seems clear: the Papua New Guinean State ensures the opening of local markets and the privatization of enterprises it owned for the benefit of private capital, especially foreign capital; the latter enters into the capital ownership structures of the country and operates the transfers of surplus from the local economy to foreign firms and banks; Australian 'cooperation' provides this State with the aid necessary to rebalance public deficits and a balance of payments disrupted by these transfers to the outside, while deepening the neoliberal strategy – and subduing, through violence, the local resistance. PNG enjoys the status of the first recipient country of Australian public aid, via the Australian Government's Overseas Aid Program – that is, more than half of the bilateral aid granted by Canberra. The adoption of neoliberal reforms, as well as the respect for 'good governance' – in a country considered one of the most corrupt in the world–, determine bilateral aid.

In this scheme, external debt plays a key role. The latter rose significantly during the 1990s, following the increase in financing requirements linked to the extension of new mining (Lihir site) and oil (Kutubu complex) activities; then again at the end of the decade, following the Asian crisis of 1998 and the appeal to international organizations. After a peak reached in 2003–2004, a decline allowed this debt to return in 2009 to its 1999 level. However, the flows caused by the service of external debt remain today higher than those of public aid received. In the 2000s, the stock of public debt, almost exclusively long-term, was roughly equivalent to the value of GDP, that is, one and a half times that of exports and three times the total State budget. Of this amount, three-quarters were owed to international organizations, the rest corresponding to bilateral public debts contracted mainly with Australia. Added to this, the commitments are also important vis-à-vis the IMF.

Nevertheless, domestic debt, the repayment of which requires more external debt, tends to increase, especially in the form of PNG Treasury bonds, held by foreign institutional investors, but also by national agents, many of whom include senior army officials. In a context where the sovereign function of national defence is partially 'delegated' to Australia and to private military companies to protect strategic sites for foreign capital, the role of some fractions of the national army was determinant in the neoliberal orientation of the course of economic policy. In parallel, Australian military aid is crucial in the device aimed at convincing the Papua New Guinean authorities to adopt a line consistent with Canberra's strategic interests.

The political evolution in PNG remains difficult to predict, especially as tensions are brewing in certain Melanesian islands. Already, during a referendum in December 2019, the inhabitants of the island (and autonomous region) of

Bougainville voted, by more than 98%, in favour of independence – the process of which is underway and which should normally intervene by 2027. The impact of external constraints and a high degree of dependence has been decisive on the trajectory taken by the Papua New Guinean economy, marked by the relative weakness and instability of its long-term economic growth.

It is again dependence on the outside world which explains certain rigidities characterizing public finances. On the revenue side, income generated by corporate tax increased (until 2008 and the outbreak of the global financial crisis), but the dividend tax regime nonetheless remains very accommodating for transnational firms, themselves encouraged by many tax incentives. On the expenditure side, public funds financing major works supporting private capital absorb disproportionate shares of the State budget, while infrastructure vital to subsistence agriculture, import substitution industries and domestic trade is neglected.

CONCLUSION

As a result, the immediate needs of the population are sacrificed and PNG's social indicators are among the worst in the world, particularly with regard to education, health, social inequalities, etc. We therefore understand both the destructive impact produced by the extension of capitalist land relations on the survival of ancestral links of solidarity and the reasons which have pushed large sections of society to revolt in recent years against the rigour of SAPs, privatization of natural resources and land status 'reforms'. This resistance raises the question of the search for alternatives to neoliberalism in the form of a strategy guaranteeing balanced, self-centred development that benefits the people. The country's dependence is certainly extreme on international lenders and donors, and the crisis has degraded the structure of trade. The government's room for manoeuver is narrow, in a country whose GDP barely exceeds half the turnover of Rio Tinto – one of the transnational firms operating on its soil. Nevertheless, they are not non-existent; especially since revenues from mining and oil exports could make it possible to consider the redistribution of rent in the direction of better satisfaction of social needs, based on a land regime where arable land still largely escapes modern capitalist laws.

REFERENCES

Herrera, R. (2007). Australie: l'impérialisme oublié. *Afrique Asie*, *7/8*, 58–61.

Herrera, R., & Tetoe, P. (2011). Le Capital étranger dans le secteur des mines en Papouasie Nouvelle–Guinée. *Économies et Sociétés*, *45*(2), 321–360.

Herrera, R., & Tetoe, P. (2012). Papouasie Nouvelle–Guinée/Australie: des relations ambivalentes. *Journal de la Société des Océanistes*, *2*(135), 201–214.

Herrera, R., & Tetoe, P. (2015). The *Papua Niugini* paradox: Land property archaism and modernity of peasant resistance? In R. Herrera & K. C. Lau (Eds.), *The struggle for food sovereignty* (pp. 119–135). Pluto Press.

THE LONG-LASTING BATTLE OF CHILE

Marcelo Dias Carcanholo and
Hugo Figueira de Souza Corrêa

Fluminense Federal University, Brazil

ABSTRACT

This chapter aims to identify in the socioeconomic evolution of Chile since the 1973 military coup and the pioneering implementation of neoliberalism in the country the reasons for the social outburst that occurred in 2019. The objective is to demonstrate that the class struggle in this long battle is based on contradictions presented by the implementation of such strategy, at first, during the military dictatorship years (1973–1990) and, after that, through what the authors argue to have been gatopardismo within the democratic transition. In conclusion, it is pointed out that Chile's long battle appears to be far from a decision.

Keywords: Chile; capitalism; neoliberalism; class struggle; social movements; '*gatopardismo*'; military dictatorship; democratic transition

INTRODUCTION

Not only the title of this article but also the argument that unfolds are inspired by Patrício Guzmán's trilogy, *La Batalla de Chile* (1975–1979). This award-winning documentary film shows the entire process of explicit class struggle preceding and leading to the election of the socialist government of Salvador Allende in 1970, as well as the coup of September 11, 1973, when the counter-revolution takes power, deepening its counter-offencive and, in brutal and genocidal ways, torturing murdering, 'disappearing' and exiling thousands of people.

Through this work, Patricio Guzmán shows us how the social dynamic of class struggle is an actual battle made up of all its social, political, economic, ideological and armed warfare elements. Our starting point here is that this Battle of Chile, that is, the social process of class struggle in what may be called the

Trajectories of Declining and Destructive Capitalism
Research in Political Economy, Volume 40, 225–239

ISSN: 0161-7230/doi:10.1108/S0161-72302025000040015

Chilean revolution, does not end with the 1973 coup. The social dynamic of the Chilean revolution spans the entire period of the military dictatorship (1973–1990), as well as the different moments of the post-dictatorship era (1990–2018) of the so-called democratic transition, when the *Concertación* governments predominated until the present day. Thus, the Chilean revolution that Patricio Guzmán called the Battle of Chile may be renamed, in light of current events, as the Long-lasting Battle of Chile.

What is most striking about the current moment of the Chilean class struggle is the process that was revealed on October 18, 2019 by the multiform social outburst (students, workers, feminists, indigenous people, indebted people, unemployed people, informal workers, etc.) which lasted for months. This heterogeneous uprising, however, was not an isolated, random, unprecedented phenomenon, nor was it without consequences. The reasons behind the so-called social outburst of 2019, both structural and conjunctural, are one of the aspects that this chapter aims to analyze. On the other hand, it was such an important social process that it produced fundamental social and political developments to this long duration of battle of Chile, which we will also try to address here.

From the outset, we must point out a question that will structure our entire journey to achieve the proposed objectives. Although the multifaceted heterogeneity of the 2019 uprising is undeniable, something must have unified this social outburst, even if not obvious or immediately apprehensible in the consciousness of the different identity specificities that made up this concrete process. What provides unity? Unfolding this might be the main objective of our chapter.

MILITARY COUP AND NEOLIBERALISM IN CHILE (1973–1990)

On September 11, 1973, the military coup led by Augusto Pinochet put an end to the Chilean experience of a declared search for the democratic road to socialism, establishing the military regime that would pioneer the implementation of a neoliberal prescription. The coup must be understood in light of the class struggle that had allowed *Unidad Popular* (henceforth UP, or People's Unity) to rise to power and determined the limits of its capacity for action.[1] It did not fall like a 'bolt from the blue:' it was the result of contradictions caused by Chilean developmentalism in the context of dependent development, especially those caused between fractions of the bourgeois class and towards the petite bourgeoisie.

The contradictions within the Chilean developmentalist project had reached clear limits under the Frei Montalva government (1964–1970), as it dissociated the interests of the working classes, the petite bourgeoisie and the high bourgeoisie. Its policies had enabled a substantial advance in the processes of monopolization of the economy and the entry of big foreign capital into the dynamic sectors of the Chilean economy. At the same time, the result of these policies had been the fostering of not only the erosion of the working classes' capacity of consumption but also the displacement of the Chilean petite bourgeoisie from positions of privilege it had become accustomed to, increasing dissatisfaction and the division between supporters of wings further to the right or to the left of the prevailing political spectrum.

From this scenario of fissure of fractions of the bourgeoisie and growing popular dissatisfaction, the electoral victory of the UP emerged. But the Allende government would have to navigate that same sea of contradictions, now even more turbulent, since the victory of the socialist project served as a catalyst for the right-wing forces that would begin to work ever harder to paralyze and overthrow the democratically elected government.

Initially, the UP responded by betting on a distributist policy, which was possible due to the idle capacity and domestic availability of industrial raw materials and foreign currency, in order to activate demand and satisfy popular and bourgeois interests. Within the proposed strategy, the positive results of this policy should enable the government to garner support for deeper reforms in the property structure, pushing ahead the agrarian reform and nationalization processes (which nevertheless affected the banking sector and some productive sectors).

Hopes of reconciling the interests of the working class with the gains of capital in an industrialist project, or of being able to push forward deeper reforms in the property structure, however, proved to be in vain. The inflationary effects of the policy based on expanding the capacity of consumption (without confronting bourgeois income more forcefully), on the one hand, and, on the other, the obstacles imposed on institutional reforms to advance the socialization of the means of production, determined the economic aspect of the impasse of the 'Chilean road' to socialism. Meanwhile, in the political field, the reorganization of the right and ultra-right, fuelled by the support of US imperialism, and the difficulty of radicalizing in defense of the socialist project on the Allendist left already pointed out the inauspicious future of the Chilean revolution. The reaction came, first in the form of boycotts of the production and distribution of goods, then in the form of a stalemate between the executive and legislative branches, and finally in the form of a coup d'État in September 1973.

The coup and the dictatorship that followed it were necessary because the crisis in the capitalist world economy at that time demanded an increase in the rate of exploitation, even more so in dependent economies like the Chilean. Furthermore, in every process of resuming capital accumulation after a crisis, the need for primitive capital accumulation is reinforced, with an increase in expropriations, privatizations and the entry of foreign capital. Neoliberalism, at that time, was a necessity for world capitalism and, with its own particularities, in dependent economies like the Chilean.

With Pinochet, it should have become clear from the outset that the kind of freedom that neoliberals were concerned about – in Chile and in the rest of the world, as would be demonstrated – was never to include democracy (not even formal democracy) and its civil and political freedoms as a necessary pillar. *Market freedom* asserted over any other form of freedom would thus become a defining feature of the times to come.[2]

The neoliberal development strategy, pioneered by the Chilean dictatorship, is largely misunderstood in at least two aspects. First, this strategy is confused with the orthodox economic policies of stabilization, contemporaneously composed of the inflation targeting regime in monetary policy, austerity in fiscal policy and the floating exchange rate regime in exchange rate policy. This is, however, a mistake. Neoliberalism is based on two basic points. Firstly, as a precondition, macroeconomic stabilization is advocated, basically concerning inflation and public spending. Nevertheless, it does not matter whether this stabilization is achieved through orthodox or heterodox policies, as long as it is achieved. Thus, for example, fundamental price control policies, such as the exchange rate, in some periods of the Chilean dictatorship as well as, in a widespread way, in Latin America in the 1990s, are not unusual to neoliberalism. What defines the correct economic policy to achieve stabilization is each particular scenario.

Having achieved the precondition of stabilization, the second and most important point is the defense of structural reforms, in the sense of increasing the commodification of social relations, promoting privatization, deregulation, liberalization and opening the main markets to international competition. These reforms, according to their advocates, would guarantee an increase in competition, productivity, investment and growth, with positive impacts on income distribution. This is the promise that neoliberalism forever touts.

The second misunderstanding about neoliberalism is considering its clumsiest and lax version valid, according to which greater market participation in the allocation of resources is synonymous with less State participation in the economy and society. On the contrary, given the fact that neoliberalism sets out from a historical context in which the State, in a very limited and specific way, takes part in the economy, it is necessary, according to neoliberals, to deconstruct the possible social gains that class struggle has brought to fractions of the working class. For this to happen, a strong, present and very active State is needed, as to provide the dismantling of these hard-won social rights with a certain aura of legitimacy. On the other hand, a strong State is also necessary to repress any social resistance and protests which will certainly arise as a result of this action.

Looking back, the limits of the UP's class conciliation policy, revealed by the Chilean military coup, find parallels with those present in central economies of the post-war period, as the turn of the 1980s would reveal although the social consequences experienced in post-1973 Chile would turn out to be somewhat more drastic due to the violence with which the neoliberal counter-revolution was established and the very dependent nature of its economy. The 'stabilization of the Cold War' and the popular reaction to the contradictions of the post-war social arrangement between the late 1960s and the 1970s, the economic crisis manifested in falling profit rates, the collapse of the Bretton Woods system, the Oil Shock, and, finally, the so-called stagflation were all clear symptoms that the tectonic plates were moving, unfortunately to the right.

Thus, anticipating the conservative wave that would sweep the world from the 1980s onwards, the Chilean military government set in motion a 'pilot project' of the neoliberal program that would spread around the world. The Pinochet dictatorship set in motion a regressive reform of the tax system (favoring indirect taxation and the reduction of taxes on wealth and capital gains, etc.), a labor reform (with the repression of unions, suspension of collective bargaining, expansion of individual and flexible contracts, restriction of the right to strike, etc.), a social security reform (with the privatization of the social security system), a broad privatization plan, a reversal of the agrarian reform promoted under the UP administration, and the processes of trade and financial opening.

The 'Chilean laboratory' of the neoliberal project was then touted as an example to be followed. The false Chilean 'miracle' was first publicized between 1977 and 1982. An average growth of 8% and the containment of inflationary trends were supposed to be the sign that the country was finally on the right track.

The neoliberal experiment in Chile was deemed extremely successful by its advocates. Mckinnon (1982, p. 159) went so far as to say that 'the order of economic liberalization laid out below approximates the successful Chilean experience after 1975, Chile is to be treated as a norm or standard of reference'. What this prestigious (at the time) author was defending was the so-called optimal sequence in the process of external economic opening, according to which the checking account should be liberalized first and only then should the capital account be liberalized. External openness was an essential part of the promise made by the neoliberal development strategy.

Reality, however, would impose itself in a different direction. Shortly after Mckinnon's statement, the currency and economic crisis hit Chile, leading to a massive capital flight. The year 1982 would reveal the impact that increased external vulnerability can have. Domestic product fell by around 12% and unemployment rates exceeded ¼ of the economically active population. It is true that this 1982 fall cannot be dissociated from the peripheral 'debt crisis', which began with the Mexican moratorium that same year, but neither can it be understood without looking at the policies that had allowed the external vulnerability of the Chilean economy to be increased through both liberalization and the increase in the servicing of the external debt that emerged as a counterpoint to the capital inflows of the period.

The post-1982 period thus inaugurated a phase of the Chilean economy in which neoliberalism was maintained as a strategic orientation, even if this involved the adoption of heterodox policies.

'GATOPARDISMO' OF THE DEMOCRATIC TRANSITION AND 'CONCERTACIÓN' GOVERNMENTS (1990–2018)[3]

The milestone for the end of the Pinochet dictatorship was the plebiscite held on October 5, 1988, when the Chilean population had to answer whether or not they agreed with Pinochet remaining in power. On that day, 54.68% of the population voted 'No', while 43.04% voted for continuity. From then on, it is often said that the process of transition from dictatorship to democracy began.

In the first place, this process was not the result of a benefaction and/or enlightenment of the dictatorship. On the contrary, the transition was necessary for the continuity of Chilean-dependent capitalism. On the one hand, because the intensification of the class struggle led to strong protests against the dictatorship, such as those that took place in 1983, 1985 and 1986. On the other hand, what is actually reinforced by the above, because the dictatorship became a real nuisance for the process of dependent accumulation in the country. So much that even the United States supported the 'No' vote in the plebiscite.

Secondly, it can be said that between the dictatorship and the 'transition' governments there was also a transition, a kind of moment of mediation. Already defeated in the plebiscite, Pinochet accepted a series of constitutional reforms, also approved through a plebiscite on July 30, 1989, and enacted by Law 18,825 of August 17th of the same year. Through these reforms, the forces represented by the dictatorship, which had been defeated at the time, were able to block any changes proposed by the new government via the Parliament. This might have been the first clear manifestation of 'gatopardismo'.

The origin of the concept of 'gatopardismo' is Giuseppe Tomasi di Lampedusa's novel *Il Gatopardo* (The Leopard), about the unification of Italy in the 19th century. The term seeks to capture processes of change of form (reform) with the intention, conscious or not, explicit or veiled, of maintaining the content. In one of this novel's most famous phrases, 'se vogliamo che tutto rimanga uguale, tutto deve cambiare' [If we want everything to remain as it is, everything must change]. We will try to demonstrate that the so-called 'democratic transition' was an illustrative example of *gatopardismo*.[4]

Nevertheless, *gatopardismo* had been going on for some time. The gestation of the democratic transition took place in the process of the formation of the *Concertación por la Democracia* (concertation for democracy) political strength, when the main party leaderships coalesced around two major agreements, clearly seeking to contain social mobilizations. The first agreement is the *Acuerdo Nacional por la Transición a la Plena Democracia* (National Agreement for the Transition to Full Democracy) of August 25, 1985, sponsored by the Catholic Church. The second, of September 8, 1986, called *Bases de Sustentación del Régimen Democrático* (Bases of Support of the Democratic Regime) was developed from the first agreement. The bases of these agreements that would form the *Concertación* are the reconciliation of the country and the 'concertación social'. These are strict neologisms. Reconciliation meant nothing but impunity for the crimes committed under and by the dictatorship. The 'concertación social', while recognizing that the Chilean economic model had produced social inequalities, did not imply breaking with it, but, taking it as a premise, proposed measures to mitigate the resulting social problems. The theoretical basis here was the so-called 'New ECLAC' (Economic Commission for Latin America and the Caribbean).[5]

The structuralist thinking of the ECLAC in the middle of the last century was based on a critical diagnosis of the orthodox economic development theory, identifying Latin America's economic and social problems in its subordinate position in the international division of labour. Its proposal was to promote a process of industrialization of the economy, based on a proactive State policy and confronting the signs of the free market, in what became known as national developmentalism.

The so-called New ECLAC, right at the end of the last century, when neoliberalism reached its practical and theoretical hegemony, sought to oppose both this hegemony and the limits that, according to it, the old structuralist thinking presented. Despite recognizing some of the economic and social problems resulting from the neoliberal strategy, its proposal was not to abandon the neoliberal reforms, but to deal with them pragmatically (*Reforming the Reforms*). Firstly, under the shameless argument that the cost of abandoning the liberalizing reforms would outweigh the benefits, it was a matter of resignedly departing from the reforms that had already been made. Secondly, taking advantage of and deepening the benefits that these reforms would bring, such as increased competition and productivity. Thirdly, in order to minimize the costs of the processes of liberalization and external economic opening, the State was to implement economic policies to manage and direct incoming foreign capital towards productive investments, mainly in sectors geared towards future exports, taking into consideration the need for mechanisms to selectively control foreign capital. Fourthly, promoting targeted and compensatory social policies in order to minimize the social problems caused by the reforms (*Transformación Productiva con Equidad*, to be translated by Productive Transformation with Equity).

In short, the conservative reformism of the New ECLAC proposed simply managing the imperfections in the functioning of markets, encouraged by neoliberal reforms, in line with the emerging new orthodoxy in macroeconomics, the new Keynesianism. The ideologues of the New ECLAC believed that it differed from neoliberalism in that the State would play an active role in regulating the economy and promoting heterodox economic policies. Their mistake is to believe that neoliberalism is defined by orthodox economic policies, on the one hand, and by minimizing the role of the State, on the other. One of the main members of the economic team of the beginning of the democratic transition went so far as to say that 'the *Concertación* governments decided to avoid radical changes in current economic policy and sought change in continuity' (Ffrench–Davis, 2002, p. 83). Change while maintaining continuity may be considered an expression of *Gatopardist* confession. Furthermore, the fact that this prestigious economist did his PhD at the University of Chicago in 1971 is no coincidence.

The formal end of the Chilean dictatorship, and therefore of what we call the transition or mediation towards a democratic transition, came with the proclamation of Patricio Aylwin as president on March 11, 1990. The elections of December 14, 1989 had given him 55.71% of the vote, compared to 29.4% for Büchi, the pro-dictatorship candidate. Aylwin was elected by the *Concertación por la Democracia*, formally founded in 1988 by the Christian Democracy Party, the Socialist Party, the Party for Democracy, and other smaller parties. As mentioned, the formal foundation was preceded by a previous articulation aimed at containing social mobilization, while at the same time seizing the leading role and the consequences of the 'No' plebiscite.

Thus, the formal end of the Chilean dictatorship did not represent a rupture and, ultimately, neither did it represent a transition. As seen before, the neoliberal development strategy implemented during the dictatorship was maintained, disguised with the renewed makeup of the New ECLAC. Furthermore, it is of no less importance that at no point was a new sovereign constituent assembly convened, which implied maintaining the Constitution imposed by the dictatorship in 1980, which not only legitimized the dictatorial government but also imposed neoliberal economic structure.

The notion of democratic transition used by these governments should at least be questioned. If we accept that a real transition towards democracy was being sought, the premise here is the existence of a certain commitment to ending what is being transitioned, however long it may be, and achieving its opposite at the end of the transition. In other words, the premise is that there has to be a break with the dictatorship (and everything that structured it) and the building of its opposite. One way or another, this is incompatible with merely 'changing' forms in order to maintain content. *Gatopardismo* is not compatible with a transition, at least not a real one. Conversely, a question arises: what would be the opposite of what structured the dictatorship? What would have to be overcome or severed?

Since real change (rupture) has never occurred, this endless character of the democratic transition is very similar to what may be called neoliberalism's self-attributed immunity syndrome.[6] Despite its promises, it turns out that, in practice, all the neoliberal experiences, especially in dependent economies, Chile being just one of them, have led to a reduction in growth, an increase in external vulnerability and dependence, and a deepening of the concentration of income and wealth. Against all counterfactual evidence, the ideologists of neoliberalism always came up with ad hoc excuses, blaming either the implementers of the policies ('it's the pilot's fault'), the adverse shocks, which in conventional economics are always exogenous and stochastic, or a combination of the two.

What is the routine neoliberal recommendation in such situations? More of the same. Making sure the economic policy managers are in fact technically prepared ('change the pilot'), preferably having been trained in universities that are not contaminated by heterodox and ludicrous economic theories, reforms are recommended, of second, third and as many generations as necessary. The premise here is that there is always the possibility of creating an additional market, a new round of privatization or liberalization.

This is what we call the self-attributed immunity syndrome. Since there is no concrete economy in which all social relations are 100% commodified, and the idealistic argument of the neoliberals is that the results that were promised – and even mathematically demonstrated – are only obtained through the free flow of prices and markets (market clearing), there is always room for a neoliberal to justify the failure of what they had proposed with the need for more reforms, *ad infinitum*.

What happens with the democratic transition is similar. As full democracy in the capitalist reality is an impossibility, the argument that the transition towards it is not over is *ad infinitum*, and the '*todavía no*' becomes 'never'.

Wood (1995), among others, has already shown that capitalism and democracy are incompatible, contrary to what neoliberal ideologists believe. Since the *Concertación* governments do not go as far as to propose an overcoming of capitalism, the democratic transition is caught in this trap. It is an endless transition, towards something that will never be complete, and which is, therefore, infinitely reset as a goal. This might have been what the *Concertación* party leaderships were aiming for, consciously or not.

From a concrete point of view, maintaining the neoliberal development strategy has meant, among other things, increasing the exploitation of labour (and its social consequences), increasing the plundering of natural resources, increasing privatization, and intensifying the dependent condition of the Chilean economy.

With regard to the deregulation of labour, the rationale of the 1979 *Plan Laboral* (Work Plan) was maintained. It questioned collective bargaining, denied the right to strike by setting a maximum of 60 days, and limited the action of trade unions. It was not until the second Bachelet government, in 2014, that a reform bill was sent to Congress, which would only soften the scope of the law. This reform was to be enacted only on August 29, 2016, and even then, the country's Constitutional Court declared a significant part of the reform inadmissible, a section which concerned union ownership, which in practice meant diluting the representativeness and reducing the power of the unions. In 2018, under the Piñera government, flexible working hours were increased and compensation for length of service was reduced.

Comparing the growth in real remuneration, in relation to the increase in the ratio between gross domestic product and the level of employment (an indicator of productivity), the former grew by 1%, 4.3% and 2.6% over the periods 1984–1989, 1990–1995 and 1996–2000, respectively. The latter, on the other hand, grew by 1.4%, 5% and 3.7% in the same periods (Carcanholo, 2004, p. 54). In other words, productivity has always grown faster than real remuneration in these periods, meaning an increase in the rate of exploitation of labour (surplus value), as taught by Marx (1991). Milanovic (2019), in turn, notes that in 2015, income inequality in Chile was greater than in almost every country of Latin America, except for Honduras and Colombia, with the poorest 5% having an income level similar to the poorest 5% in Mongolia, and the richest 2% similar to the richest 2% in Germany. The concentration of wealth is even greater than the concentration of income. According to Chancel et al. (2022, p. 189), the richest 1% in Chile have 26.5% of the income and 49.6% of the wealth. The richest 10%, on the other hand, hold 58.9% and 80.4%, respectively.

As for privatization, the best illustration was the creation of the *Admnistradoras de Fondos de Pensiones* (AFPs, or Administrators of Pension Funds), created by a Law of 1980, which came into force on May 1st, 1981. This was actually an imposition of individual contributions and private management of pension funds, contrary to the principle of intergenerational solidarity and social security. The loss of social rights for pensioners and insured people is so blatant that the armed forces themselves, agents of the dictatorship, did not take part in the AFP scheme.

The very formula for calculating final pensions makes the AFPs logic explicit and clarifies what a great step backwards they were. Final pensions are obtained by dividing the capitalization of individual contributors by the average life expectancy of the whole population. On the one hand, the administration of funds collected individually is carried out by private administrators, according to the speculative logic of financial markets. Given the speculative nature of this constitution of capital, this is an extremely volatile and uncertain value, regardless of the contribution collected during a person's whole life. On the other hand, treating life expectancy as an average for all individuals ends up deepening inequality, as it disregards the fact that life expectancy is lower for the working class, reducing the value of workers' final pensions by including a life expectancy that does not correspond to them.

The process of external economic opening was resumed after a brief period of pragmatic retreat responding to the 1982–1983 crisis. The implication was a deepening of the external vulnerability and dependence of the Chilean economy. Between 1996 and 2003, for example, the proportion of net interest to foreign countries, when compared to exports, rose from 0.94 to 2.78. In the same period, net external debt as a percentage of the GDP went from 16.48 to 38.5. Compared to the volume of exports, it went from 0.63 to 1.28 in proportion. The servicing of this external debt, in relation to exports, which was 29.55 in 1996, rose to 38.13 in 2003 (Carcanholo, 2004, p. 52). This external vulnerability (dependency) has only increased since then (Montoro, 2023, pp. 293–295).

One must never forget how heavily Chilean exports rely on mining resources, especially copper. This gives the Chilean economy a clear behaviour which is typical of (neo)colonial economies, largely dependent on how these commodities are priced on international markets. Such prices are, in contemporary capitalism, established on future markets, according to the fictitious valuation of capital. It goes without saying that the Chilean economy's ability to interfere in this determination is inversely proportional to the degree of its dependence.

The maintenance and deepening of the logic of the two structural pillars of the Chilean dictatorship (i.e., neoliberalism and the Pinochetist Constitution) characterized the entire period of the governments of the so-called democratic transition. It is not surprizing, therefore, that the increase in the exploitation of labour, social inequality and economic dependence in Chile are the explanatory elements behind the social protests against this model. The *gatopardismo* of the *Concertación* governments was not enough to demobilize the Chilean population.

THE OUTBURST OF SOCIAL STRUGGLES IN 2019 AND CURRENT EVENTS

Some of the questions proposed by this chapter have already been answered. The outburst of social struggles in 2019 comes as no surprize if we consider the entire period encompassed by both the dictatorship and the *gatopardismo* of the governments of the democratic transition. Popular rejection of constitutive elements of the dictatorship which were maintained, especially neoliberalism and the Pinochetist Constitution, is the answer. But that should come as no surprize if we remember that the social uprising did not start in 2019.

A huge high school student mobilization took place in 2006 (*los pinguinitos*, or the penguins), which led to the formation of the *Asamblea Nacional de Estudiantes Secundários* (ANES, or National Assembly of High School Students).[7]

They were already protesting the privatization of education and transport, and the movement went so far as to stop 400 schools. In a general strike on May 30, 600,000 students were involved.

In 2011, another youth mobilization, this time at university level, deepened the struggles against the privatization of education. The accumulation of forces through class struggle is evident here. Many of the students who had been involved in the 2006 protests were now part of the university student movements. In addition, high school students also joined this movement, which brought together a million people to march in O'Higgins Park on August 21st.

In 2017, there was a strong movement against the AFPs. The protests against the privatization of the pension system brought together 800,000 people in Santiago and 2 million across the country on March 26.

Going back in time, we must not forget the intense protests of 1983 and 1986 that led to the October 1988 plebiscite on whether or not Pinochet, the dictator, should remain in power. The fact that the accumulation of forces built up there was betrayed by party leaderships, leading to the conciliation promoted by the *Concertación*, does not diminish the concrete nature of these protests.

Despite this important background, the social outburst of 2019 is special not only because of its magnitude but also because of its particular meaning, which has, at the same time, provided it with great opportunities and set limitations to its scope.

The worsening of social problems throughout this period of promised democratic transition is almost a consensus in explaining the social outburst of 2019.[8] The revolt was triggered on October 6th, when a 30 peso increase in the price of public transport was announced. It was the fourth in less than 2 years, in a year in which electricity, gas and water, among other basic prices, had already risen considerably. Juan Andrés Fontaine, Minister of Economy, suggested waking up earlier to take advantage of a discount in the early hours of the morning, a real provocation. Thousands of students began the protests. Students from the so-called 'emblematic schools' had already been in conflict with the government, fighting the *Safe Classroom Bill* of late 2018, which provided for the expulsion of students involved in 'violent acts'.

The following day, the first 'turnstile jumping' action was promoted, with the aim of challenging the privatization of services. The process unfolds with large gatherings and strong police repression. Little by little, the extent of the demands became clear ('no son 30 pesos, son 30 años', which means 'it's not 30 pesos, it's 30 years'), highlighting the rejection of neoliberalism and the democratic transition.

On October 18, social revolt erupted, with protests intensifying and leading to the closure of the Metro. The following day, President Piñera decreed a state of emergency and a curfew in greater Santiago. That weekend, between the 19th and 20th, ended with the release of an audio by the first lady (Cecilia Morel), expressing the government's desperation and what was really at stake: 'it's like a foreign invasion, an alien invasion, and we don't have the tools to fight it. (...) [W]e're going to have to reduce our privileges and share with the rest'. On the 19th, the suspension of the increase in transport fares was decreed.

On October 23rd, both the state of emergency and the curfew were already in force in 15 of Chile's 16 regional capitals. Government responses did not put an end to the movement and two days later the largest demonstration in Chilean history took place, gathering 1.2 million people in Santiago and many more across the country. The following month, on the 12th, a general strike broke out.

The Piñera government really found itself in check during this period, and on December 23rd it was forced to call for the draughting of a constitution. Decades of *gatopardismo* had left their mark and, even under questioning, the government, through Law 21.200, in its article 135, established that it would not modify: (i) international treaties ratified by Chile (which maintains the neoliberal economic openness); (ii) enforced court decisions (which ensures great impunity for the crimes committed by the dictatorship). This was all agreed in what may be called the second major moment of *gatopardismo*, when on November 15, 2019 the main political parties set these principles in the *Acuerdo por la paz y la nueva constitución* (Comprehensive Peace Agreement and Interim Constitution). On October 25, 2020, 78.28% of the votes of the plebiscite are in favour of a new Constitution; 79% are in favour of the constituent assembly being elected in its entirety.

On October 15 and 16, 2021, the new constituent assembly was elected, with most of its members having no party ties and in some way reflecting the amalgam of the social movements that made up the social outburst of two years earlier. It seemed that one of the main pillars of the false democratic transition, the Pinochetist constitution, was about to fall.

Tinta Limón (2021) interviewed various leaders of some of the movements taking part in the social outburst of 2019, and wondered who the subject of this social explosion is, so heterogeneous and furious. The answer is, dialectically, all of them and none of them at the same time. This vast and even diffuse composition has allowed the social outburst to escape the control of party leaderships, the true subjects of *gatopardismo*, and, from there, to seriously challenge the way the dictatorship's legacy remained in the foundations of the democratic transition.

On the other hand, the same heterogeneity and diffusion of the composition of this subject of the social outburst posed clear limits to the possibilities of social transformation. This is most concretely expressed in the proposal for a new constitution, which was also diffuse, fragmented, with some achievements, but with less class cohesion than necessary to confront neoliberalism. As the proposed constitution failed to make this confrontation concrete enough, it was already too limited to achieve the purposes it set out to.

In the same context of apparent victories from the 2019 social uprising, on December 19, 2021, Gabriel Boric, a former student leader, was elected president in the second round with 55.8% of the votes. The inauguration took place on March 11, 2022. There were many who, at this point, saw the social uprising as largely victorious.

But the strength of Chilean *gatopardismo* did not take long to show itself. On October 4, 2022, after intense political work by the Chilean right (among other elements) exploiting the disjunctions in the formation of the social subject of the uprising, some of them expressed in the constitutional proposal itself, 61.89% of Chileans rejected the proposal in a plebiscite. This stage of the long battle of Chile was a combination of the demobilization of the buildup of protests, the actions of the right, and the aggiornamento of the political parties.

The Boric government, in its turn, did not lag behind. That same year, 2022, it announced a proposal regarding the AFPs which, it said, would meet some of the demands. However, it was only a rebranding (*Gestoras de Inversión Privada*, or Private Investment Managers). In terms of content, the proposal increased the role of the private sector, since the final pension would be provided by private insurance companies!

With regard to the economic openness, Boric ratified Chile's incorporation into the TPP-11 (or CPTPP, for Comprehensive and Progressive Agreement for Trans-Pacific Partnership), which had been agreed by Bachelet in 2018. Among other things, this free trade agreement between countries in the Pacific Basin protects the activities of multinational companies.

The apparent victory of the 2019 social uprising was quickly accommodated by the official system of Chilean *gatopardismo*, working for the maintenance of neoliberalism as well as for the validity of the constitution inherited from the dictatorship.

CONCLUSION

The long battle of Chile will not end in 2023. Neither will the strength of conservative reactionism. Following the rejection of the constitutional proposal, a parliamentary council, made up of 51 parliamentarians, 33 of whom are from right-wing parties, was assigned for drawing up a new proposal which was also be subject to a plebiscite, in December 17, 2023.

The obvious backwardness of this proposal is evidenced by ideas of a retreat in abortion rights, the immediate expulsion of immigrants, and increased privatization of health, education and transport. The capitalist counter-offencive in the Chilean class struggle explicitly seeks to bring together the two constituent elements of the dictatorship's legacy, neoliberalism warranted and shielded by a new constitution, now backed by a supposed democracy, which was never actually achieved by the transition.

Resistance has already taken shape, represented by movements such as *Chile vota en contra* (Chile votes against). With the rejection of this proposal, the constitutional vacuum would remain, with the dictatorship's constitution still formally in force and the bitter taste of a promise (the New Constitution) which is once again unfulfilled. With the approval of the right-wing constitutional proposal, the shielding of the Chilean model inherited from the dictatorship would seem complete. The Chilean people rejected this second proposal for a new constitution with 56% of the votes unfavourable, and various social movements now call for a new social outburst.

Just as it was after the 1973 coup, social resistance has succeeded, through comings and goings, in putting the social process in check. Workers and social movements, within their possibilities and limitations, stubbornly refuse to surrender. Sometimes it may be all they have left. It may be enough.

NOTES

1. *Unidad Popular* was a coalition of left-wing parties that enlisted support from broad sectors of the Chilean society, which therefore included the Chilean Communist Party, and also less radical tendencies.

2. Milton Friedman has tried numerous times to disassociate himself from any relationship with the Chilean military regime and the Chicago Boys. However, the most prominent actor in the implementation of this project was actually a much less well-known character called Arnold 'Al' Harberger. Nevertheless, Friedman's attempt to downplay his connection to the Chilean military regime must be viewed with at least a few reservations (Edwards, 2003, chapter 5; and Ffrench–Davis, 2004).

3. To be accurate, this whole period was not entirely one of governments of the *Concertación*. From 2010 to 2014, and then again from 2018 to 2022, Chile was governed by Sebastián Piñera, the political heir and economic benefactor of the Chilean dictatorship.

4. Montoro (2023), in the same sense as here, prefers the term 'transición lampedusiana'.

5. The ECLAC, a commission linked to the United Nations, has its headquarters in Santiago de Chile. The analytical framework of the 'New ECLAC' can be found in Ffrench–Davis (2000) and ECLAC (1990).

6. Curiously, the expression '*todavia no*' ('not yet') has become widely and frequently used whenever the issue of the democratic transition was raised. Had it been completed? Had the governments committed to it already accomplished their missions, forcing them to either withdraw from the electoral contest, or to propose something more than a mere democratic transition? '*Todavia no*'.

7. The term refers to the fact that Chilean high school uniforms, black and white, closely resemble penguins.

8. Hadzi–Vaskov and Ricci (2021), in an International Monetary Fund (IMF) working paper, recognize this explanation for what happened in 2019. However, they have the intellectual dishonesty to claim that inequality was not exactly the cause, because, according to them, it had been reduced. However, perhaps not to the extent required and/or the improvements had not been perceived by the population. According to them, the solution lies in improving the communication of results, and one of the elements for this is to deepen competition!

REFERENCES

Carcanholo, M. D. (2004). A Falsa via chilena. *Revista da Sociedade Brasileira de Economia Política*, *15*, 34–61.

Chancel, L., Piketty, T., Saez, E., & Zucman, G. (2022). *World inequality report 2022*. World Inequality Lab. https://wid.world/document/world-inequality-report-2022/

ECLAC. (1990). *Changing production patterns with social equity: The prime task of Latin American and Caribean development in the 1990s*. Economic Commission for Latin America and the Caribbean–United Nations.

Edwards, S. (2003). *The Chile project: The story of the Chicago boys and the downfall of neoliberalism*. Princeton University Press.

Ffrench–Davis, R. (2000). *Reforming the reforms in Latin America: Macroeconomics, trade, finance*. Palgrave Mcmillan.

Ffrench–Davis, R. (2002). Chile, neoliberalismo y el crecimiento con equidad. *Revista de Economia Política*, *22*(4), 88.

Ffrench–Davis, R. (2004). *Entre el neoliberalismo y el crecimiento con equidad: tres décadas de política económica en Chile*. Siglo XXI.

Hadzi–Vaskov, M., & Ricci, L. A. (2021). *Understanding Chile's social unrest in an international perspective*. IMF Working Paper, 21/174. International Monetary Fund.

Limón, T. (2021). *Chile desperto: la revuelta antineoliberal*. Tinta Limón Ediciones.

Marx, K. (1991). *Capital: A critique of political economy*. Penguin Classics.

Mckinnon, R. (1982). The order of economic liberalization: Lessons from Chile and Argentina. In K. Brunner & A. Meltzer (Eds.), *Economic policy in a world of change*. Elsevier.

Milankovic, B. (2019). *Global inequality: A new approach for the age of globalization*. Harvard University Press.

Montoro, X. (2023). *Chile: milagro o quimera - Significado histórico del modelo económico de la dictadura a 50 años del golpe*. Instituto Marxista de Economía.

Wood, E. M. (1995). *Democracy against capitalism: Renewing historical materialism*. Cambridge University Press.

AFTERWORD

AFTERWORD: THE ISRAELI GENOCIDE OF PALESTINIANS, THE UKRAINE WAR, AND DANGERS AHEAD

By Paul Zarembka, July 10, 2024

The Israeli genocide of Palestinians is the most open, widely exposed genocide ever occurring as it is unfolding. You can read some of the evidence even in mainstream media, while the appropriate noun is avoided, armaments to Israel continue, and any humanity of Palestinians a minor footnote to the 'Enlightenment' we are supposed to be living through.

Could, perhaps, the leaders of the countries sponsoring and engaging in the colonialisms we all know about have simply made a mistake regarding Israel – relative to their own interests? Had they not understood or did not sufficiently care – in their own interests – what they had created under the slogan, 'a country for a people without a country'? Even so, do they know how to get out of the box?

Israel has been important because the United Kingdom and the United States make it important. Back in 1948, the alternative to a religious state was a secular one, an alternative that had been on the agenda of the United Nations. This would have been more consistent with the claimed ideals of the secular republics that were determining the outcome. Furthermore, one did not need to be an Einstein to realize the danger, needing only to be able to think independently and with integrity.[1]

The state of Israel has lost whatever credibility it may have had. Continuing to support it undermines the credibility of those states continuing their support in 2024. On the other hand, major countries like South Africa, Brazil and China benefit with their objections towards the Israeli genocide.

The Palestine resistance is not being defeated. Therefore, under its stated agenda, Israel is losing. Is there any scenario for it to claim 'victory'? Can Israel accept defeat? Or, will it only accept defeat when all come down, including itself, perhaps even with the use of nuclear options?

Consider October 7, 2023. There is plenty of evidence that Israel knew of the plans of the Palestinian resistance to launch an attack on Israel.[2] Rather than prepare to stop it in its tracks, Israeli authorities did the opposite, weakening its own border with Gaza ahead of the event, and failing to respond immediately once it had begun. The border became wide open in several places, and incursions into Israel were almost unobstructed for a significant period of time, including into an Israeli military base. It took three days to restore Israeli control over the penetrated territory. Apart from resistance groups, it is difficult to know exactly who had crossed the border from Gaza, and there were certainly elements that were unconnected to any group. Deaths and injuries among those on the Israeli side surely did include non-combatants, but accurately ascribing causes are difficult, particularly as Israel also had a tactic of unconcern whether its military response would be killing some of their own. The numbers of those killed that were not soldiers or security personnel were identified in December to be 695 Israel civilians and 71 foreigners (most Thai), without being able to precise who engaged in the killing.[3] In any case, the context of the conflict is important: For the decade and a half beforehand, *i.e.*, between January 24, 2008 and October 6, 2023, the United Nations reports that Palestinian fatalities had been 6,336, 20 times the Israeli fatalities of 310.[4]

October 7 was not a 'false flag' on the part of Israel. A 'false flag' would involve Israeli combatants wearing identities of the opposite and attacking Israel.[5] Nevertheless, Israel's behaviour into October 7, 2023, can certainly be described as Machiavellian. And I have not seen a claim that Israel's reduction of its defenses into October 7 went beyond Israel's own internal decisions. In other words, Israeli political leaders operated with their anticipations of what major supporters like the United Stated and the United Kingdom would do after October 7, anticipating the product of prior reactions by such powers to events in the Middle East, particularly those connected to Israel. They were not wrong, even after the Israeli continuing attacks on Gaza, militarily and anti-humanitarian, were decided by the International Court of Justice to plausibly be a genocide – with a US-appointed judge presiding no less. Later it ruled – however, with no effect – that the attack on Rafah stop immediately, and needed humanitarian aid be allowed into Gaza.

Since October 8, 2023, Israeli civilian fatalities have involved some hostages, but, on the Palestinian side, tens of thousands of non-combatants have suffered death from the Israeli assaults, mostly in Gaza but also expanding into the West Bank. Many more tens of thousands have suffered injuries, while starvation is rampant and there is scarcely a Palestinian not tragically traumatized. After a long wait, the International Criminal Court finally moved towards arrest warrants against two Israeli principals, Prime Minister Benjamin Netanyahu and Defence Minister Yoav Gallant (along with three resistance leaders). As of this writing, those warrants are yet to be approved.

Turn to the US Government and its material aid of this genocide. Can it allow – in its own interests – Israel to engage in the complete destruction of Gaza and the West Bank, whoever forms the Israeli Government? Can it cut its losses? For myself, I could see this as possible. The propaganda around the necessity to defeat communism in Vietnam was no less powerful, yet the nuclear option was not deployed to try to avoid that defeat. Nonetheless, the world configuration has moved greatly in the half century, including the end of apartheid in South Africa, the fall of the Soviet empire but eventual restoration of Russian power, the rise of Chinese power, the Modi repression of Muslims in India, increased ties of most European governments to US hegemony, . . .

The depravity of the Israeli behaviour is so beyond cruel and outlandish that even some of the strongest critics of Zionism were rather unprepared for how far it has already gone. I can make the case that the commoditisation of people by capitalism, described by Marx, is the fountain of this genocide. And it is unmasked. It is even clearer than the nuclear bombing by the United States on Hiroshima and Nagasaki since the genocide in Gaza is seen in detail by hundreds of millions worldwide on an hourly basis. The Western powers, led by the United States, the United Kingdom and Germany in their full-throated support of Israel, don't care in the slightest and publicly accept Israeli officials lying without bothering to check the evidence.

Thus, the commoditisation of Palestinians is openly presented. Humanity of Palestinians is ignored. We have leading capitalist governments exposed naked, the essence of capitalism shining brightly. A half millennium of historical development is illuminated, within this interconnected world of news being transmitted anywhere in mere seconds.

While the powers behind Israel are weakened, they will not accept their decline in a quiet vote at the United Nations, with a 'thanks for the good times.' Still, Israel itself is out of control, and nothing it might do is off the table. It could happen at any time. How powers behind Israel would react is too speculative for this short piece.

We might more creditably consider the Ukraine war. One perspective, offering attention to the 1648 Peace of Westphalia, argues:

> The Ukraine War that threatens to destroy the planet in a nuclear holocaust is a symptom of a wider crisis in the international system. After enjoying hegemony for five centuries and constructing and imposing global rules to serve Western interests, there is now a spectacular realignment of power in the world. The global majority seeks multipolarity in accordance with a Westphalian world order, while the West, under Washington's leadership, attempts to restore its dominant position in the world. The U.S. has accurately identified China and Russia as the main challengers that have created a gravitational pull to reorganise the world order towards multipolarity. (Diesen, 2024, p. 351))

The point is clear enough if we understand Diesen to mean that the initial Peace of Westphalia was within Europe, later encompassing North America, that was to dominate the world. The new order would refer a projected Westphalian world order to include Asia, particularly China, also including the importance of BRICS, as a counterweight to the West.

Diesen points to argumentation by Henry Kissinger as a background for his own argument, a type not uncommon among bourgeois historians critical of the Western drive for the war, but who also exhibit no concern for class exploitation and oppression. I can also think of John Mearsheimer's promotion of his concept of real politics in commentaries on the Ukraine war and on Israel, although he does give some attention to morality. The interventions by Jeffery Sachs who has direct, personal knowledge of the period after the collapse of the

Soviet Union, and of Ukraine in particular, does exhibit concern for the lives of workers, albeit limited by a 'developmentalist' perspective.

There seems to be little reason to object to such attentions to the high level of danger we are in, even recognizing their bourgeois perspectives. We cannot skip over the possibility of nuclear war. Our current danger seems similar to the Cuban missile crisis for which a nuclear annihilation was avoided partly by the particular individuals leading the Soviet Union and the United States at the time, and partly (sorry to say) by 'luck,' namely, one naval officer who happened to have a command on one Soviet submarine that had lost all communications and otherwise was on a 'go' by two other officers for a nuclear attack on the United States.

I want to conclude with the uncomfortable: Our theory is not comprehensive enough to direct us precisely in the present conjuncture. We are too ignorant. Still, we do have pointers: We do have our studies of history and of the working classes; we do have certain guides, often before the nuclear age ('combined and uneven development' being one example[6]); we do know the need to contest the exploiters; and we do know what we don't want. But the people are not in power. And those that are in power are extremely dangerous, inclusive of nuclear blackmail or use.

NOTES

1. 'The most famous Jewish scientist in history [Albert Einstein] knew from its bloody conception that an Israel created and run by right-wing, gun-wielding zealots was not viable. It shouldn't have taken a genius to tell us that, but it did.' (Ridley, Y. [2021, June 4]. The 'final' downfall of Israel was predicted by Einstein. *Middle East Monitor*). https://www.middleeastmonitor.com/20210604-the-final-downfall-of-israel-was-predicted-by-einstein

2. Report: New evidence reveals IDF had detailed prior knowledge of Hamas plan to raid Israel. Fink, R. (2024, June 18). https://www.haaretz.com/israel-news/2024-06-18/ty-article/report-new-evidence-reveals-idf-had-detailed-prior-knowledge-of-hamas-plan-to-raid-israel/00000190-2afb-d2de-af9e-6ffbdf700000. It also mentions this report as 'but one in a long list of reports which points to the extent to which military officials were warned of Hamas' plans to attack Israel.'

3. Israel social security data reveal the true picture of Oct 7 deaths. *France* 24, December 12, 2023. www.france24.com/en/live-news/20231215-israel-social-security-data-reveals-true-picture-of-oct-7-deaths

4. Data on casualties. *United Nations Office for the Coordination of Humanitarian Affairs*. www.ochaopt.org/data/casualties. Accessed on May 20, 2024.

5. Discussion of types of state conspiracies is offered in Zarembka (2021, Chapter 10).

6. Alexander (2024) utilizes this concept in consideration of the current Middle East.

REFERENCES

Alexander, A. (2024). Revisiting the dynamics of imperialism in the Middle East. *International Socialism*, 37–56.

Diesen, G. (2024). *The Ukraine war & the Eurasian world order*. Clarity Press, Kindle Edition.

Zarembka, P. (2021). *Key elements of social theory revolutionized by Marx*. Brill or Haymarket paperback. Chinese translation in preparation.

INDEX

Printed and bound by CPI Group (UK) Ltd, Croydon, CR0 4YY

01/06/2026

14890745-0003